NARUTO VOL. 64
SHONEN JUMP Manga Edition

STORY AND ART BY MASASHI KISHIMOTO

Translation/Mari Morimoto
Touch-up Art & Lettering/John Hunt
Design/Sam Elzway
Editor/Alexis Kirsch

Published by VIZ Media, LLC
P.O. Box 77010
San Francisco, CA 94107

10 9 8 7 6 5 4 3 2 1
First printing, January 2014

www.viz.com

THE WORLD'S
MOST POPULAR MANGA

SHONEN JUMP
www.shonenjump.com

Oh, man... Yeah...
I can't think of anything to write in the comments section anymore... Which is why, right this very moment, I'm going to just scribble down the first thought that comes to me while I sit here at my desk staring outside...
"These clouds are pretty gray!!"

岸本斉史

—Masashi Kishimoto, 2013

Author/artist Masashi Kishimoto was born in 1974 in rural Okayama Prefecture, Japan. After spending time in art college, he won the Hop Step Award for new manga artists with his manga **Karakuri** (Mechanism). Kishimoto decided to base his next story on traditional Japanese culture. His first version of **Naruto**, drawn in 1997, was a one-shot story about fox spirits; his final version, which debuted in **Weekly Shonen Jump** in 1999, quickly became the most popular ninja manga in Japan.

SHONEN JUMP MANGA EDITION

NARUTO

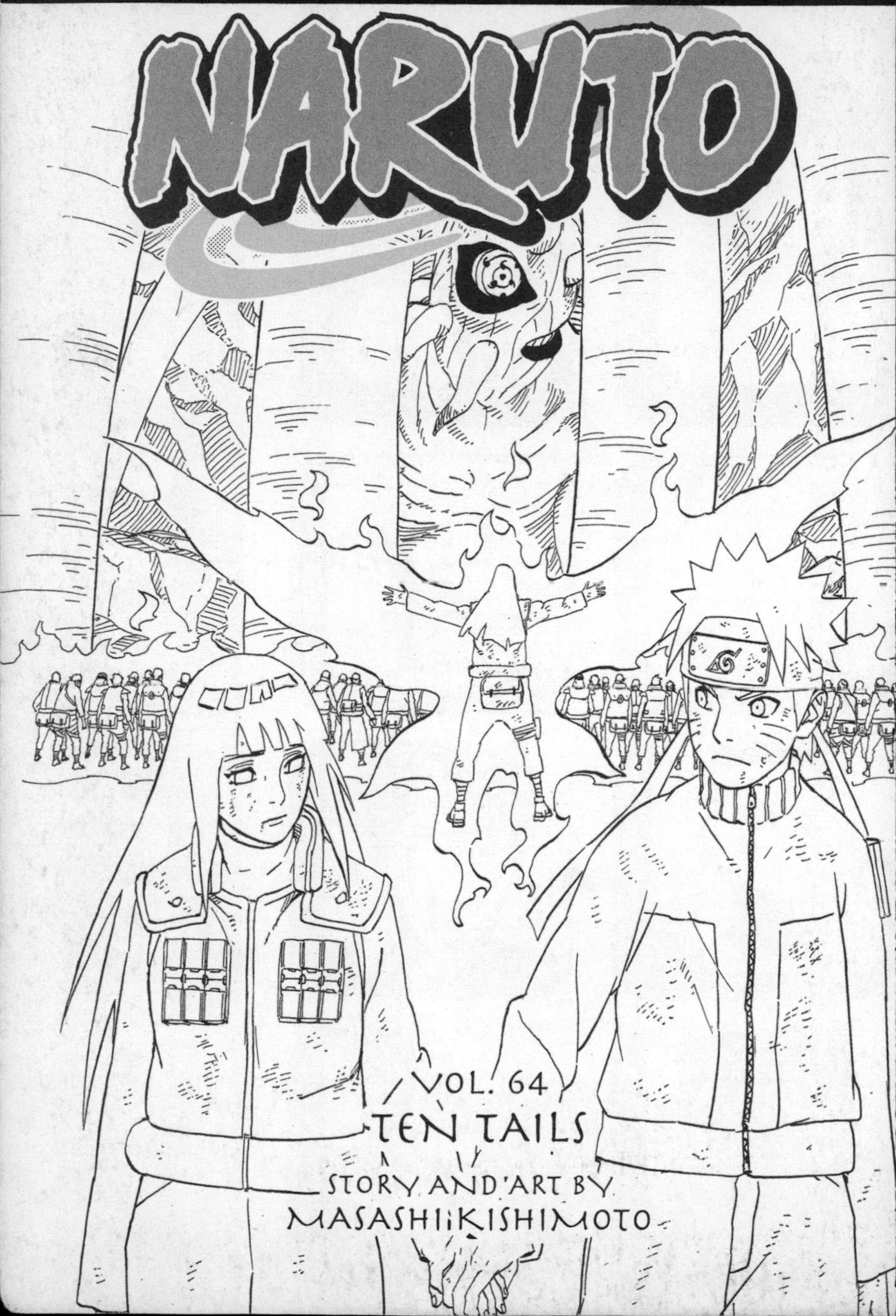

VOL. 64

TEN TAILS

STORY AND ART BY
MASASHI KISHIMOTO

CHARACTERS

Naruto うずまきナルト

Sasuke うちはサスケ

Kakashi はたけカカシ

Sakura 春野サクラ

Sai サイ

Yamato ヤマト

Kurama 九喇嘛

Obito うちはオビト

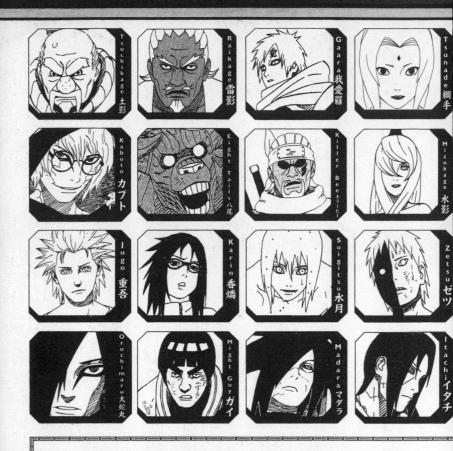

Tsunade 綱手
Gaara 我愛羅
Raikage 雷影
Tsuchikage 土影
Mizukage 水影
Killer Bee キラービー
Eight Tails 八尾
Kabuto カブト
Zetsu ゼツ
Suigetsu 水月
Karin 香燐
Jugo 重吾
Itachi イタチ
Madara マダラ
Might Guy ガイ
Orochimaru 大蛇丸

THE STORY SO FAR...

Naruto, the biggest troublemaker at the Ninja Academy in the Village of Konohagakure, finally becomes a ninja along with his classmates Sasuke and Sakura. They grow and mature through countless trials and battles. However, Sasuke, unable to give up his quest for vengeance, leaves Konohagakure to seek Orochimaru and his power…

Two years pass. Naruto grows up and engages in fierce battles against the Tailed Beast-targeting Akatsuki. Elsewhere, after winning the heroic battle against Itachi and learning his older brother's true intentions, Sasuke allies with the Akatsuki and sets out to destroy Konoha.

The Fourth Great Ninja War against the Akatsuki begins. Having stopped the Edotensei jutsu with the help of his brother, Sasuke now heads off with Orochimaru to fullfil a new objective. Meanwhile, the man trying to revive Ten Tails is revealed as Kakashi's old teammate, Uchiha Obito. Now Naruto and Kakashi go up against the man who wants to end the world as we know it!

CONTENTS

Number 608: Kakashi's Resolve

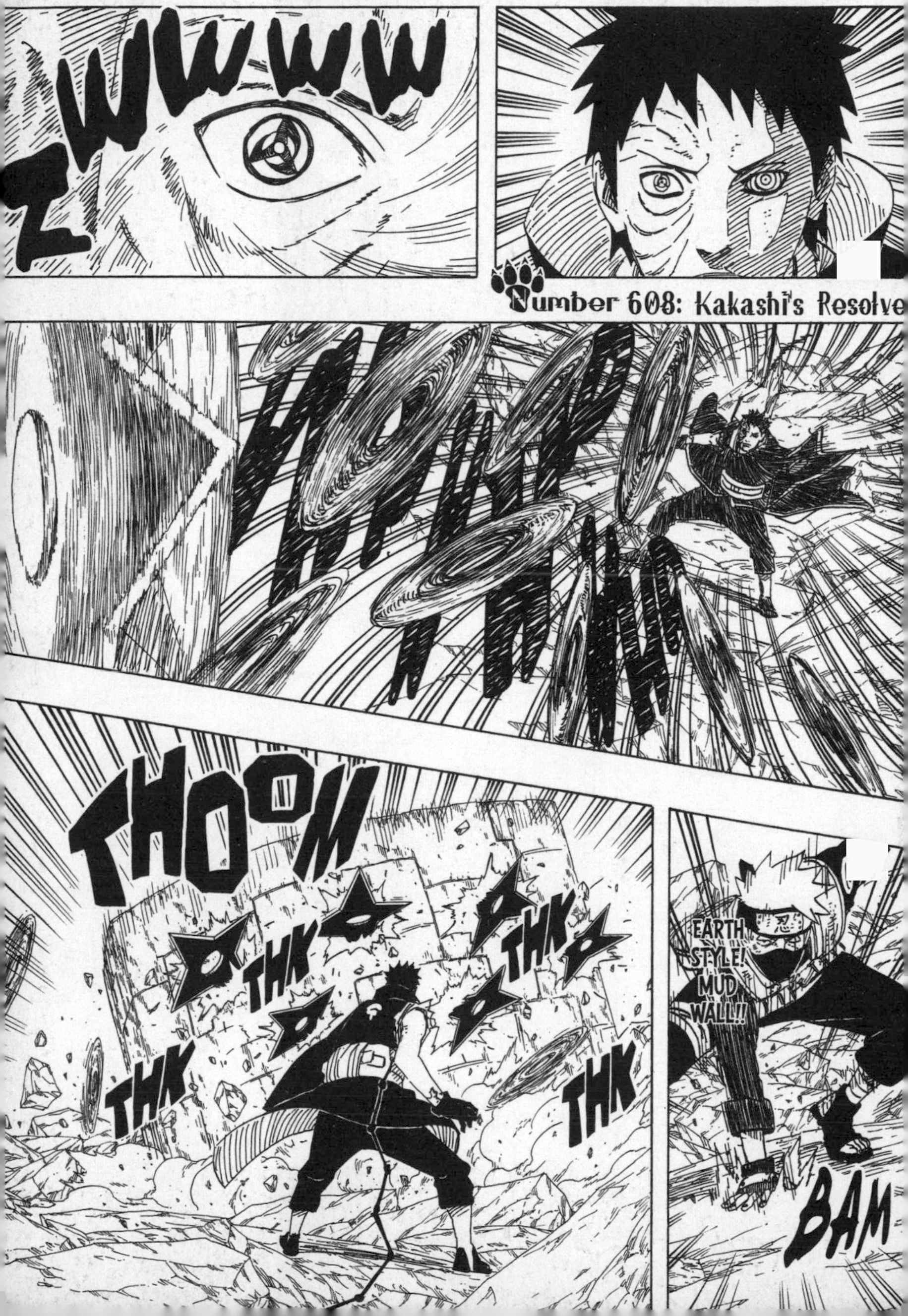
EARTH STYLE! MUD WALL!!
BAM
THOOM
THK
THK
THK
THK
THK

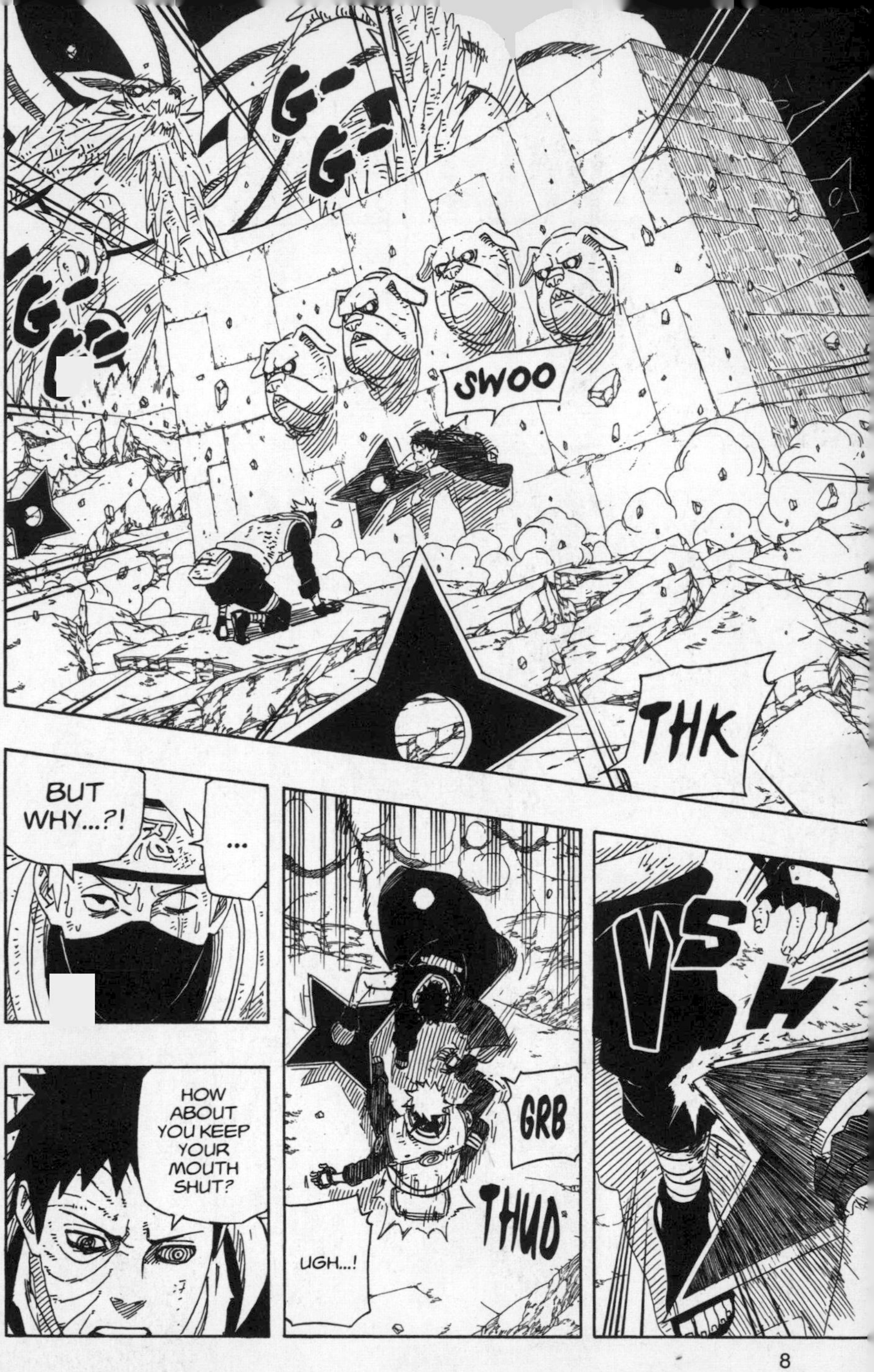

G-G-
G-G-
SWOO
THK
VSH
GRB
THUD
UGH...!
BUT WHY...?!
...
HOW ABOUT YOU KEEP YOUR MOUTH SHUT?

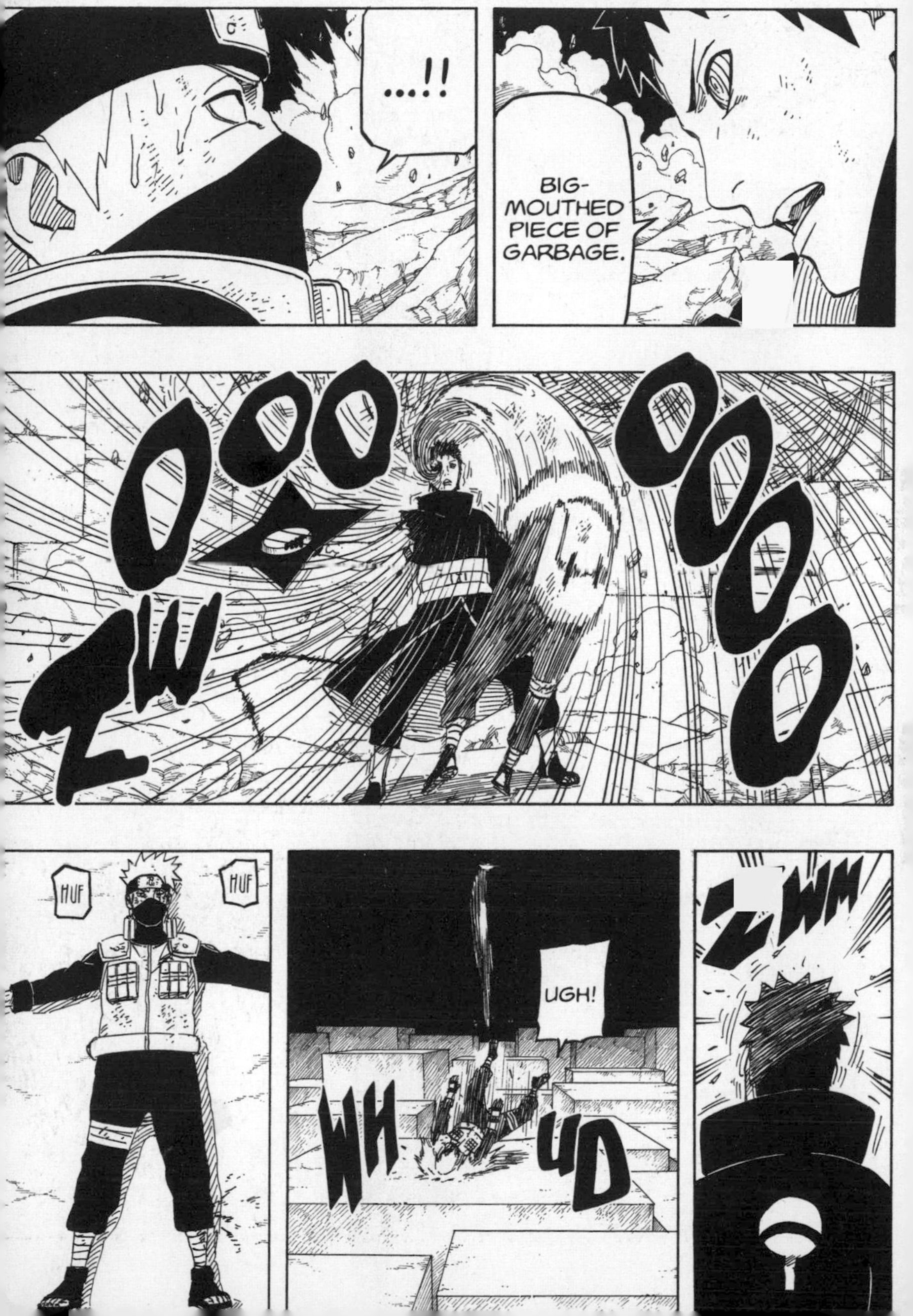
BIG-MOUTHED PIECE OF GARBAGE.
...!!
ZWOOOOOOOO
ZWM
UGH!
WHUD
HUF
HUF

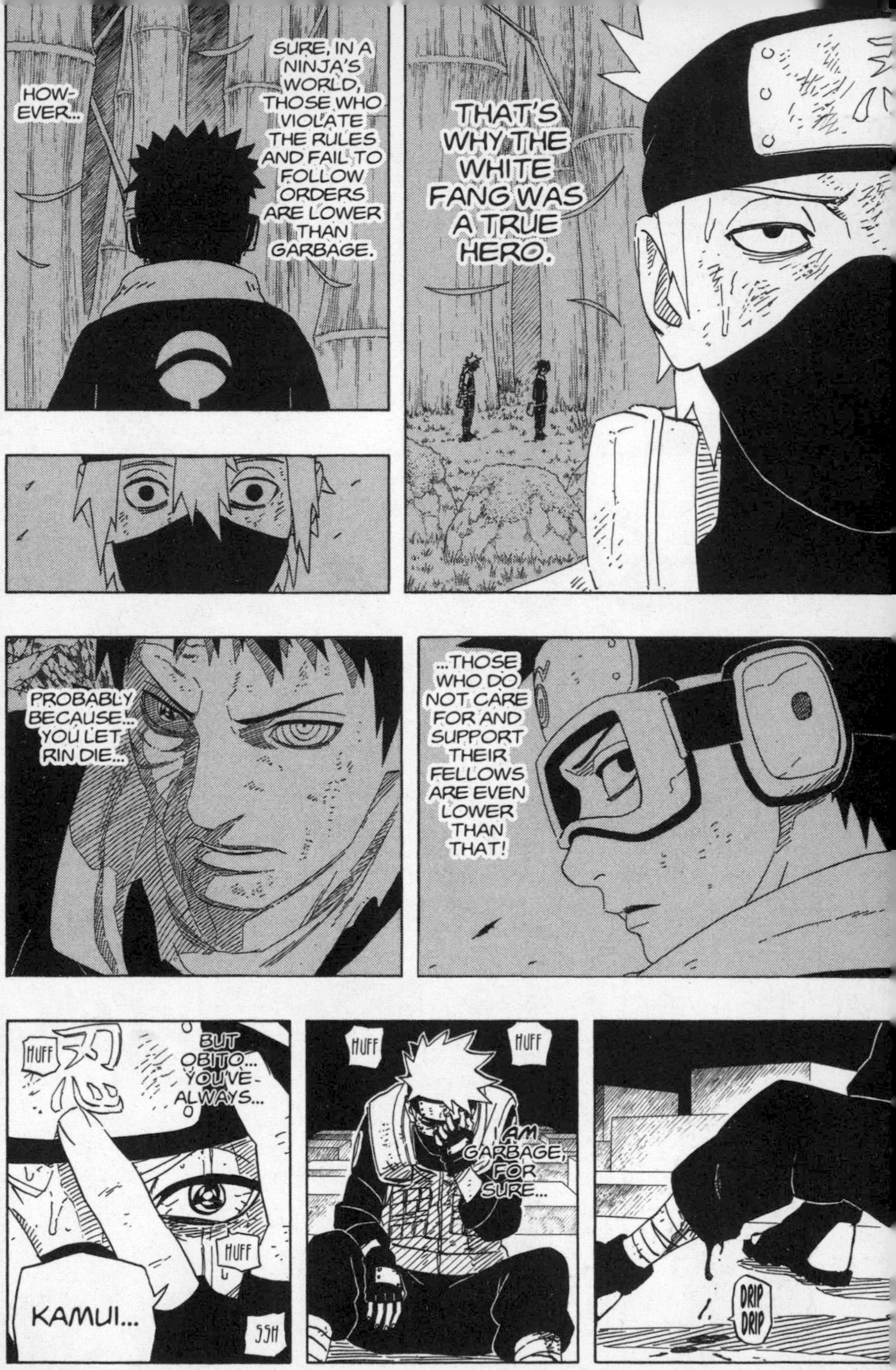
THAT'S WHY THE WHITE FANG WAS A TRUE HERO.
SURE, IN A NINJA'S WORLD, THOSE WHO VIOLATE THE RULES AND FAIL TO FOLLOW ORDERS ARE LOWER THAN GARBAGE.
HOW-EVER...
...THOSE WHO DO NOT CARE FOR AND SUPPORT THEIR FELLOWS ARE EVEN LOWER THAN THAT!
PROBABLY BECAUSE... YOU LET RIN DIE...
DRIP DRIP
HUFF
HUFF
I AM GARBAGE, FOR SURE...
BUT OBITO... YOU'VE ALWAYS...
HUFF
HUFF
KAMUI...
SSH

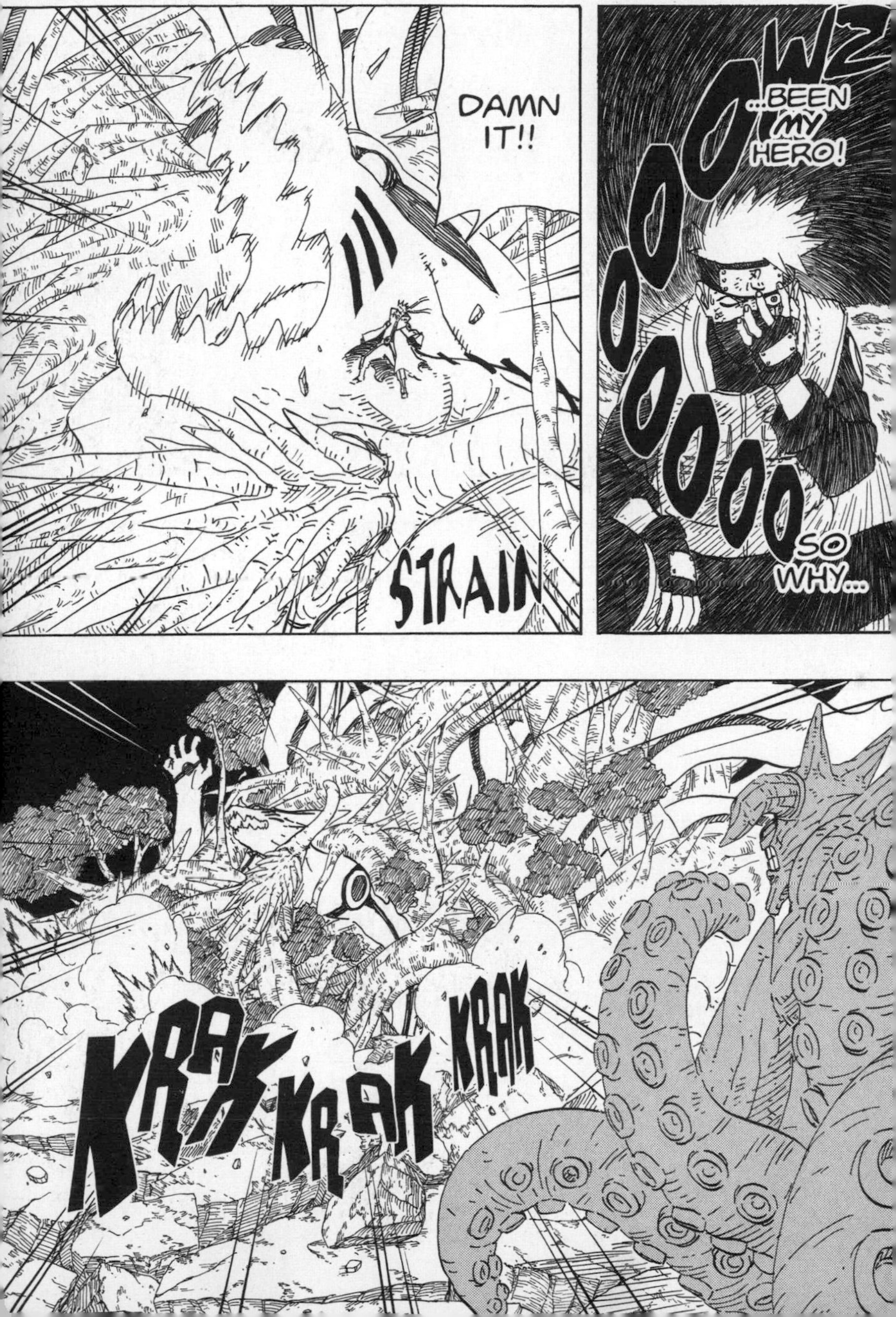
...BEEN MY HERO!
SO WHY...
DAMN IT!!
STRAIN
KRAK
KRAK
KRAK

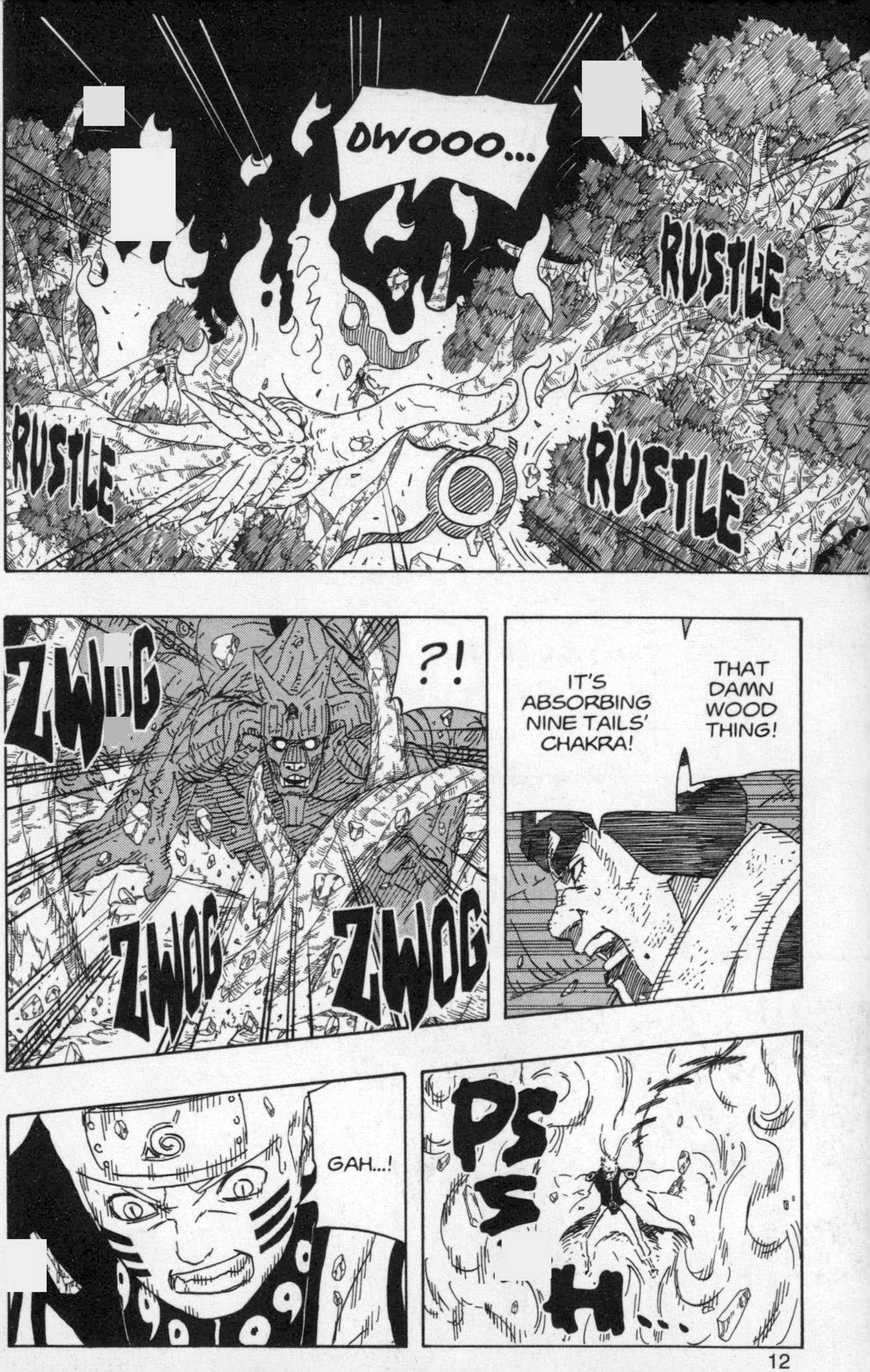
DWOOO...
RUSTLE
RUSTLE
RUSTLE
THAT DAMN WOOD THING!
IT'S ABSORBING NINE TAILS' CHAKRA!
?!
ZWOG
ZWOG
ZWOG
PSSH...
GAH...!

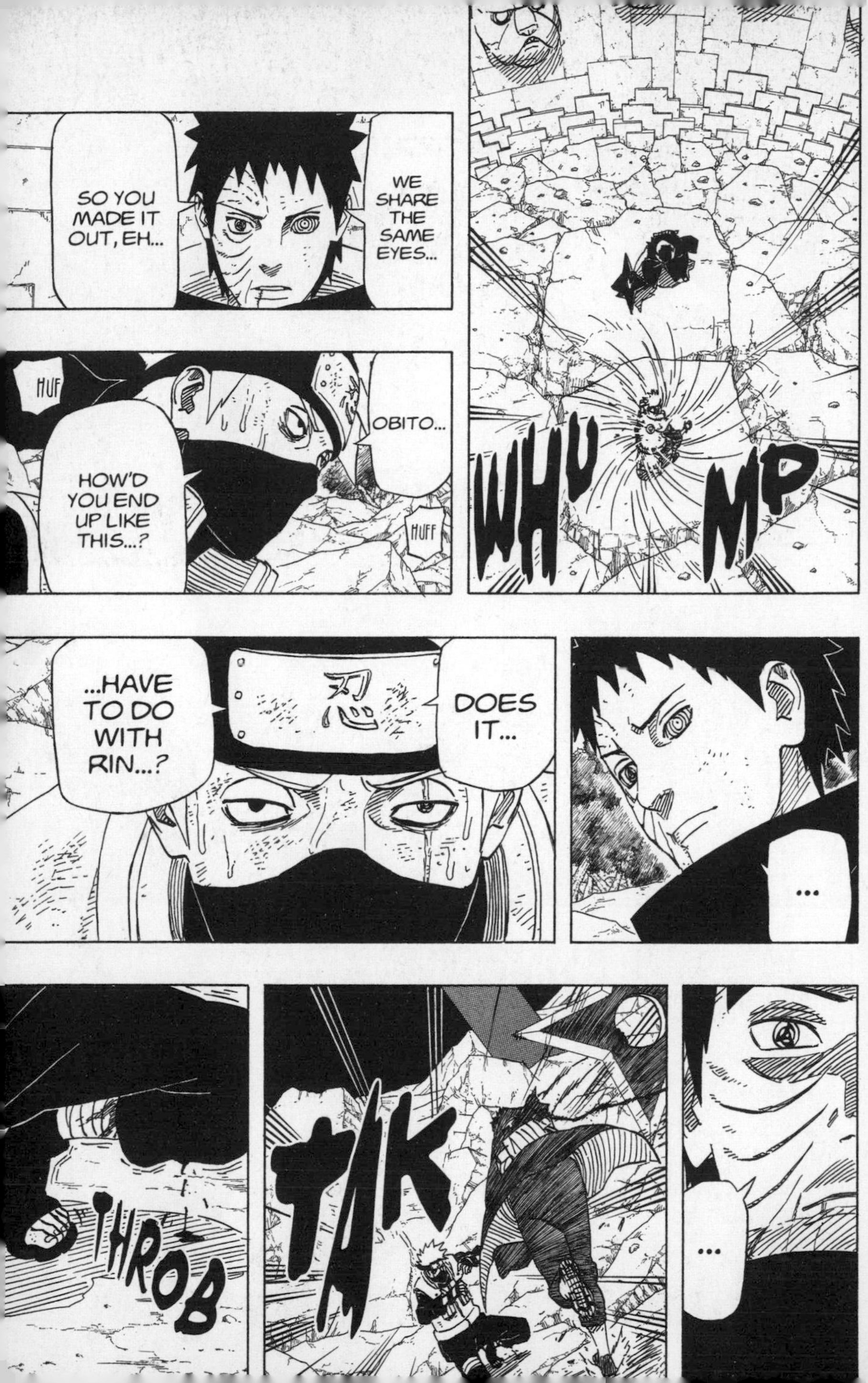
WHUMP
WE SHARE THE SAME EYES...
SO YOU MADE IT OUT, EH...
OBITO...
HUFF
HUF
HOW'D YOU END UP LIKE THIS...?
...
DOES IT...
...HAVE TO DO WITH RIN...?
...
TAK
THROB

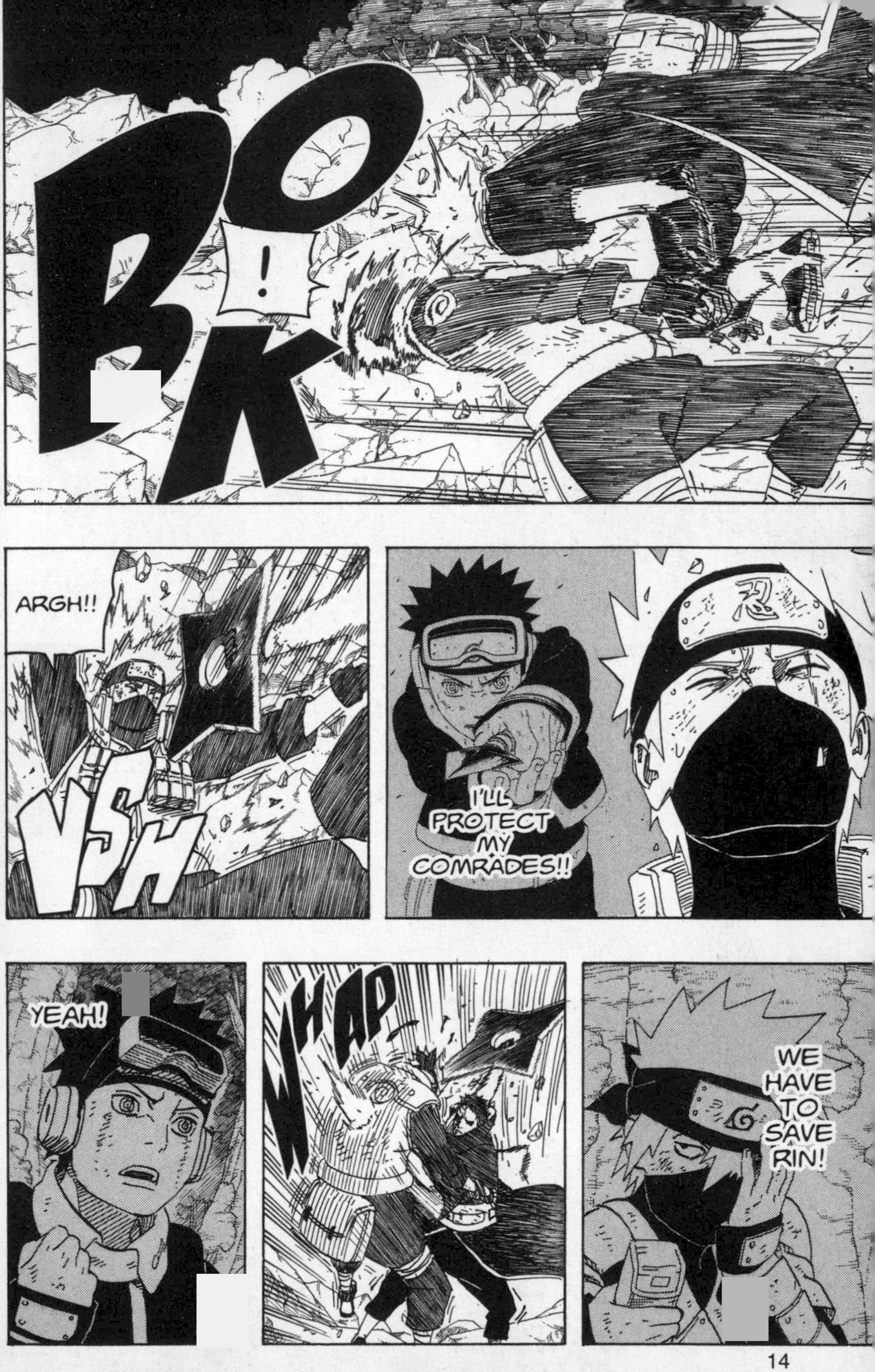
BOK
!
I'LL PROTECT MY COMRADES!!
ARGH!!
VSH
WE HAVE TO SAVE RIN!
WHAP
YEAH!

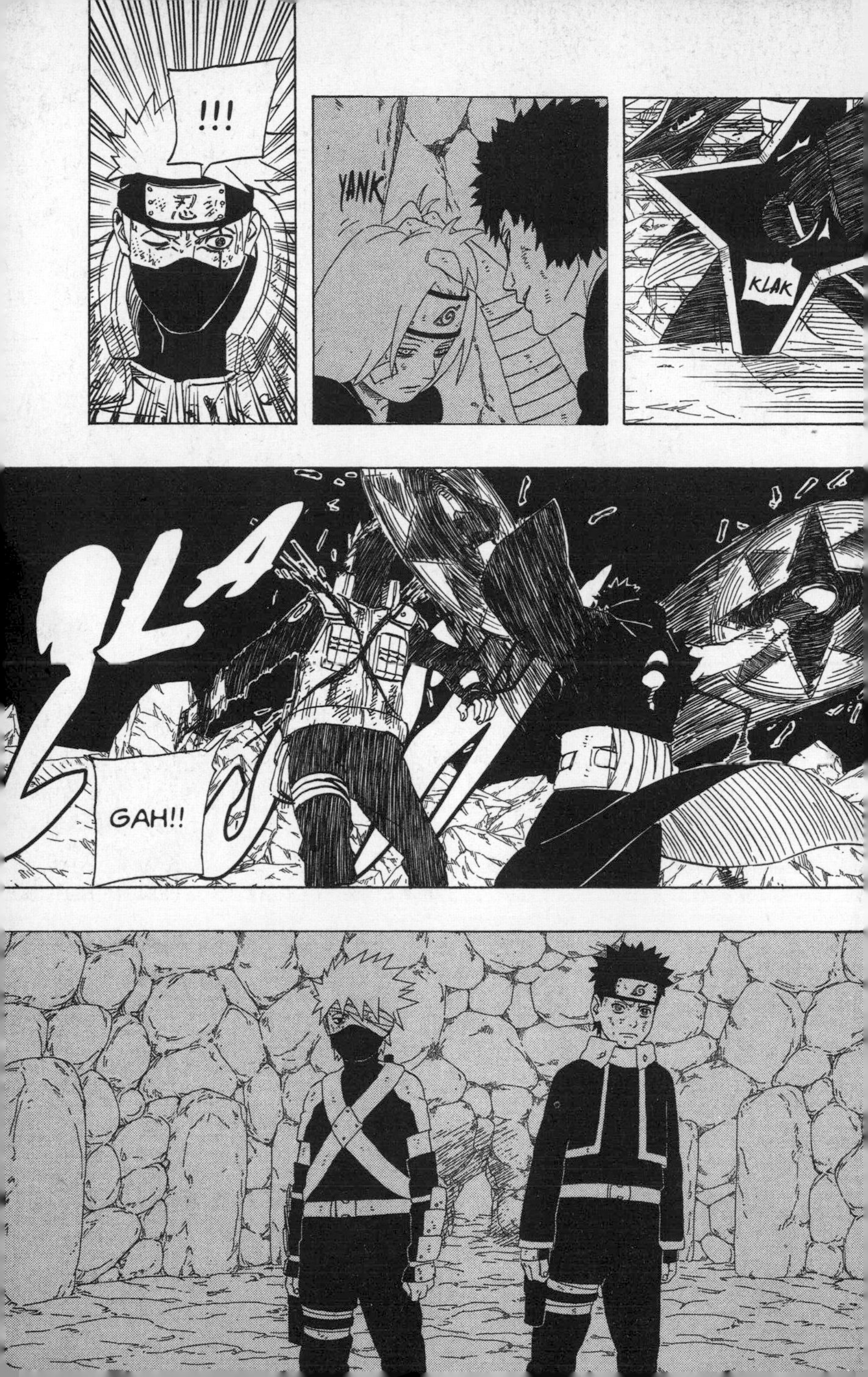
KLAK
YANK
!!!
GAH!!

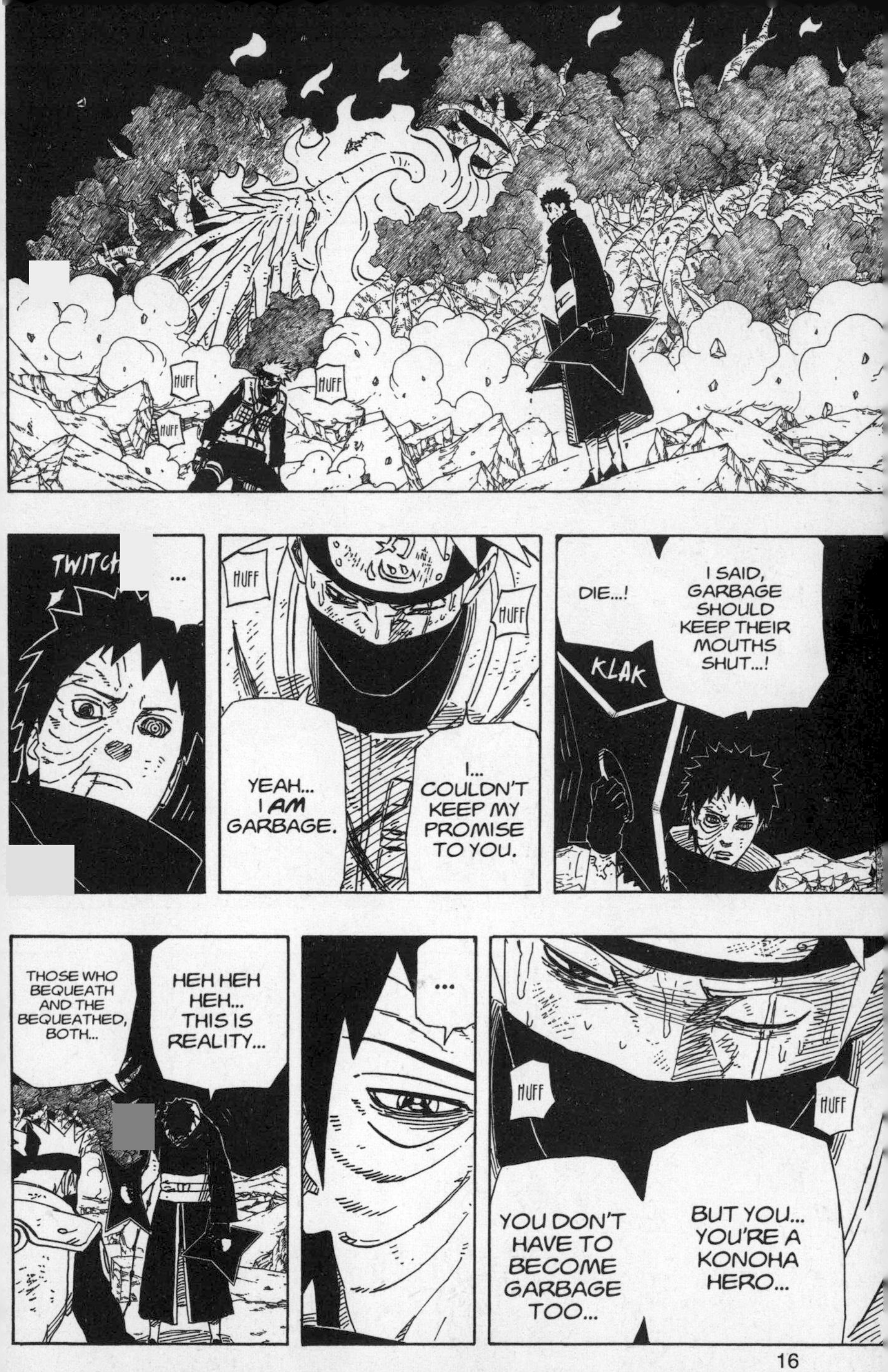
HUFF
HUFF
HUFF
I SAID, GARBAGE SHOULD KEEP THEIR MOUTHS SHUT...!
DIE...!
KLAK
HUFF
HUFF
I... COULDN'T KEEP MY PROMISE TO YOU.
YEAH... I AM GARBAGE.
TWITCH
...
BUT YOU... YOU'RE A KONOHA HERO...
YOU DON'T HAVE TO BECOME GARBAGE TOO...
HUFF
HUFF
...
HEH HEH HEH... THIS IS REALITY...
THOSE WHO BEQUEATH AND THE BEQUEATHED, BOTH...

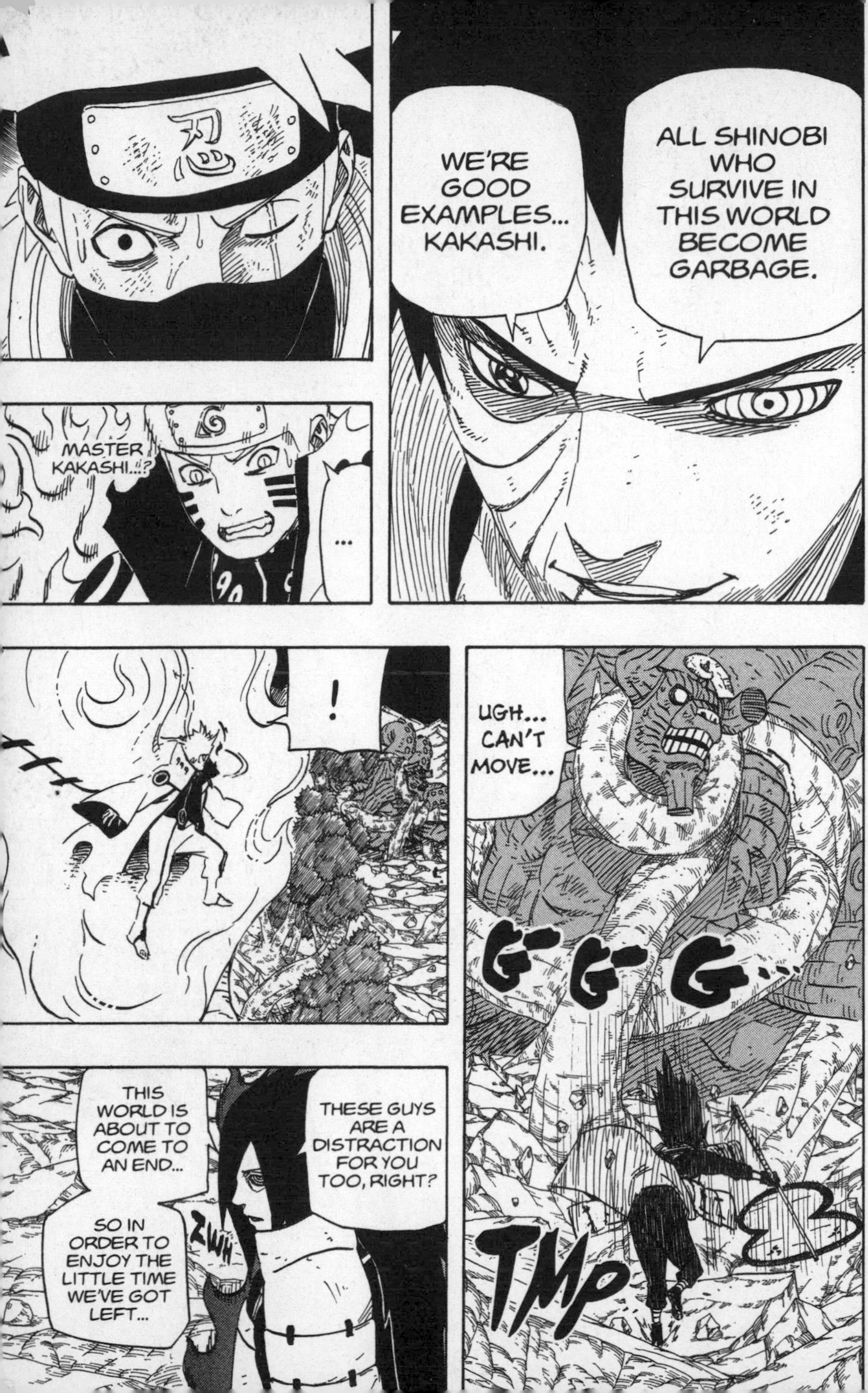
ALL SHINOBI WHO SURVIVE IN THIS WORLD BECOME GARBAGE.
WE'RE GOOD EXAMPLES... KAKASHI.
MASTER KAKASHI...?
...
UGH... CAN'T MOVE...
G-G-G...
TMP
!
THESE GUYS ARE A DISTRACTION FOR YOU TOO, RIGHT?
THIS WORLD IS ABOUT TO COME TO AN END...
SO IN ORDER TO ENJOY THE LITTLE TIME WE'VE GOT LEFT...
ZWH

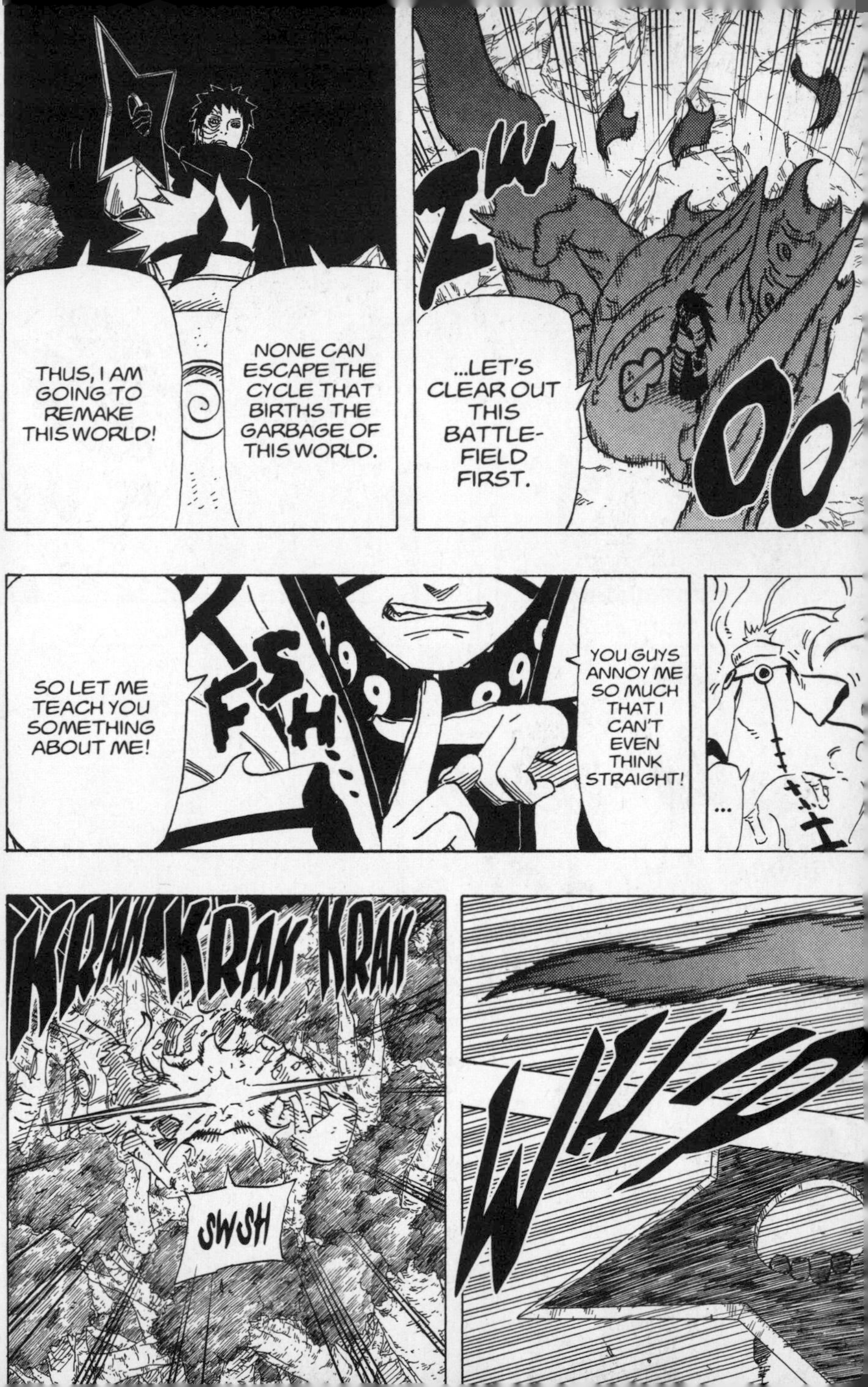
ZWOO
...LET'S CLEAR OUT THIS BATTLE-FIELD FIRST.
NONE CAN ESCAPE THE CYCLE THAT BIRTHS THE GARBAGE OF THIS WORLD.
THUS, I AM GOING TO REMAKE THIS WORLD!
...
YOU GUYS ANNOY ME SO MUCH THAT I CAN'T EVEN THINK STRAIGHT!
FSH
SO LET ME TEACH YOU SOMETHING ABOUT ME!
WHP
KRAK KRAK KRAK
SWSH

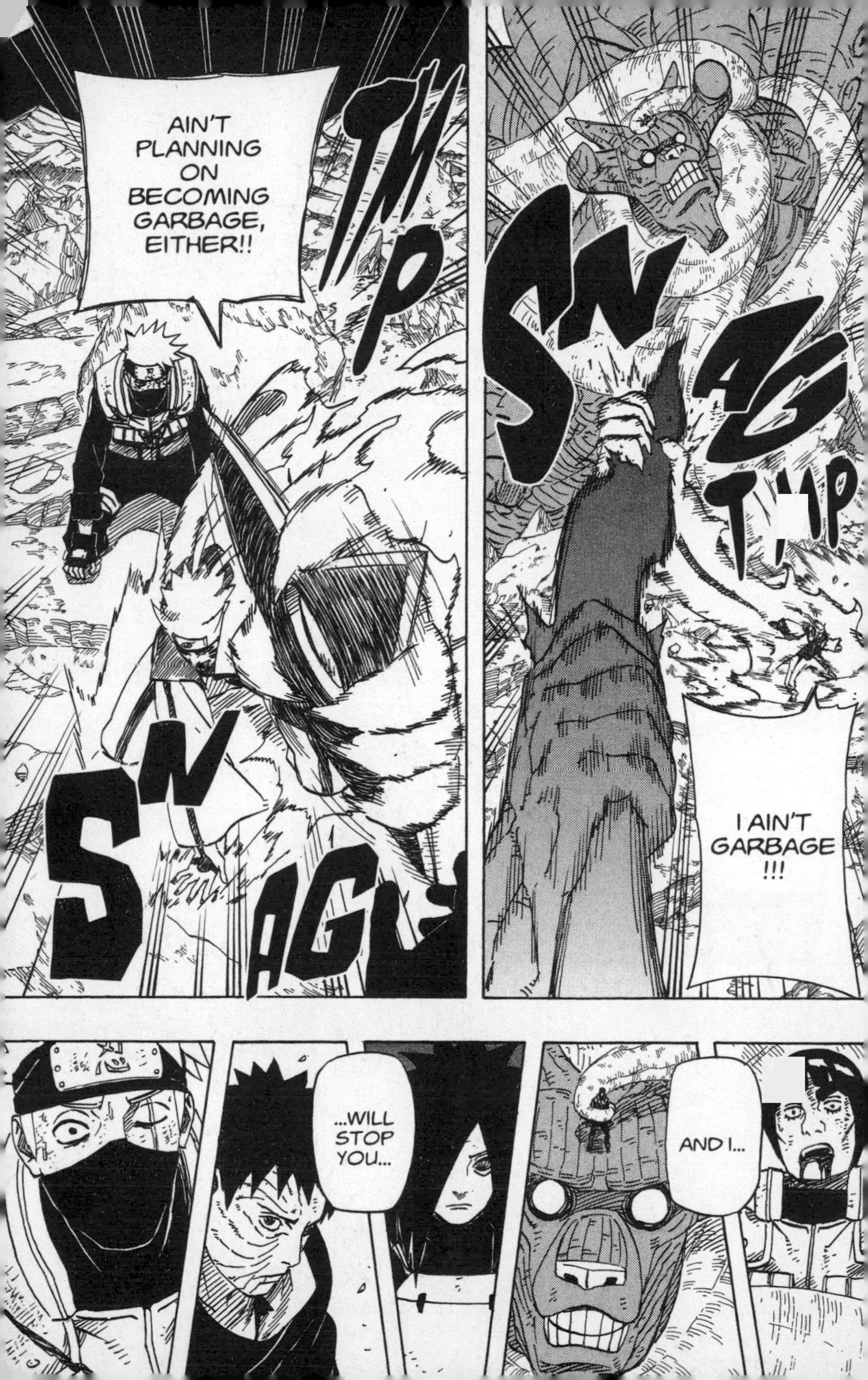
SNAG
THP
I AIN'T GARBAGE !!!
AIN'T PLANNING ON BECOMING GARBAGE, EITHER!!
THP
SNAG
AND I...
...WILL STOP YOU...

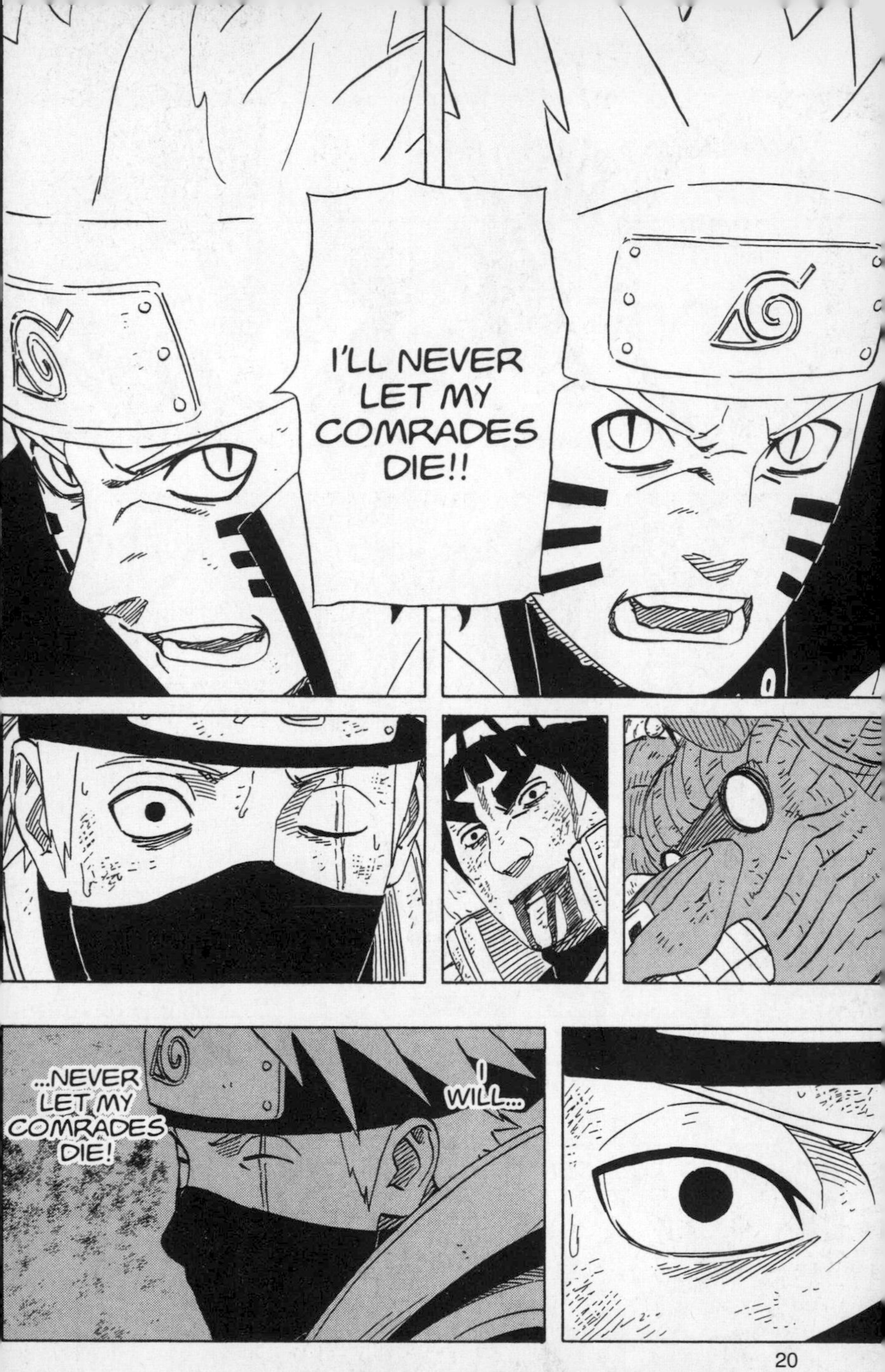
I'LL NEVER LET MY COMRADES DIE!!
I WILL...
...NEVER LET MY COMRADES DIE!

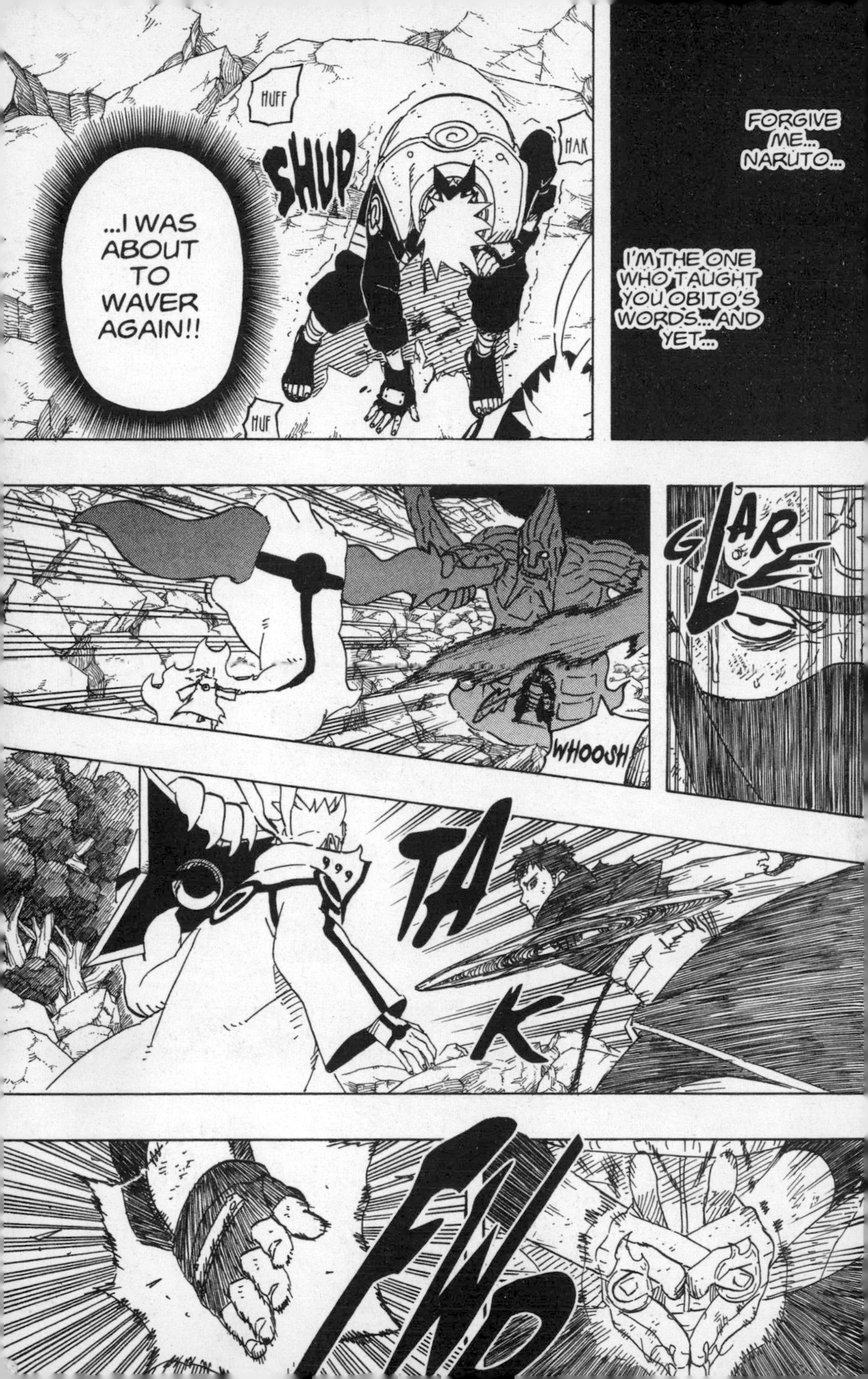
FORGIVE ME... NARUTO...
I'M THE ONE WHO TAUGHT YOU OBITO'S WORDS... AND YET...
HUFF
HAK
SHUP
...I WAS ABOUT TO WAVER AGAIN!!
HUF
GLARE
WHOOSH
TAK

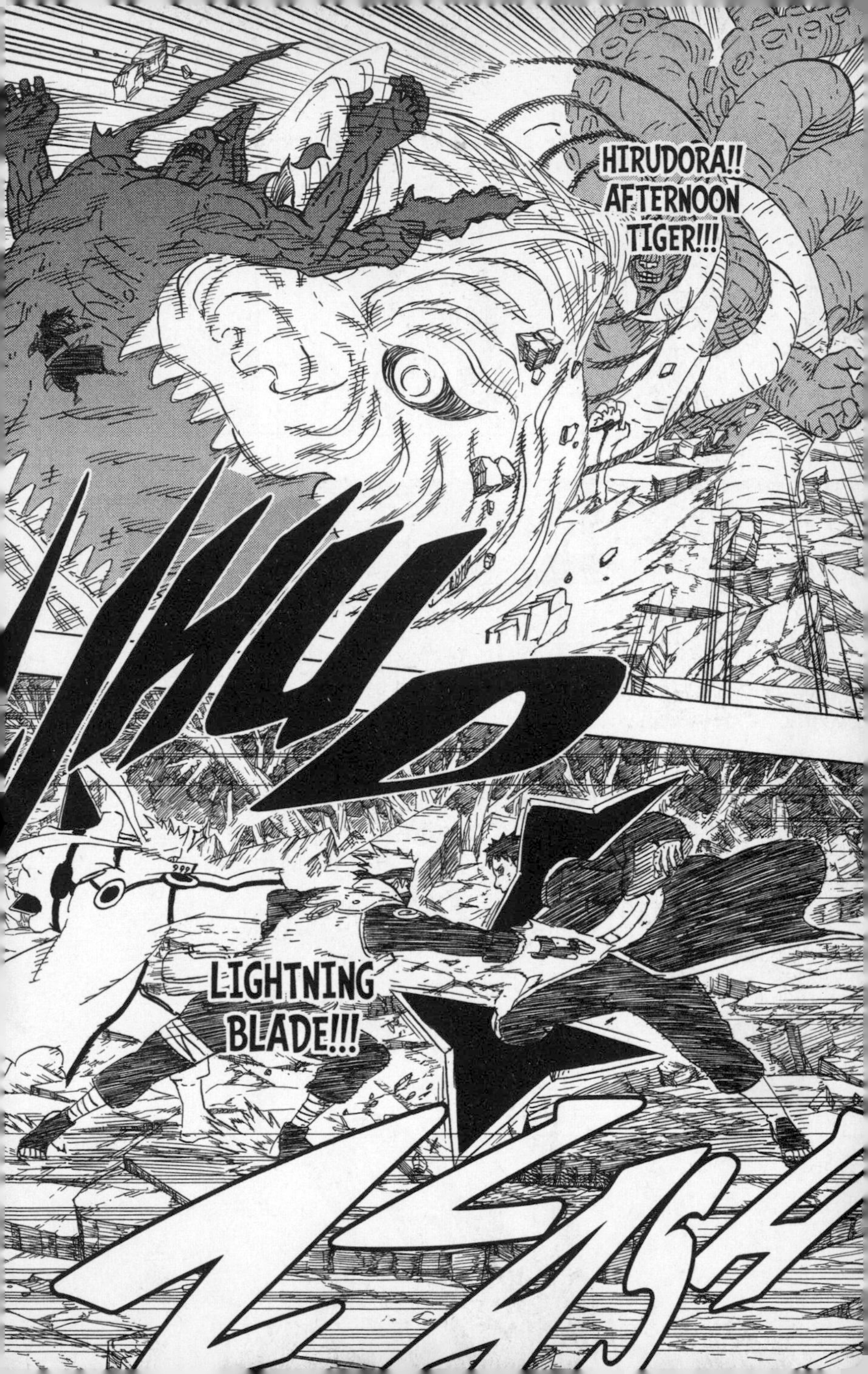
HIRUDORA!! AFTERNOON TIGER!!!
LIGHTNING BLADE!!!

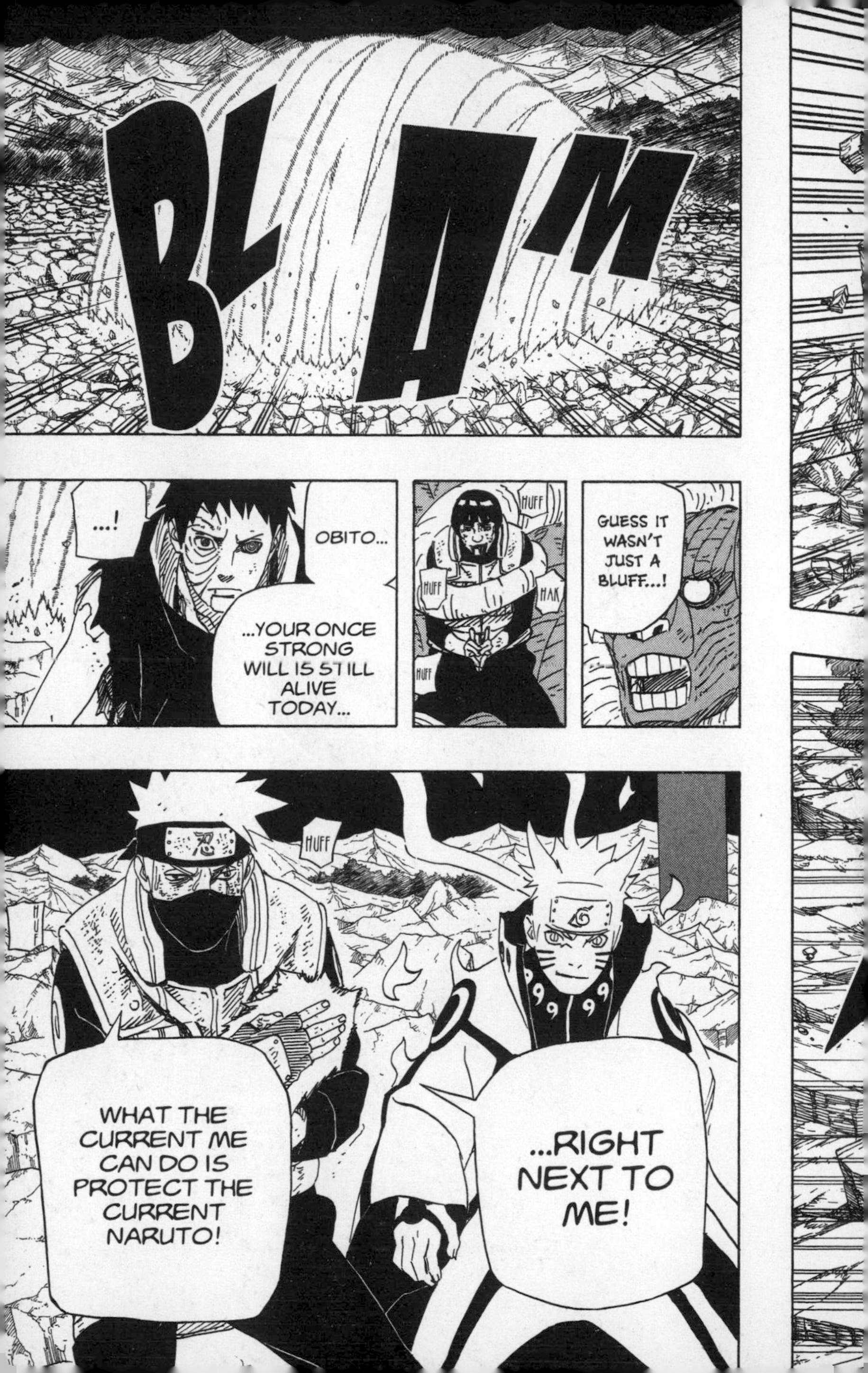
BLAM
GUESS IT WASN'T JUST A BLUFF...!
HUFF
HUFF
HAK
HUFF
...!
OBITO...
...YOUR ONCE STRONG WILL IS STILL ALIVE TODAY...
HUFF
HUF
WHAT THE CURRENT ME CAN DO IS PROTECT THE CURRENT NARUTO!
...RIGHT NEXT TO ME!

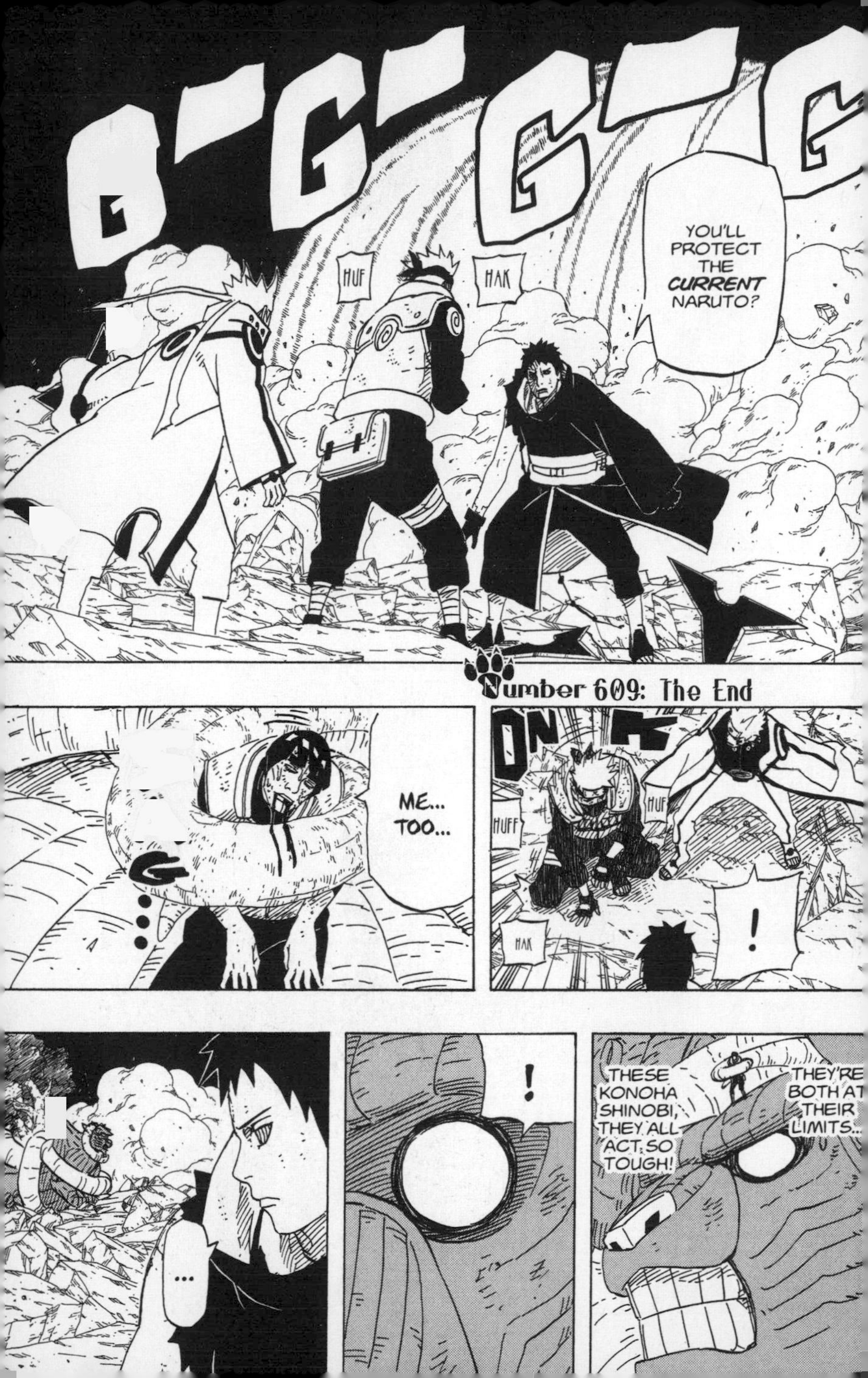
G-G-G-G
YOU'LL PROTECT THE *CURRENT* NARUTO?
HAK
HUF
Number 609: The End
HUF
HUFF
!
HAK
ME... TOO...
G
...
THEY'RE BOTH AT THEIR LIMITS...
THESE KONOHA SHINOBI, THEY ALL ACT SO TOUGH!
!
...

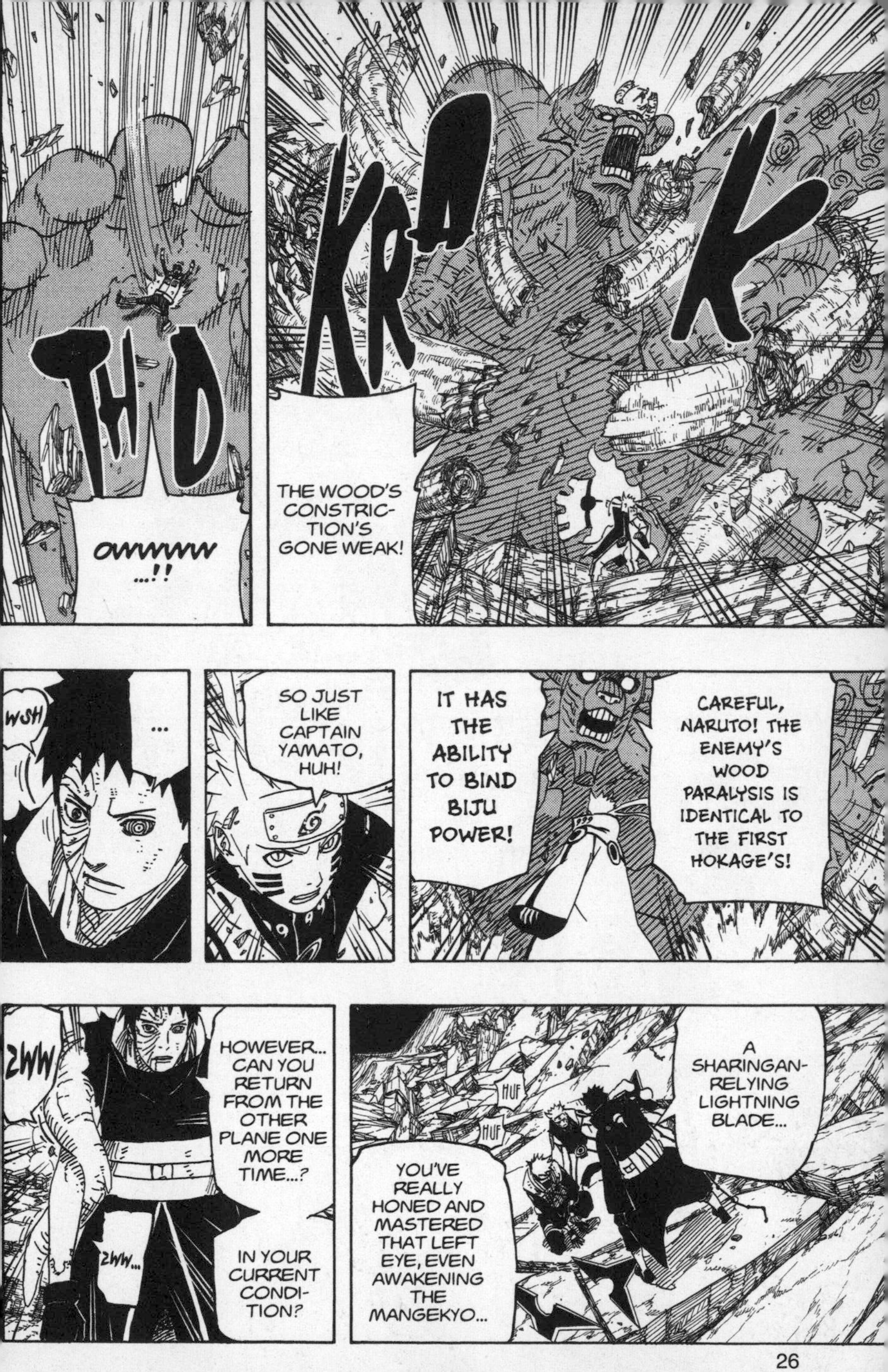
KRAAK
THE WOOD'S CONSTRICTION'S GONE WEAK!
THUD
OWWWW ...!!
CAREFUL, NARUTO! THE ENEMY'S WOOD PARALYSIS IS IDENTICAL TO THE FIRST HOKAGE'S!
IT HAS THE ABILITY TO BIND BIJU POWER!
SO JUST LIKE CAPTAIN YAMATO, HUH!
WSH
...
A SHARINGAN-RELYING LIGHTNING BLADE...
HUF
HUF
YOU'VE REALLY HONED AND MASTERED THAT LEFT EYE, EVEN AWAKENING THE MANGEKYO...
ZWW
HOWEVER... CAN YOU RETURN FROM THE OTHER PLANE ONE MORE TIME...?
IN YOUR CURRENT CONDITION?
ZWW...

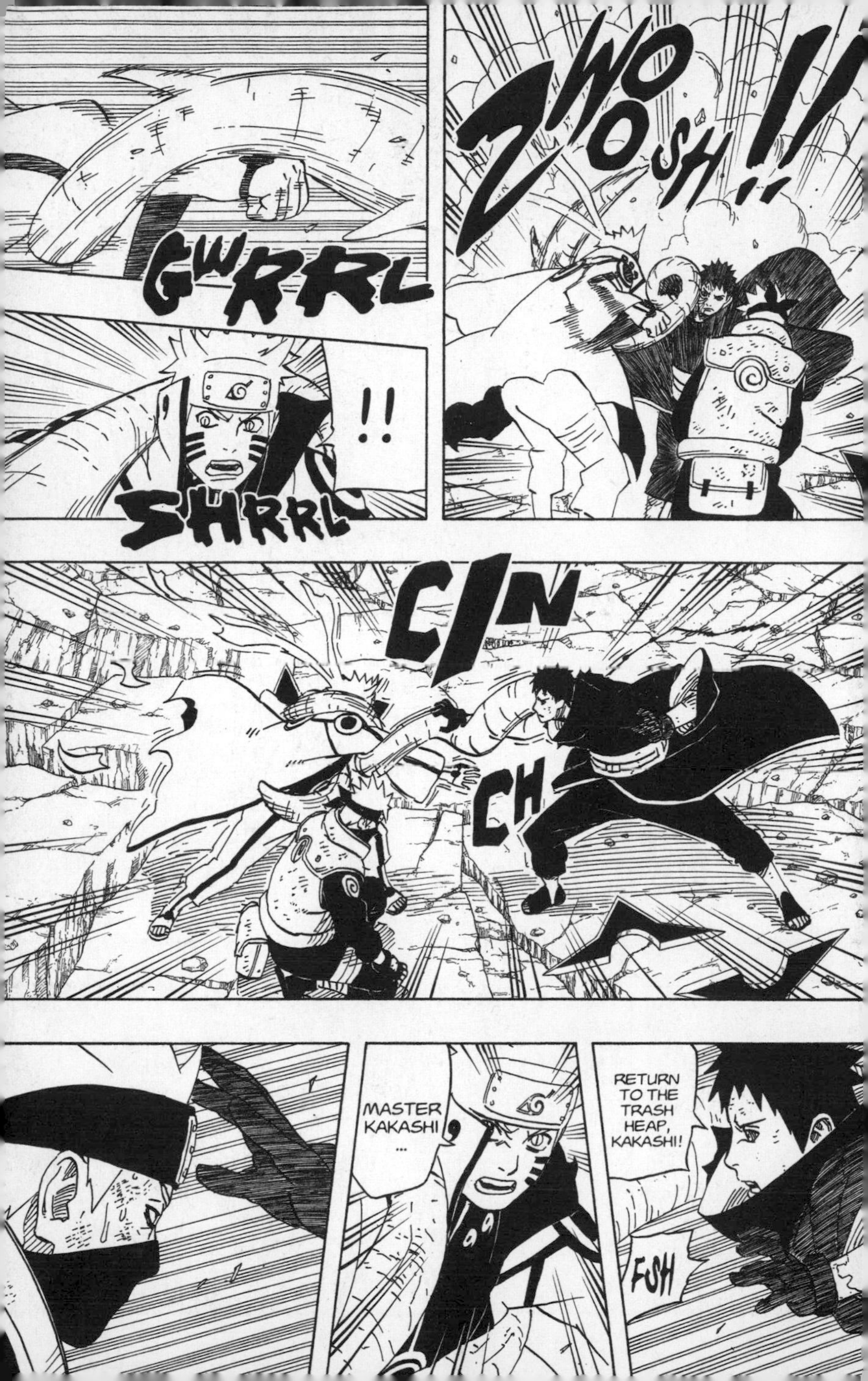
ZWOOSH!!
GWRRRL
!!
SHRRL
CINCH
RETURN TO THE TRASH HEAP, KAKASHI!
FSH
MASTER KAKASHI ...

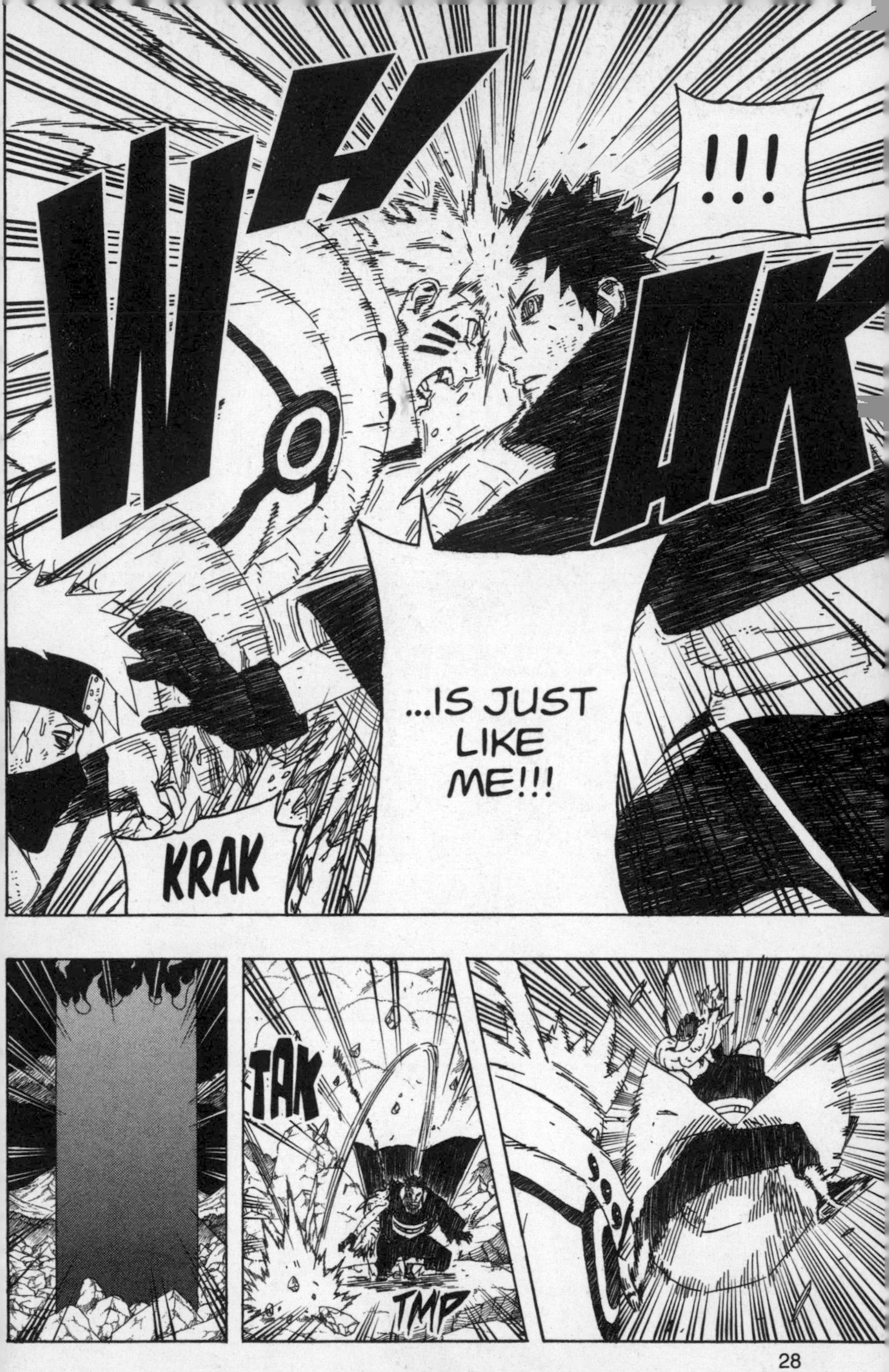
!!!
WHAK
...IS JUST LIKE ME!!!
KRAK
TAK
TMP

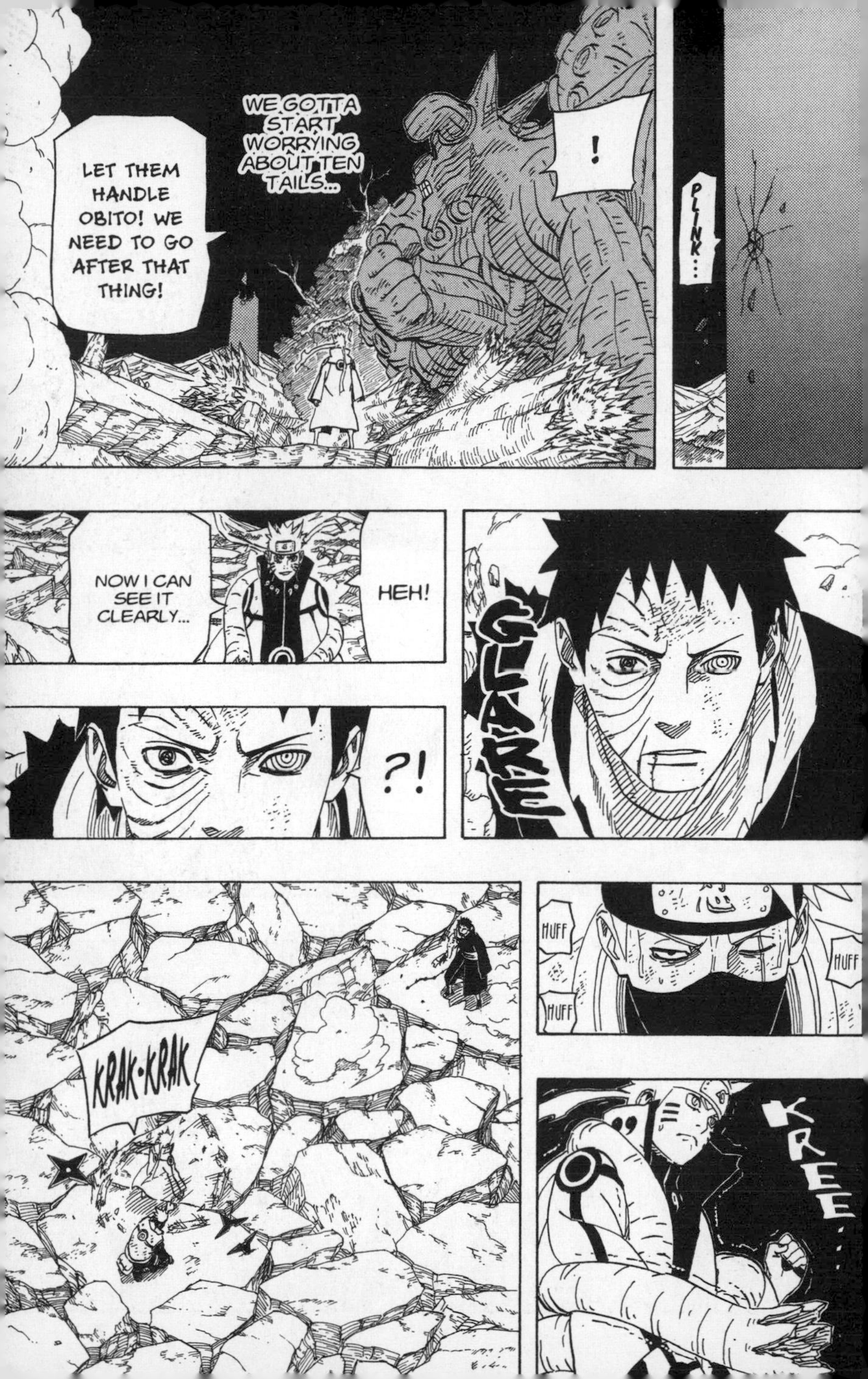
PLINK...
!
WE GOTTA START WORRYING ABOUT TEN TAILS...
LET THEM HANDLE OBITO! WE NEED TO GO AFTER THAT THING!
GLARE
HEH!
NOW I CAN SEE IT CLEARLY...
?!
HUFF
HUFF
HUFF
KREE...
KRAK-KRAK

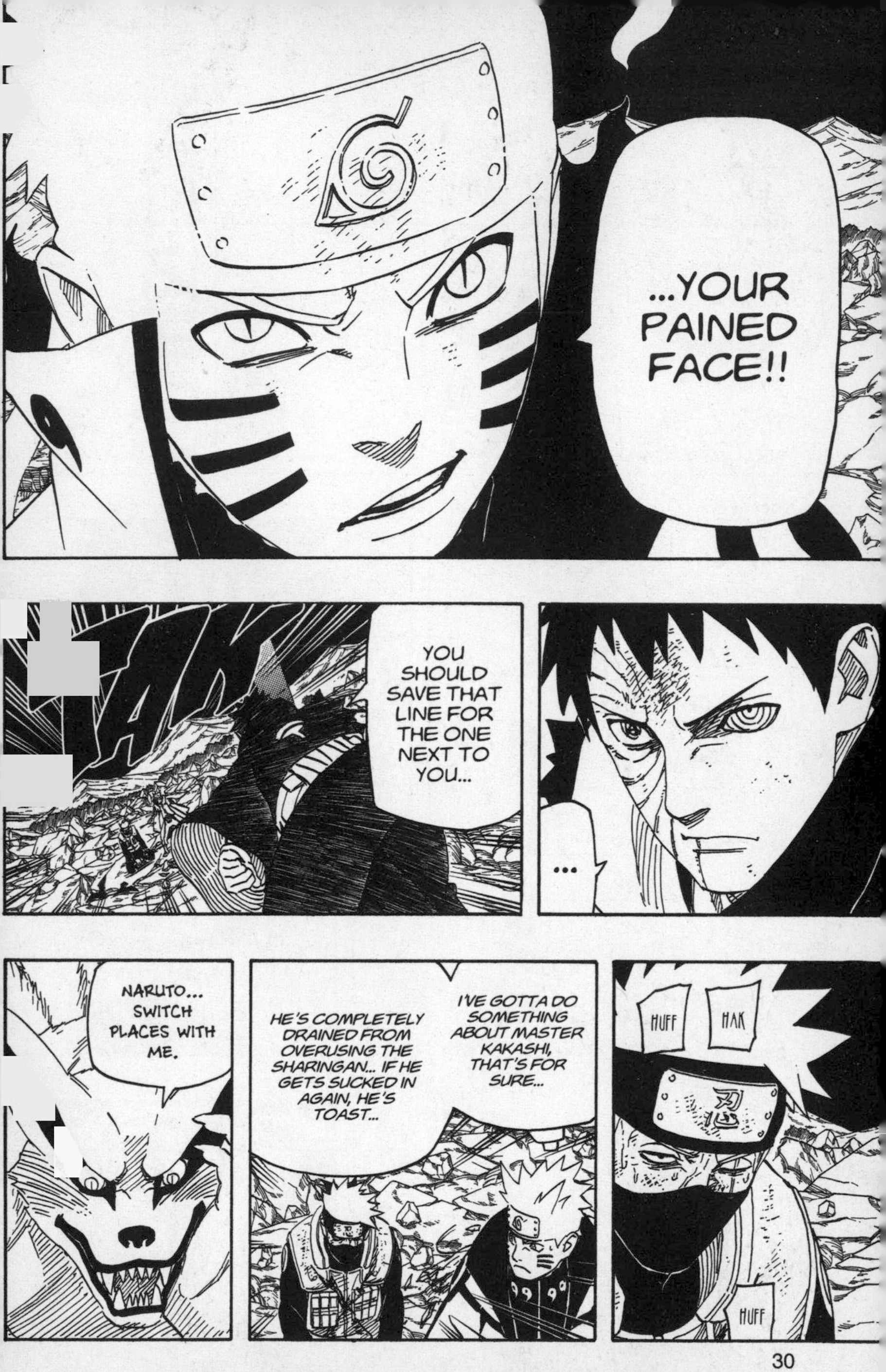
...YOUR PAINED FACE!!
...
YOU SHOULD SAVE THAT LINE FOR THE ONE NEXT TO YOU...
HUFF
HAK
HUFF
I'VE GOTTA DO SOMETHING ABOUT MASTER KAKASHI, THAT'S FOR SURE...
HE'S COMPLETELY DRAINED FROM OVERUSING THE SHARINGAN... IF HE GETS SUCKED IN AGAIN, HE'S TOAST...
NARUTO... SWITCH PLACES WITH ME.

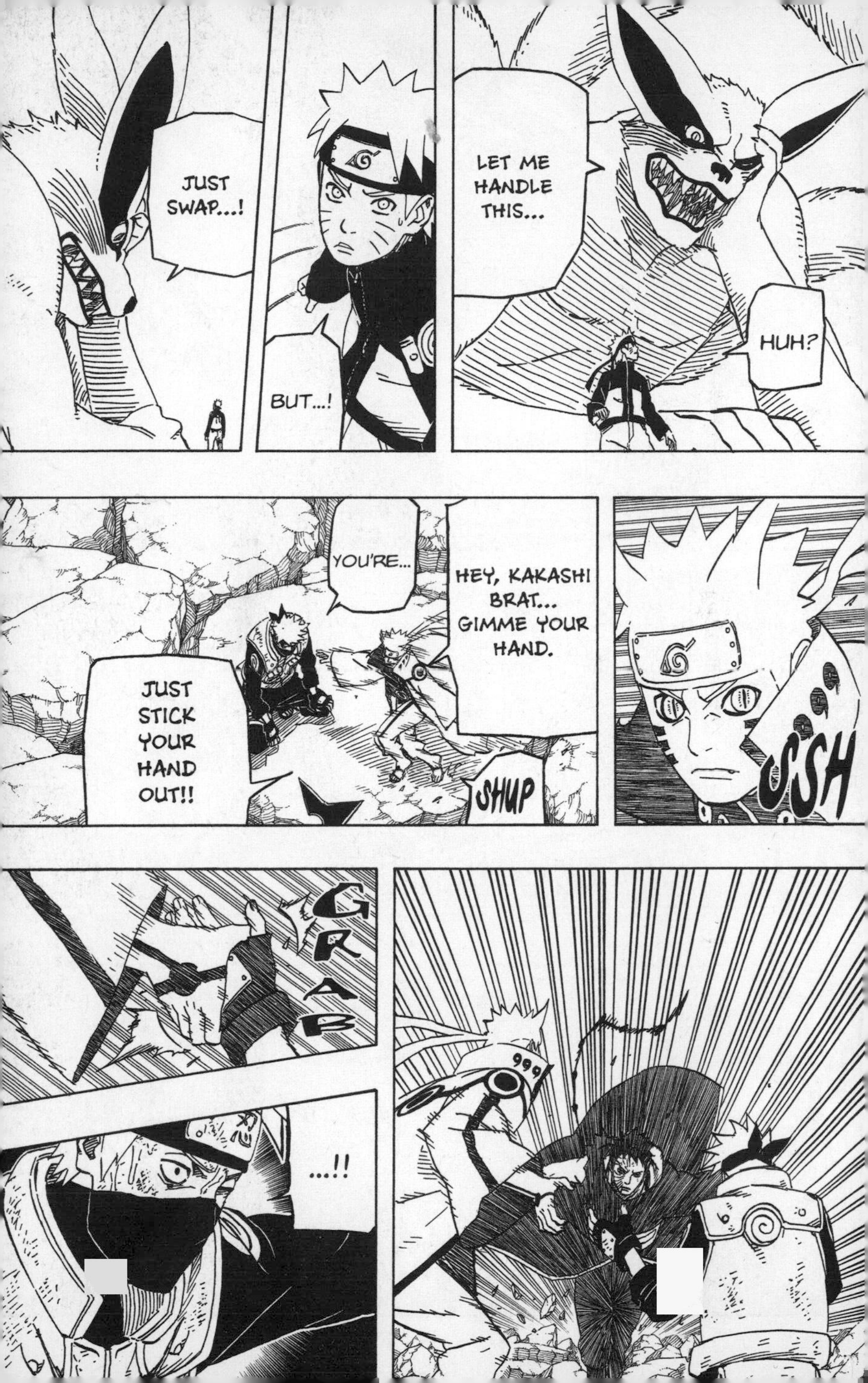
LET ME HANDLE THIS...
HUH?
BUT...!
JUST SWAP...!
SSH
HEY, KAKASHI BRAT... GIMME YOUR HAND.
YOU'RE...
JUST STICK YOUR HAND OUT!!
SHUP
GRAB
...!!

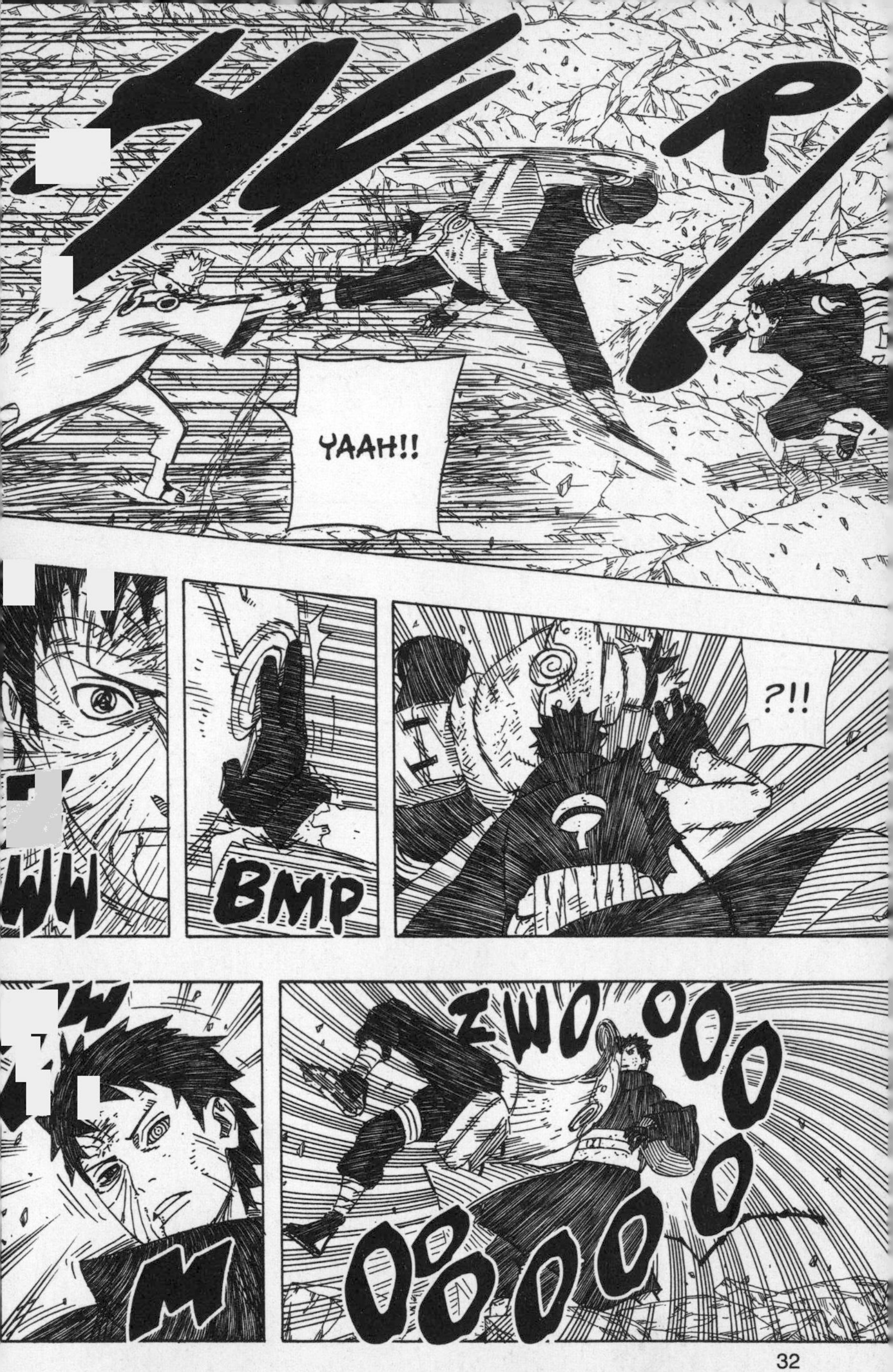
YAAH!!
?!!
BMP

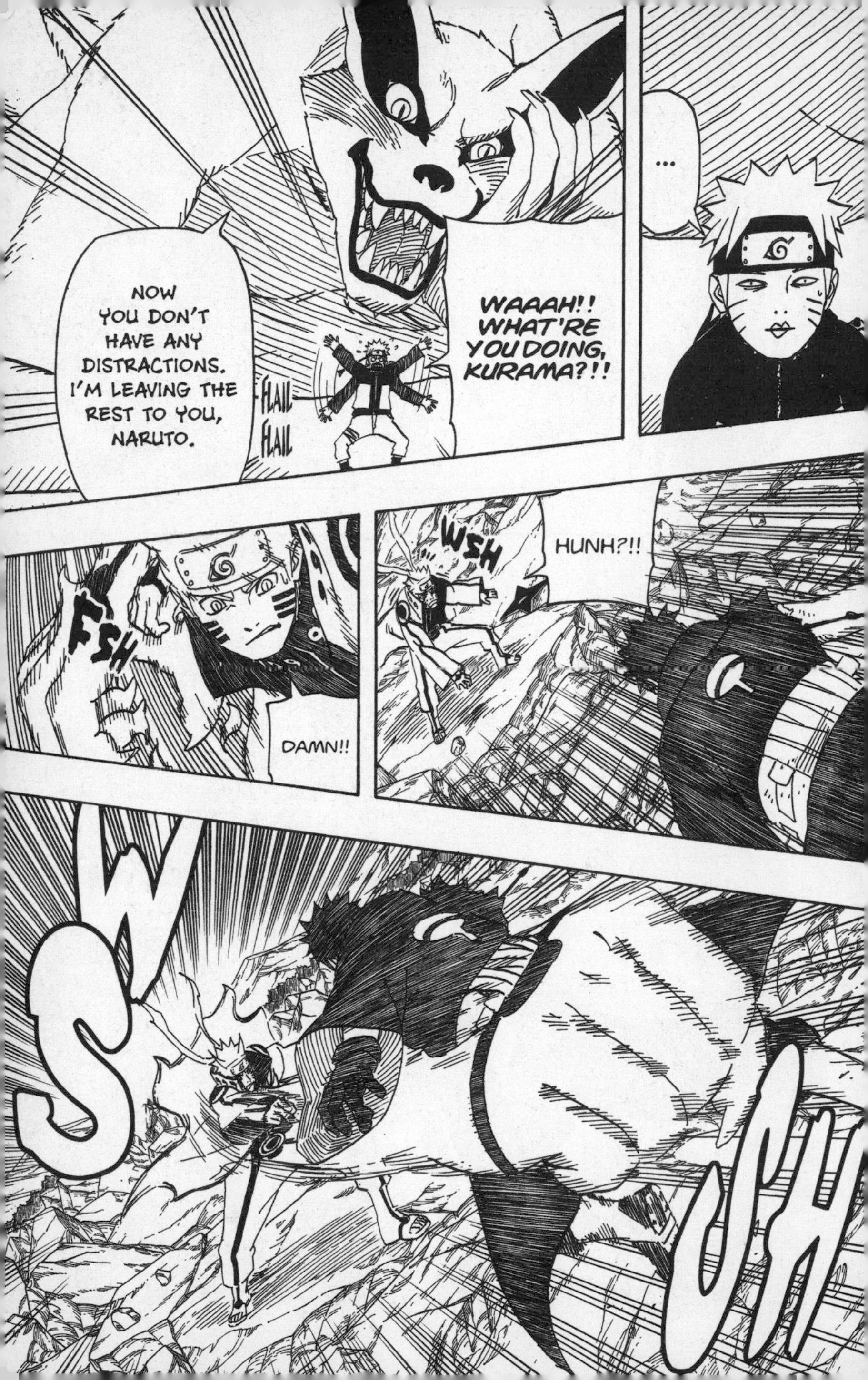
...
WAAAH!! WHAT'RE YOU DOING, KURAMA?!!
FLAIL FLAIL
NOW YOU DON'T HAVE ANY DISTRACTIONS. I'M LEAVING THE REST TO YOU, NARUTO.
WSH
HUNH?!!
FSH
DAMN!!

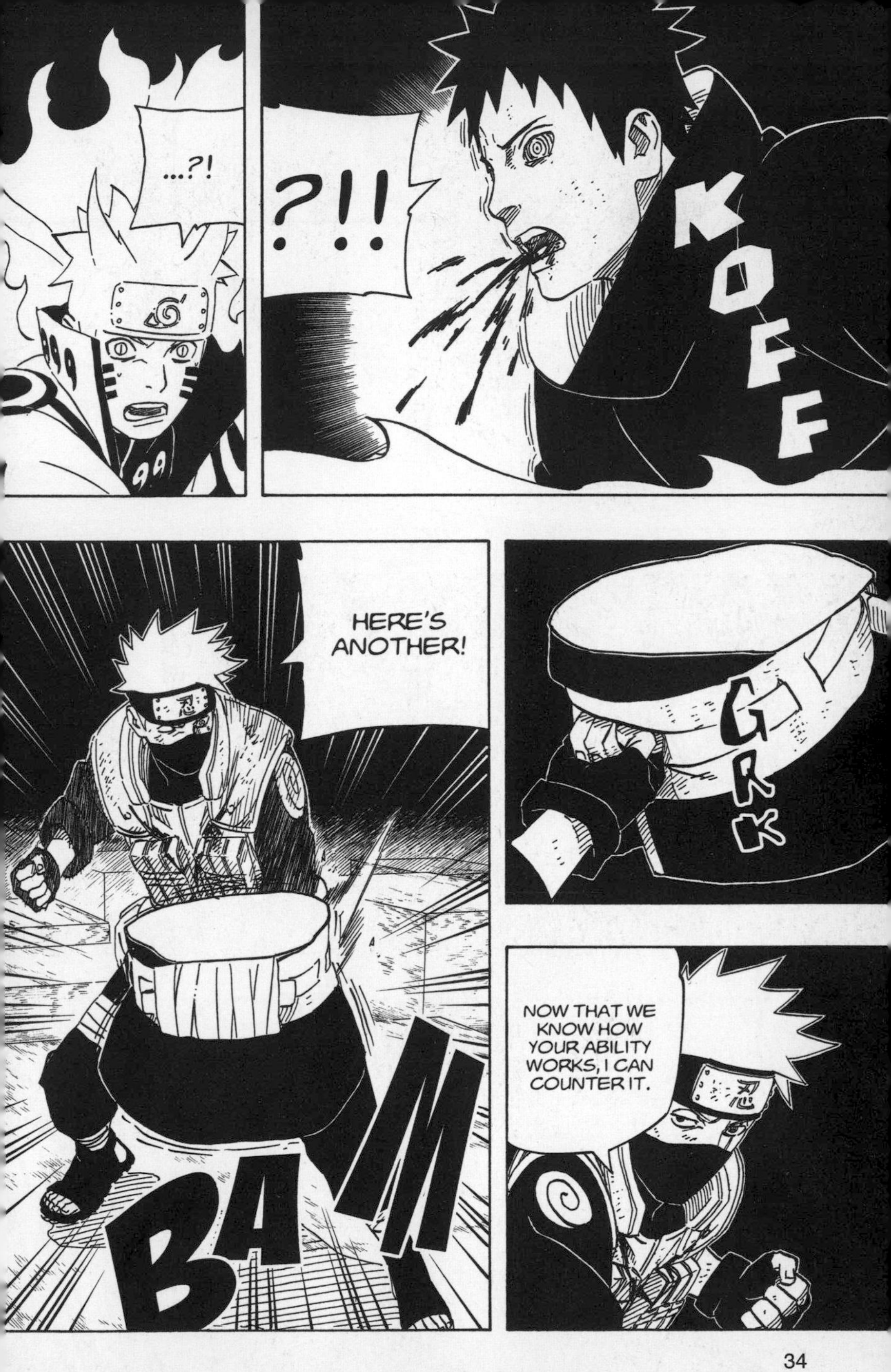
?!!
KOFF
...?!
GRK
NOW THAT WE KNOW HOW YOUR ABILITY WORKS, I CAN COUNTER IT.
HERE'S ANOTHER!
BAM

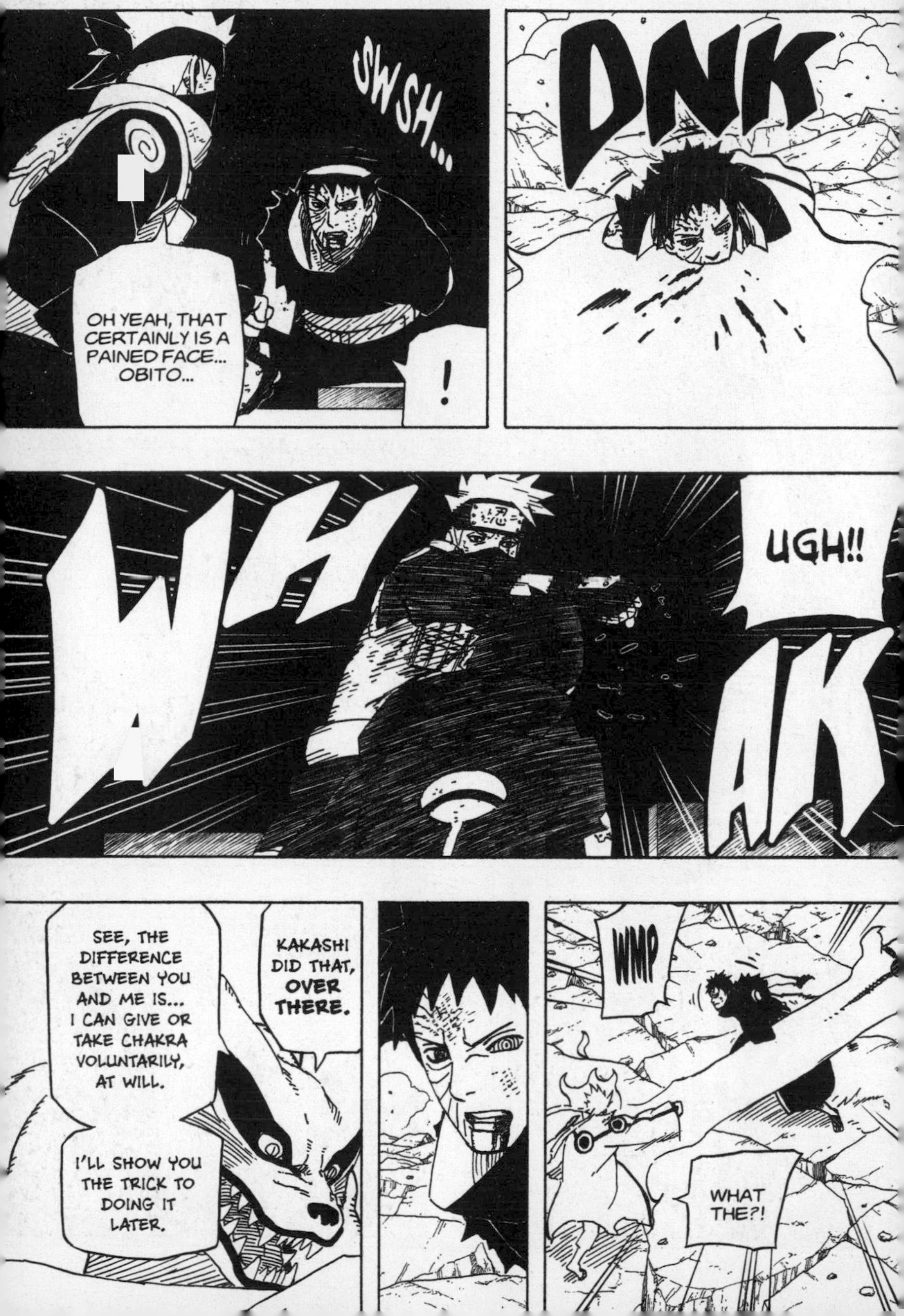
DNK
SWSH...
OH YEAH, THAT CERTAINLY IS A PAINED FACE... OBITO...
!
UGH!!
WHAK
WMP
WHAT THE?!
KAKASHI DID THAT, OVER THERE.
SEE, THE DIFFERENCE BETWEEN YOU AND ME IS... I CAN GIVE OR TAKE CHAKRA VOLUNTARILY, AT WILL.
I'LL SHOW YOU THE TRICK TO DOING IT LATER.

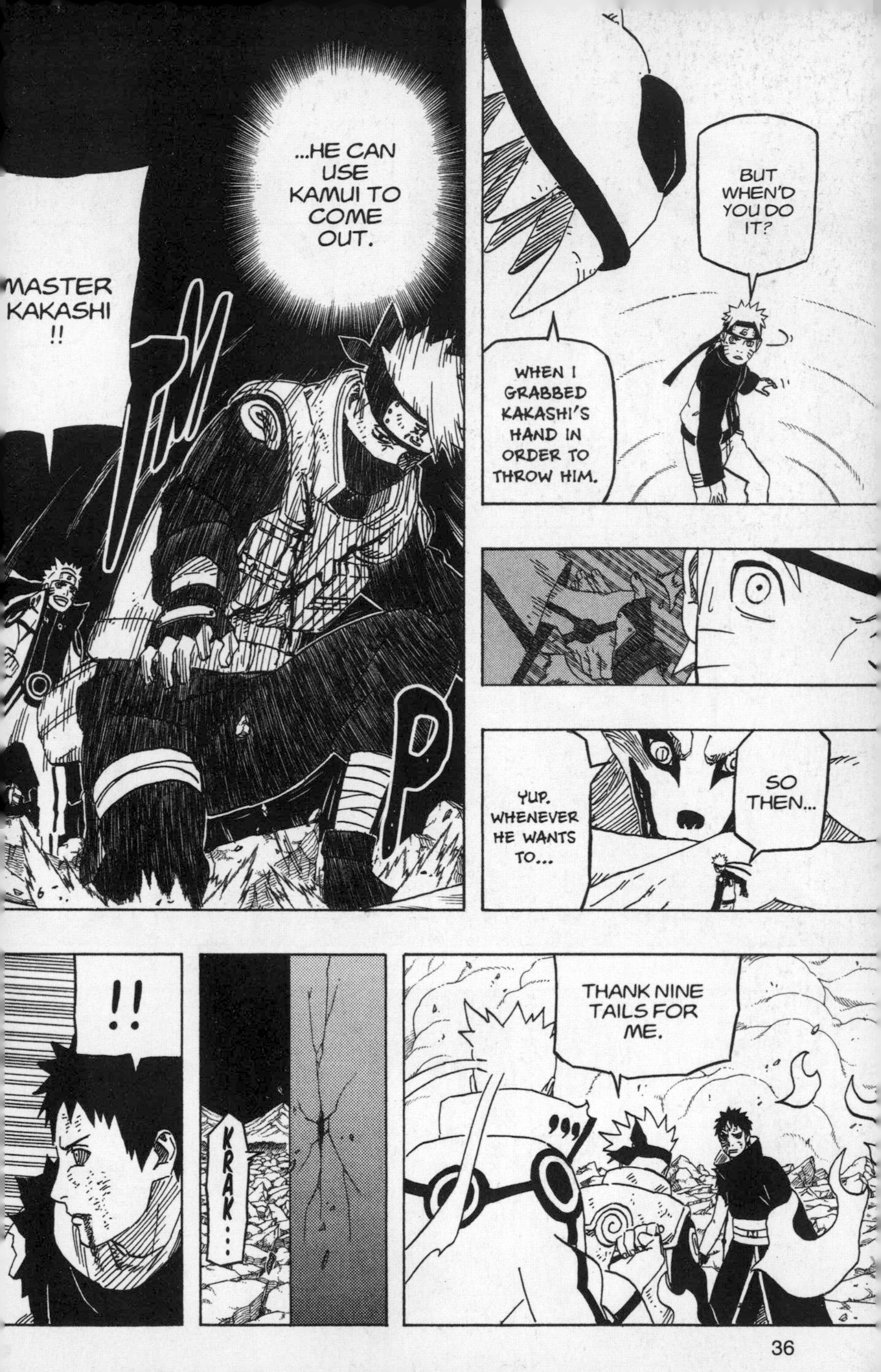

BUT WHEN'D YOU DO IT?
WHEN I GRABBED KAKASHI'S HAND IN ORDER TO THROW HIM.
SO THEN...
YUP. WHENEVER HE WANTS TO...
...HE CAN USE KAMUI TO COME OUT.
MASTER KAKASHI !!
THANK NINE TAILS FOR ME.
KRAK...
!!

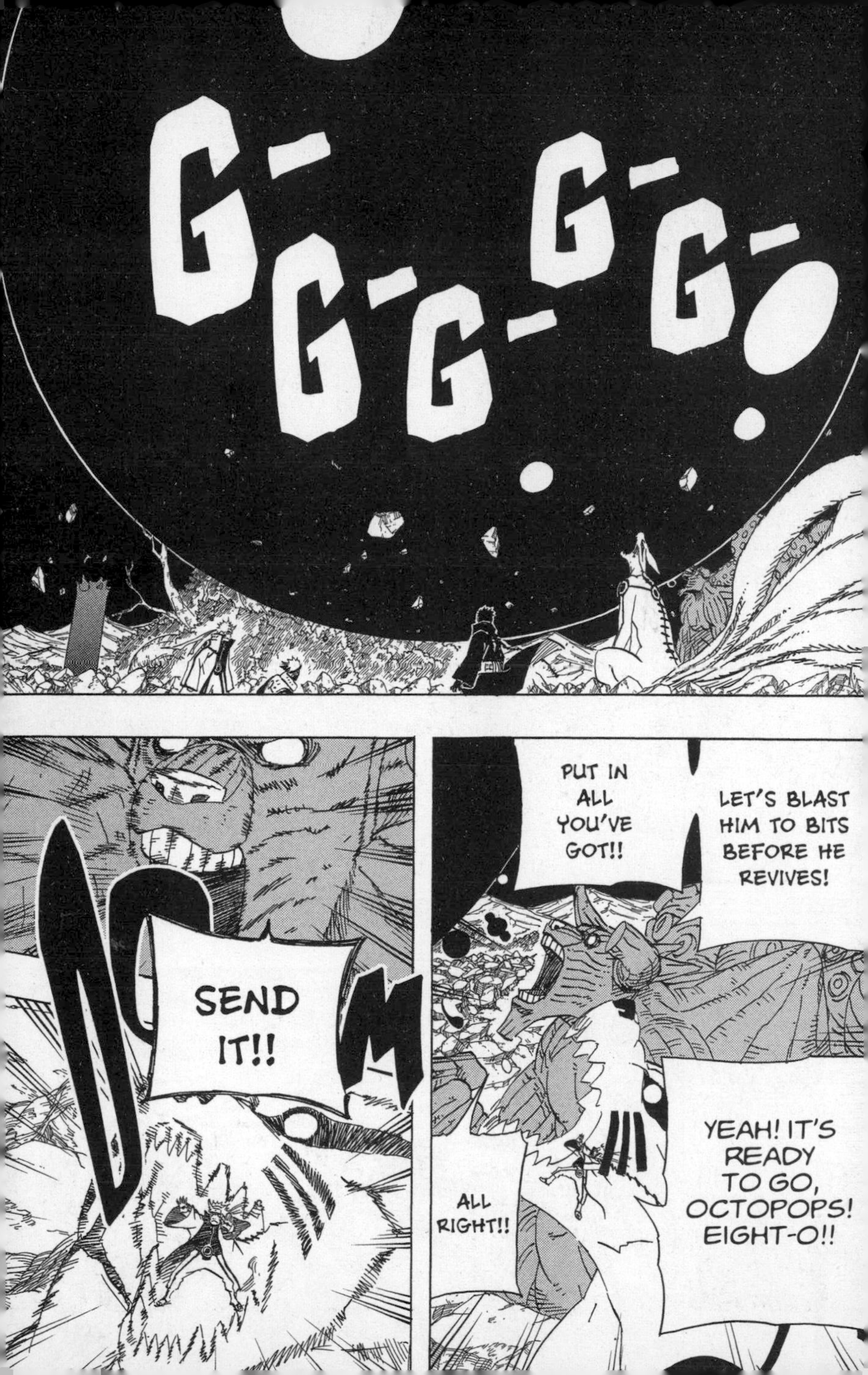
G-G-G-G-G-O!
LET'S BLAST HIM TO BITS BEFORE HE REVIVES!
PUT IN ALL YOU'VE GOT!!
YEAH! IT'S READY TO GO, OCTOPOPS! EIGHT-O!!
ALL RIGHT!!
SEND IT!!

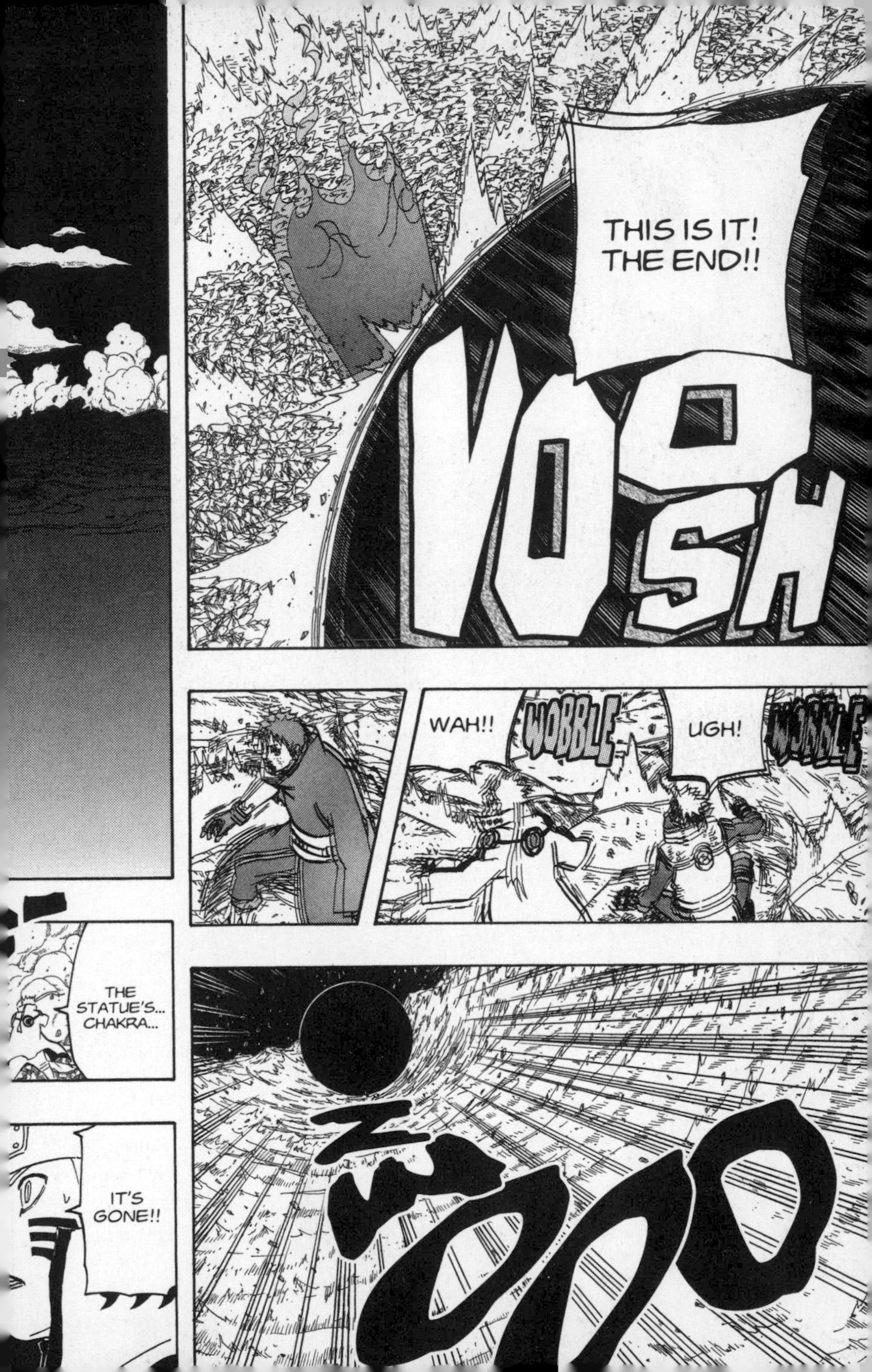
THIS IS IT! THE END!!
VOOSH
WOBBLE
UGH!
WOBBLE
WAH!!
THE STATUE'S... CHAKRA...
IT'S GONE!!

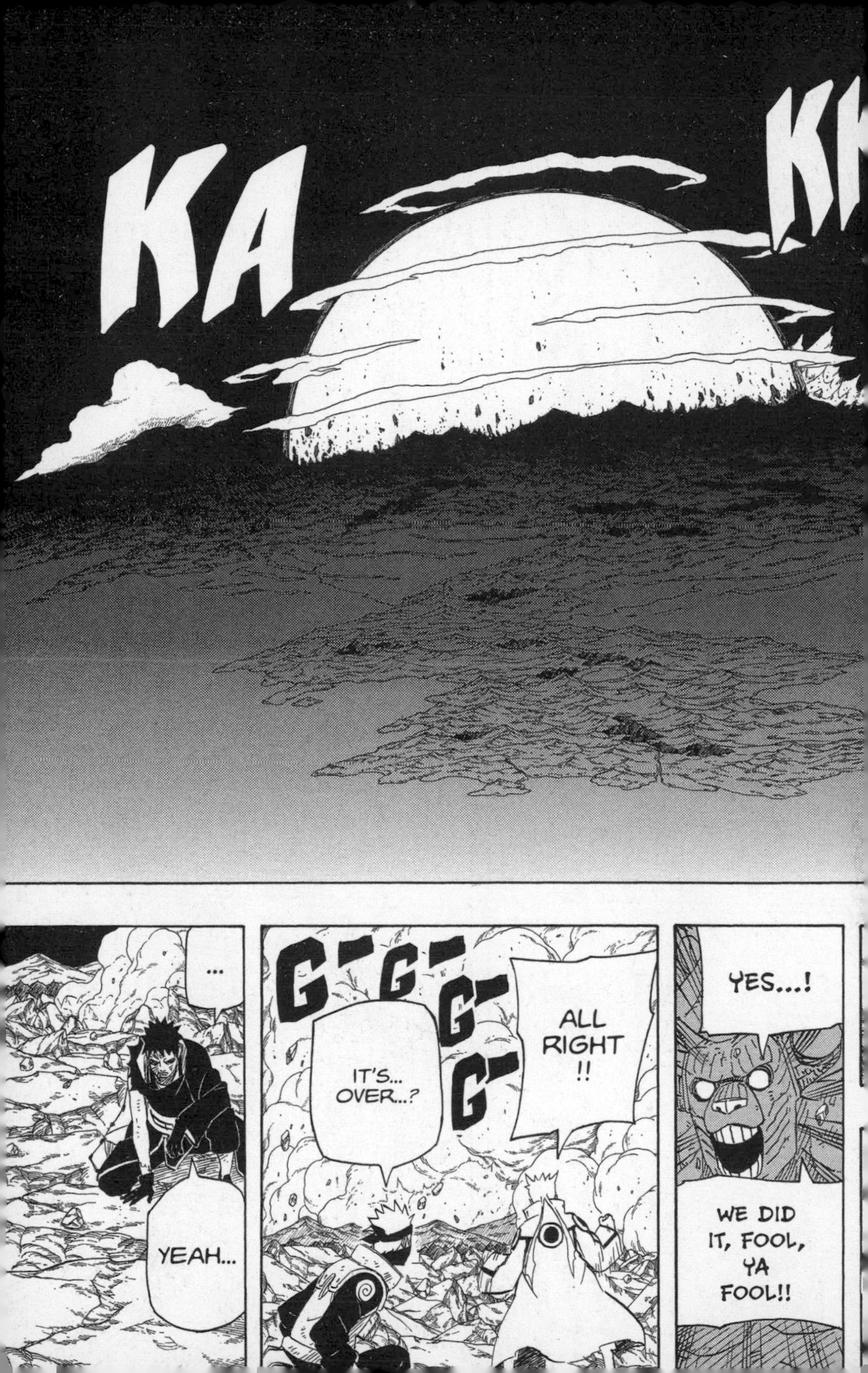
KA
KK
YES...!
WE DID IT, FOOL, YA FOOL!!
ALL RIGHT !!
G-G-G-G-
IT'S... OVER...?
...
YEAH...

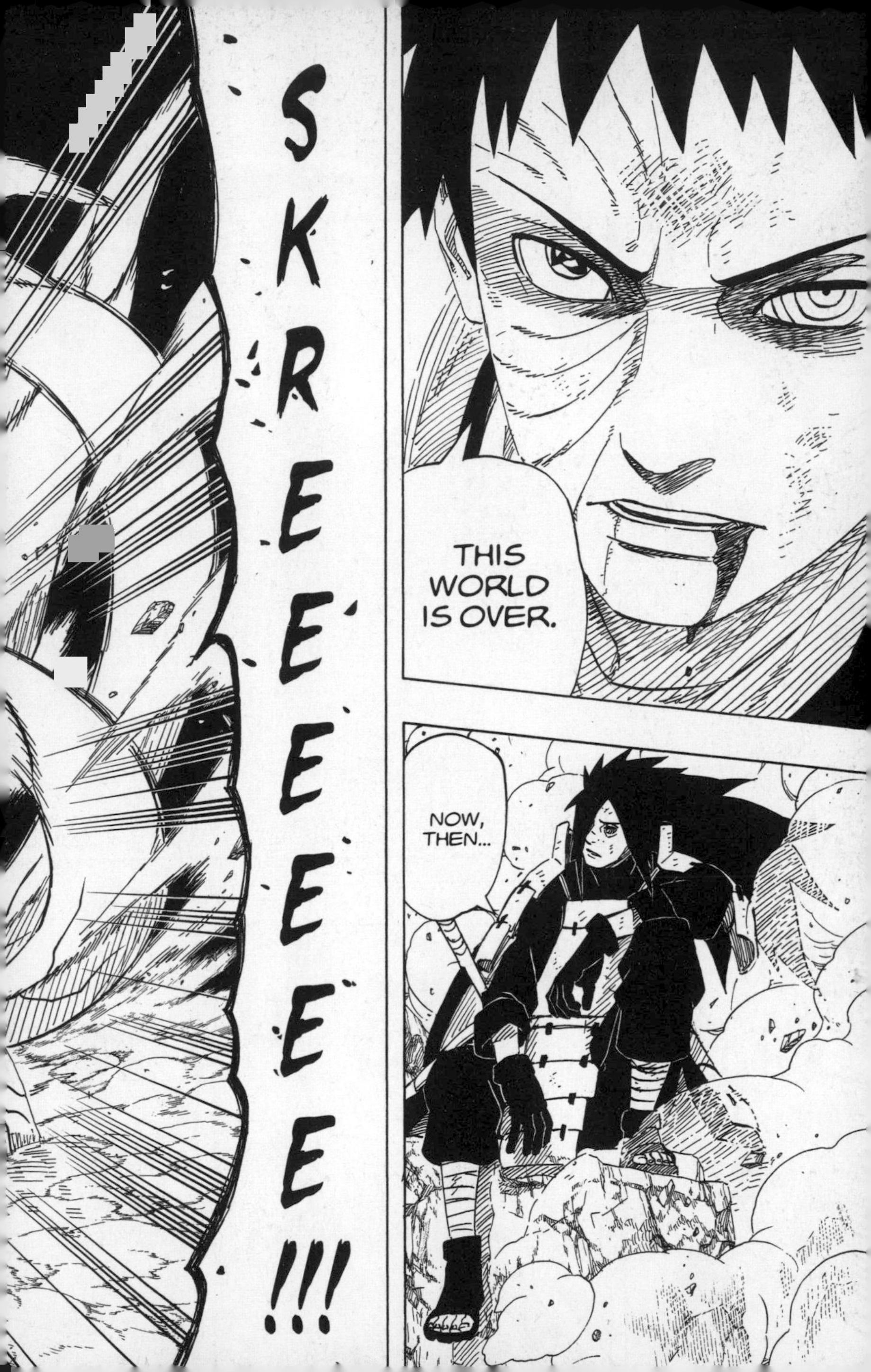
THIS WORLD IS OVER.
NOW, THEN...
SKREEEEEE!!!

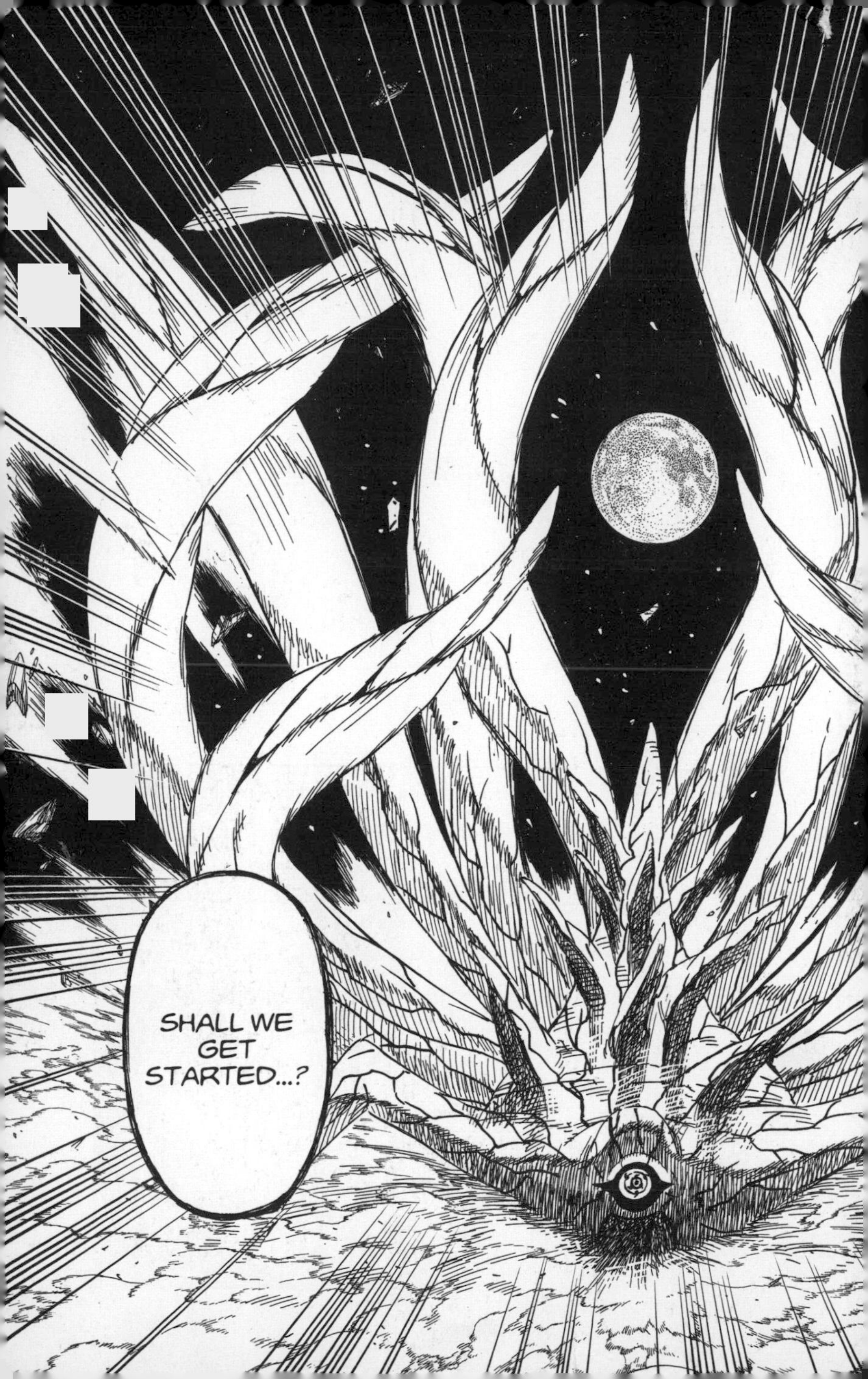
SHALL WE GET STARTED...?

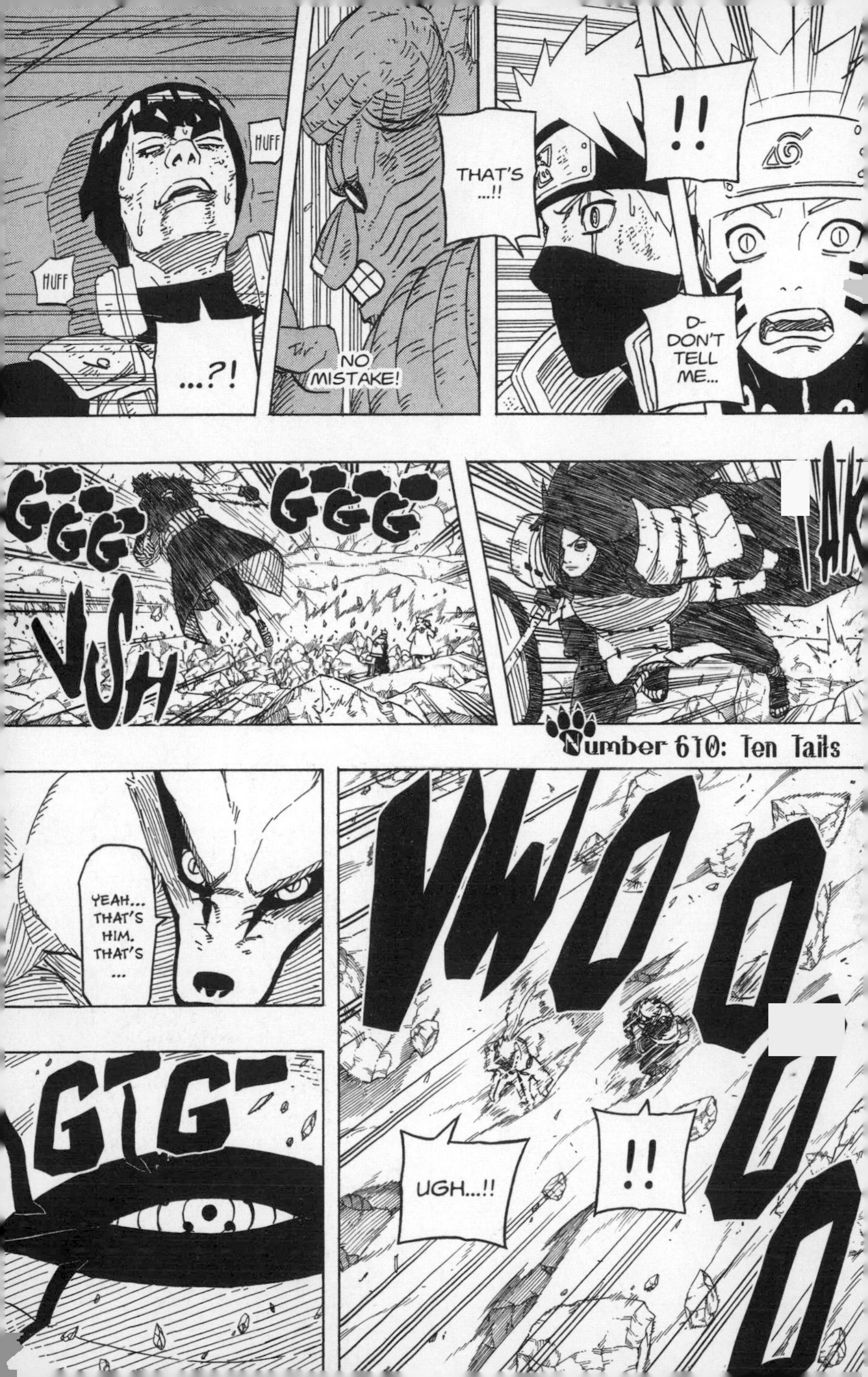
!!
THAT'S ...!!
D-DON'T TELL ME...
NO MISTAKE!
HUFF
HUFF
...?!
GGG
GGG
VSH
Number 610: Ten Tails
VWOOOO
!!
UGH...!!
YEAH... THAT'S HIM. THAT'S ...
GIG-

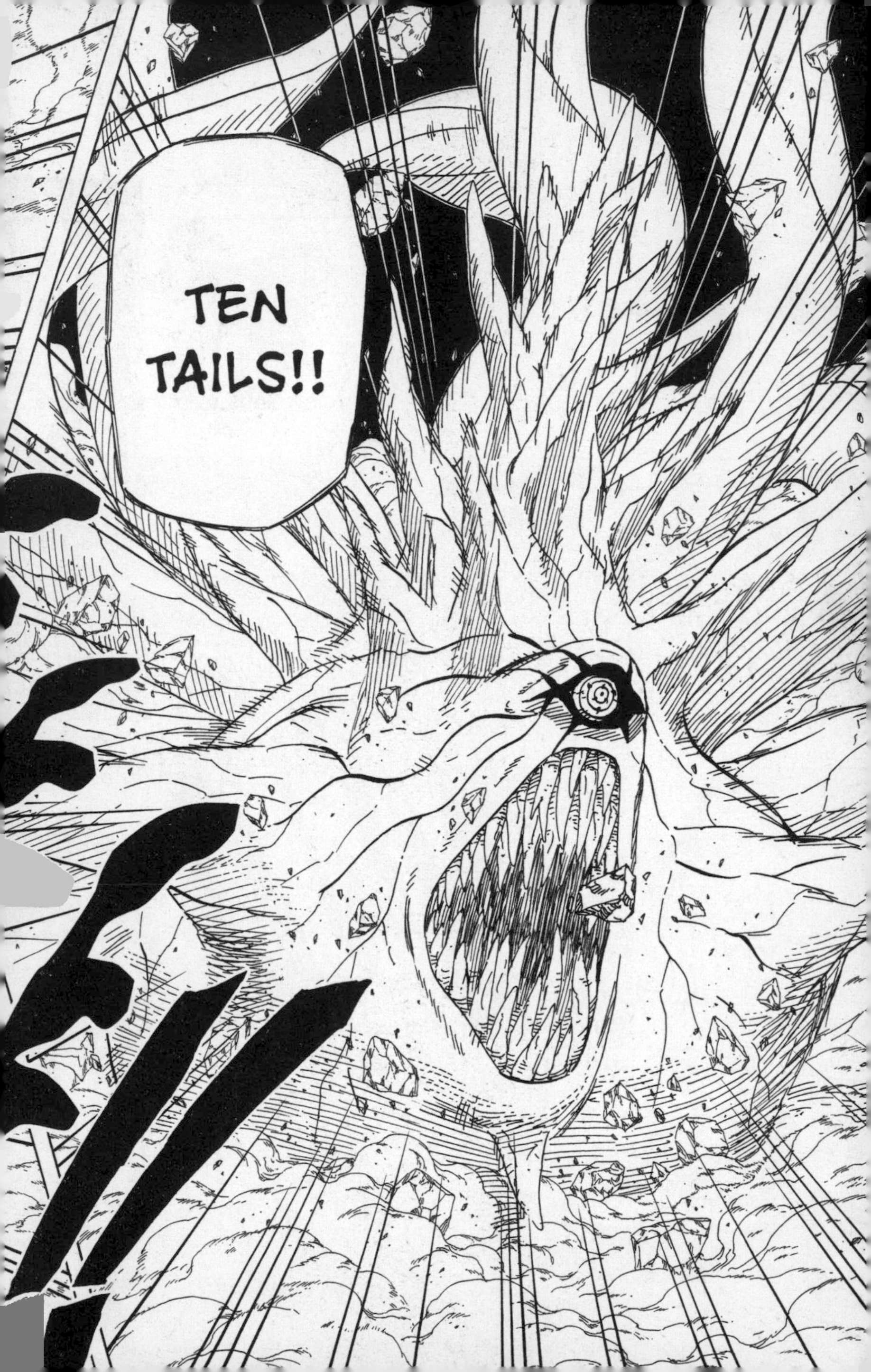
TEN TAILS!!

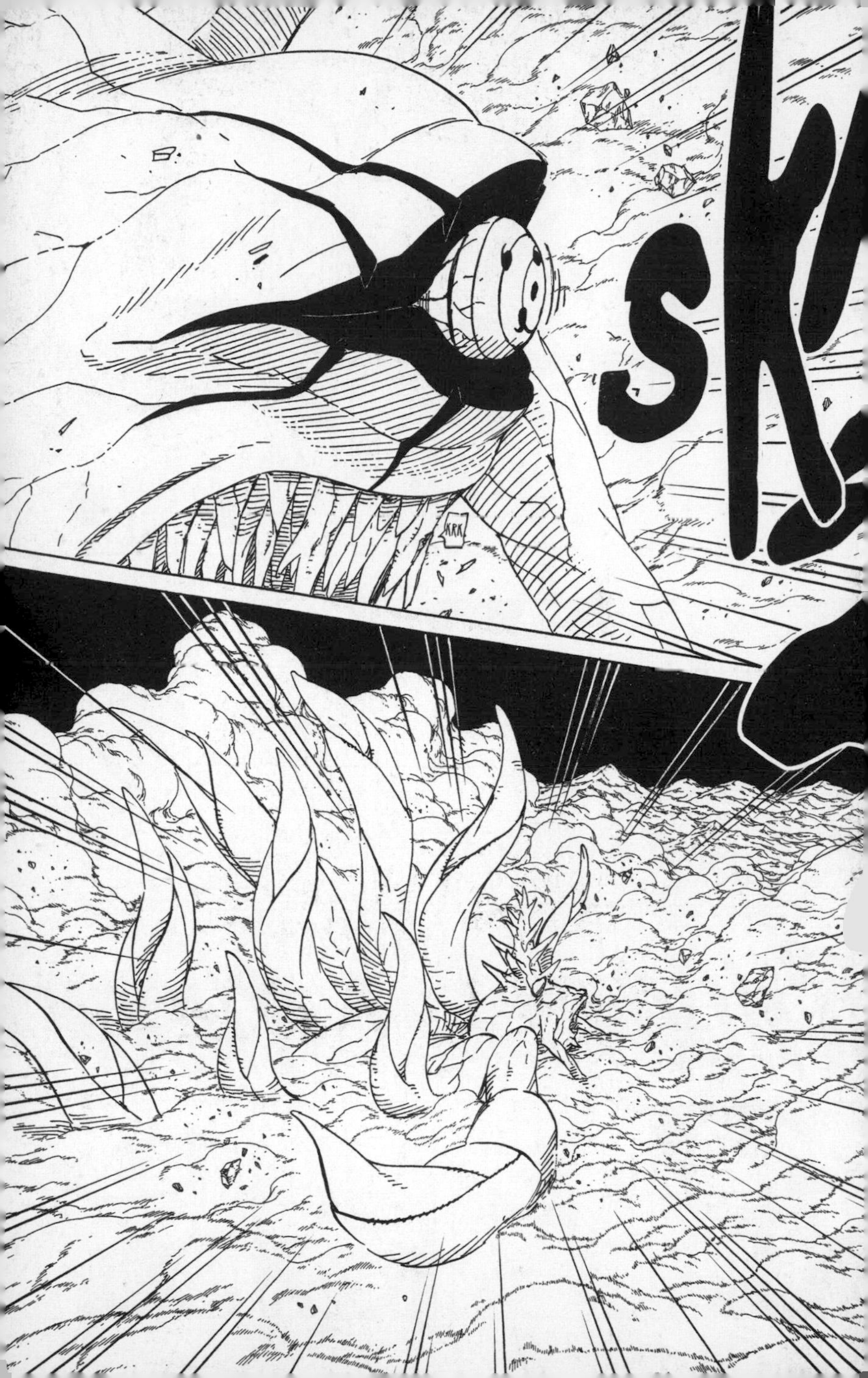
SK
KRK

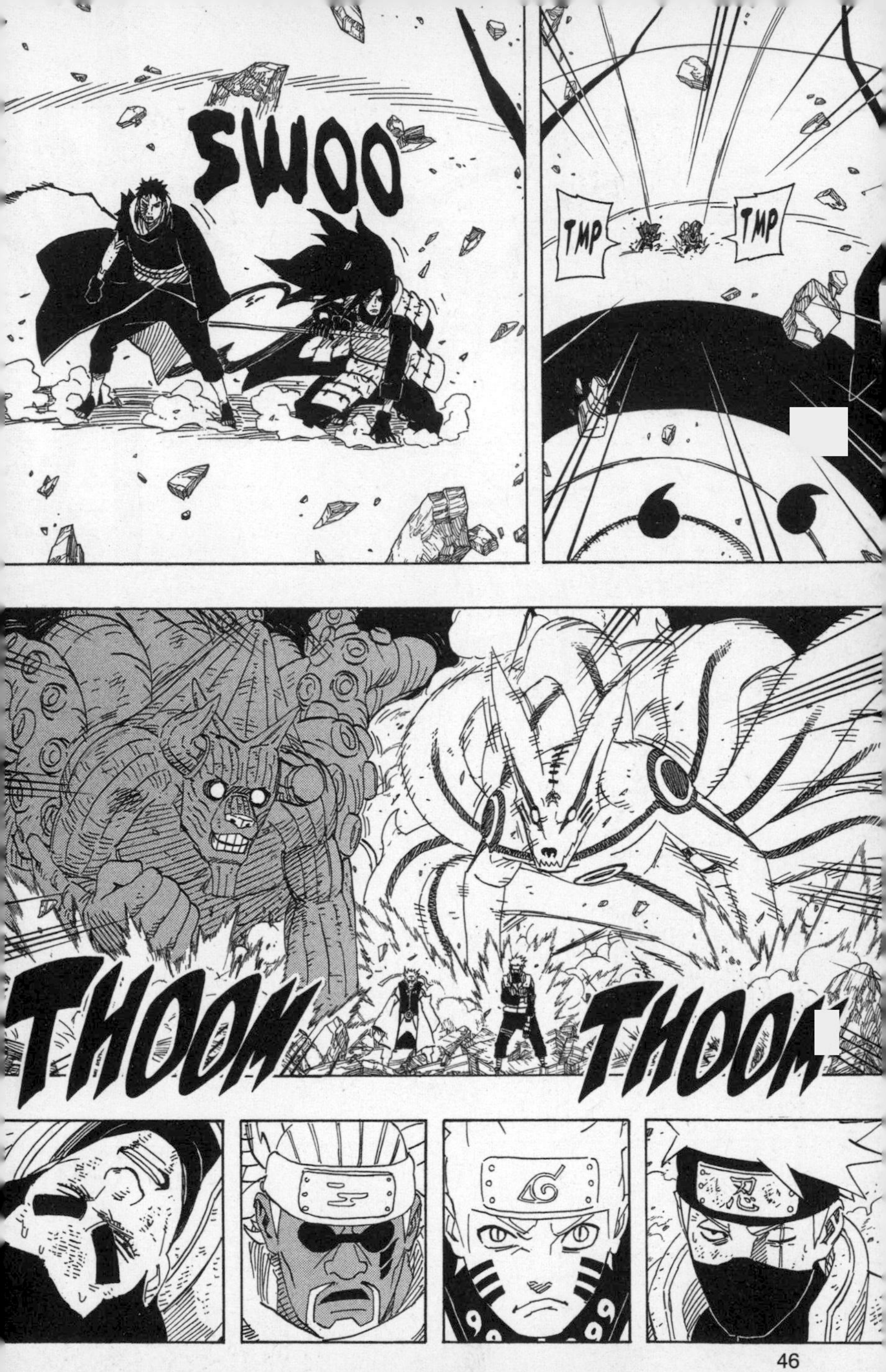
TMP
TMP
SWOO
THOOM
THOOM

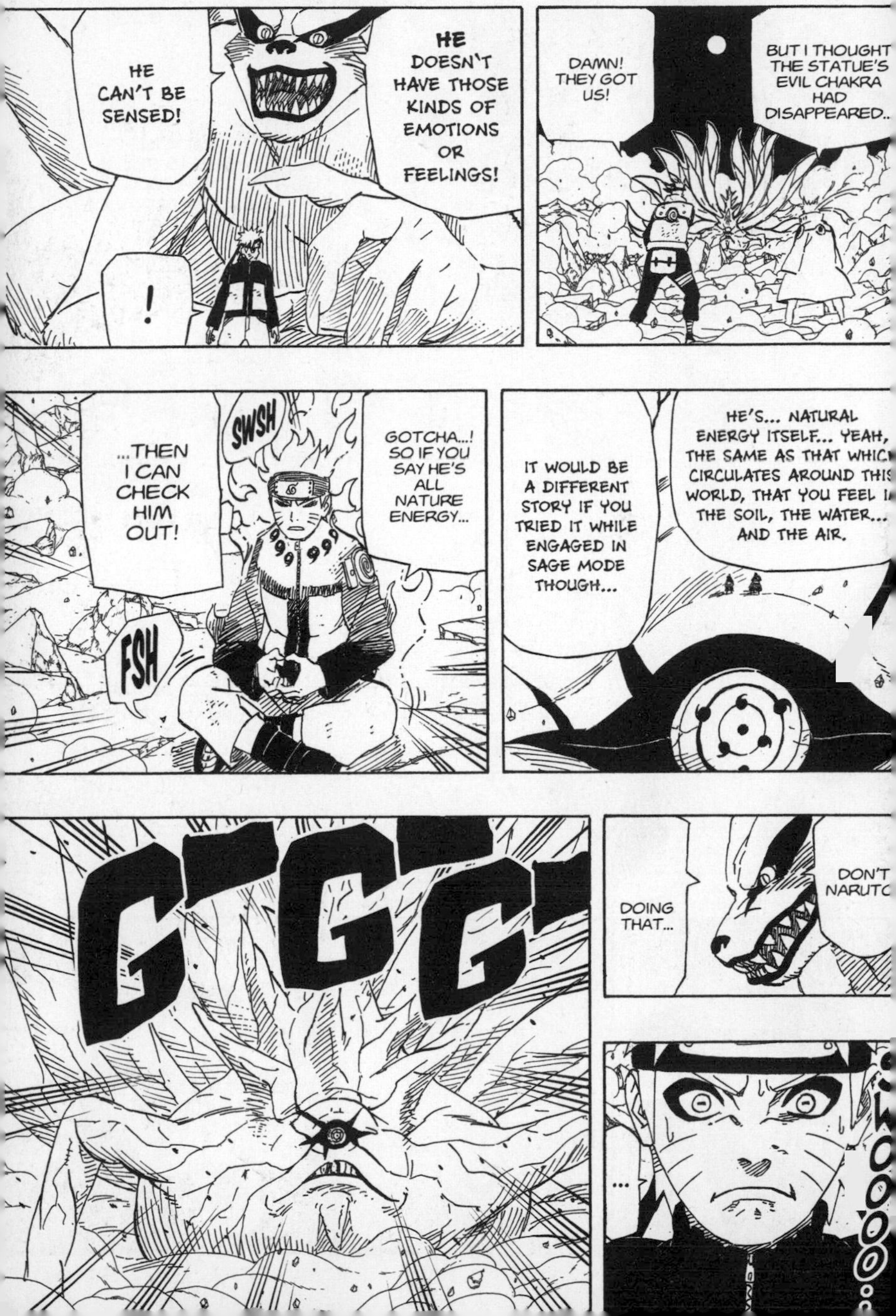
BUT I THOUGHT THE STATUE'S EVIL CHAKRA HAD DISAPPEARED..
DAMN! THEY GOT US!
HE DOESN'T HAVE THOSE KINDS OF EMOTIONS OR FEELINGS!
HE CAN'T BE SENSED!
!
HE'S... NATURAL ENERGY ITSELF... YEAH, THE SAME AS THAT WHIC CIRCULATES AROUND THIS WORLD, THAT YOU FEEL I THE SOIL, THE WATER... AND THE AIR.
IT WOULD BE A DIFFERENT STORY IF YOU TRIED IT WHILE ENGAGED IN SAGE MODE THOUGH...
GOTCHA...! SO IF YOU SAY HE'S ALL NATURE ENERGY...
SWSH
...THEN I CAN CHECK HIM OUT!
FSH
DON'T NARUTC
DOING THAT...
...
GGG

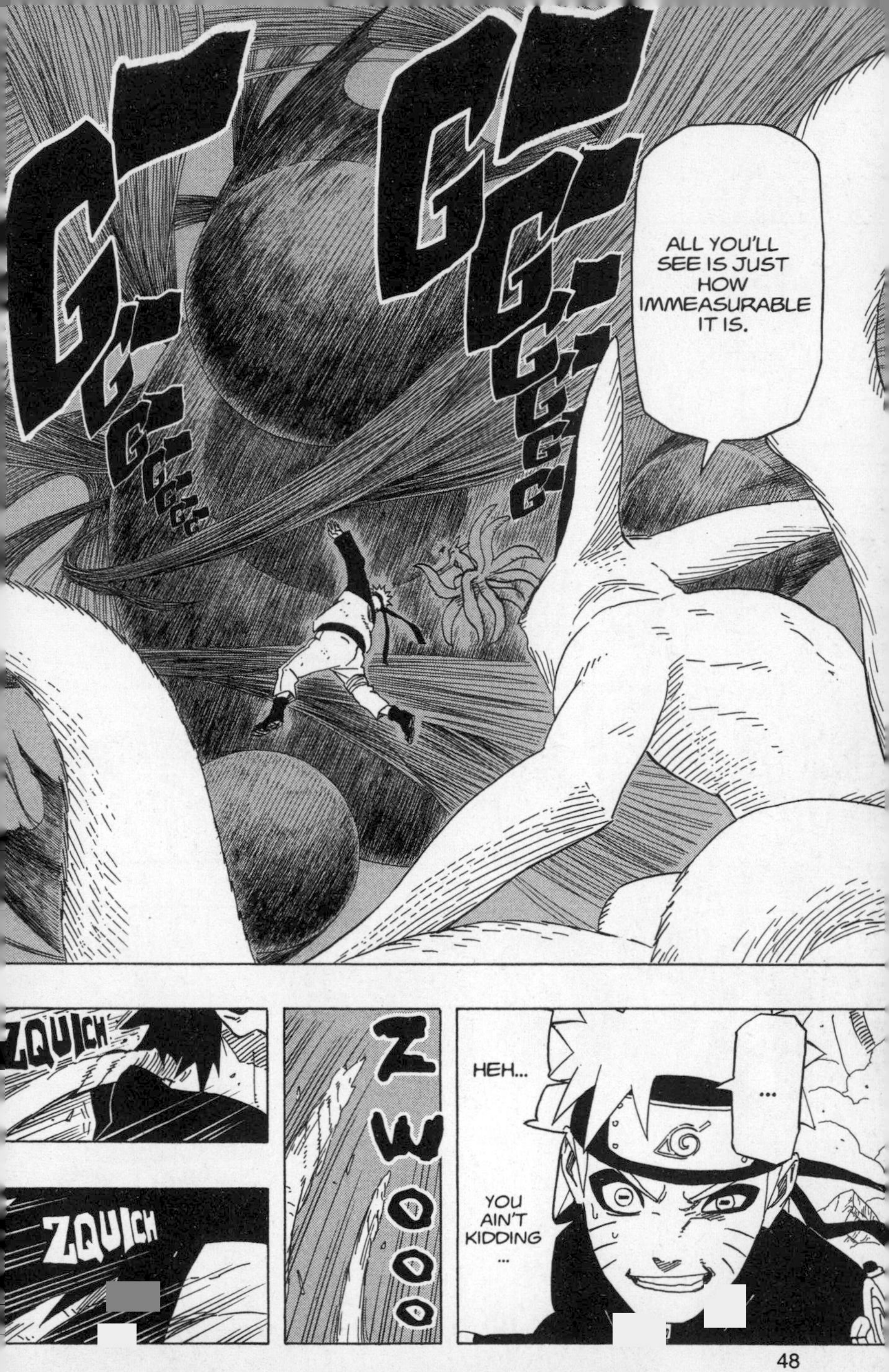
ALL YOU'LL SEE IS JUST HOW IMMEASURABLE IT IS.
...
HEH...
YOU AIN'T KIDDING ...
ZWOOO
ZQUICH
ZQUICH

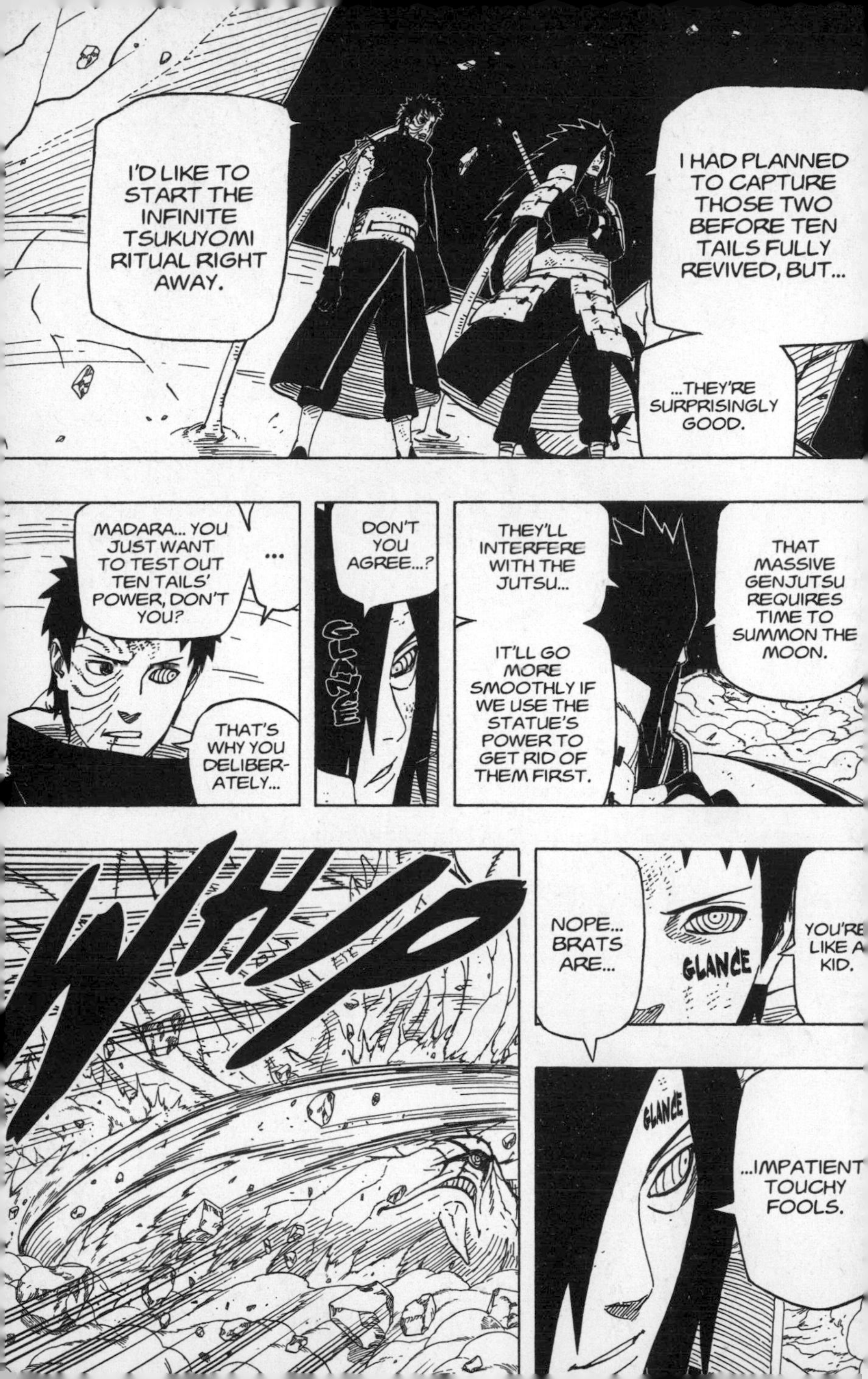
I HAD PLANNED TO CAPTURE THOSE TWO BEFORE TEN TAILS FULLY REVIVED, BUT...
...THEY'RE SURPRISINGLY GOOD.
I'D LIKE TO START THE INFINITE TSUKUYOMI RITUAL RIGHT AWAY.
THAT MASSIVE GENJUTSU REQUIRES TIME TO SUMMON THE MOON.
THEY'LL INTERFERE WITH THE JUTSU...
IT'LL GO MORE SMOOTHLY IF WE USE THE STATUE'S POWER TO GET RID OF THEM FIRST.
DON'T YOU AGREE...?
GLANCE
...
MADARA... YOU JUST WANT TO TEST OUT TEN TAILS' POWER, DON'T YOU?
THAT'S WHY YOU DELIBER-ATELY...
YOU'RE LIKE A KID.
GLANCE
NOPE... BRATS ARE...
GLANCE
...IMPATIENT TOUCHY FOOLS.
WHIP

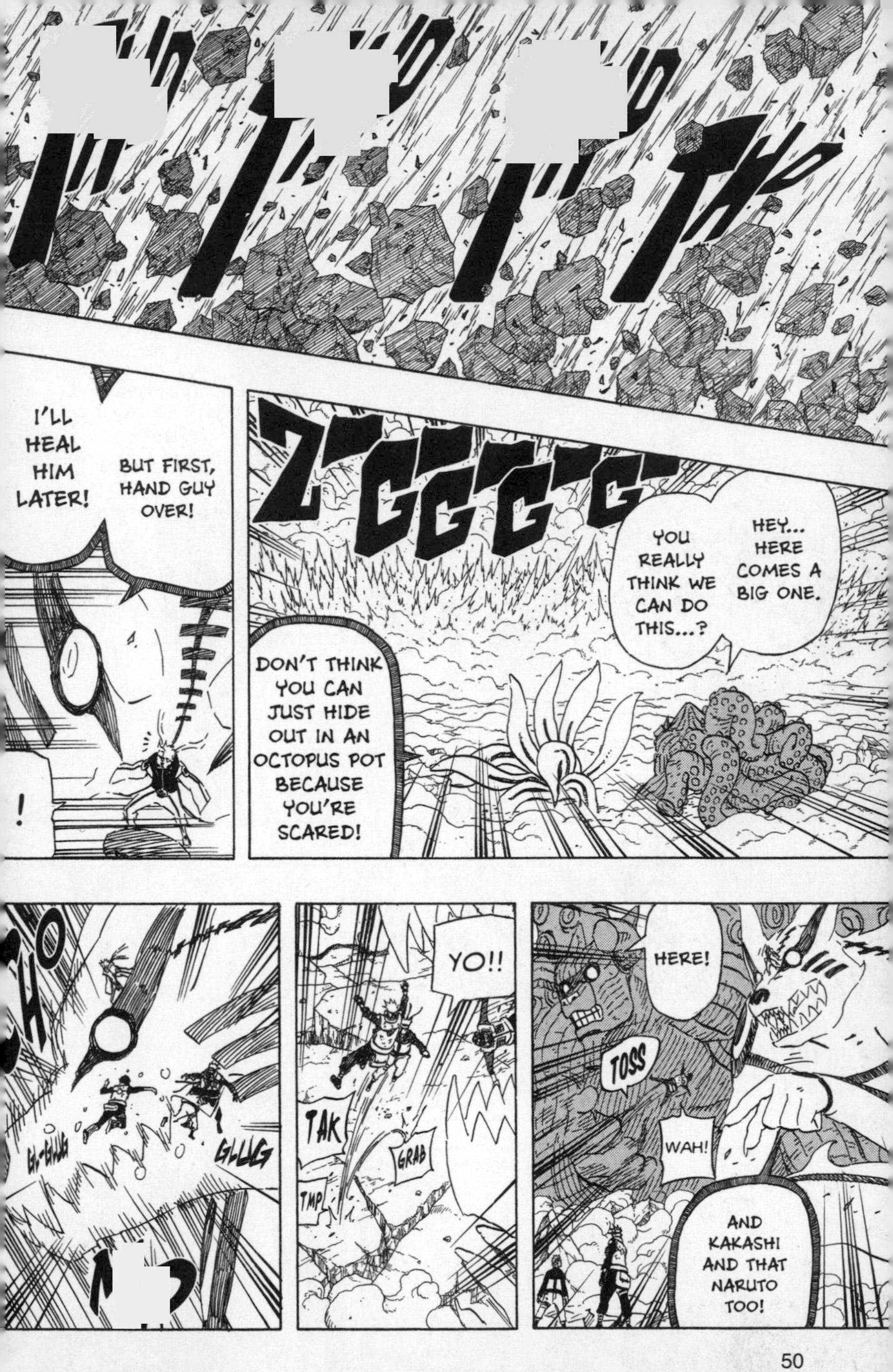

HEY... HERE COMES A BIG ONE.
YOU REALLY THINK WE CAN DO THIS...?
DON'T THINK YOU CAN JUST HIDE OUT IN AN OCTOPUS POT BECAUSE YOU'RE SCARED!
I'LL HEAL HIM LATER!
BUT FIRST, HAND GUY OVER!
!
HERE!
TOSS
WAH!
AND KAKASHI AND THAT NARUTO TOO!
YO!!
TAK
GRAB
TMP
GLUG
GL-GLUG

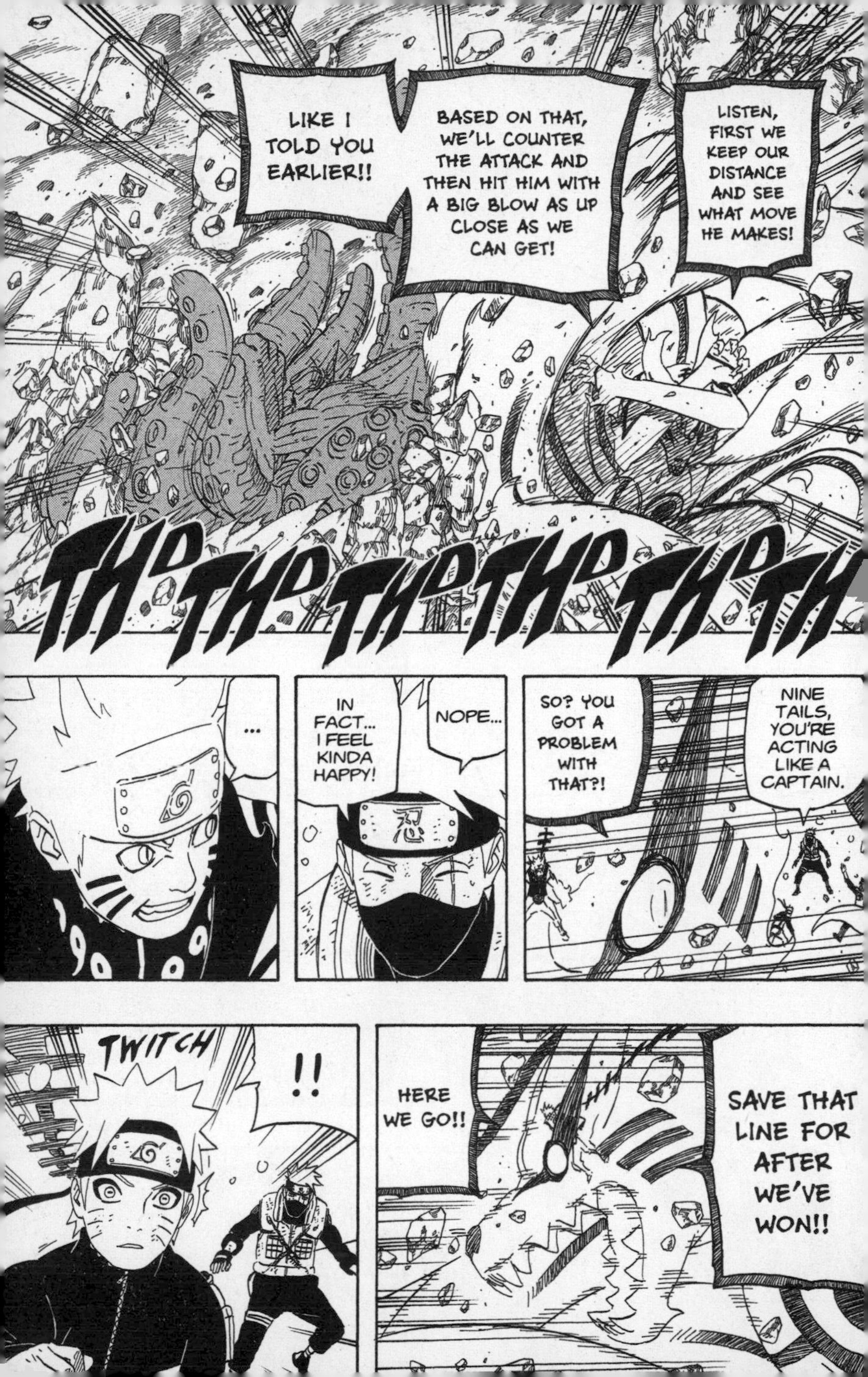

LISTEN, FIRST WE KEEP OUR DISTANCE AND SEE WHAT MOVE HE MAKES!
BASED ON THAT, WE'LL COUNTER THE ATTACK AND THEN HIT HIM WITH A BIG BLOW AS UP CLOSE AS WE CAN GET!
LIKE I TOLD YOU EARLIER!!
THP THP THP THP THP TH
NINE TAILS, YOU'RE ACTING LIKE A CAPTAIN.
SO? YOU GOT A PROBLEM WITH THAT?!
NOPE...
IN FACT... I FEEL KINDA HAPPY!
...
SAVE THAT LINE FOR AFTER WE'VE WON!!
HERE WE GO!!
!!
TWITCH

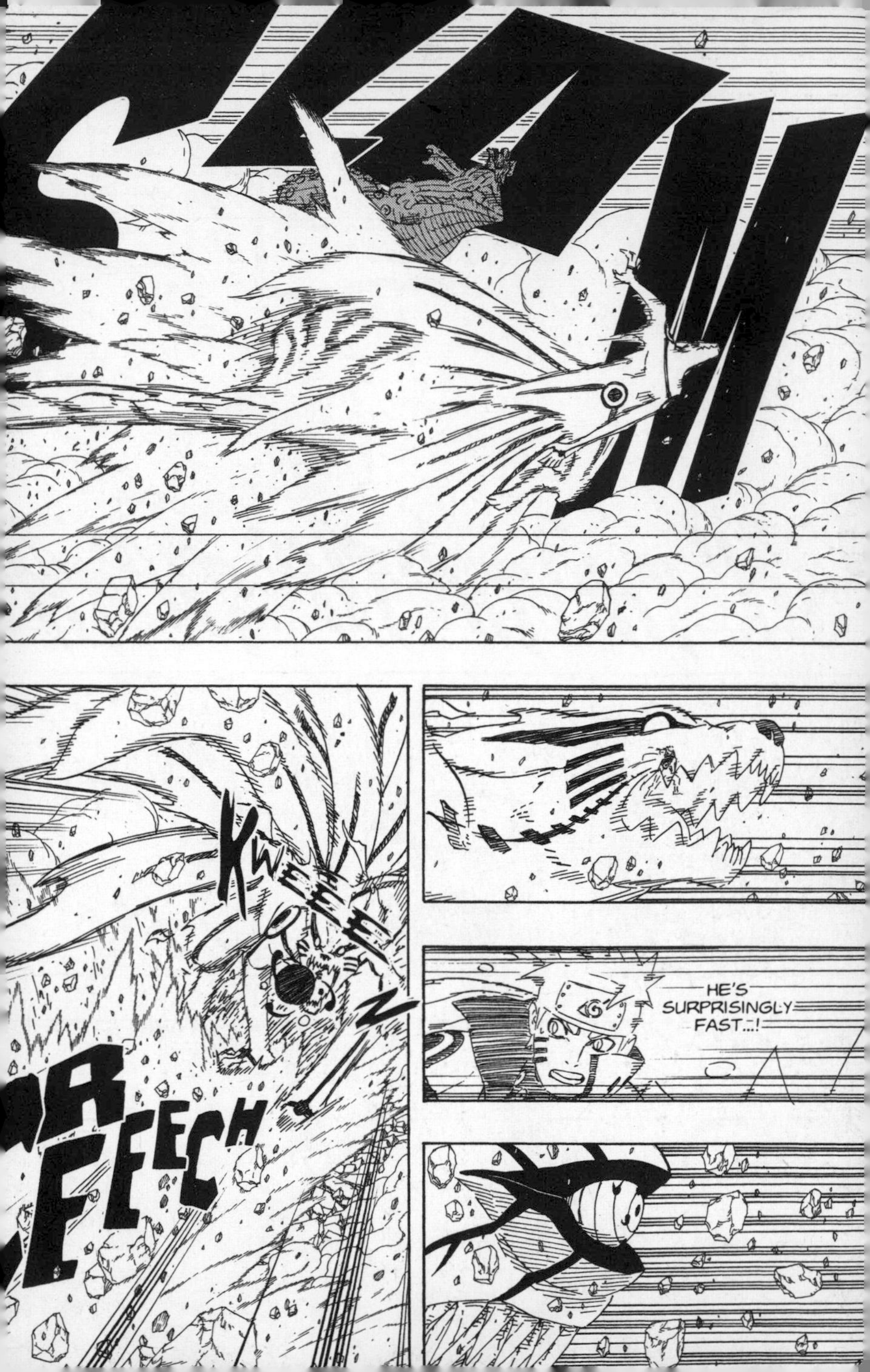
SLAM
HE'S SURPRISINGLY FAST...!
KWEEEE

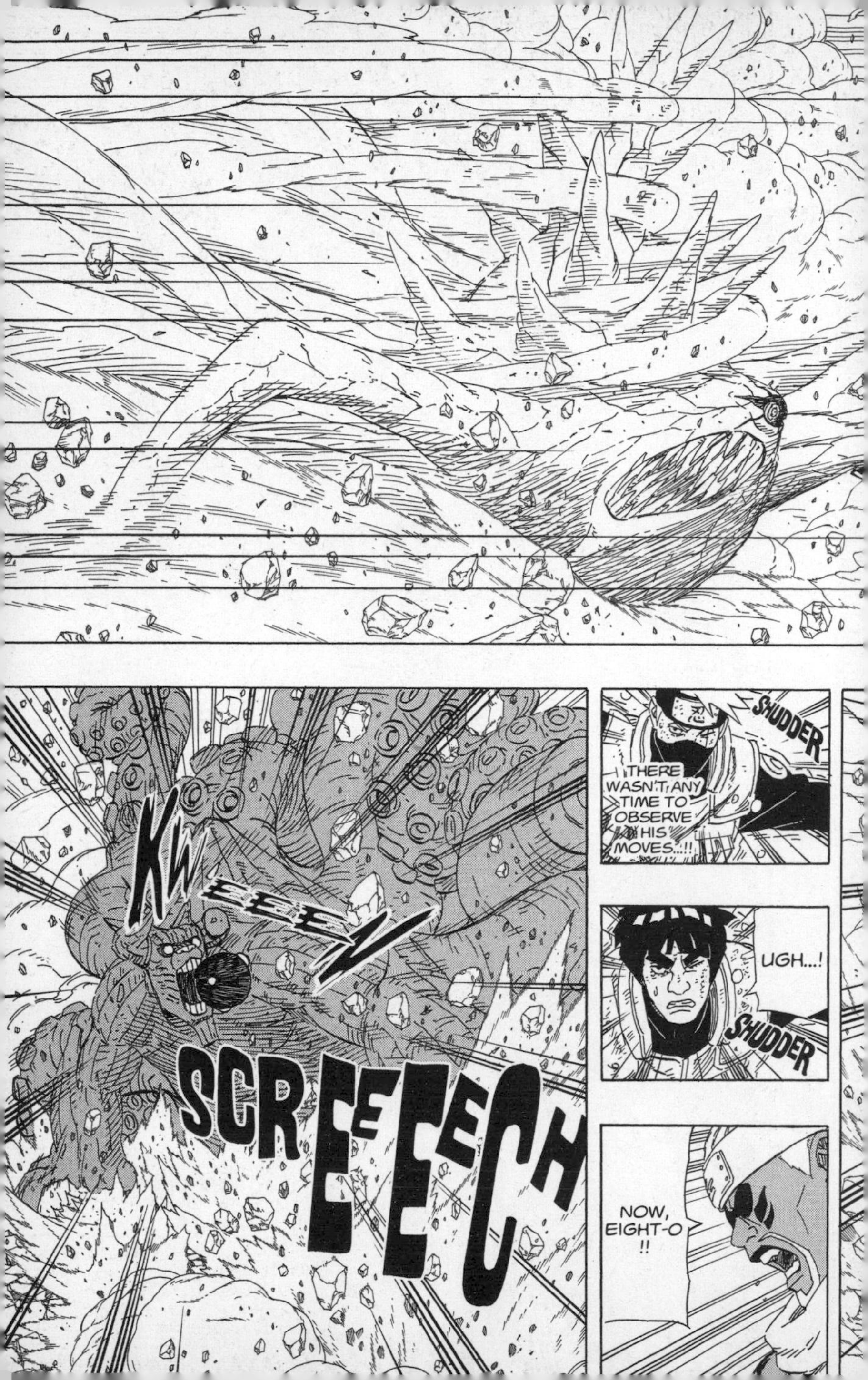
SHUDDER
THERE WASN'T ANY TIME TO OBSERVE HIS MOVES...!!
UGH...!
SHUDDER
NOW, EIGHT-O !!
KWEEEN
SCREEEECH

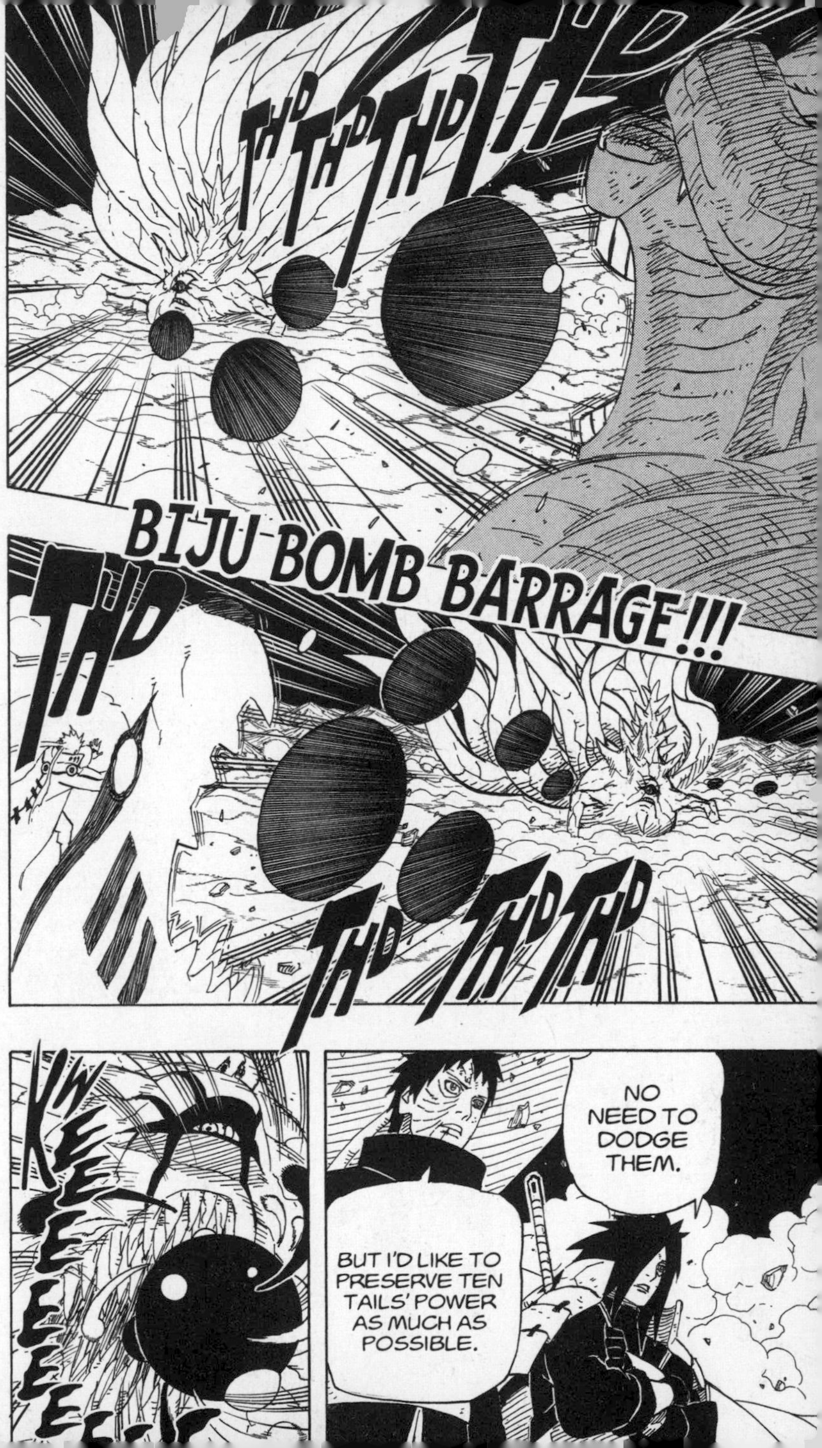
THD THD THD THD
BIJU BOMB BARRAGE!!!
THD
THD THD THD
NO NEED TO DODGE THEM.
BUT I'D LIKE TO PRESERVE TEN TAILS' POWER AS MUCH AS POSSIBLE.
KWEEEEEEEE

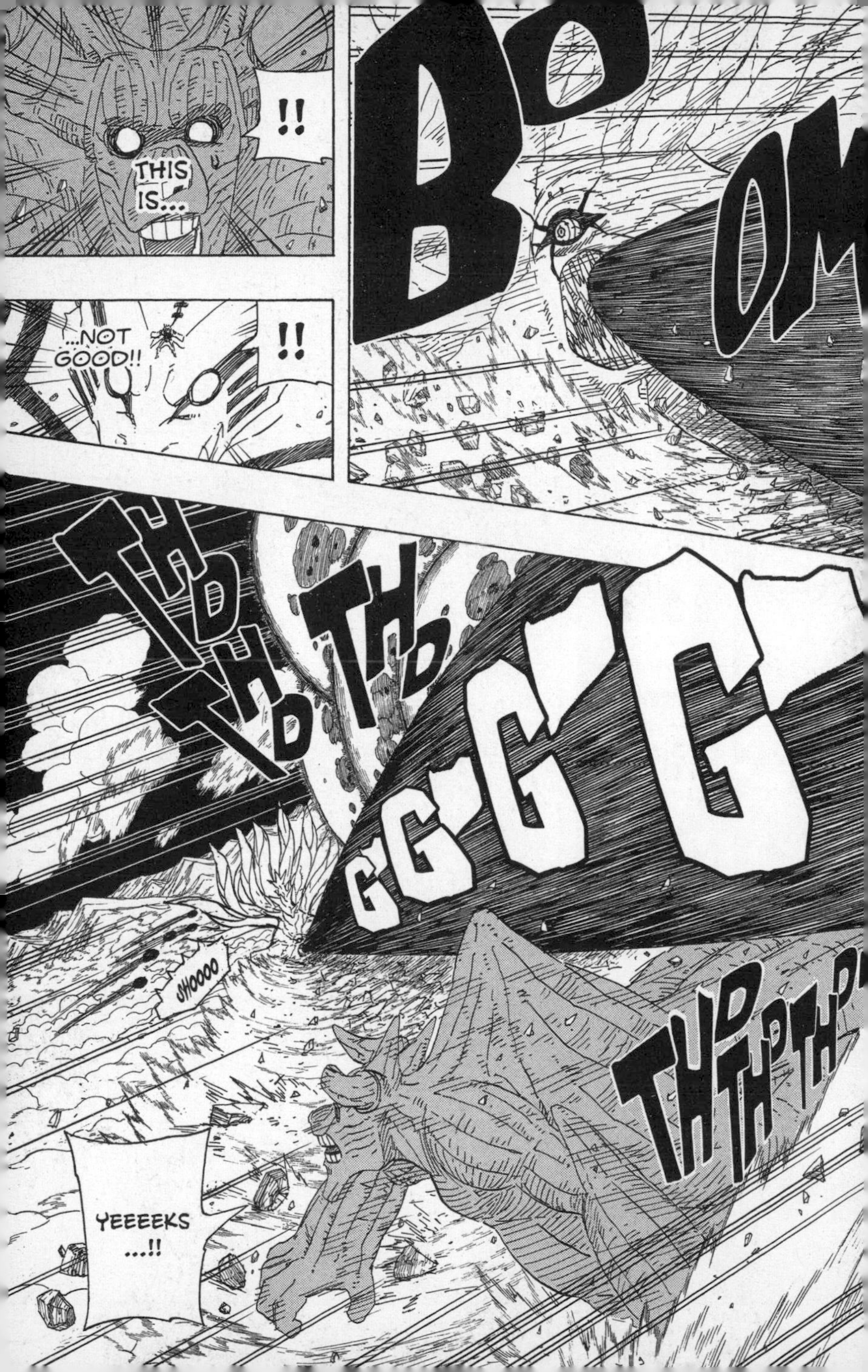

BOOM
!!
THIS IS...
!!
...NOT GOOD!!
GGGG
THD
THD THD
THD THP THP
SHOOOO
YEEEEKS ...!!

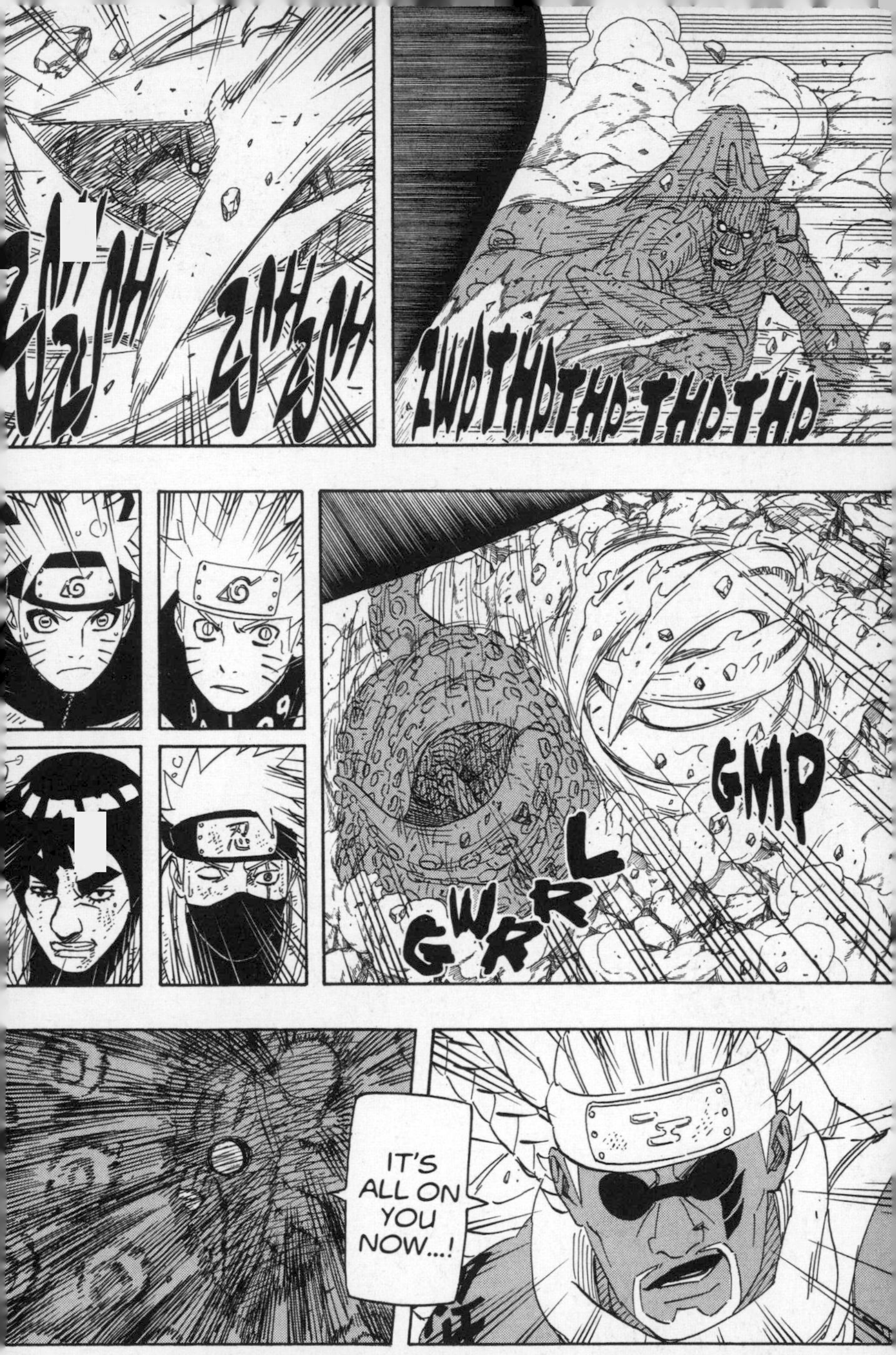
ZWDTHDTHD THDTHD
ZSHZSH
ZSHZSH
GMP
GWRRL
IT'S ALL ON YOU NOW...!

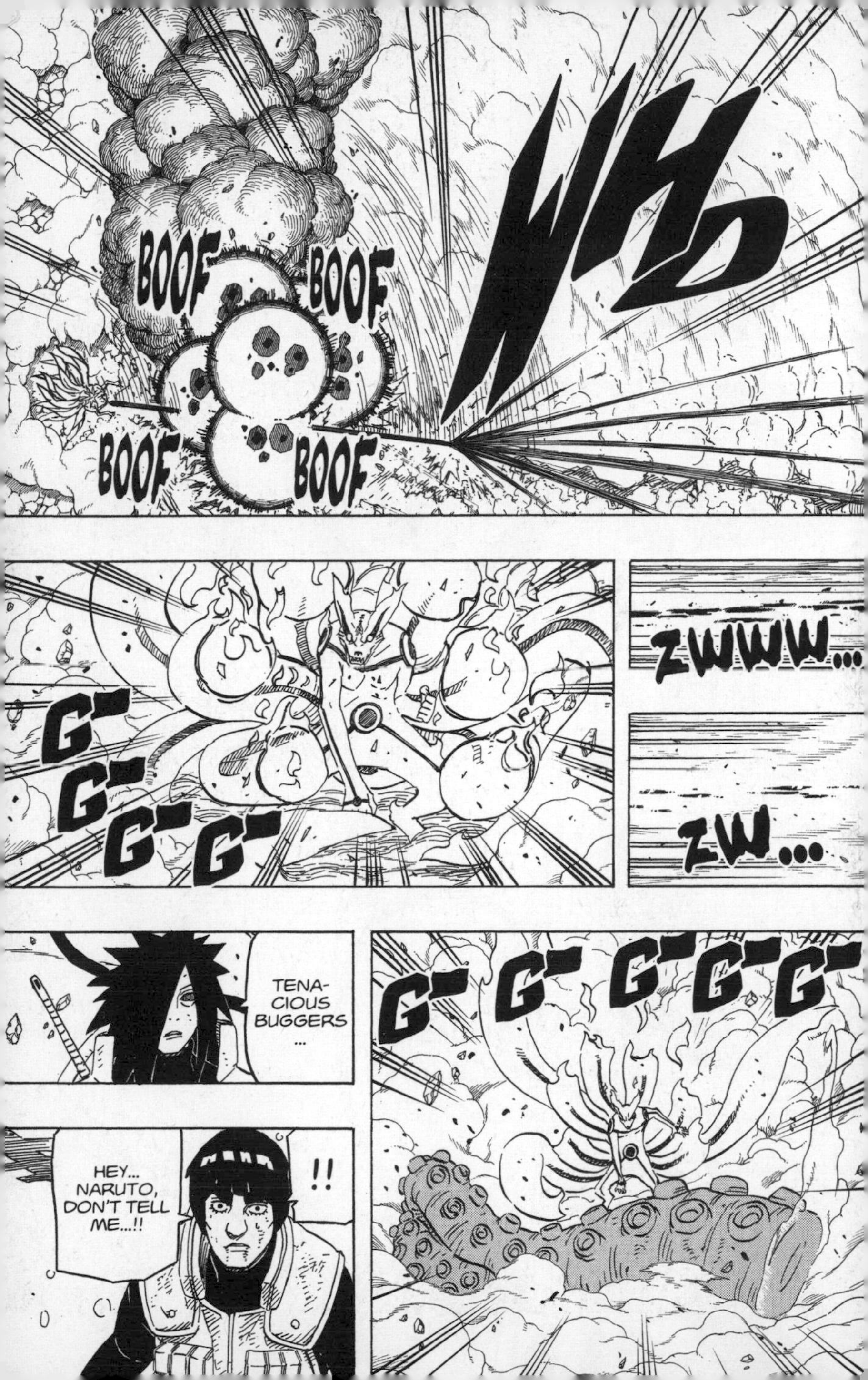
BOOF
BOOF
BOOF
BOOF
ZWWW...
ZW...
G- G- G- G-
G- G- G- G- G-
TENACIOUS BUGGERS ...
!!
HEY... NARUTO, DON'T TELL ME...!!

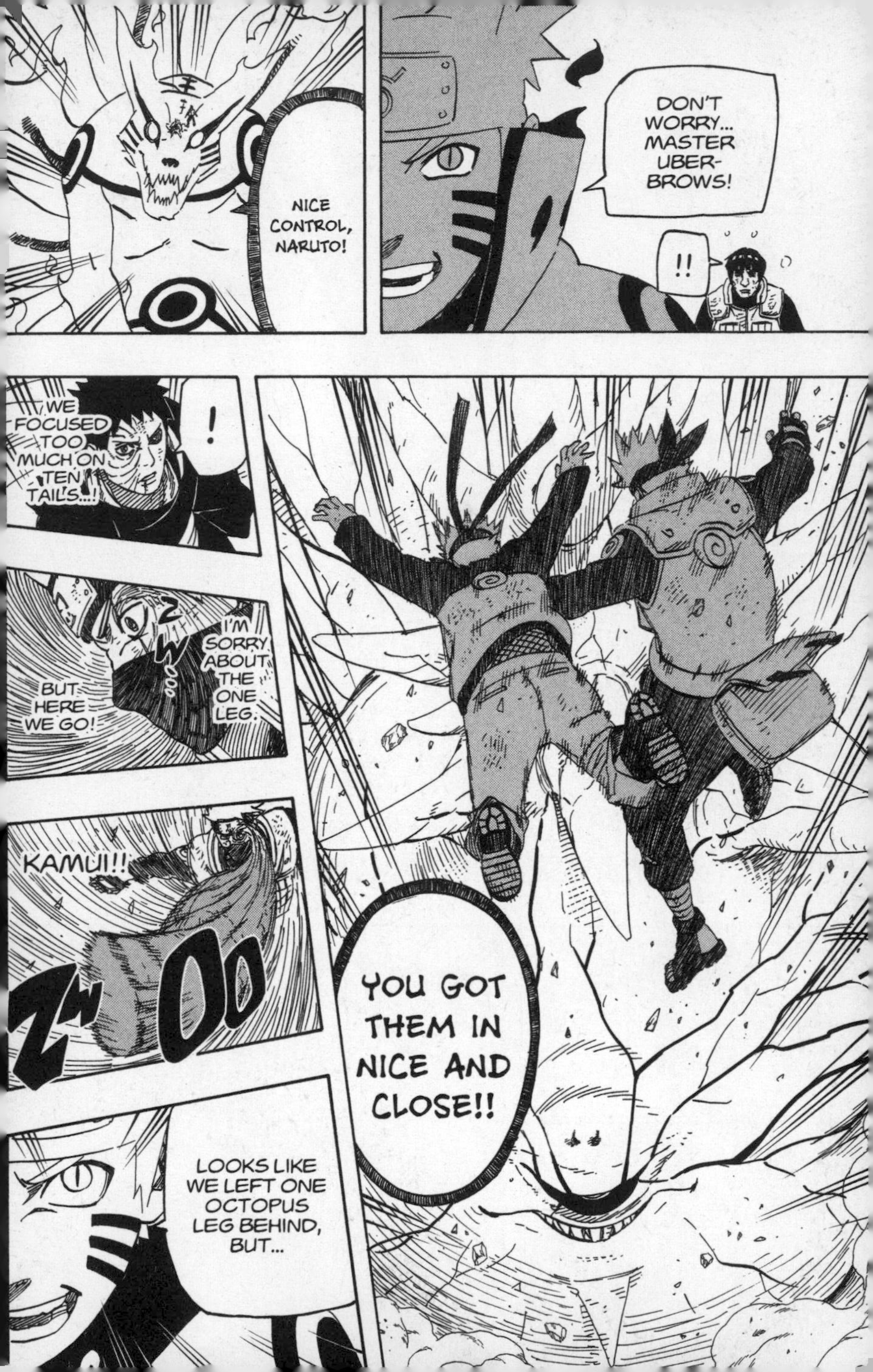
DON'T WORRY... MASTER UBER-BROWS!
!!
NICE CONTROL, NARUTO!
YOU GOT THEM IN NICE AND CLOSE!!
!
WE FOCUSED TOO MUCH ON TEN TAILS...!
I'M SORRY ABOUT THE ONE LEG.
BUT HERE WE GO!
KAMUI!!
ZWOO
LOOKS LIKE WE LEFT ONE OCTOPUS LEG BEHIND, BUT...

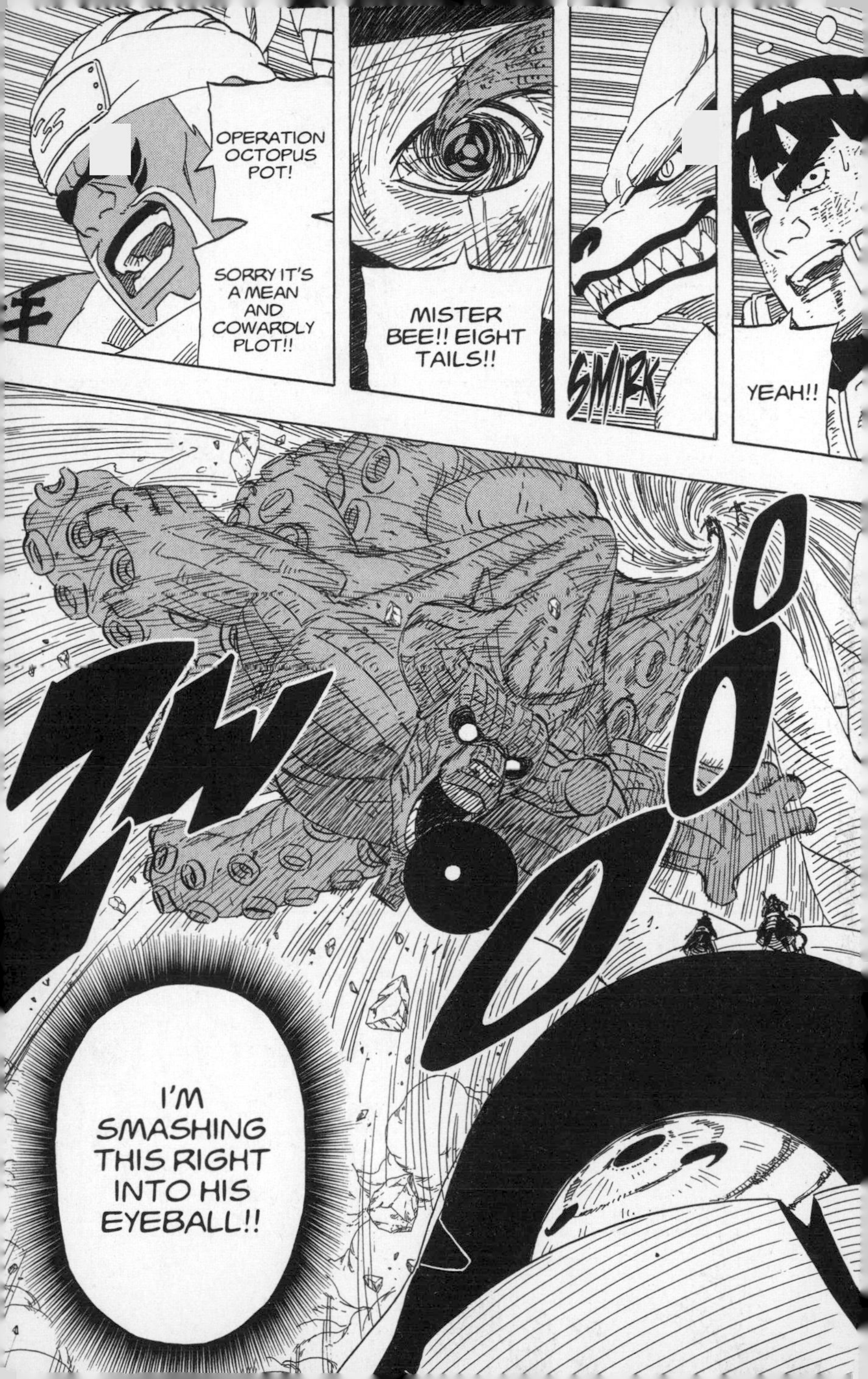
YEAH!!
SMIRK
MISTER BEE!! EIGHT TAILS!!
OPERATION OCTOPUS POT!
SORRY IT'S A MEAN AND COWARDLY PLOT!!
ZWOOOO
I'M SMASHING THIS RIGHT INTO HIS EYEBALL!!

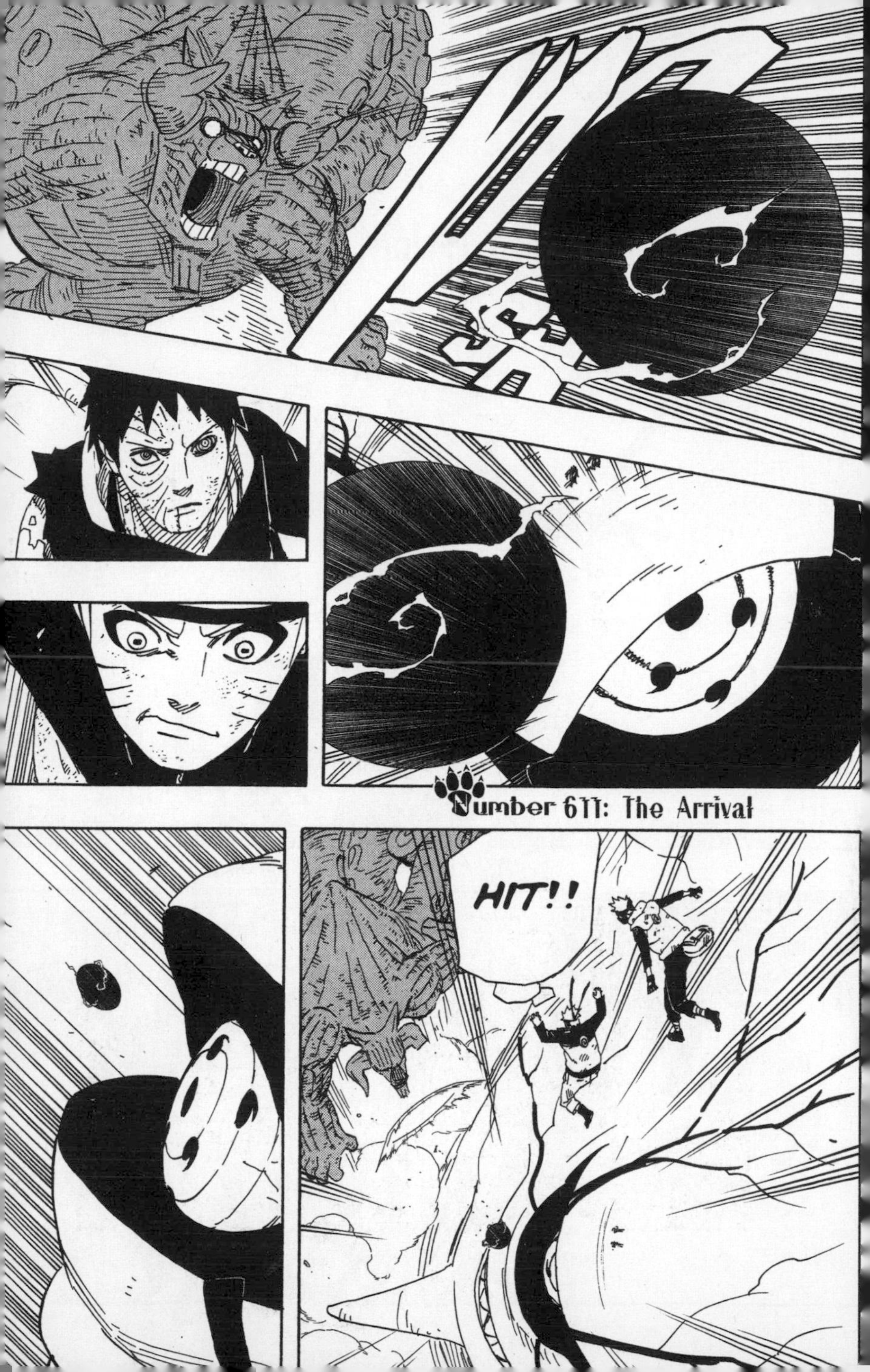
Number 611: The Arrival
HIT!!

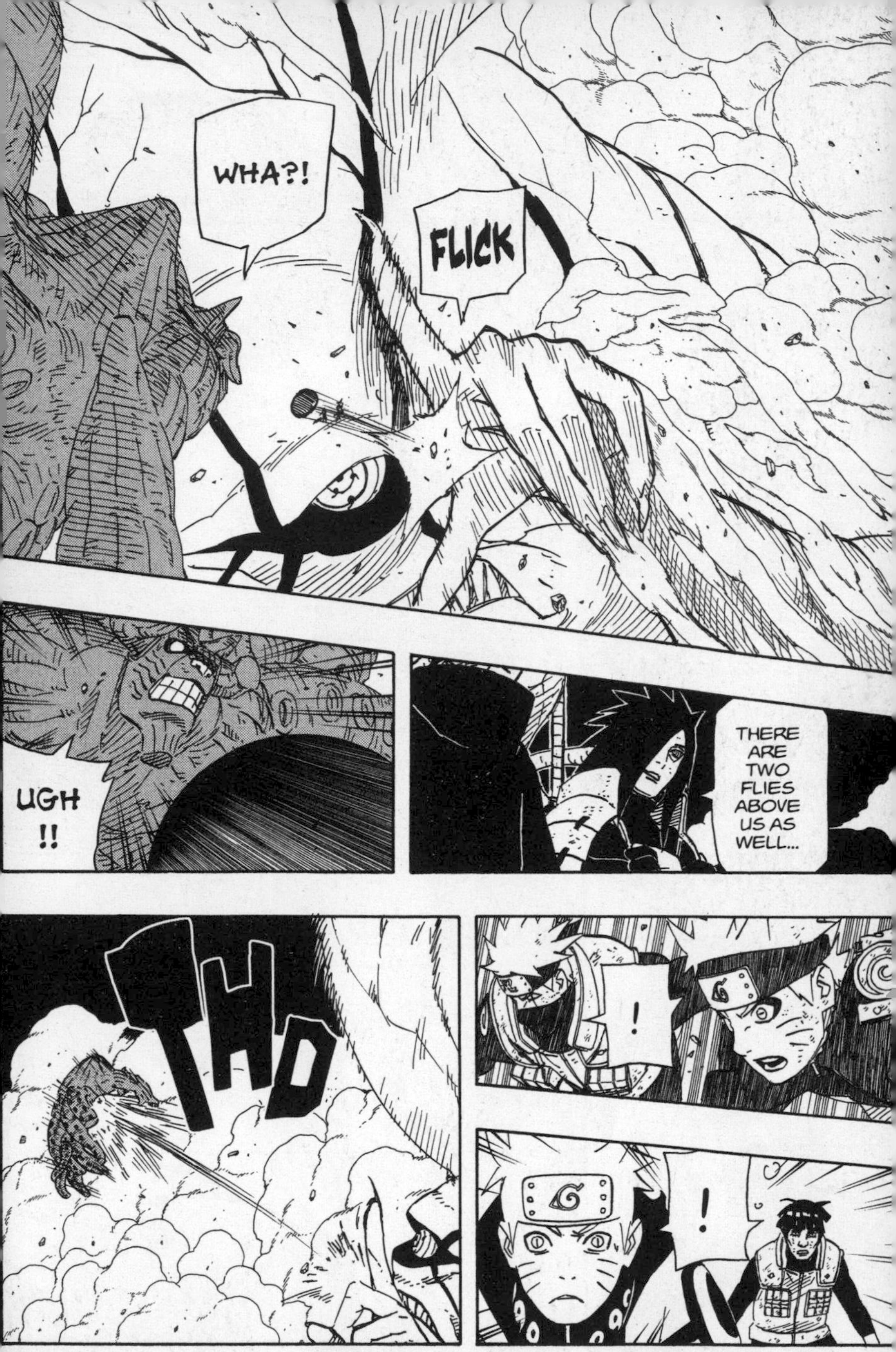
FLICK
WHA?!
THERE ARE TWO FLIES ABOVE US AS WELL...
UGH !!
!
!
THD

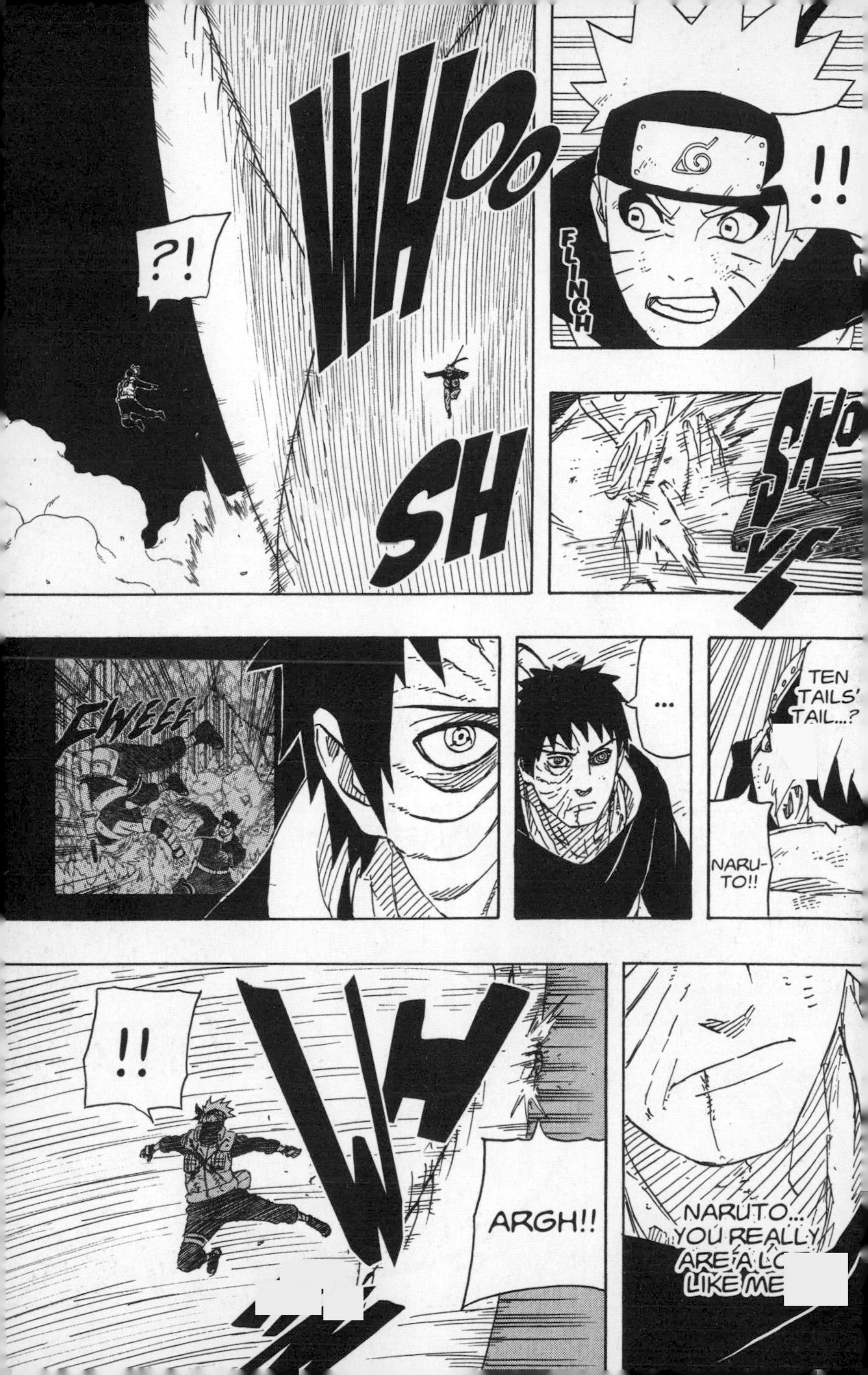
!!
FLINCH
SHO
?!
WHOO
SH
TEN TAILS' TAIL...?
NARU-TO!!
...
CWEEE
NARUTO... YOU REALLY ARE A LOT LIKE ME
ARGH!!
!!
WH

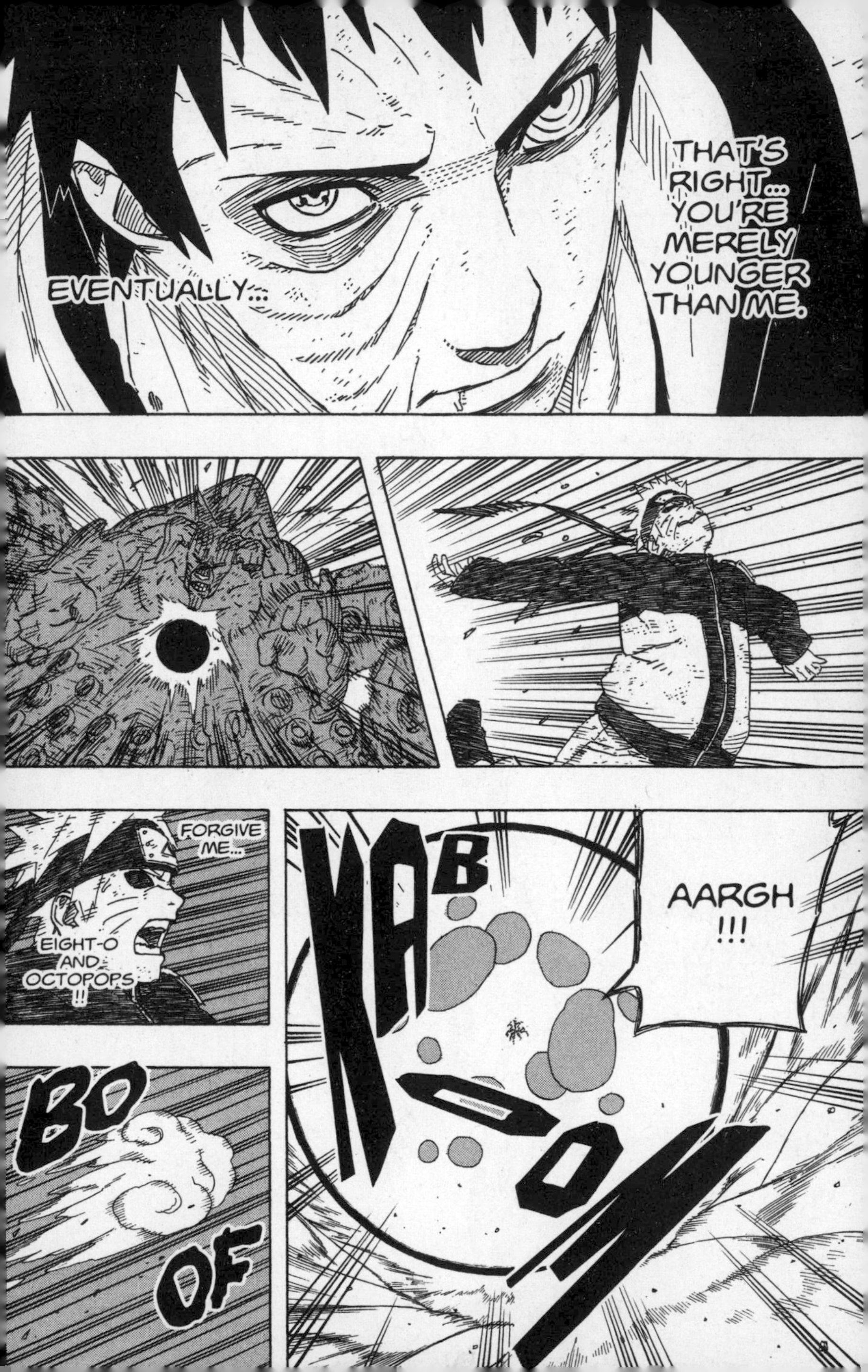
THAT'S RIGHT... YOU'RE MERELY YOUNGER THAN ME.
EVENTUALLY...
KABOOM
AARGH!!!
FORGIVE ME...
EIGHT-O AND OCTOPOPS!!
BOOF

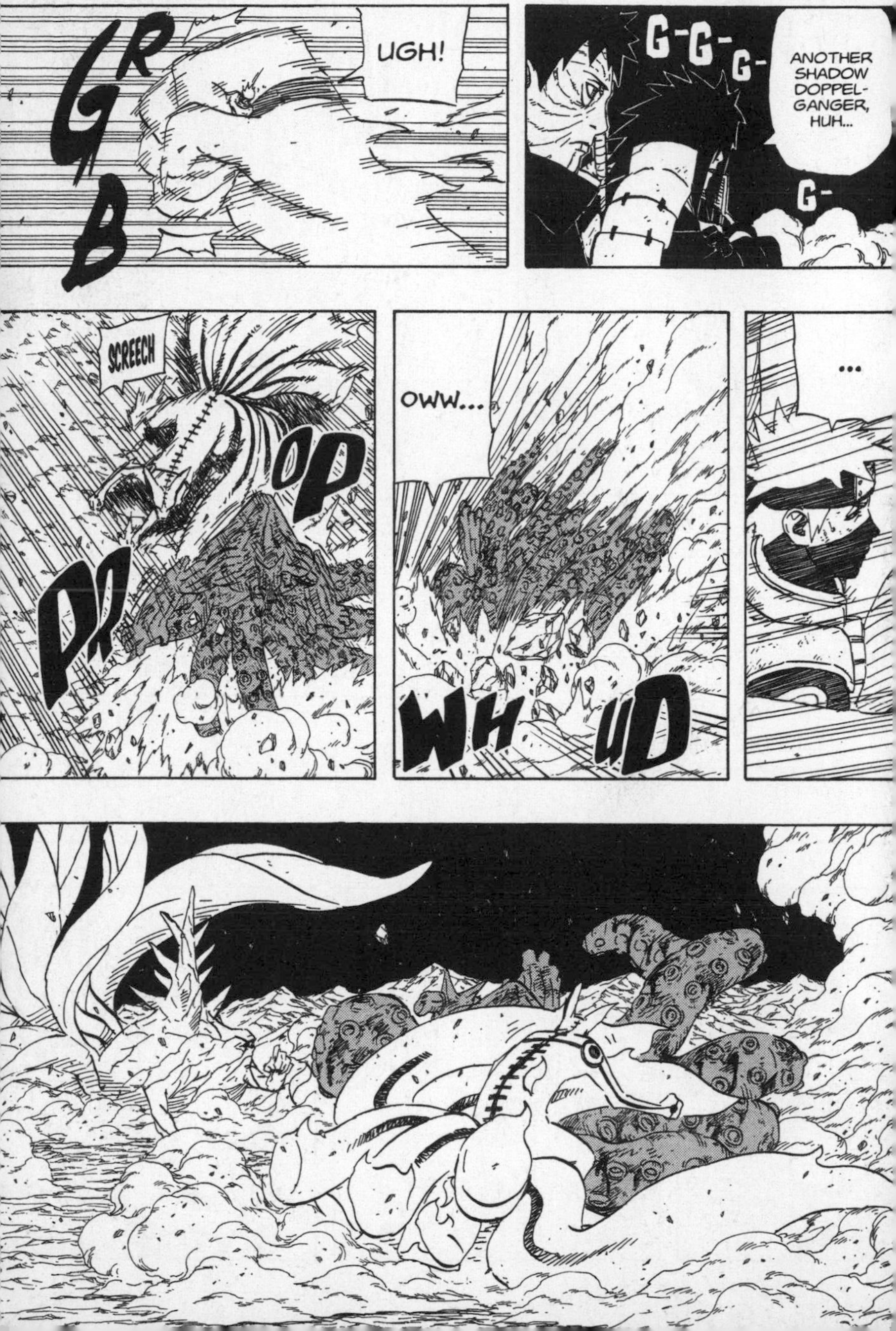
G-G-G-
ANOTHER SHADOW DOPPELGANGER, HUH...
G-
GRAB
UGH!
...
OWW...
WHUD
SCREECH
POP

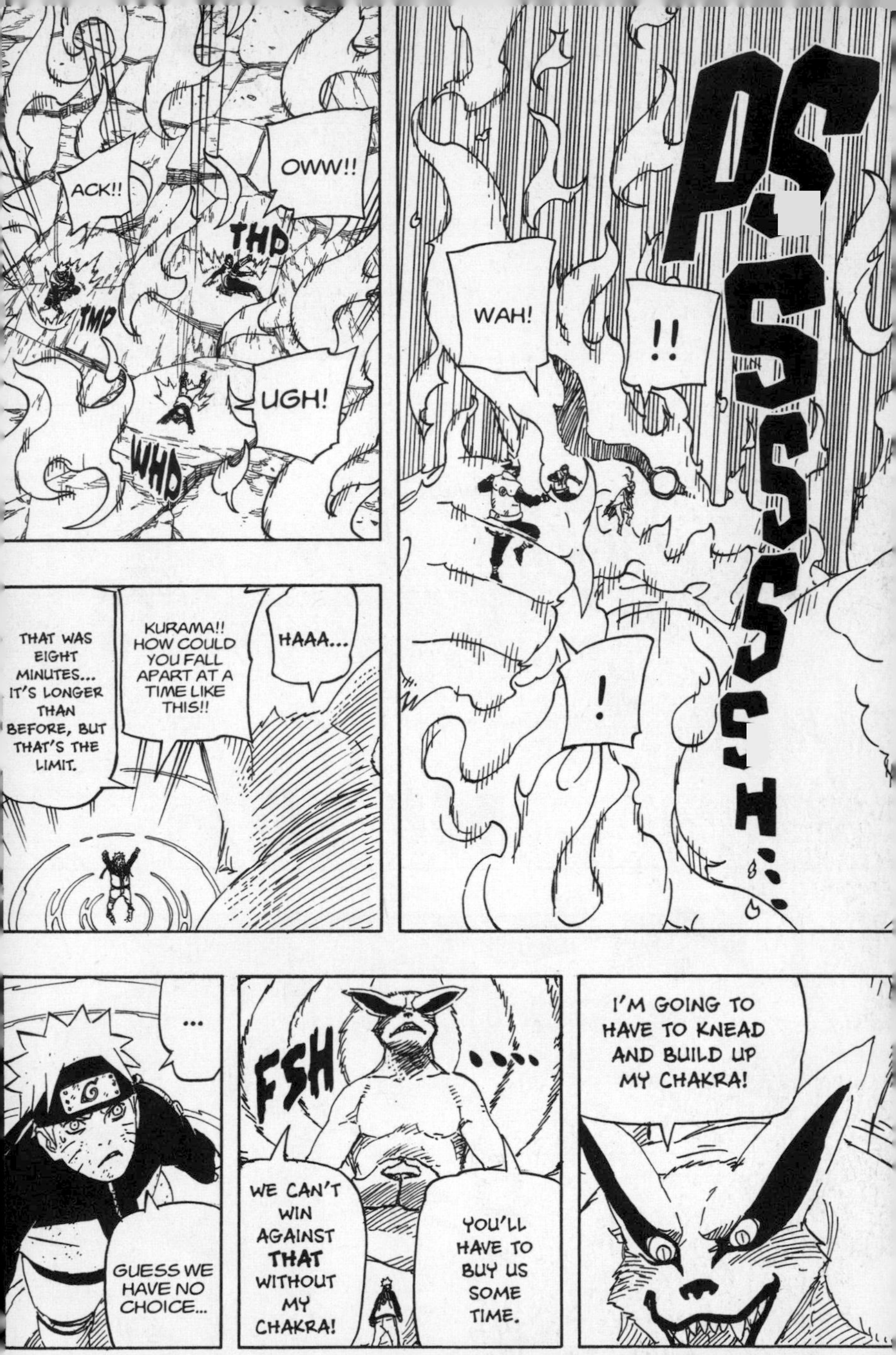

PSSSSSH
!!
WAH!
!
OWW!!
ACK!!
THD
UGH!
TMP
WHD
HAAA...
KURAMA!! HOW COULD YOU FALL APART AT A TIME LIKE THIS!!
THAT WAS EIGHT MINUTES... IT'S LONGER THAN BEFORE, BUT THAT'S THE LIMIT.
I'M GOING TO HAVE TO KNEAD AND BUILD UP MY CHAKRA!
....
FSH
YOU'LL HAVE TO BUY US SOME TIME.
WE CAN'T WIN AGAINST **THAT** WITHOUT MY CHAKRA!
...
GUESS WE HAVE NO CHOICE...

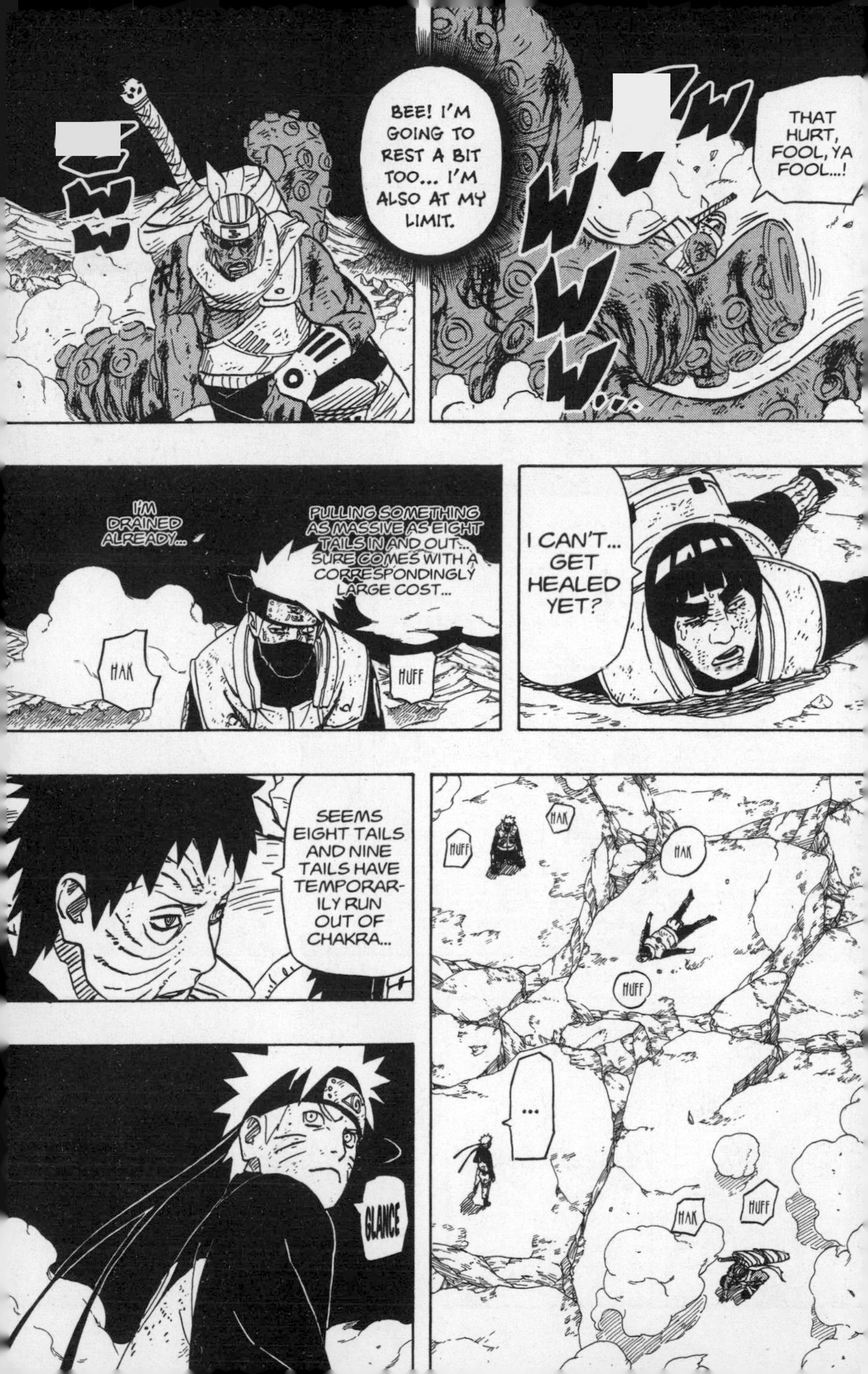
WWWW...
THAT HURT, FOOL, YA FOOL...!
BEE! I'M GOING TO REST A BIT TOO... I'M ALSO AT MY LIMIT.
WWW
I CAN'T... GET HEALED YET?
PULLING SOMETHING AS MASSIVE AS EIGHT TAILS IN AND OUT... SURE COMES WITH A CORRESPONDINGLY LARGE COST...
I'M DRAINED ALREADY...
HUFF
HAK
HAK
HUFF
HAK
HUFF
...
HUFF
HAK
SEEMS EIGHT TAILS AND NINE TAILS HAVE TEMPORARILY RUN OUT OF CHAKRA...
GLANCE

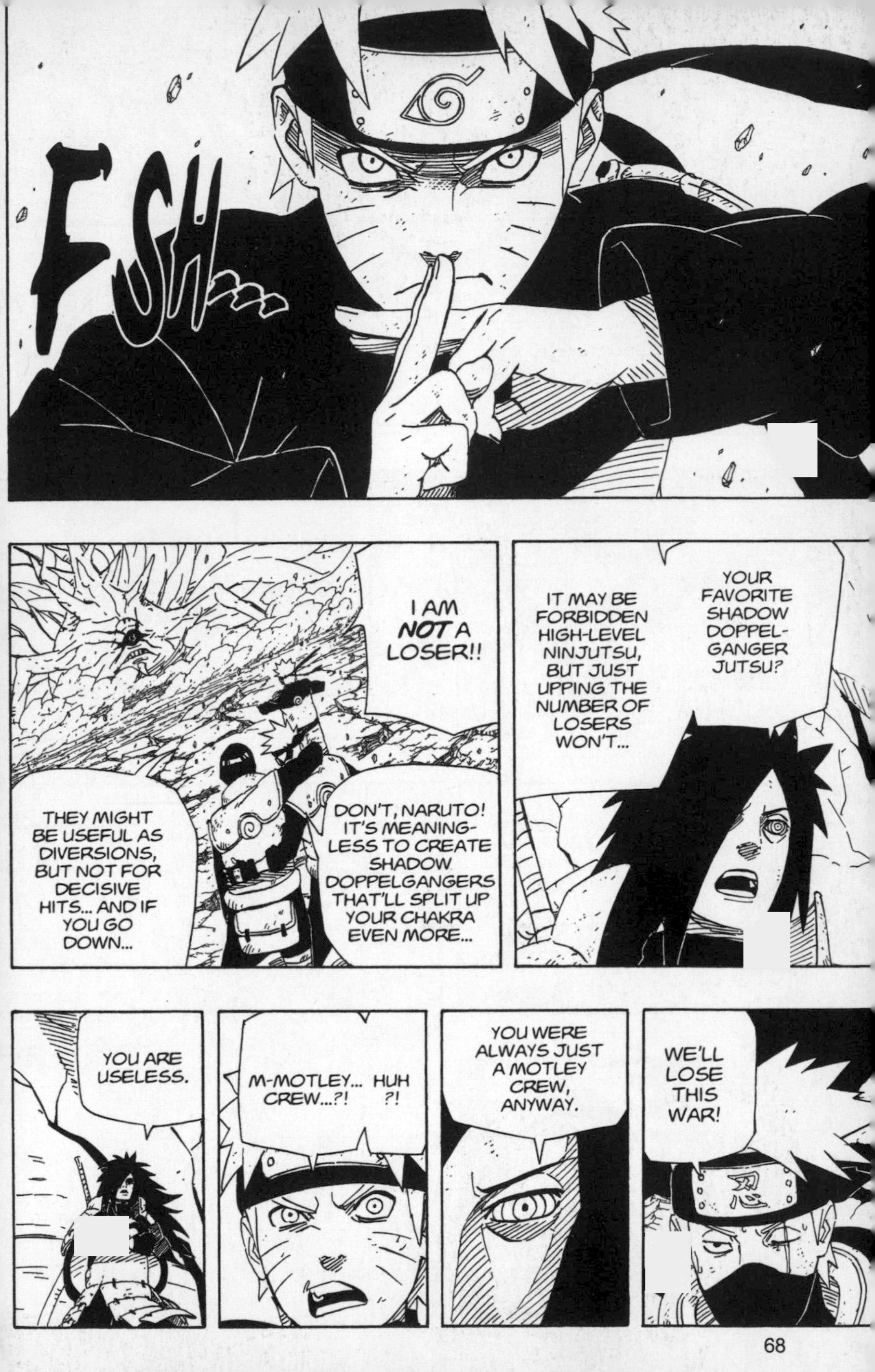
FSH
YOUR FAVORITE SHADOW DOPPEL-GANGER JUTSU?
IT MAY BE FORBIDDEN HIGH-LEVEL NINJUTSU, BUT JUST UPPING THE NUMBER OF LOSERS WON'T...
I AM *NOT* A LOSER!!
DON'T, NARUTO! IT'S MEANING-LESS TO CREATE SHADOW DOPPELGANGERS THAT'LL SPLIT UP YOUR CHAKRA EVEN MORE...
THEY MIGHT BE USEFUL AS DIVERSIONS, BUT NOT FOR DECISIVE HITS... AND IF YOU GO DOWN...
WE'LL LOSE THIS WAR!
YOU WERE ALWAYS JUST A MOTLEY CREW, ANYWAY.
HUH ?!
M-MOTLEY... CREW...?!
YOU ARE USELESS.

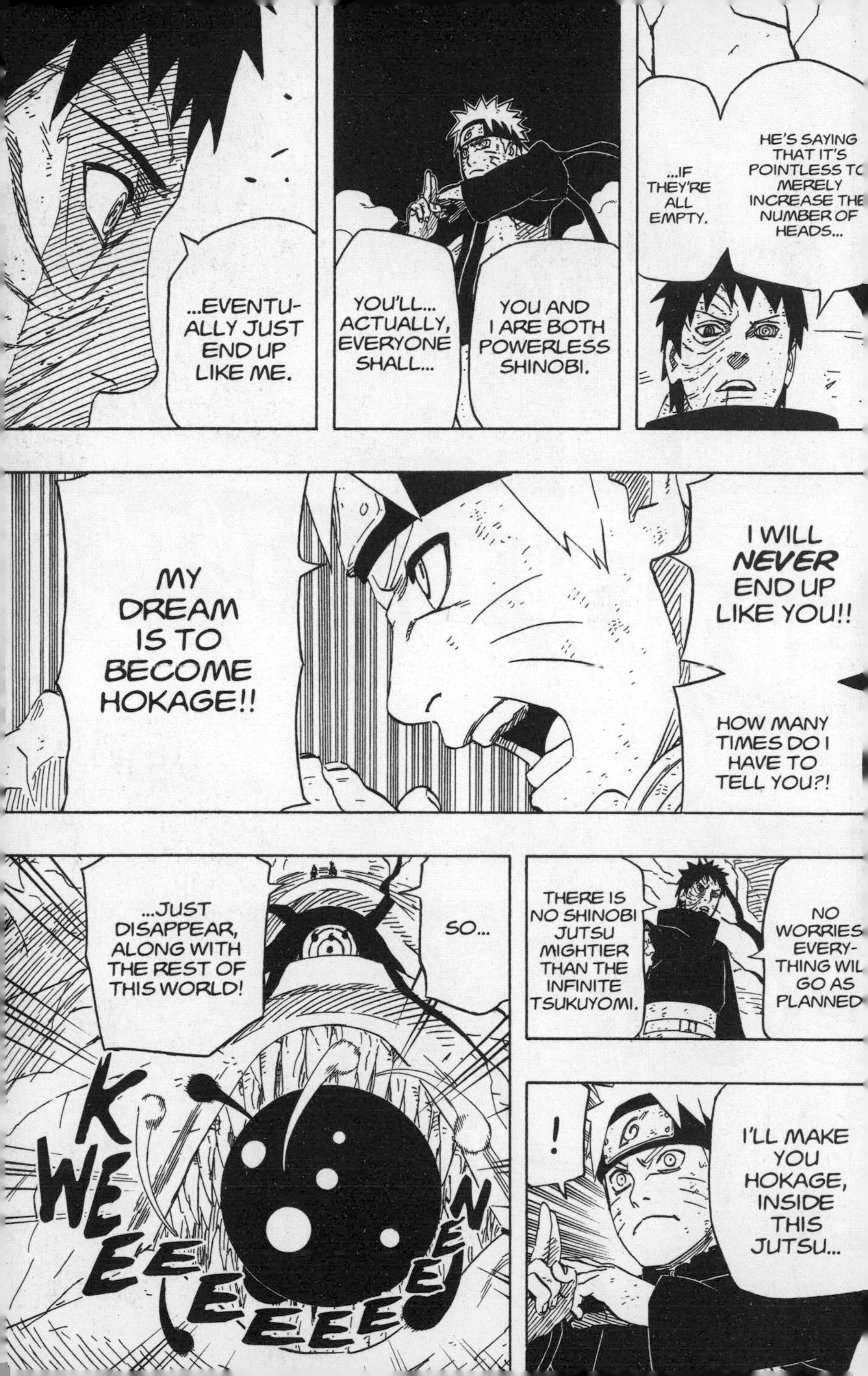
HE'S SAYING THAT IT'S POINTLESS TO MERELY INCREASE THE NUMBER OF HEADS...
...IF THEY'RE ALL EMPTY.
YOU AND I ARE BOTH POWERLESS SHINOBI.
YOU'LL... ACTUALLY, EVERYONE SHALL...
...EVENTUALLY JUST END UP LIKE ME.
I WILL *NEVER* END UP LIKE YOU!!
HOW MANY TIMES DO I HAVE TO TELL YOU?!
MY DREAM IS TO BECOME HOKAGE!!
NO WORRIES EVERYTHING WIL GO AS PLANNED
THERE IS NO SHINOBI JUTSU MIGHTIER THAN THE INFINITE TSUKUYOMI.
I'LL MAKE YOU HOKAGE, INSIDE THIS JUTSU...
!
SO...
...JUST DISAPPEAR, ALONG WITH THE REST OF THIS WORLD!
KWEEEEEEEEEEN

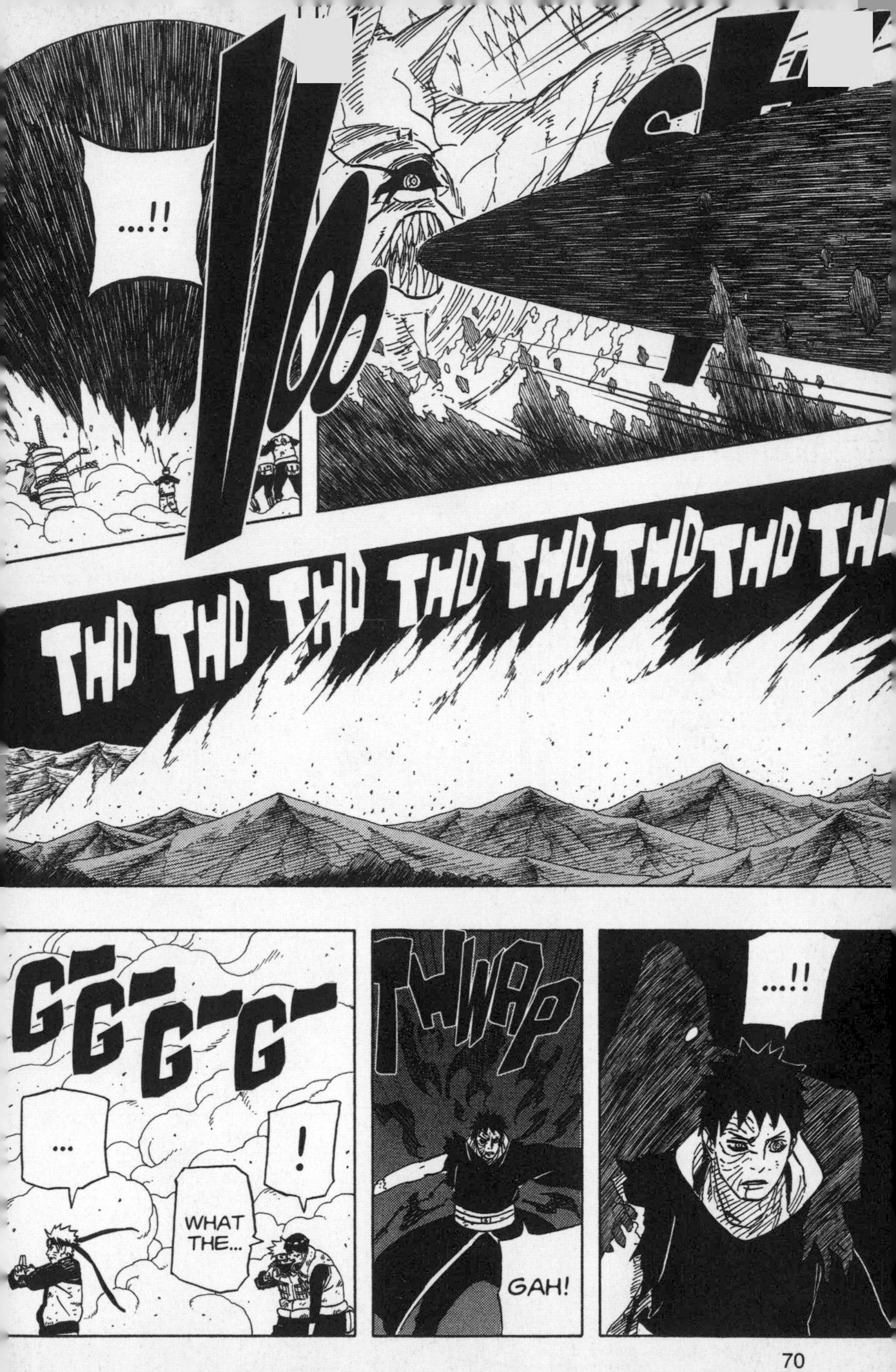
...!!
THD THD THD THD THD THD THD TH
...!!
THWAP
GAH!
G-G-G-G-
!
WHAT THE...
...

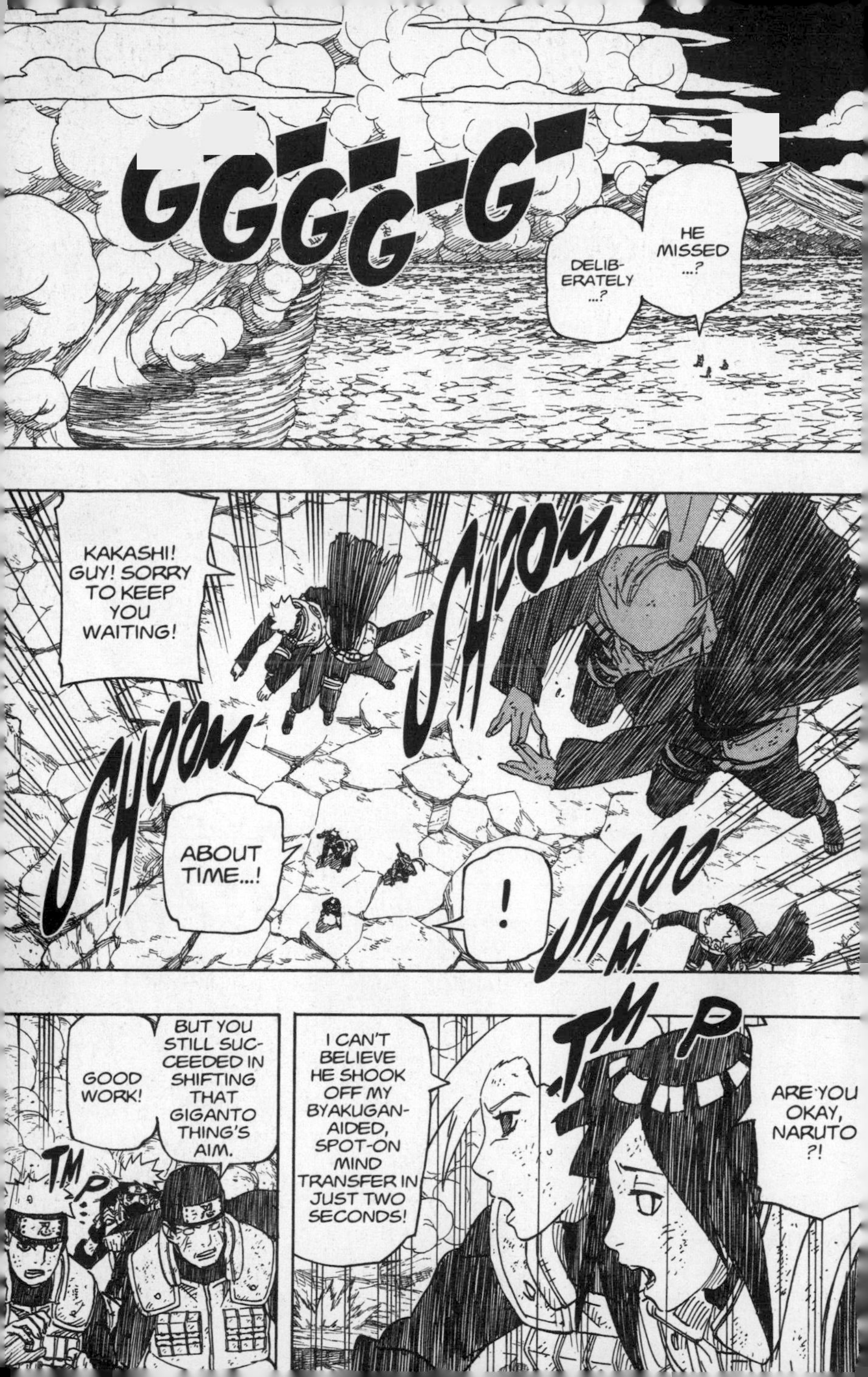
GGGGG
HE MISSED ...?
DELIBERATELY ...?
SHOOM
KAKASHI! GUY! SORRY TO KEEP YOU WAITING!
SHOOM
ABOUT TIME...!
!
SHOOM
TMP
ARE YOU OKAY, NARUTO?!
I CAN'T BELIEVE HE SHOOK OFF MY BYAKUGAN-AIDED, SPOT-ON MIND TRANSFER IN JUST TWO SECONDS!
TMP
BUT YOU STILL SUCCEEDED IN SHIFTING THAT GIGANTO THING'S AIM.
GOOD WORK!

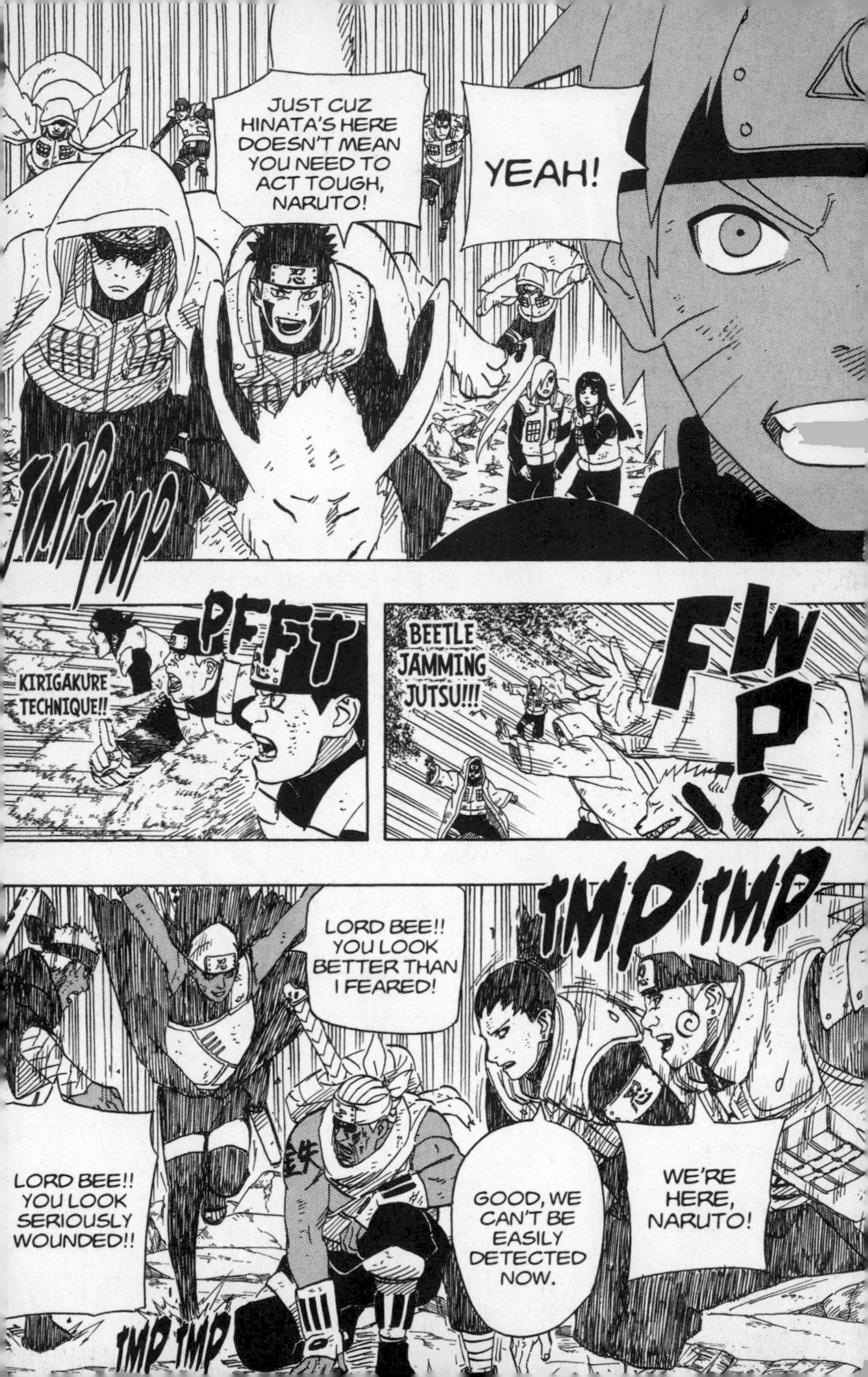
YEAH!
JUST CUZ HINATA'S HERE DOESN'T MEAN YOU NEED TO ACT TOUGH, NARUTO!
TMP TMP
FWP
BEETLE JAMMING JUTSU!!!
PFFT
KIRIGAKURE TECHNIQUE!!
TMP TMP
WE'RE HERE, NARUTO!
GOOD, WE CAN'T BE EASILY DETECTED NOW.
LORD BEE!! YOU LOOK BETTER THAN I FEARED!
LORD BEE!! YOU LOOK SERIOUSLY WOUNDED!!
TMP TMP

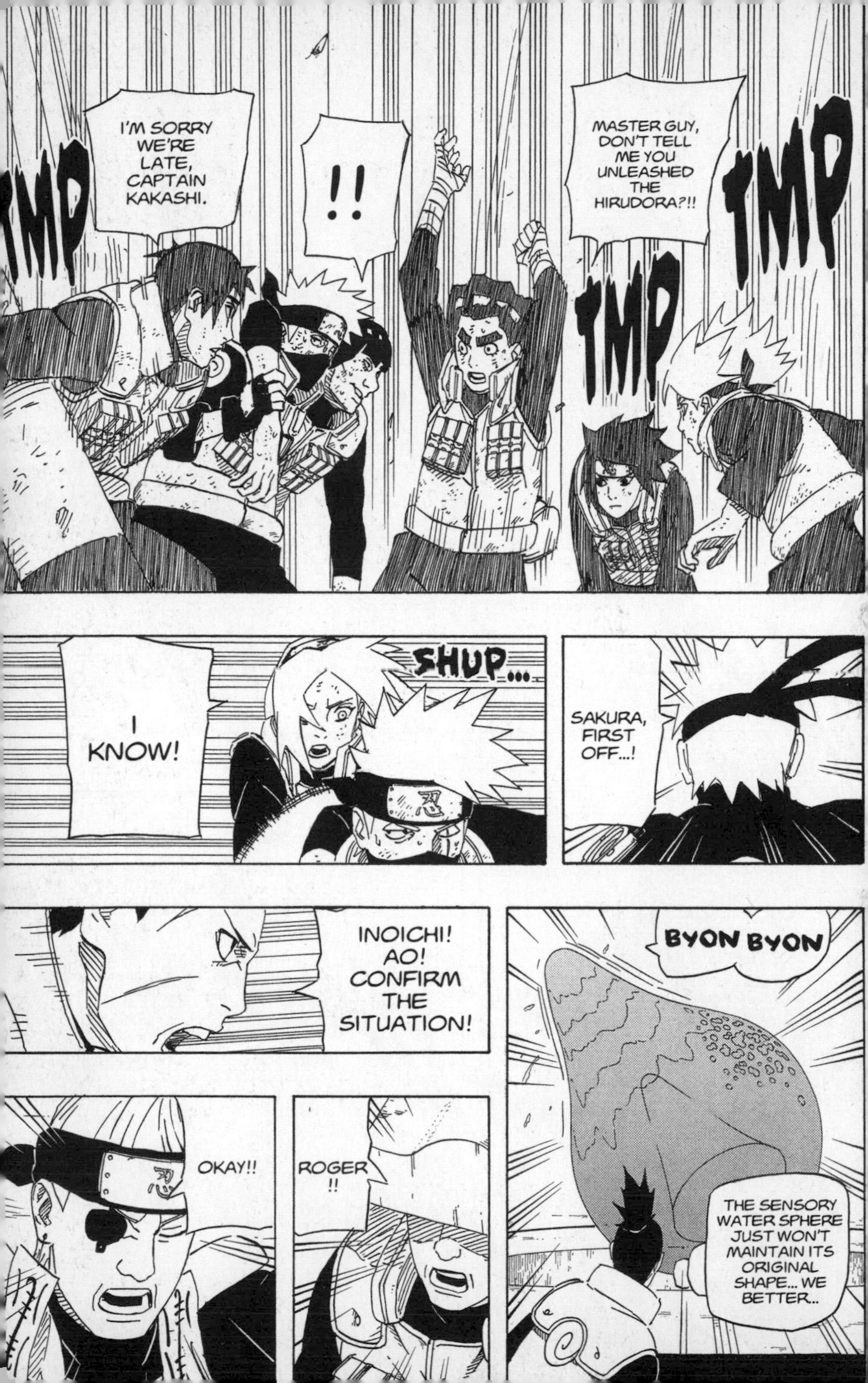
TMP
MASTER GUY, DON'T TELL ME YOU UNLEASHED THE HIRUDORA?!!
TMP
!!
I'M SORRY WE'RE LATE, CAPTAIN KAKASHI.
SAKURA, FIRST OFF...!
SHUP...
I KNOW!
BYON BYON
THE SENSORY WATER SPHERE JUST WON'T MAINTAIN ITS ORIGINAL SHAPE... WE BETTER...
INOICHI! AO! CONFIRM THE SITUATION!
ROGER!!
OKAY!!

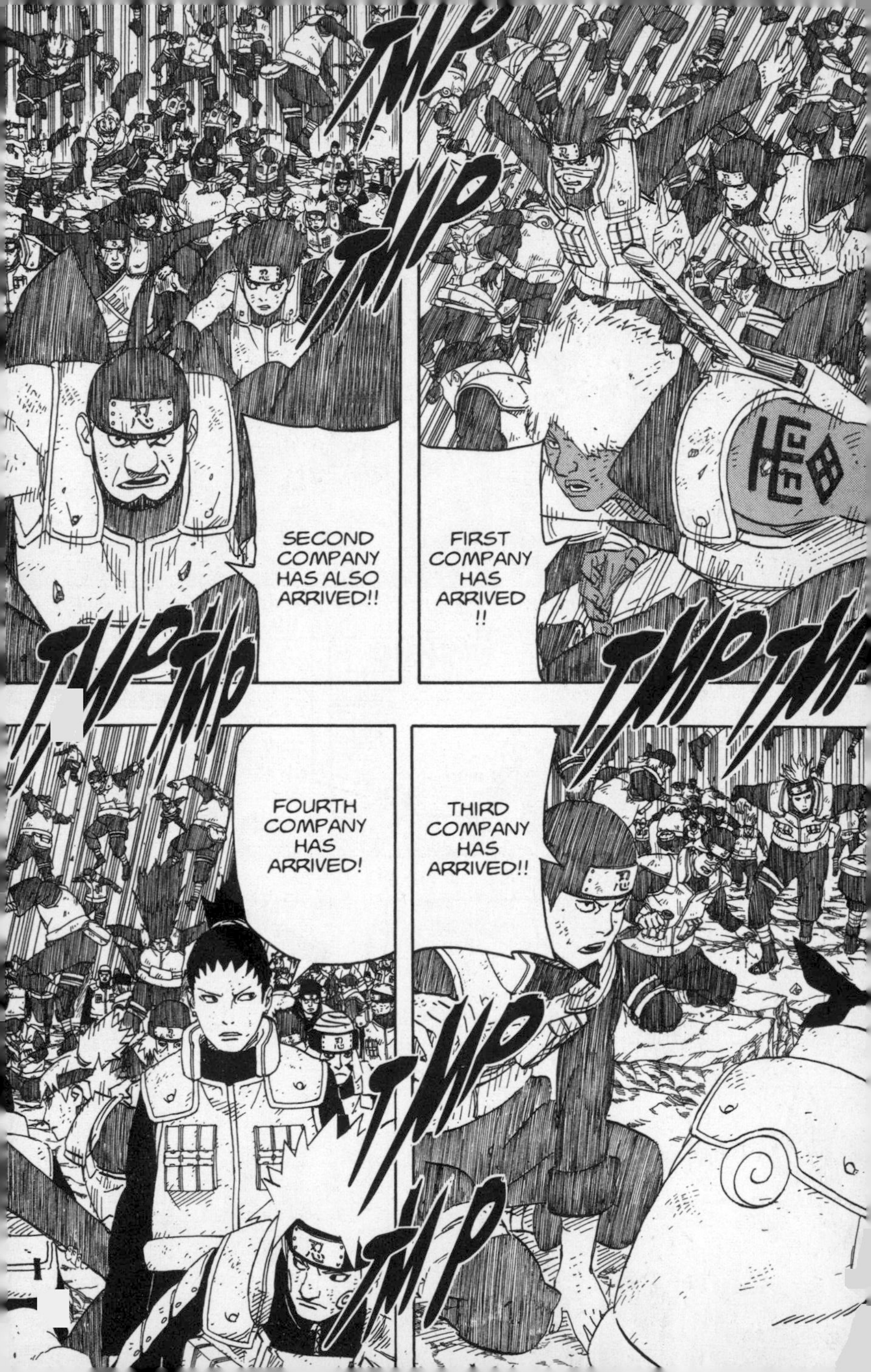
TMP TMP
FIRST COMPANY HAS ARRIVED !!
TMP TMP
SECOND COMPANY HAS ALSO ARRIVED!!
TMP TMP
TMP TMP
THIRD COMPANY HAS ARRIVED!!
TMP TMP
FOURTH COMPANY HAS ARRIVED!

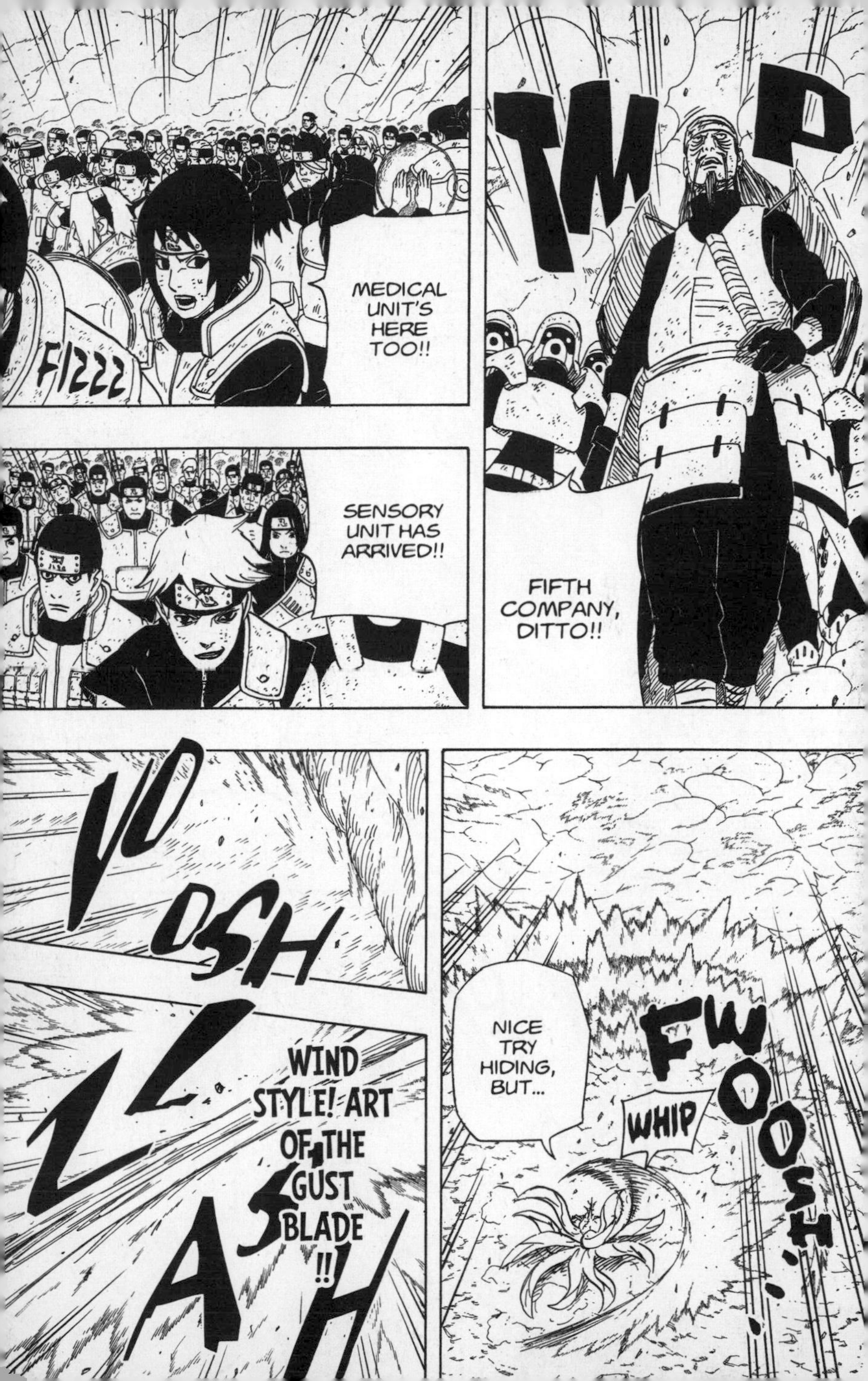
TWP
FIFTH COMPANY, DITTO!!
MEDICAL UNIT'S HERE TOO!!
FIZZZ
SENSORY UNIT HAS ARRIVED!!
NICE TRY HIDING, BUT...
FWOOSH
WHIP
VOOSH
ZASH
WIND STYLE! ART OF THE GUST BLADE!!

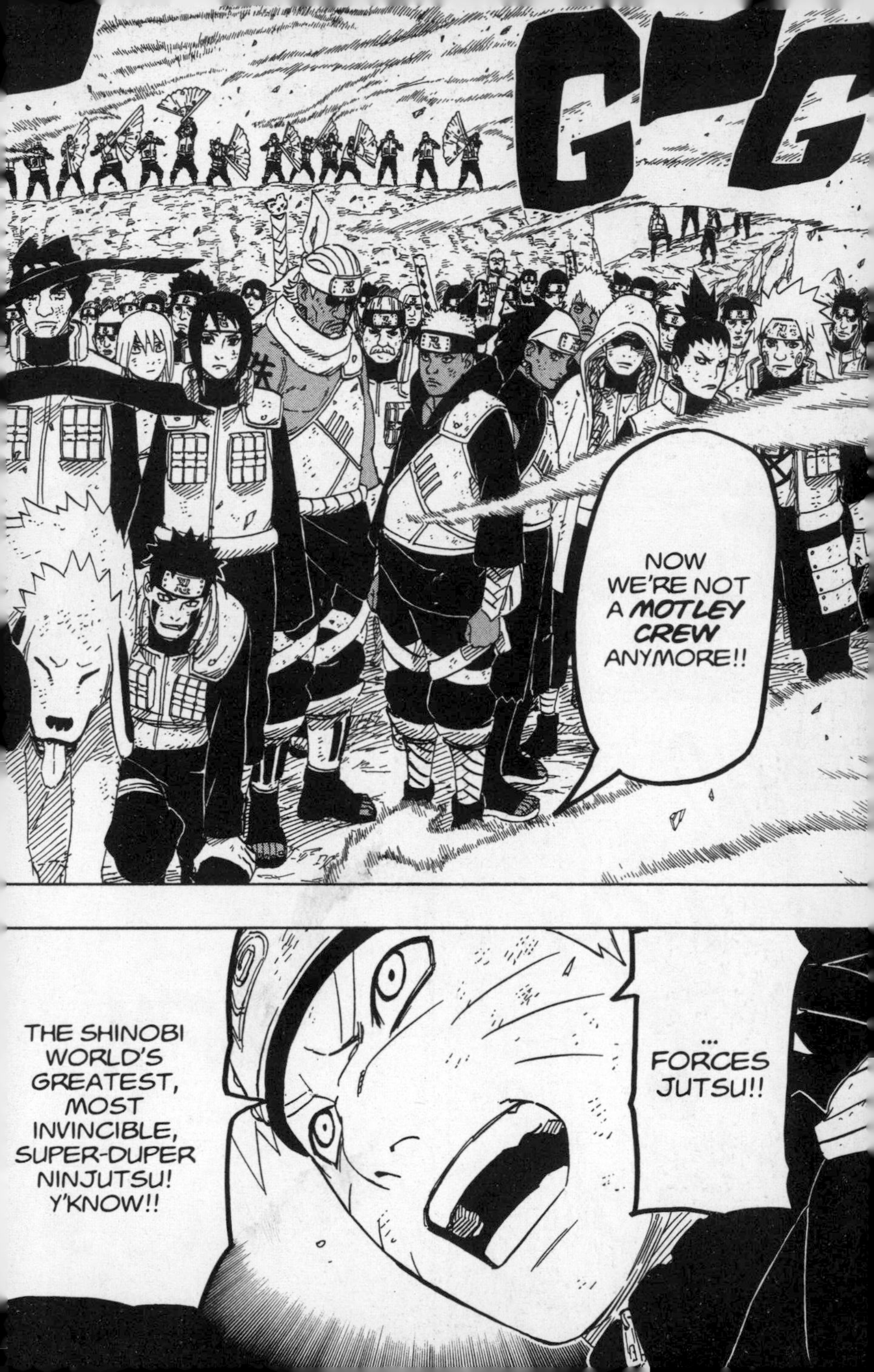
NOW WE'RE NOT A MOTLEY CREW ANYMORE!!
... FORCES JUTSU!!
THE SHINOBI WORLD'S GREATEST, MOST INVINCIBLE, SUPER-DUPER NINJUTSU! Y'KNOW!!

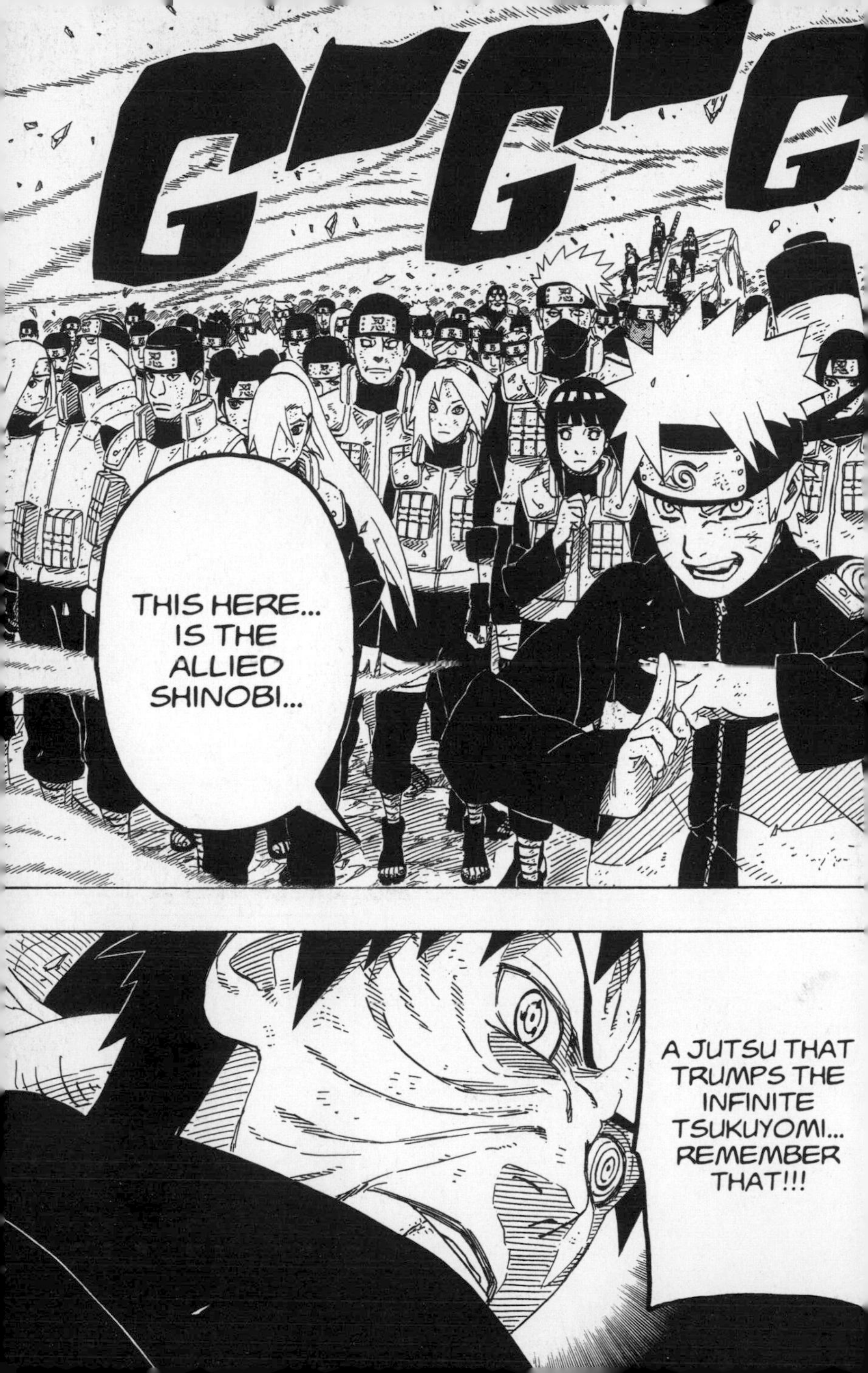
GGG
THIS HERE... IS THE ALLIED SHINOBI...
A JUTSU THAT TRUMPS THE INFINITE TSUKUYOMI... REMEMBER THAT!!!

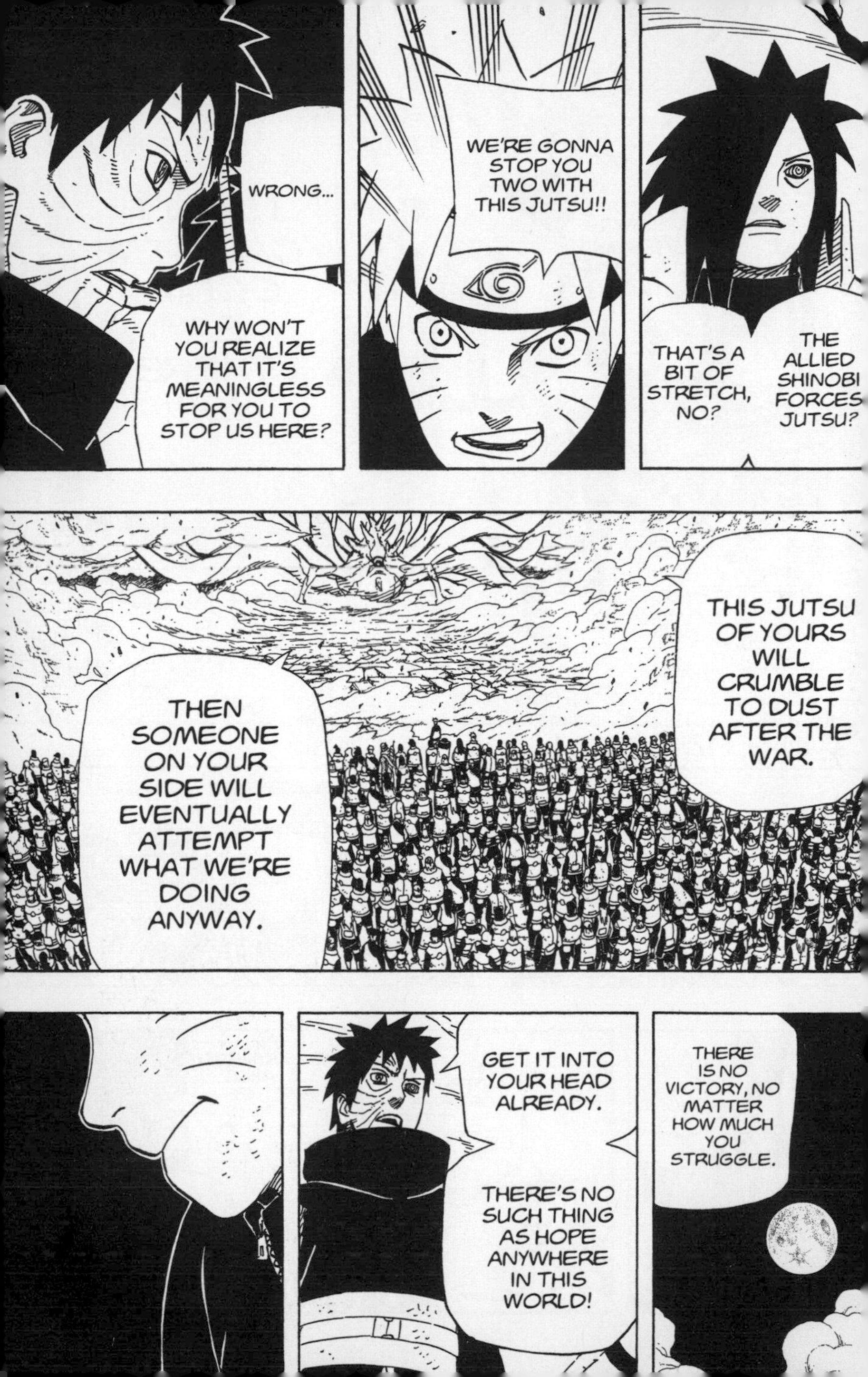
THE ALLIED SHINOBI FORCES JUTSU?
THAT'S A BIT OF STRETCH, NO?
WE'RE GONNA STOP YOU TWO WITH THIS JUTSU!!
WRONG...
WHY WON'T YOU REALIZE THAT IT'S MEANINGLESS FOR YOU TO STOP US HERE?
THIS JUTSU OF YOURS WILL CRUMBLE TO DUST AFTER THE WAR.
THEN SOMEONE ON YOUR SIDE WILL EVENTUALLY ATTEMPT WHAT WE'RE DOING ANYWAY.
THERE IS NO VICTORY, NO MATTER HOW MUCH YOU STRUGGLE.
GET IT INTO YOUR HEAD ALREADY.
THERE'S NO SUCH THING AS HOPE ANYWHERE IN THIS WORLD!

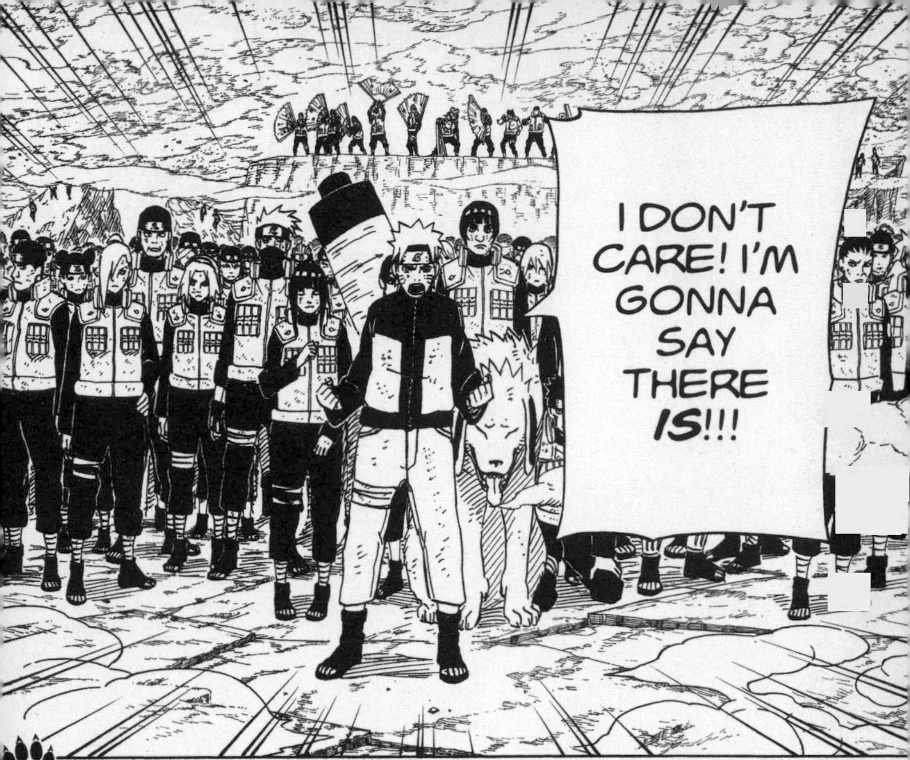
I DON'T CARE! I'M GONNA SAY THERE *IS*!!!

Number 612: The Allied Shinobi Forces Jutsu!!

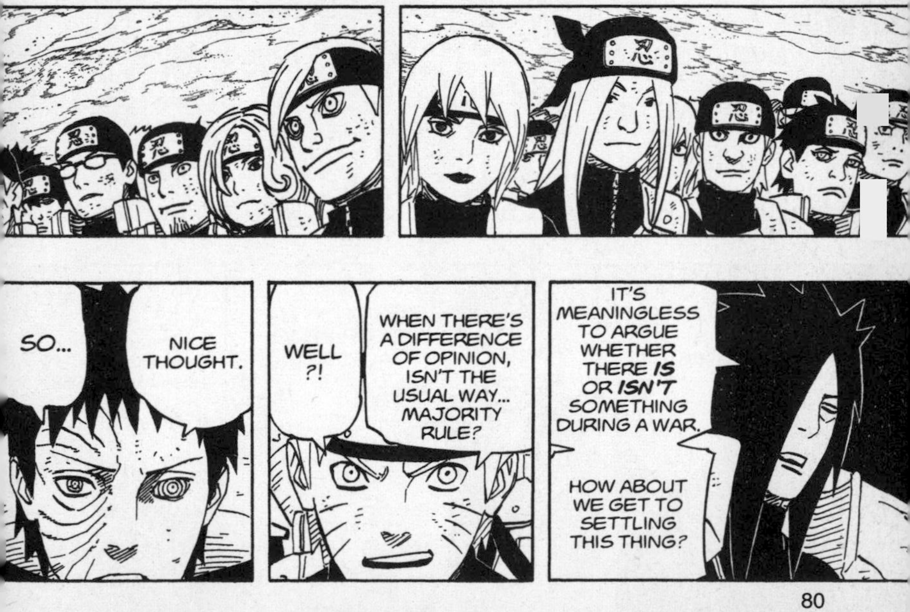
IT'S MEANINGLESS TO ARGUE WHETHER THERE *IS* OR *ISN'T* SOMETHING DURING A WAR.
HOW ABOUT WE GET TO SETTLING THIS THING?
WHEN THERE'S A DIFFERENCE OF OPINION, ISN'T THE USUAL WAY... MAJORITY RULE?
WELL ?!
NICE THOUGHT.
SO...

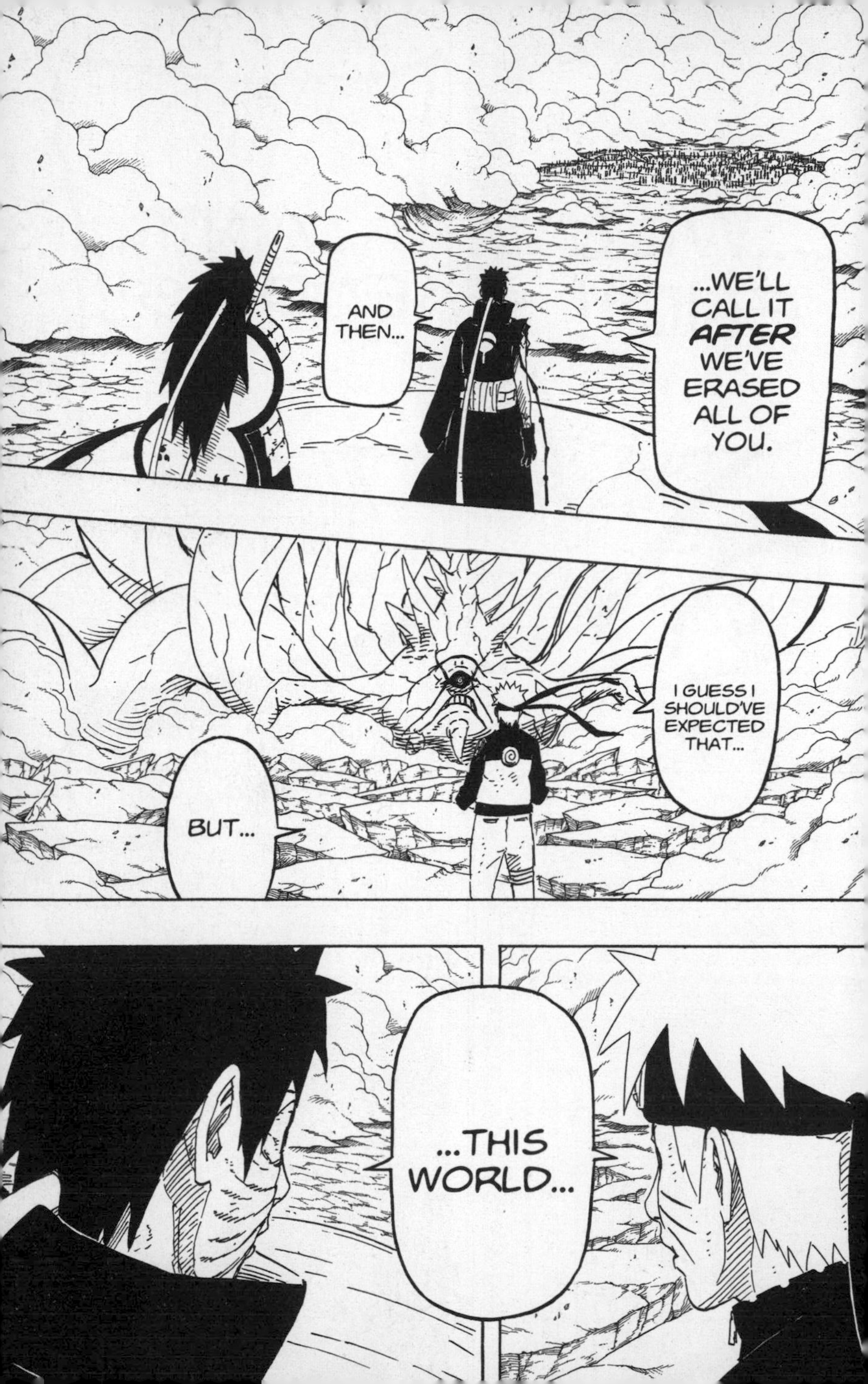
...WE'LL CALL IT AFTER WE'VE ERASED ALL OF YOU.
AND THEN...
I GUESS I SHOULD'VE EXPECTED THAT...
BUT...
...THIS WORLD...

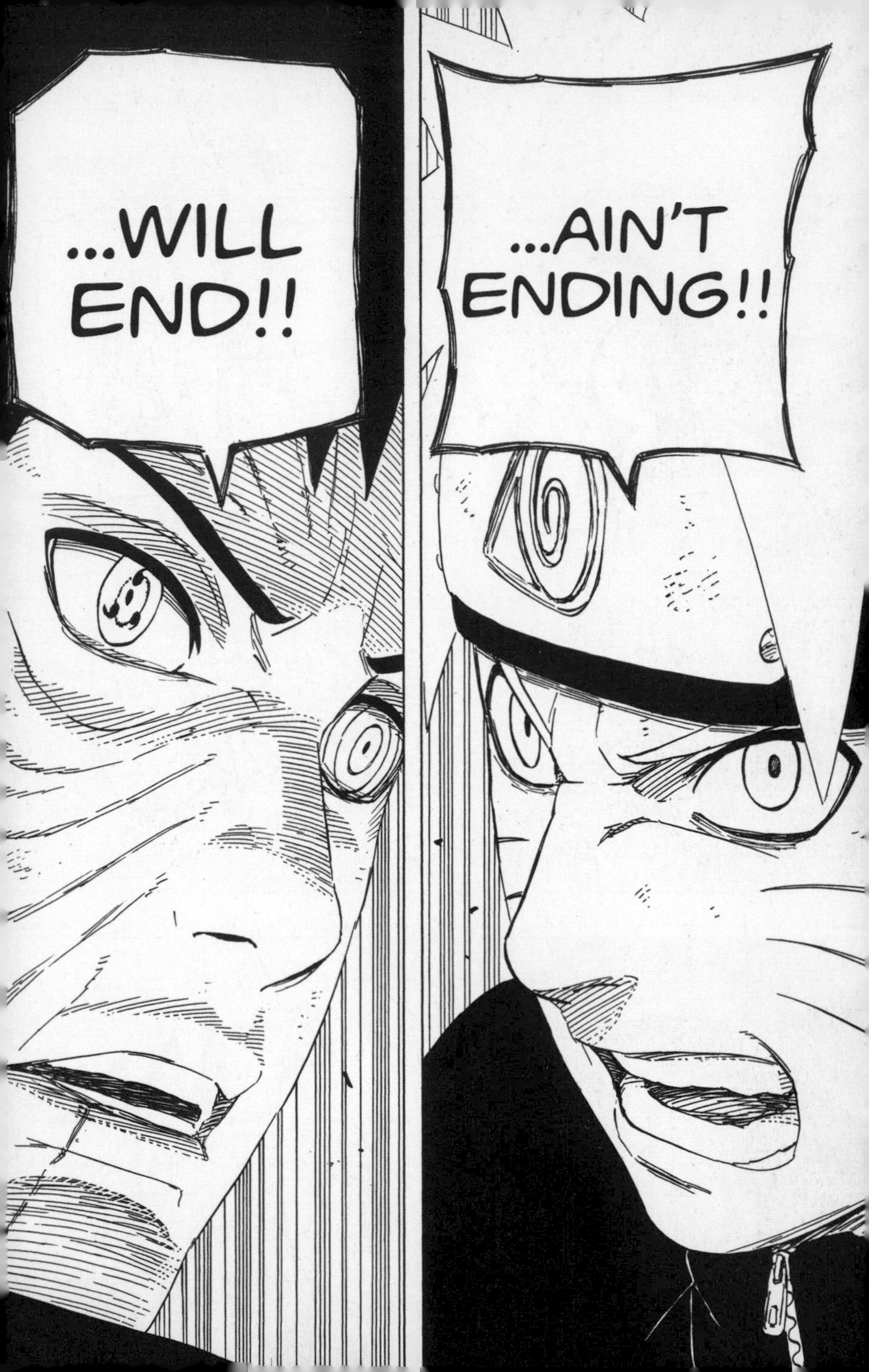
...AIN'T ENDING!!
...WILL END!!

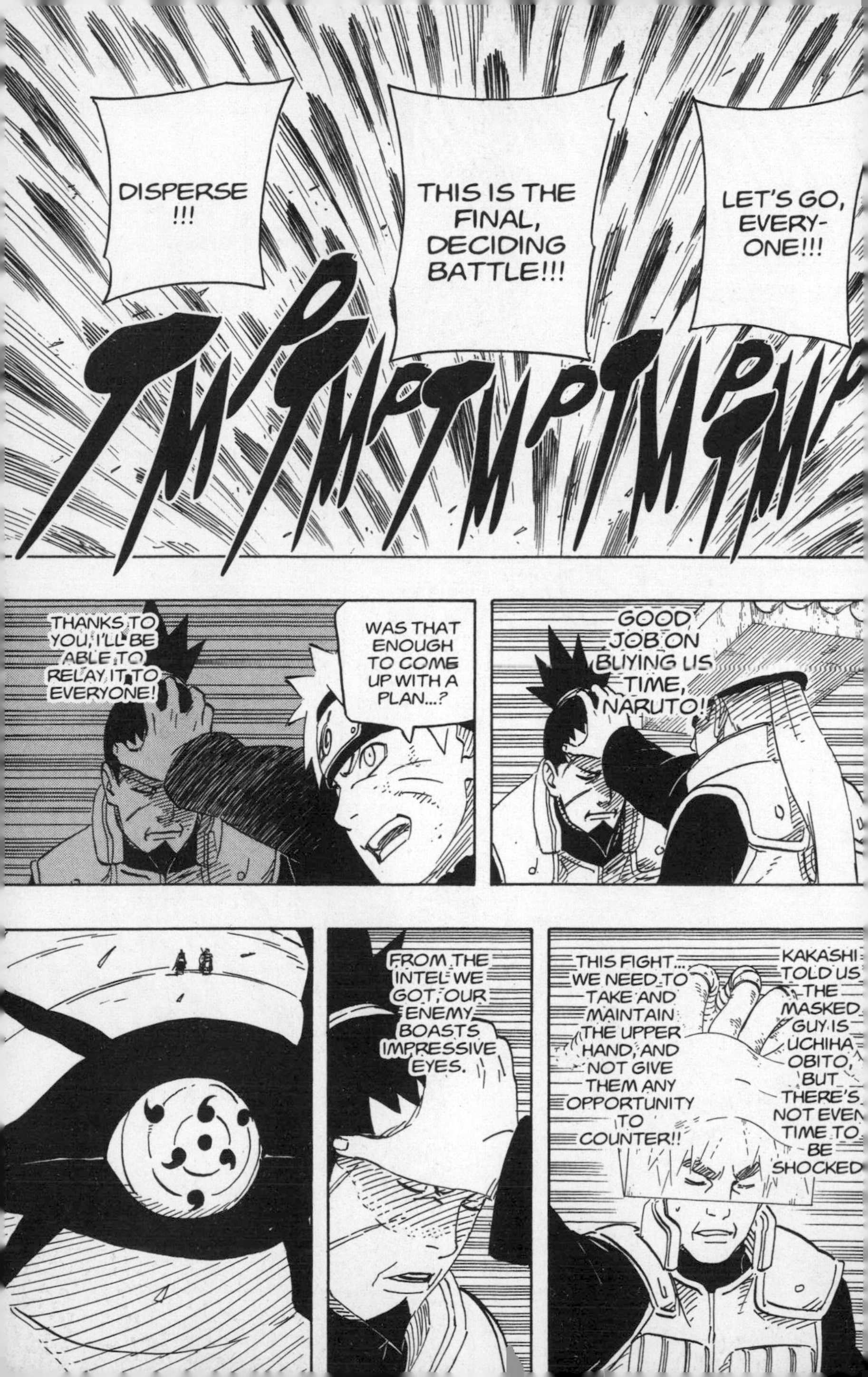
LET'S GO, EVERY-ONE!!!
THIS IS THE FINAL, DECIDING BATTLE!!!
DISPERSE!!!
GOOD JOB ON BUYING US TIME, NARUTO!
WAS THAT ENOUGH TO COME UP WITH A PLAN...?
THANKS TO YOU, I'LL BE ABLE TO RELAY IT TO EVERYONE!
KAKASHI TOLD US THE MASKED GUY IS UCHIHA OBITO, BUT THERE'S NOT EVEN TIME TO BE SHOCKED
THIS FIGHT... WE NEED TO TAKE AND MAINTAIN THE UPPER HAND, AND NOT GIVE THEM ANY OPPORTUNITY TO COUNTER!!
FROM THE INTEL WE GOT, OUR ENEMY BOASTS IMPRESSIVE EYES.

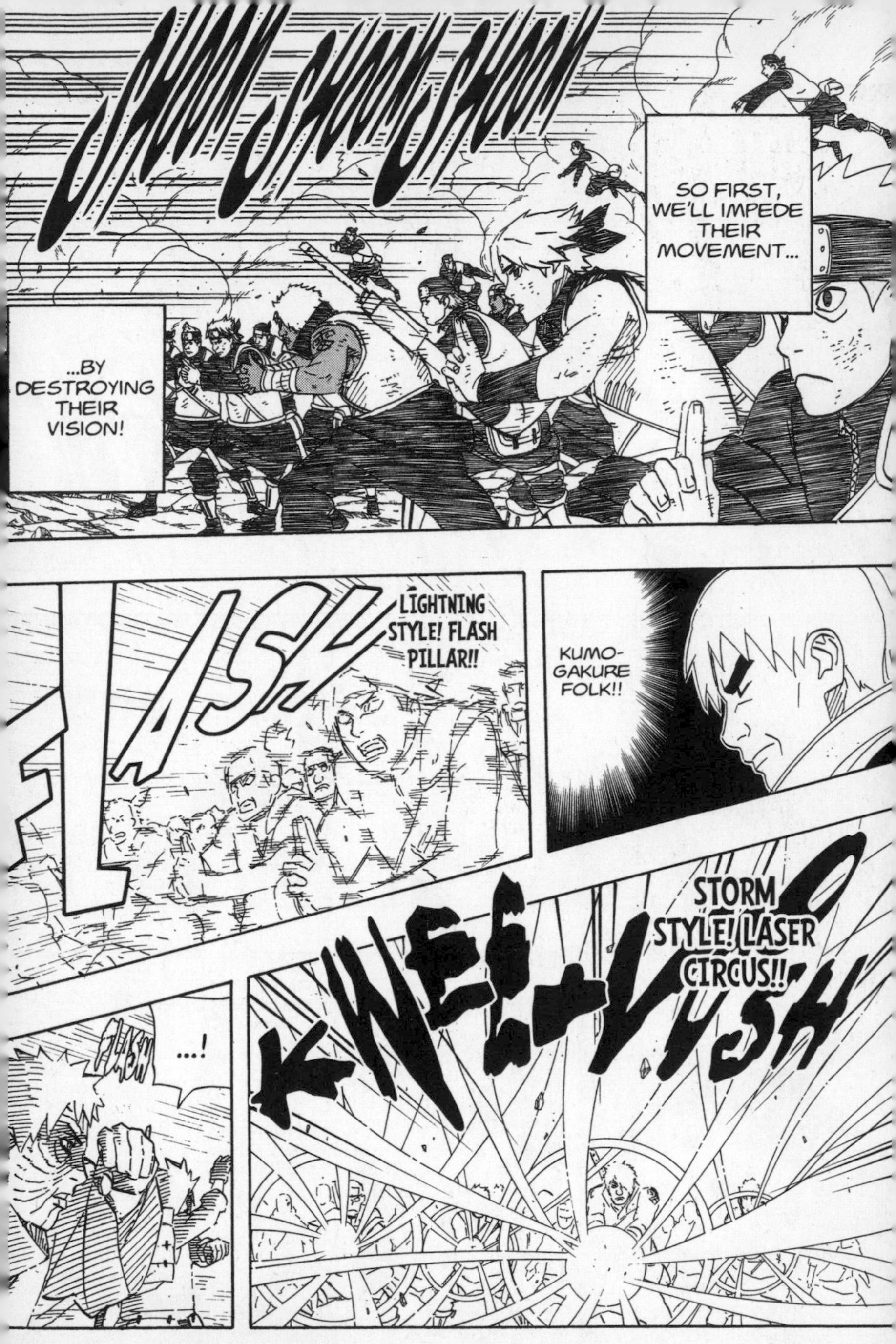
SO FIRST, WE'LL IMPEDE THEIR MOVEMENT...
...BY DESTROYING THEIR VISION!
KUMO-GAKURE FOLK!!
LIGHTNING STYLE! FLASH PILLAR!!
FLASH
STORM STYLE! LASER CIRCUS!!
FLASH
...!

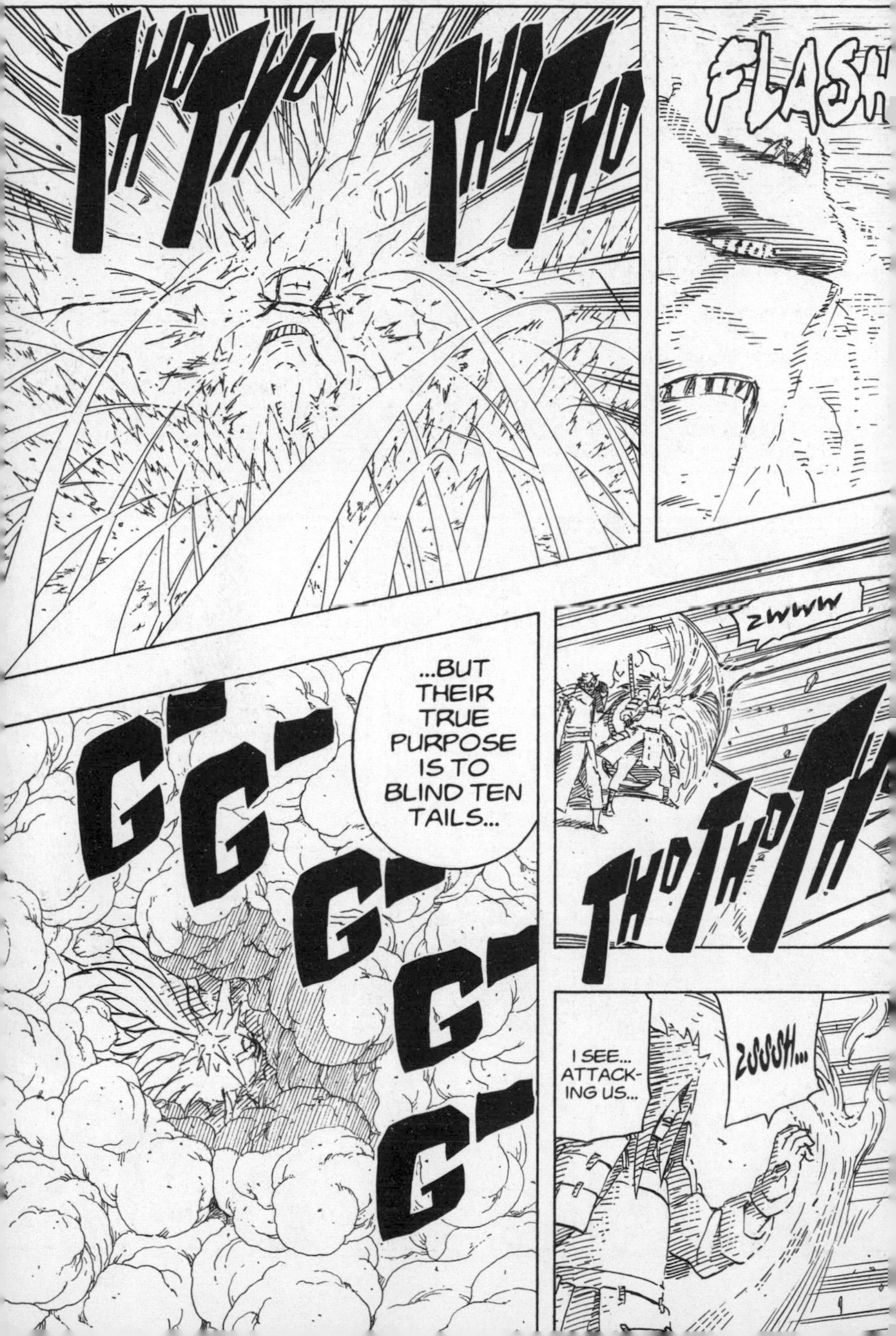
FLASH
THOTHO THOTHO
ZWWW
THOTHOTH
I SEE... ATTACKING US...
ZOSSSH...
...BUT THEIR TRUE PURPOSE IS TO BLIND TEN TAILS...
G- G- G- G- G- G-

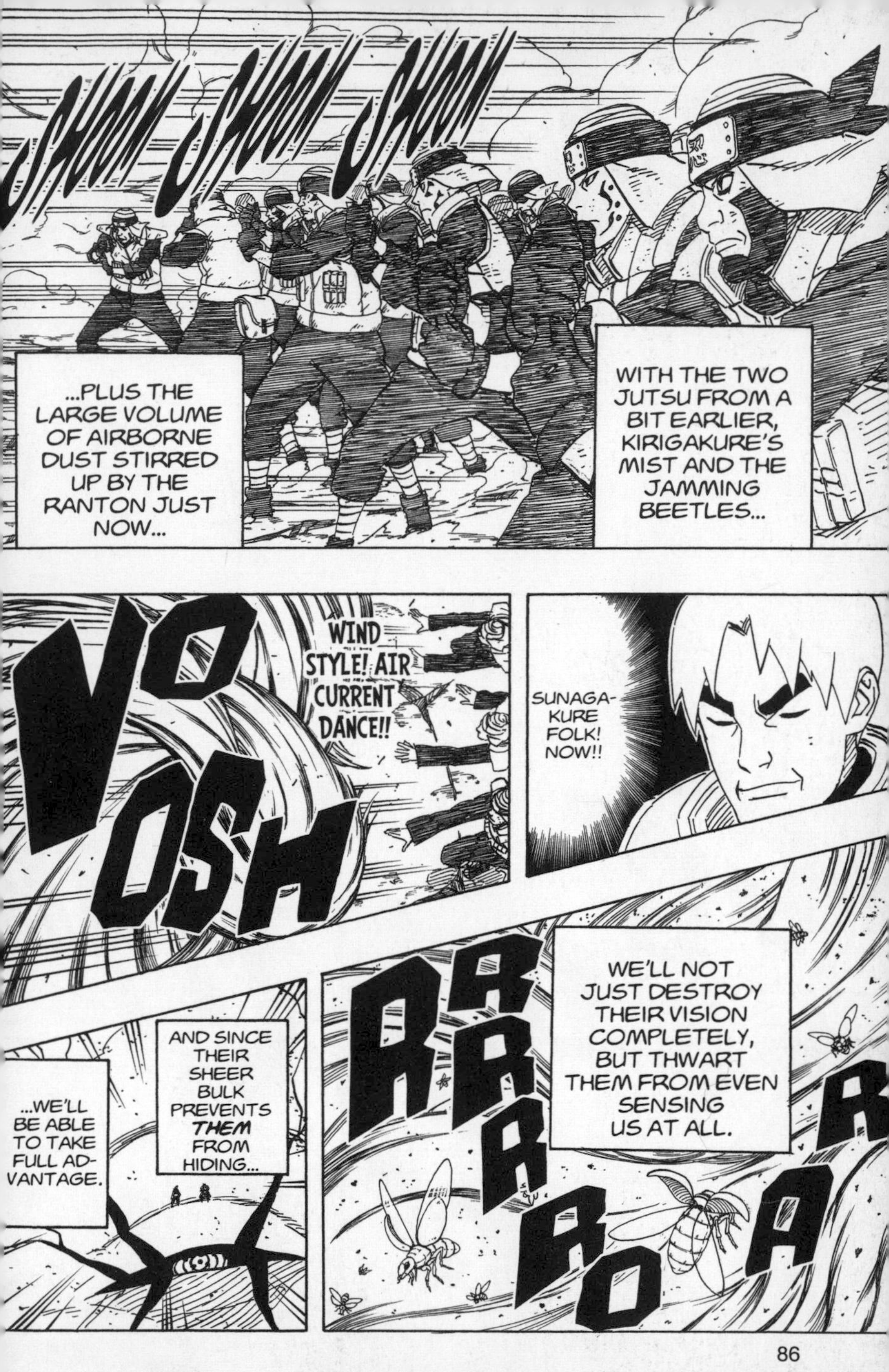
SHOOM SHOOM SHOOM
WITH THE TWO JUTSU FROM A BIT EARLIER, KIRIGAKURE'S MIST AND THE JAMMING BEETLES...
...PLUS THE LARGE VOLUME OF AIRBORNE DUST STIRRED UP BY THE RANTON JUST NOW...
SUNAGAKURE FOLK! NOW!!
WIND STYLE! AIR CURRENT DANCE!!
VOOSH
WE'LL NOT JUST DESTROY THEIR VISION COMPLETELY, BUT THWART THEM FROM EVEN SENSING US AT ALL.
RRRRROAR
AND SINCE THEIR SHEER BULK PREVENTS *THEM* FROM HIDING...
...WE'LL BE ABLE TO TAKE FULL ADVANTAGE.

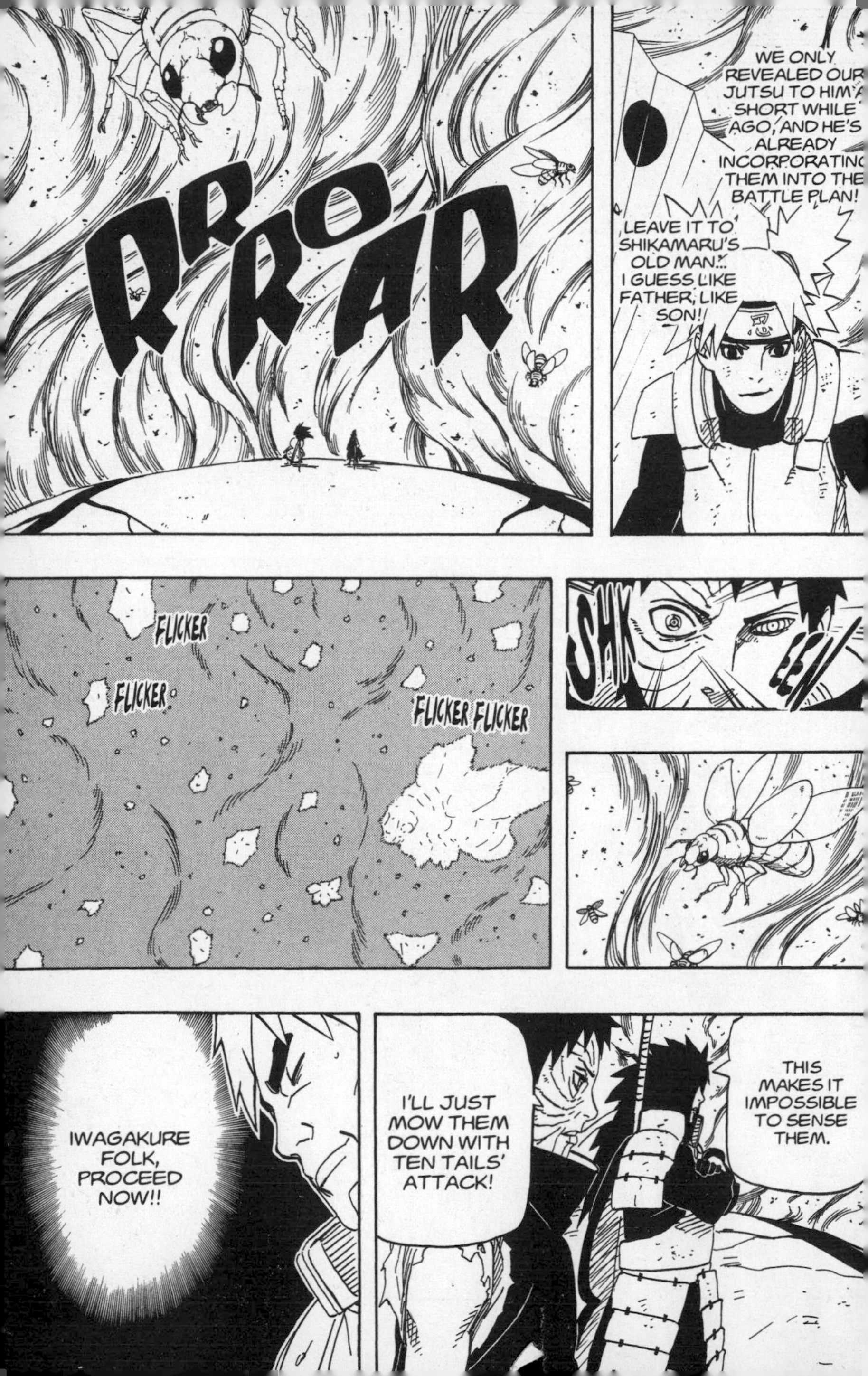
WE ONLY REVEALED OUR JUTSU TO HIM A SHORT WHILE AGO, AND HE'S ALREADY INCORPORATING THEM INTO THE BATTLE PLAN!
LEAVE IT TO SHIKAMARU'S OLD MAN... I GUESS LIKE FATHER, LIKE SON!
DRROAR
SHK
EEN
FLICKER
FLICKER
FLICKER FLICKER
THIS MAKES IT IMPOSSIBLE TO SENSE THEM.
I'LL JUST MOW THEM DOWN WITH TEN TAILS' ATTACK!
IWAGAKURE FOLK, PROCEED NOW!!

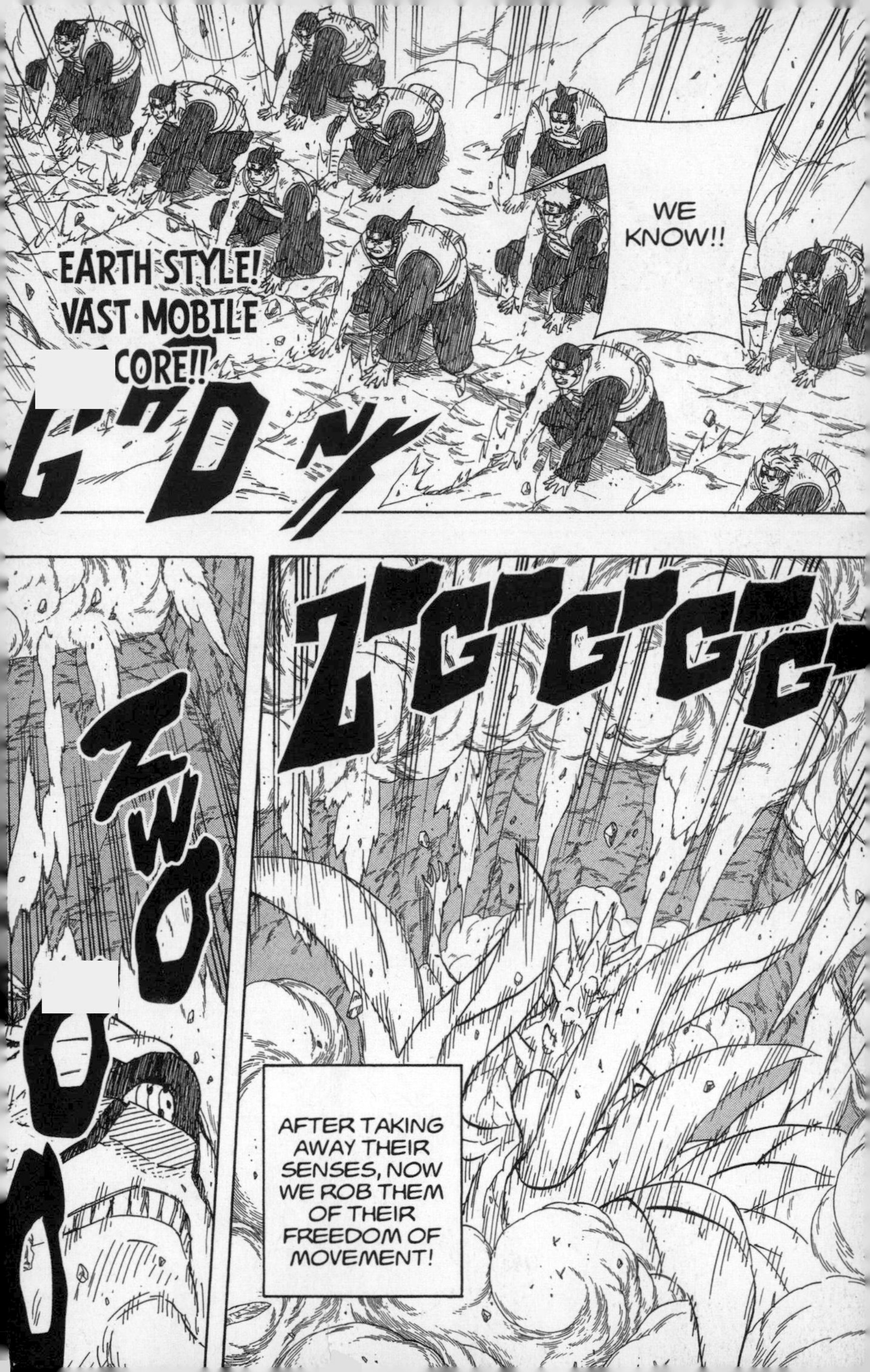
WE KNOW!!
EARTH STYLE! VAST MOBILE CORE!!
AFTER TAKING AWAY THEIR SENSES, NOW WE ROB THEM OF THEIR FREEDOM OF MOVEMENT!

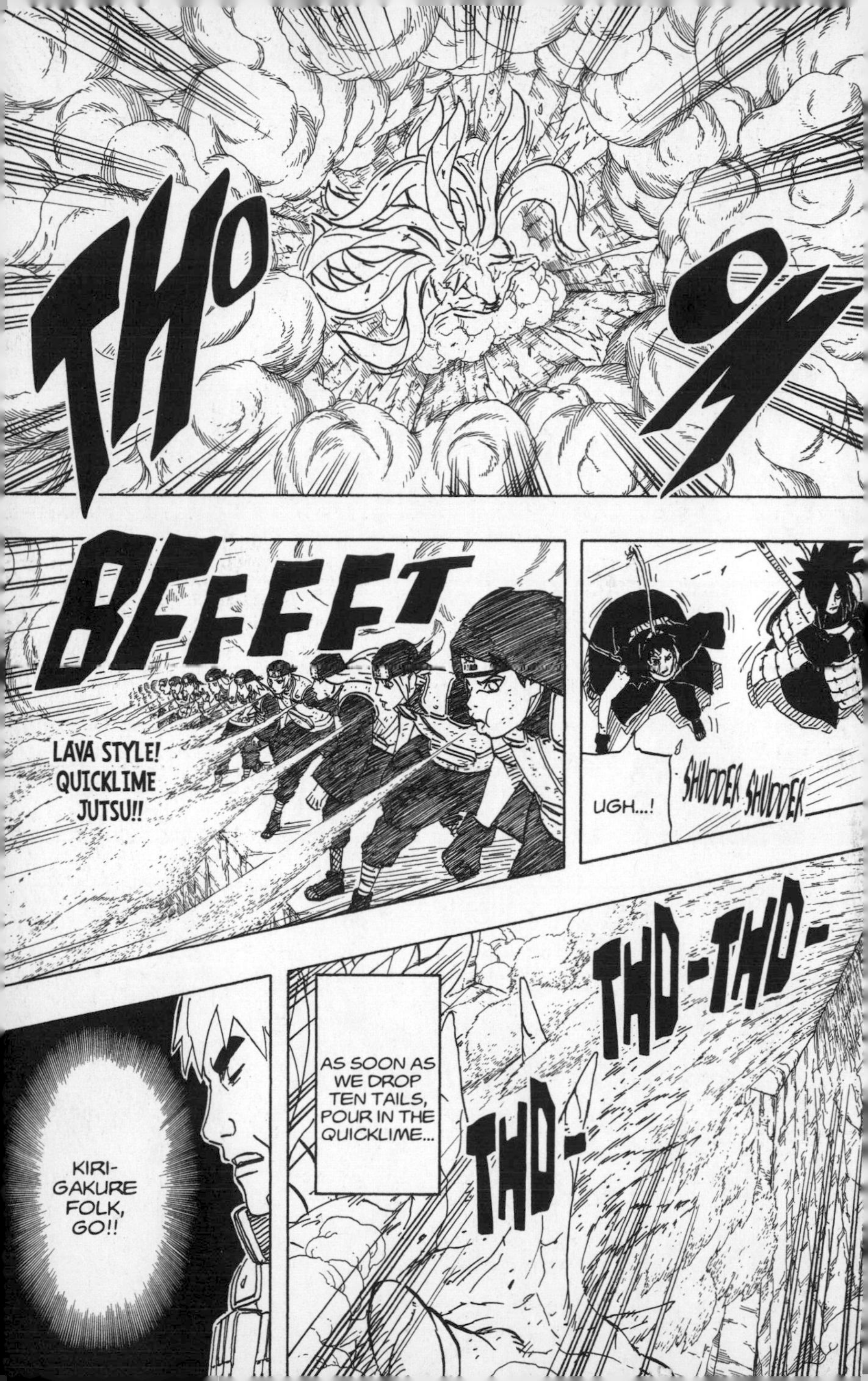
THO
SHUDDER SHUDDER
UGH...!
BFFFFT
LAVA STYLE! QUICKLIME JUTSU!!
THD-THD-
AS SOON AS WE DROP TEN TAILS, POUR IN THE QUICKLIME...
THD-
KIRI-GAKURE FOLK, GO!!

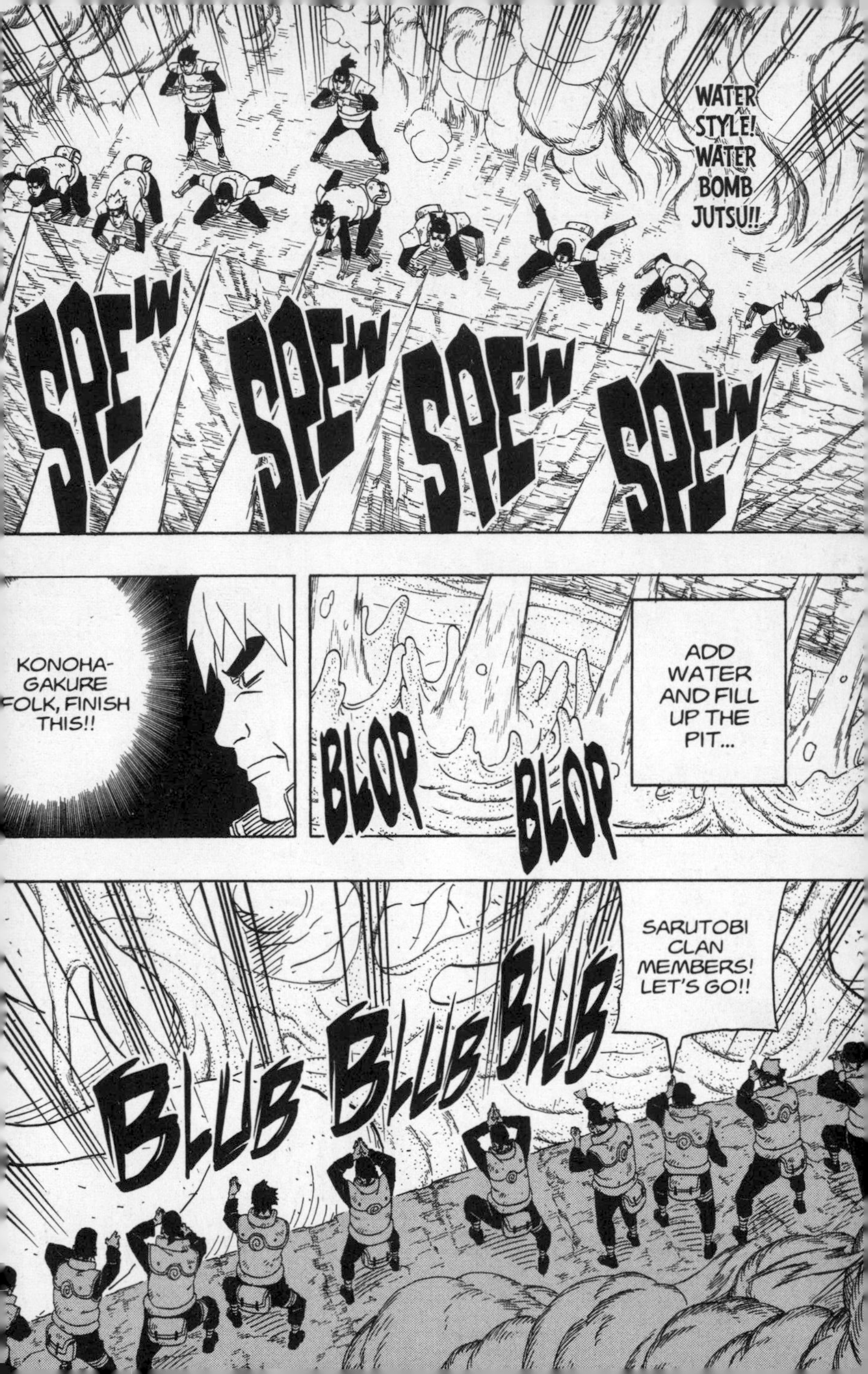
WATER STYLE! WATER BOMB JUTSU!!
SPEW SPEW SPEW SPEW
ADD WATER AND FILL UP THE PIT...
BLOP BLOP
KONOHA-GAKURE FOLK, FINISH THIS!!
SARUTOBI CLAN MEMBERS! LET'S GO!!
BLUB BLUB BLUB

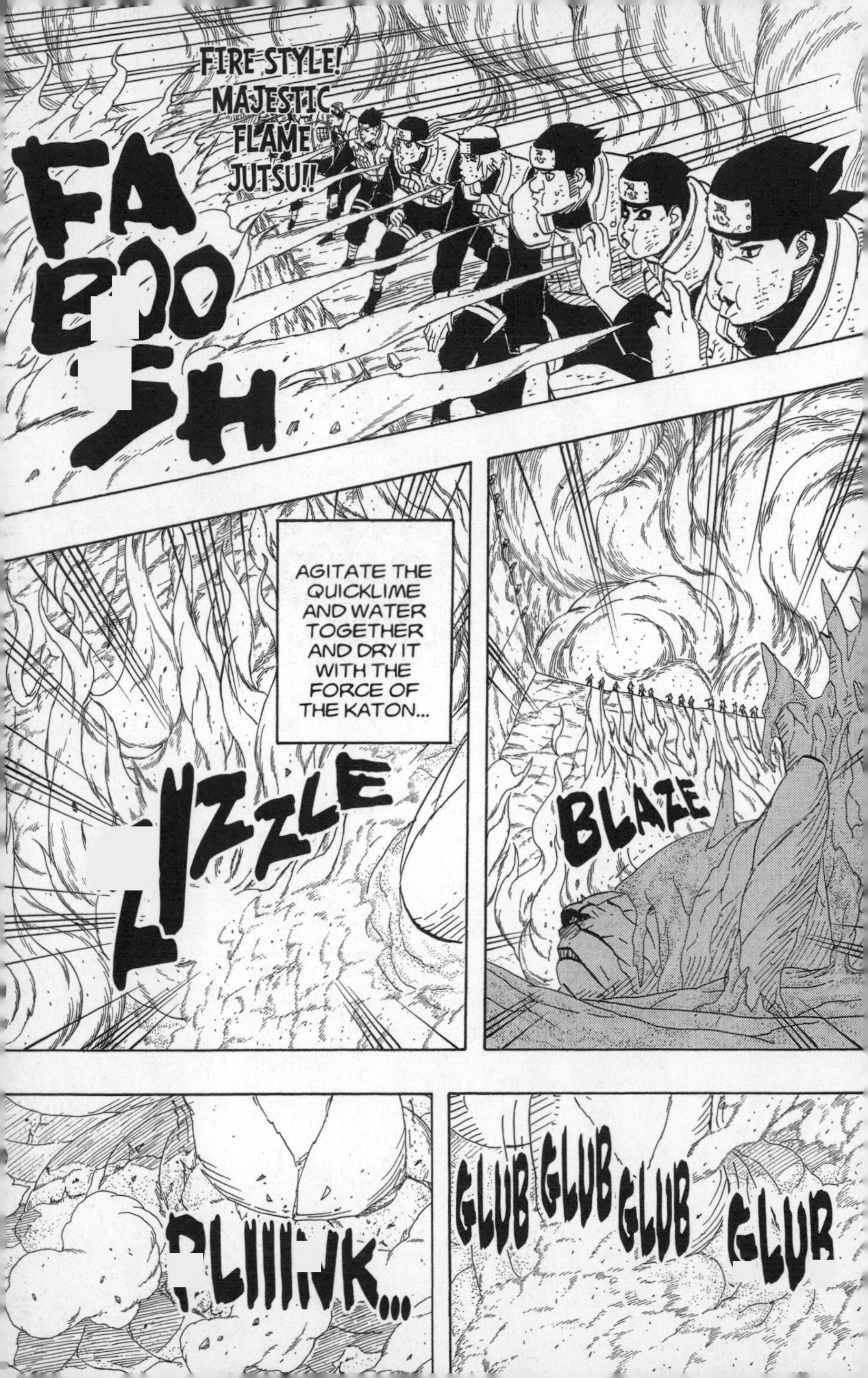
FIRE STYLE! MAJESTIC FLAME JUTSU!!
BLAZE
AGITATE THE QUICKLIME AND WATER TOGETHER AND DRY IT WITH THE FORCE OF THE KATON...
GLUB GLUB GLUB GLUB

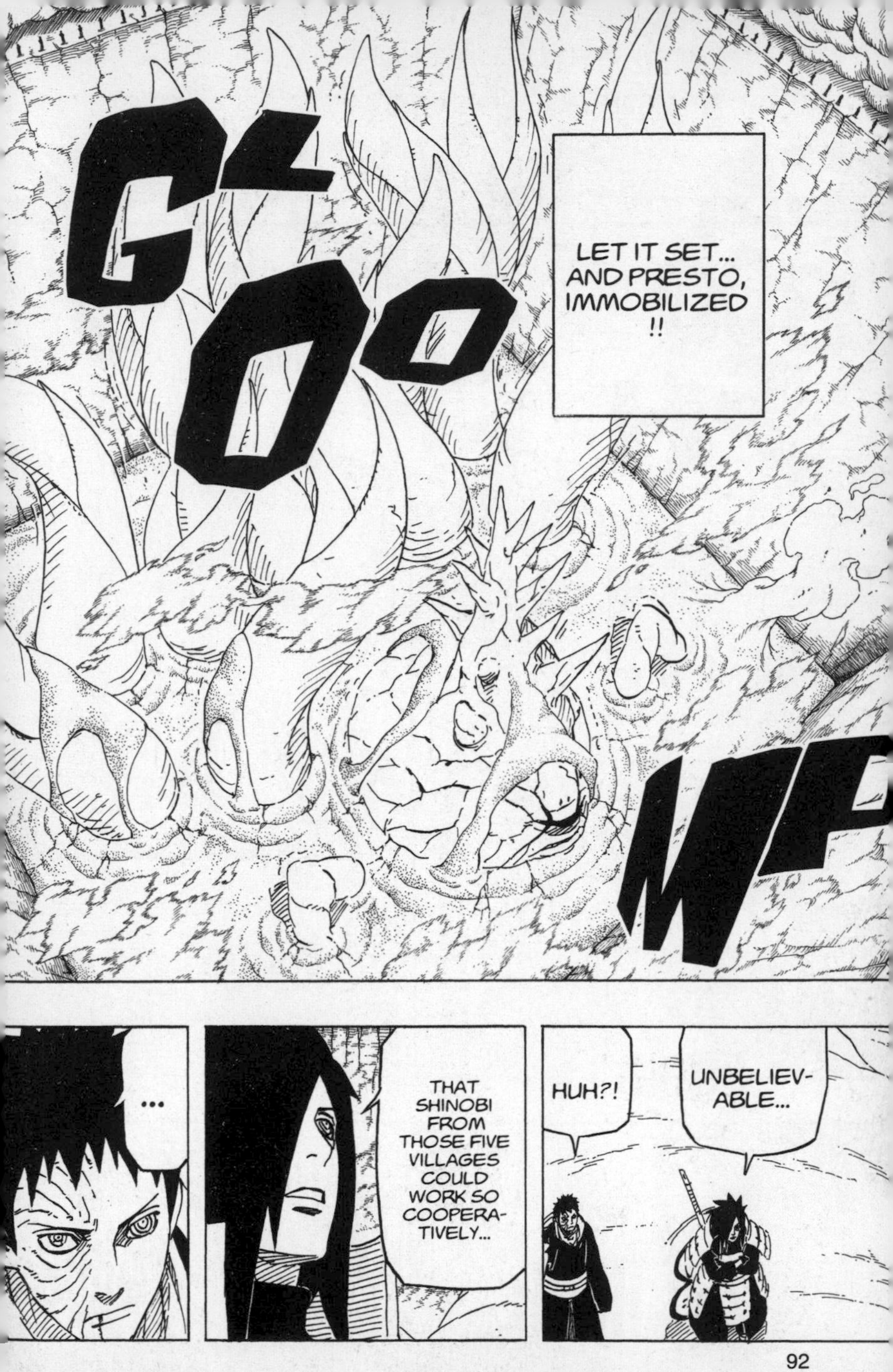
GOO
LET IT SET... AND PRESTO, IMMOBILIZED!!
UNBELIEV-ABLE...
HUH?!
THAT SHINOBI FROM THOSE FIVE VILLAGES COULD WORK SO COOPERA-TIVELY...
...

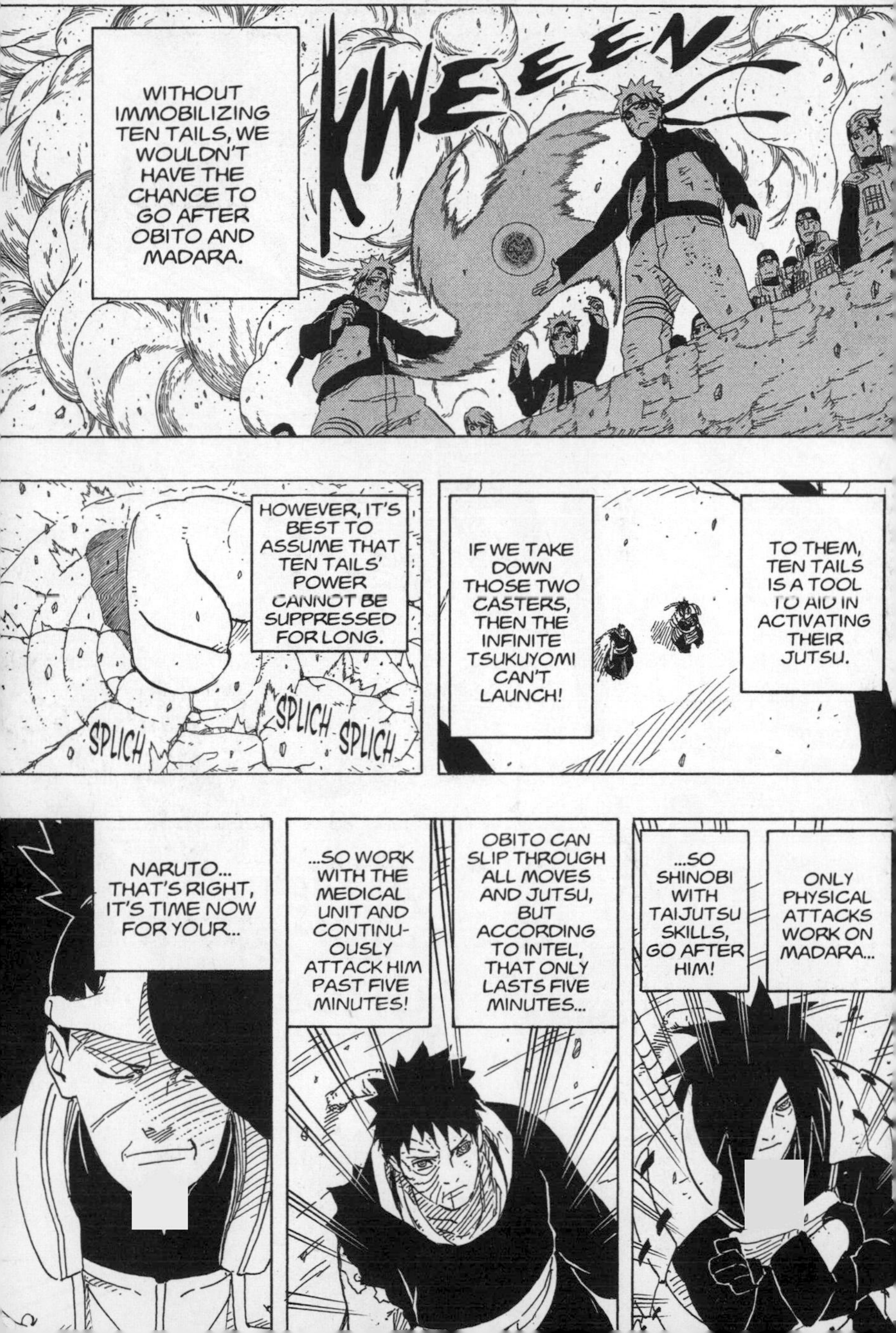
KWEEEN
WITHOUT IMMOBILIZING TEN TAILS, WE WOULDN'T HAVE THE CHANCE TO GO AFTER OBITO AND MADARA.
TO THEM, TEN TAILS IS A TOOL TO AID IN ACTIVATING THEIR JUTSU.
IF WE TAKE DOWN THOSE TWO CASTERS, THEN THE INFINITE TSUKUYOMI CAN'T LAUNCH!
HOWEVER, IT'S BEST TO ASSUME THAT TEN TAILS' POWER CANNOT BE SUPPRESSED FOR LONG.
SPLICH
SPLICH
SPLICH
ONLY PHYSICAL ATTACKS WORK ON MADARA...
...SO SHINOBI WITH TAIJUTSU SKILLS, GO AFTER HIM!
OBITO CAN SLIP THROUGH ALL MOVES AND JUTSU, BUT ACCORDING TO INTEL, THAT ONLY LASTS FIVE MINUTES...
...SO WORK WITH THE MEDICAL UNIT AND CONTINU-OUSLY ATTACK HIM PAST FIVE MINUTES!
NARUTO... THAT'S RIGHT, IT'S TIME NOW FOR YOUR...

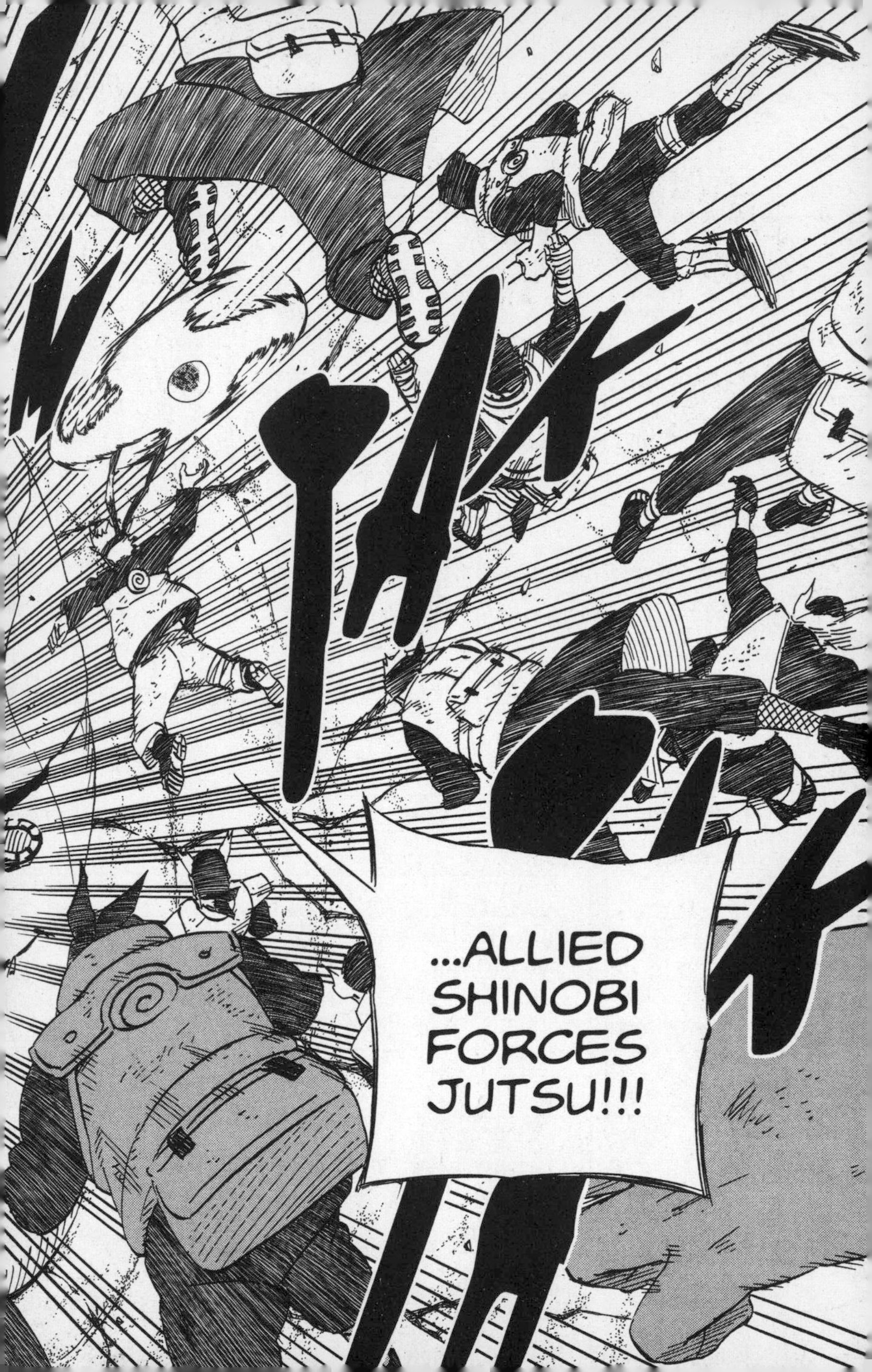
...ALLIED SHINOBI FORCES JUTSU!!!

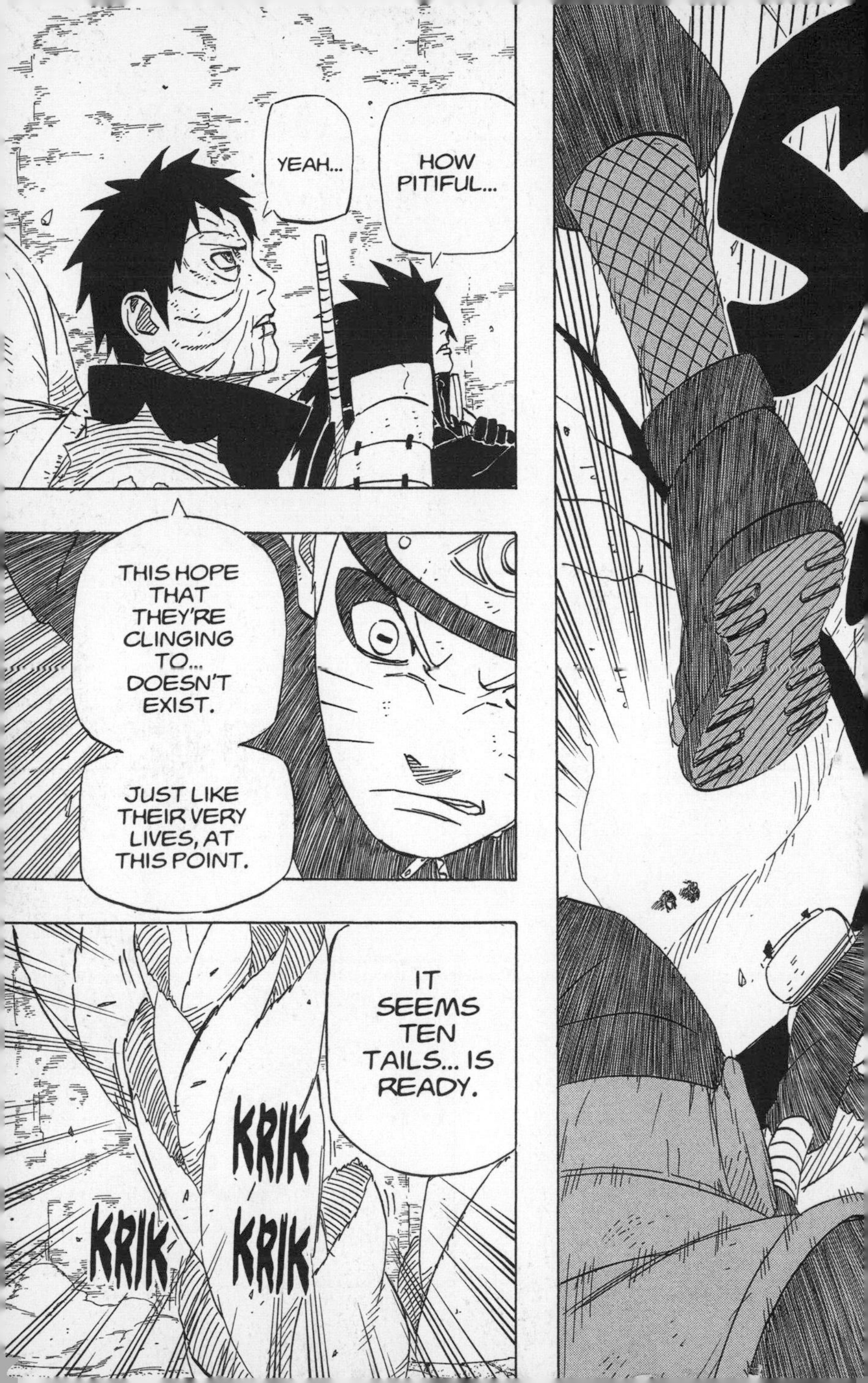
HOW PITIFUL...
YEAH...
THIS HOPE THAT THEY'RE CLINGING TO... DOESN'T EXIST.
JUST LIKE THEIR VERY LIVES, AT THIS POINT.
IT SEEMS TEN TAILS... IS READY.
KRIK KRIK
KRIK KRIK

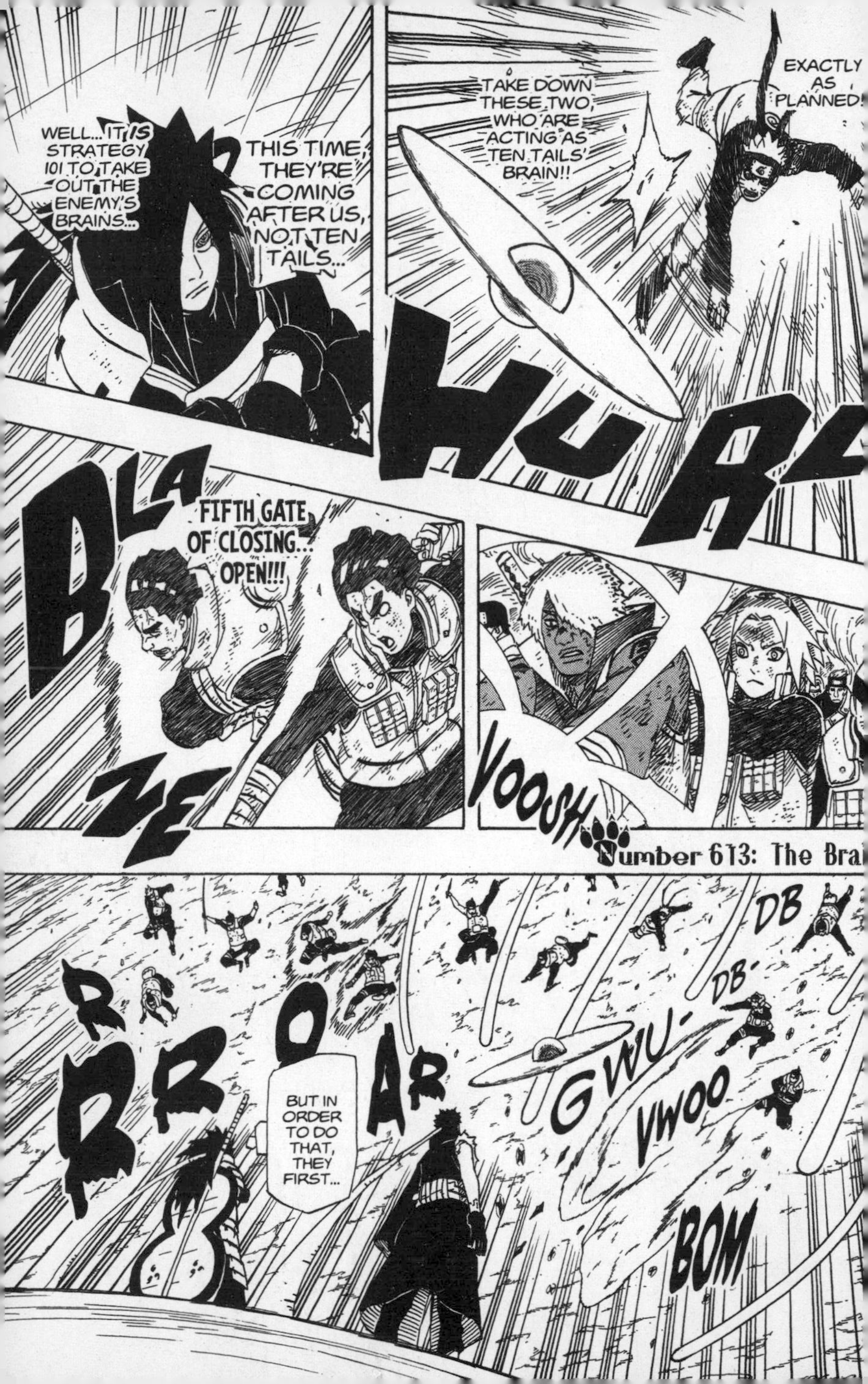
EXACTLY AS PLANNED!
TAKE DOWN THESE TWO, WHO ARE ACTING AS TEN TAILS' BRAIN!!
THIS TIME, THEY'RE COMING AFTER US, NOT TEN TAILS...
WELL... IT IS STRATEGY 101 TO TAKE OUT THE ENEMY'S BRAINS...
VOOSH
FIFTH GATE OF CLOSING... OPEN!!!
BLAZE
Number 613: The Bra
DB
DB
GWU-
VWOO
BOM
RRROAR
BUT IN ORDER TO DO THAT, THEY FIRST...

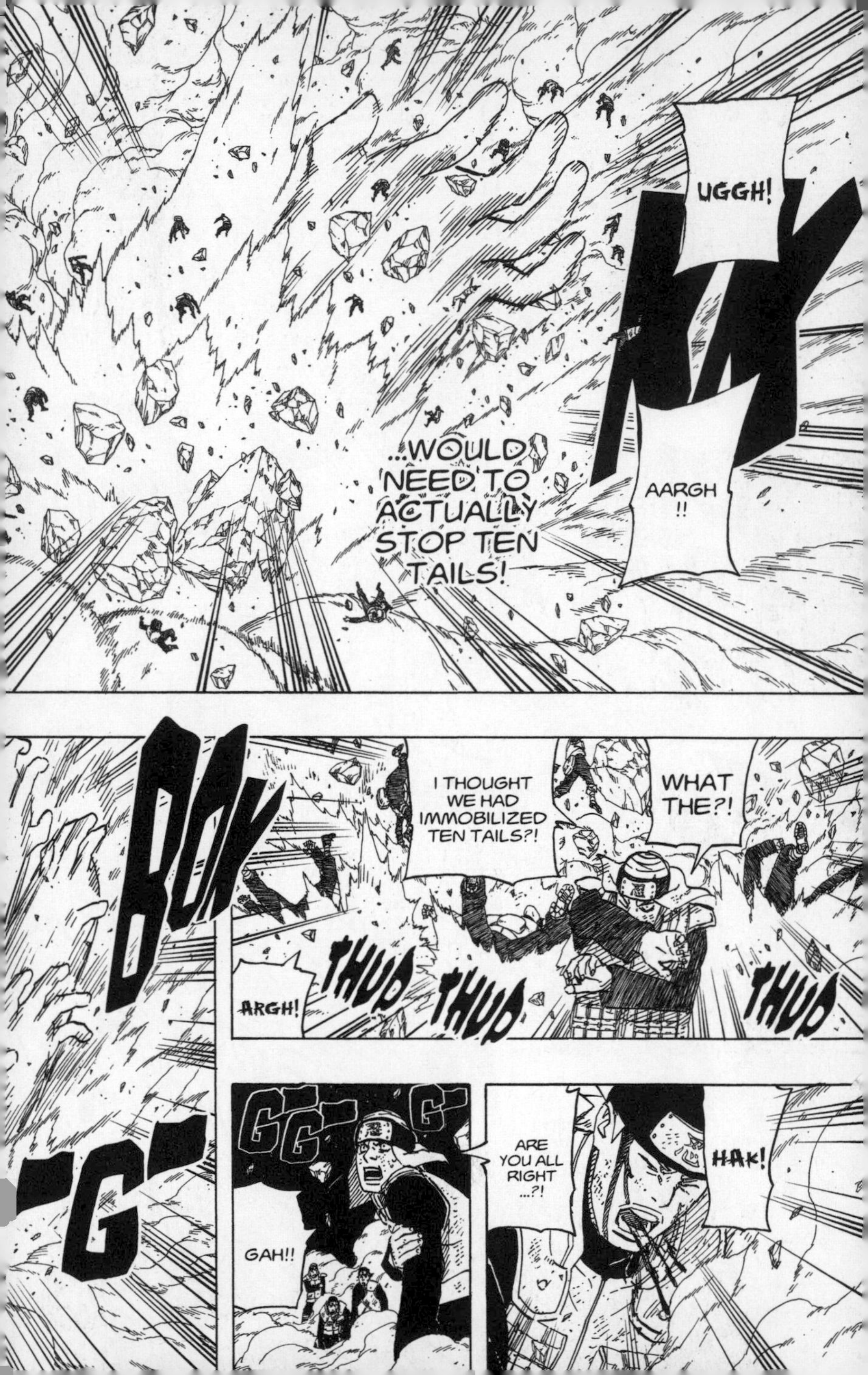
UGGH!
AARGH !!
...WOULD NEED TO ACTUALLY STOP TEN TAILS!
WHAT THE?!
I THOUGHT WE HAD IMMOBILIZED TEN TAILS?!
THUD
THUD
THUD
ARGH!
HAK!
ARE YOU ALL RIGHT ...?!
GAH!!

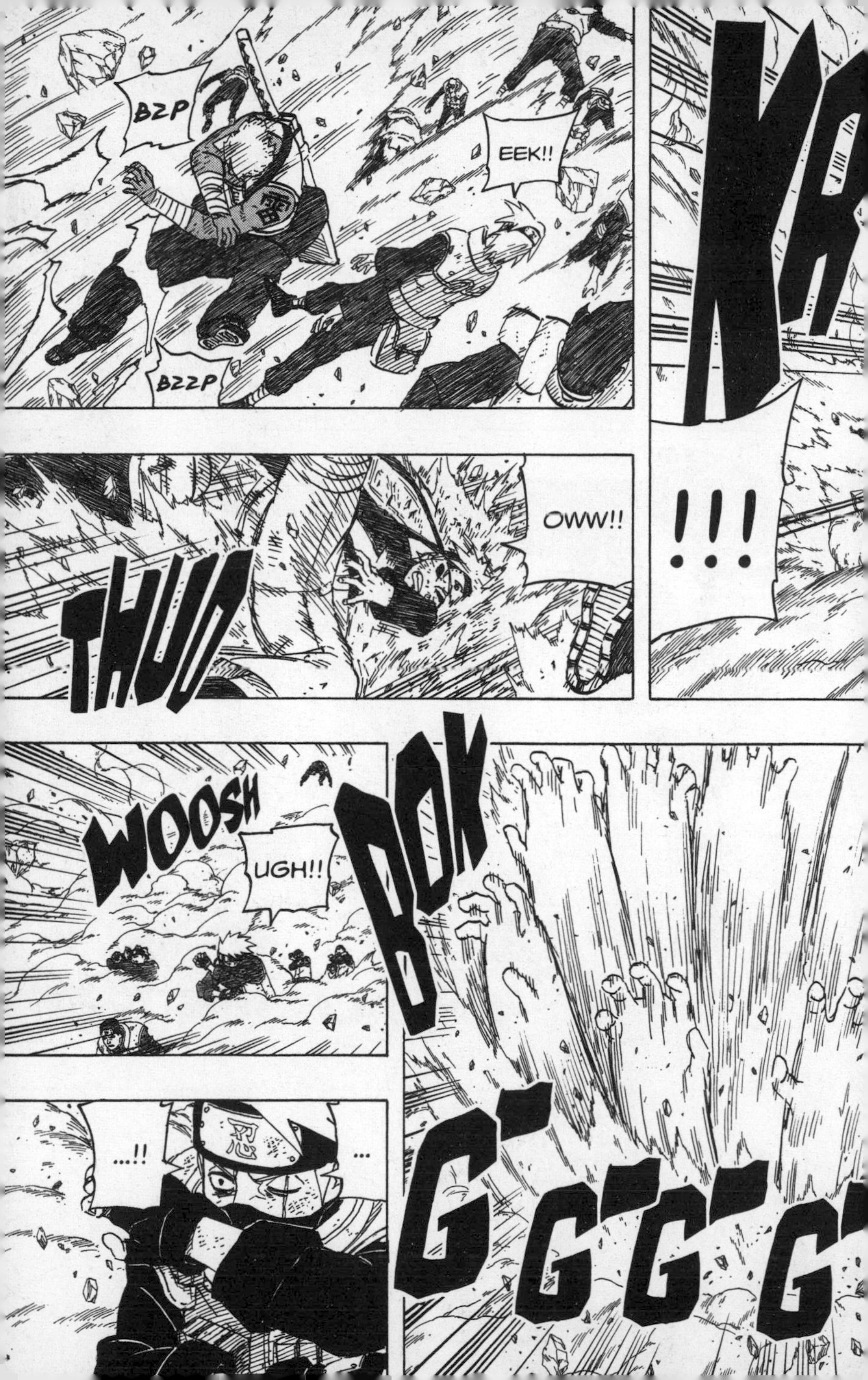
!!!
EEK!!
BZP
BZZP
OWW!!
THUD
BOK
G'G'G'
UGH!!
WOOSH
...
...!!

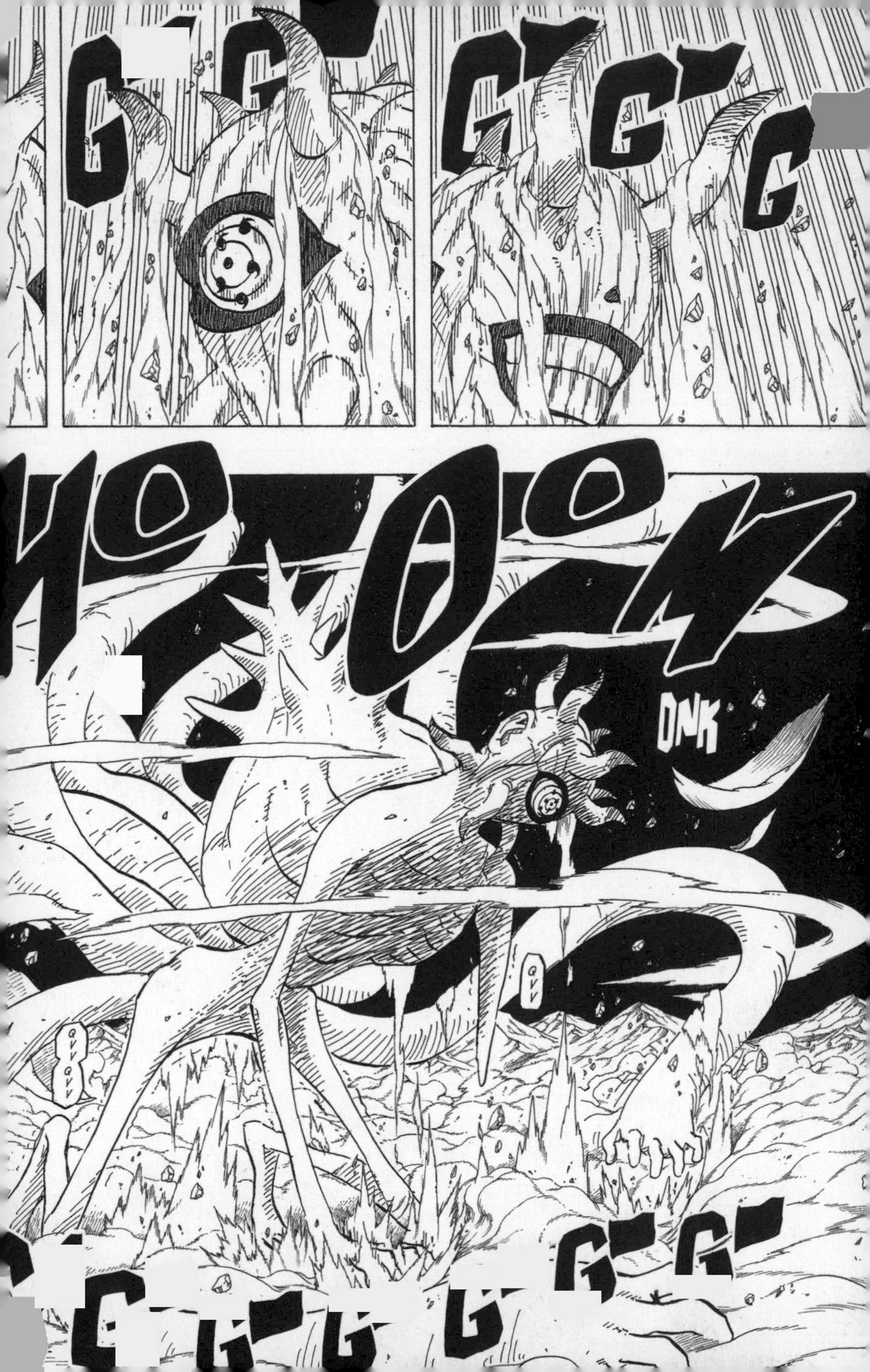
DNK

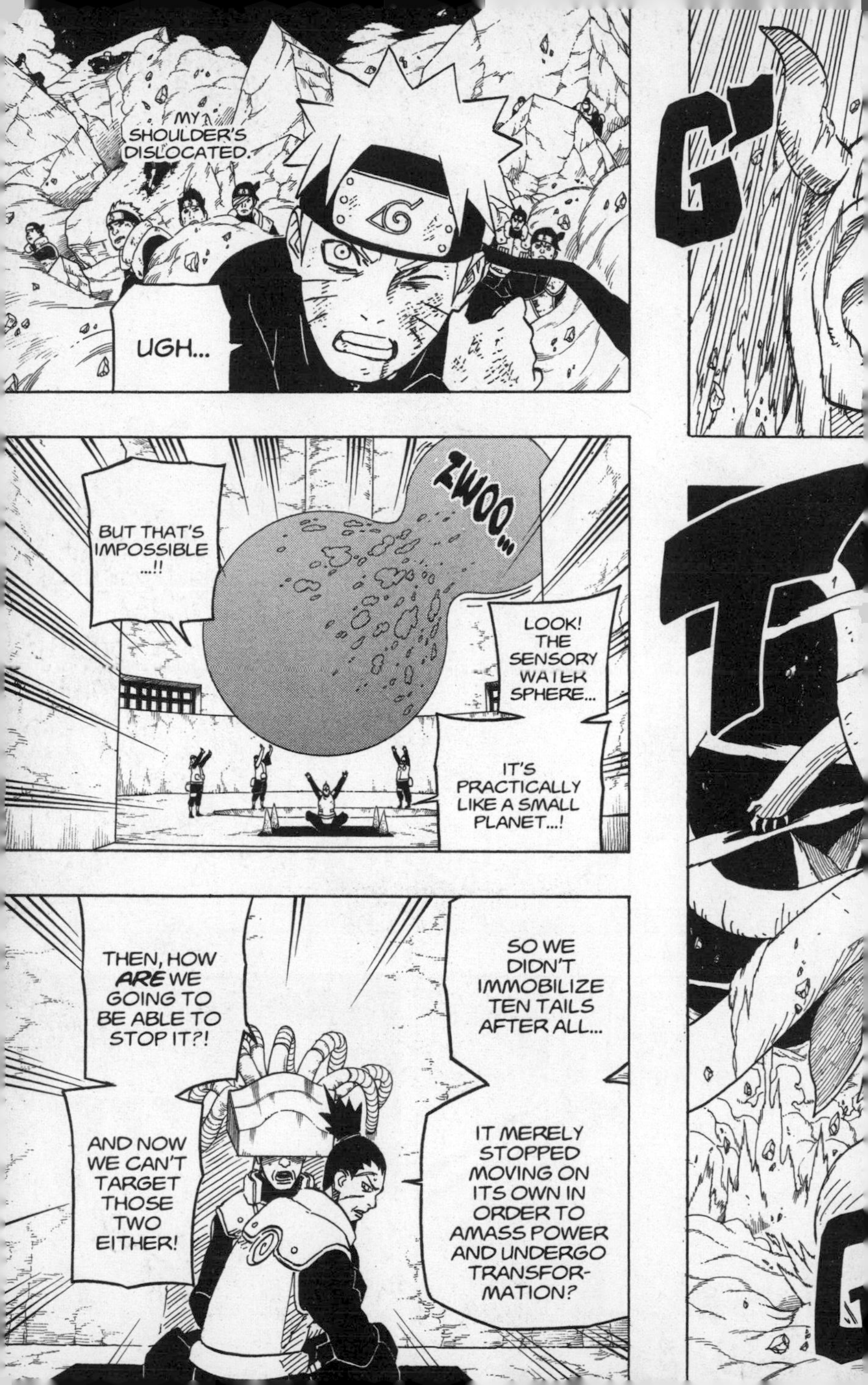
G
T
G
MY SHOULDER'S DISLOCATED.
UGH...
ZWOO...
LOOK! THE SENSORY WATER SPHERE...
IT'S PRACTICALLY LIKE A SMALL PLANET...!
BUT THAT'S IMPOSSIBLE ...!!
SO WE DIDN'T IMMOBILIZE TEN TAILS AFTER ALL...
IT MERELY STOPPED MOVING ON ITS OWN IN ORDER TO AMASS POWER AND UNDERGO TRANSFORMATION?
THEN, HOW *ARE* WE GOING TO BE ABLE TO STOP IT?!
AND NOW WE CAN'T TARGET THOSE TWO EITHER!

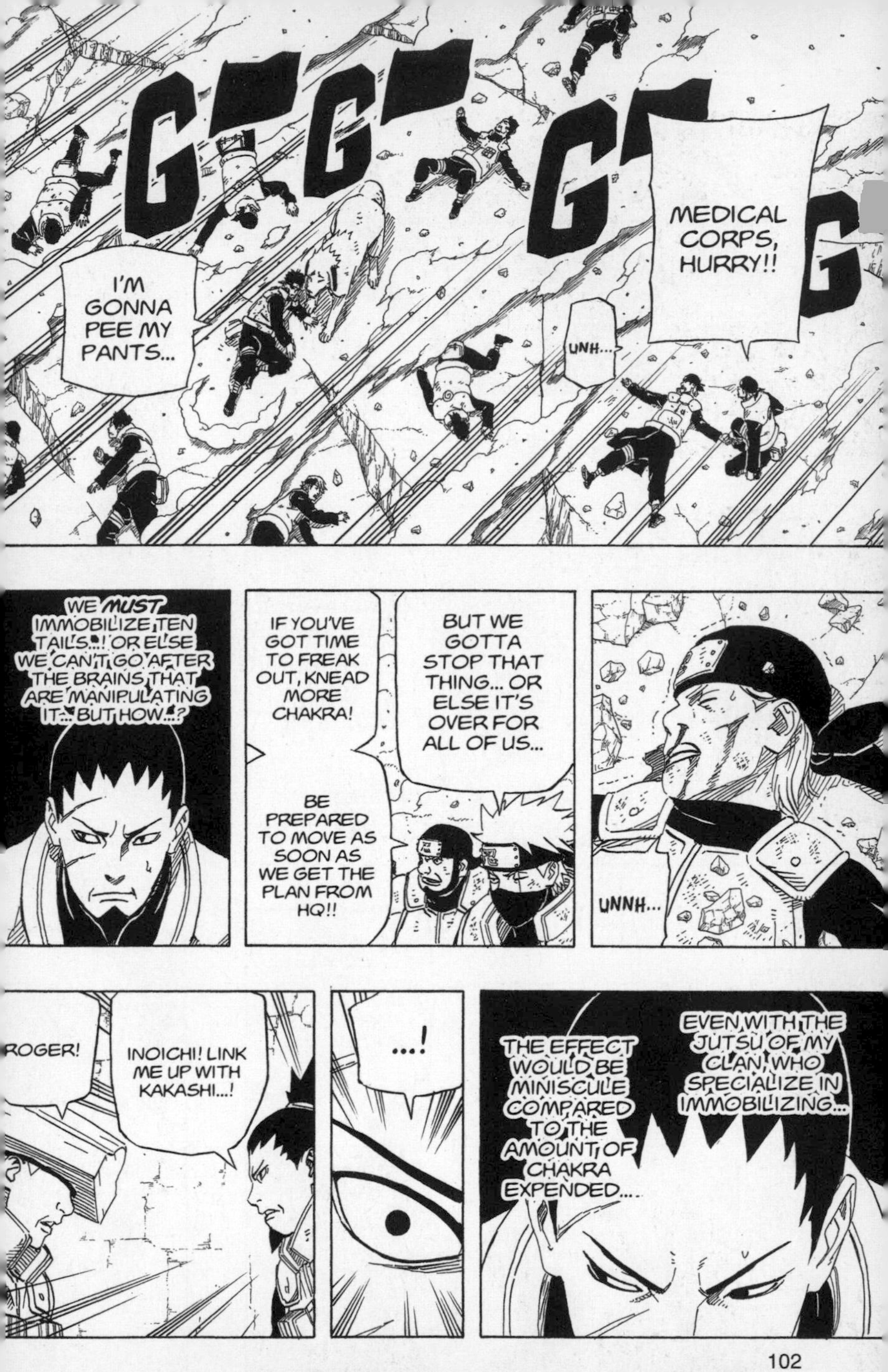
MEDICAL CORPS, HURRY!!
GGGG
UNH...
I'M GONNA PEE MY PANTS...
UNNH...
BUT WE GOTTA STOP THAT THING... OR ELSE IT'S OVER FOR ALL OF US...
IF YOU'VE GOT TIME TO FREAK OUT, KNEAD MORE CHAKRA!
BE PREPARED TO MOVE AS SOON AS WE GET THE PLAN FROM HQ!!
WE MUST IMMOBILIZE TEN TAILS...! OR ELSE WE CAN'T GO AFTER THE BRAINS THAT ARE MANIPULATING IT... BUT HOW...?
EVEN WITH THE JUTSU OF MY CLAN, WHO SPECIALIZE IN IMMOBILIZING...
THE EFFECT WOULD BE MINISCULE COMPARED TO THE AMOUNT OF CHAKRA EXPENDED...
...!
INOICHI! LINK ME UP WITH KAKASHI...!
ROGER!

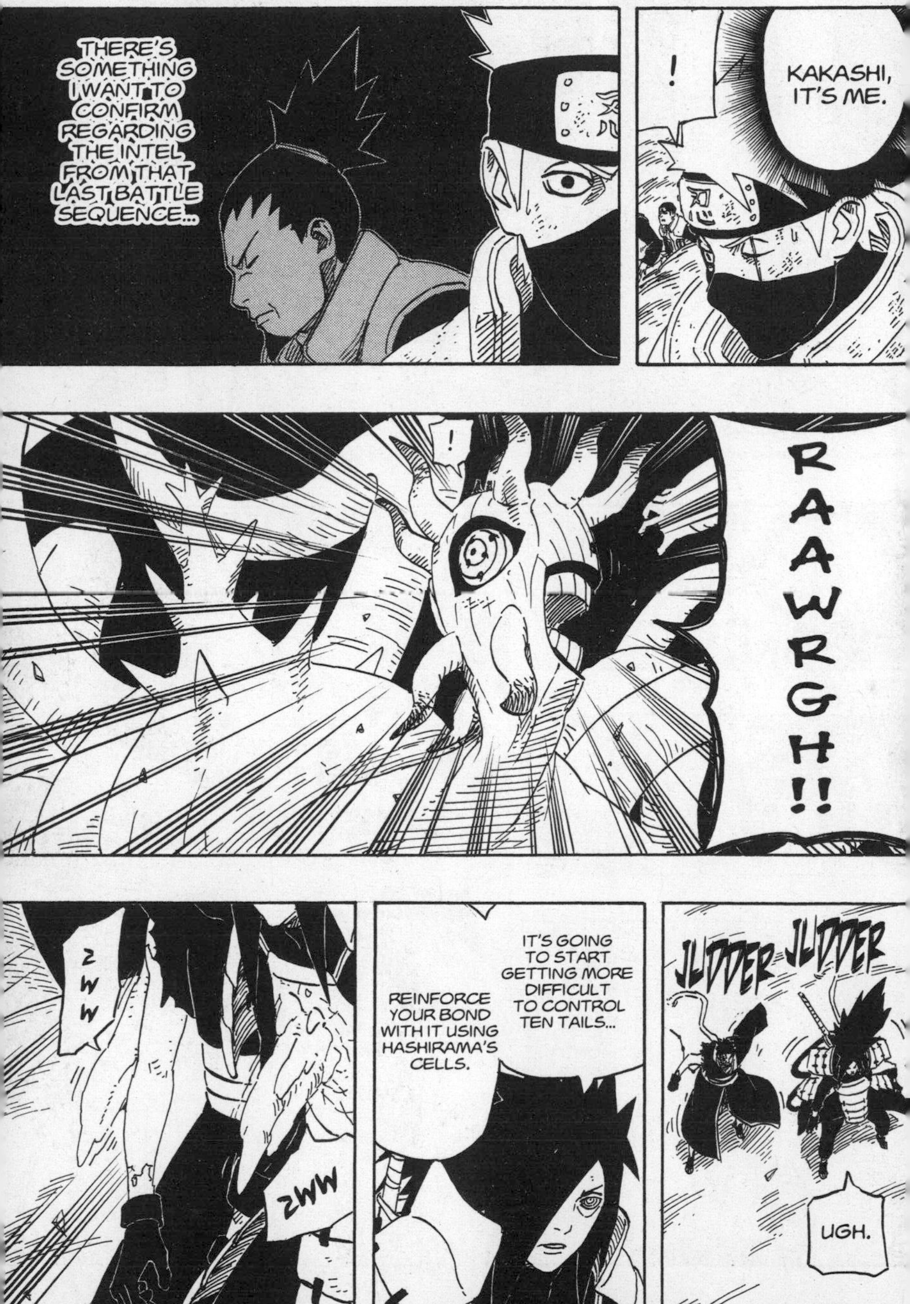
!
KAKASHI, IT'S ME.
THERE'S SOMETHING I WANT TO CONFIRM REGARDING THE INTEL FROM THAT LAST BATTLE SEQUENCE...
RAAWRGH!!
!
JUDDER JUDDER
UGH.
IT'S GOING TO START GETTING MORE DIFFICULT TO CONTROL TEN TAILS...
REINFORCE YOUR BOND WITH IT USING HASHIRAMA'S CELLS.

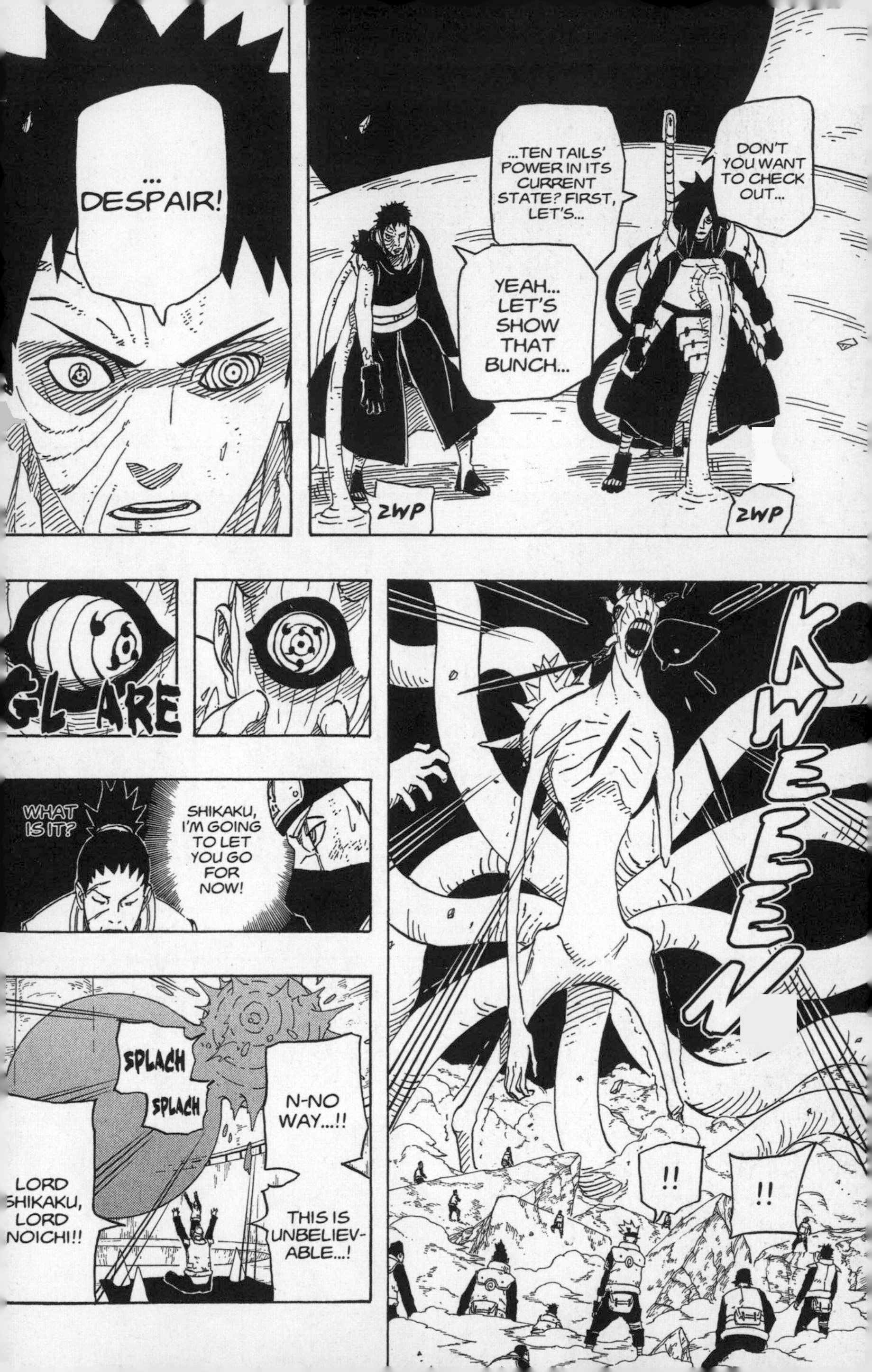
DON'T YOU WANT TO CHECK OUT...
...TEN TAILS' POWER IN ITS CURRENT STATE? FIRST, LET'S...
YEAH... LET'S SHOW THAT BUNCH...
ZWP
ZWP
... DESPAIR!
KWEEEEN
!!
!!
GLARE
SHIKAKU, I'M GOING TO LET YOU GO FOR NOW!
WHAT IS IT?
SPLACH
SPLACH
N-NO WAY...!!
THIS IS UNBELIEV-ABLE...!
LORD SHIKAKU, LORD NOICHI!!

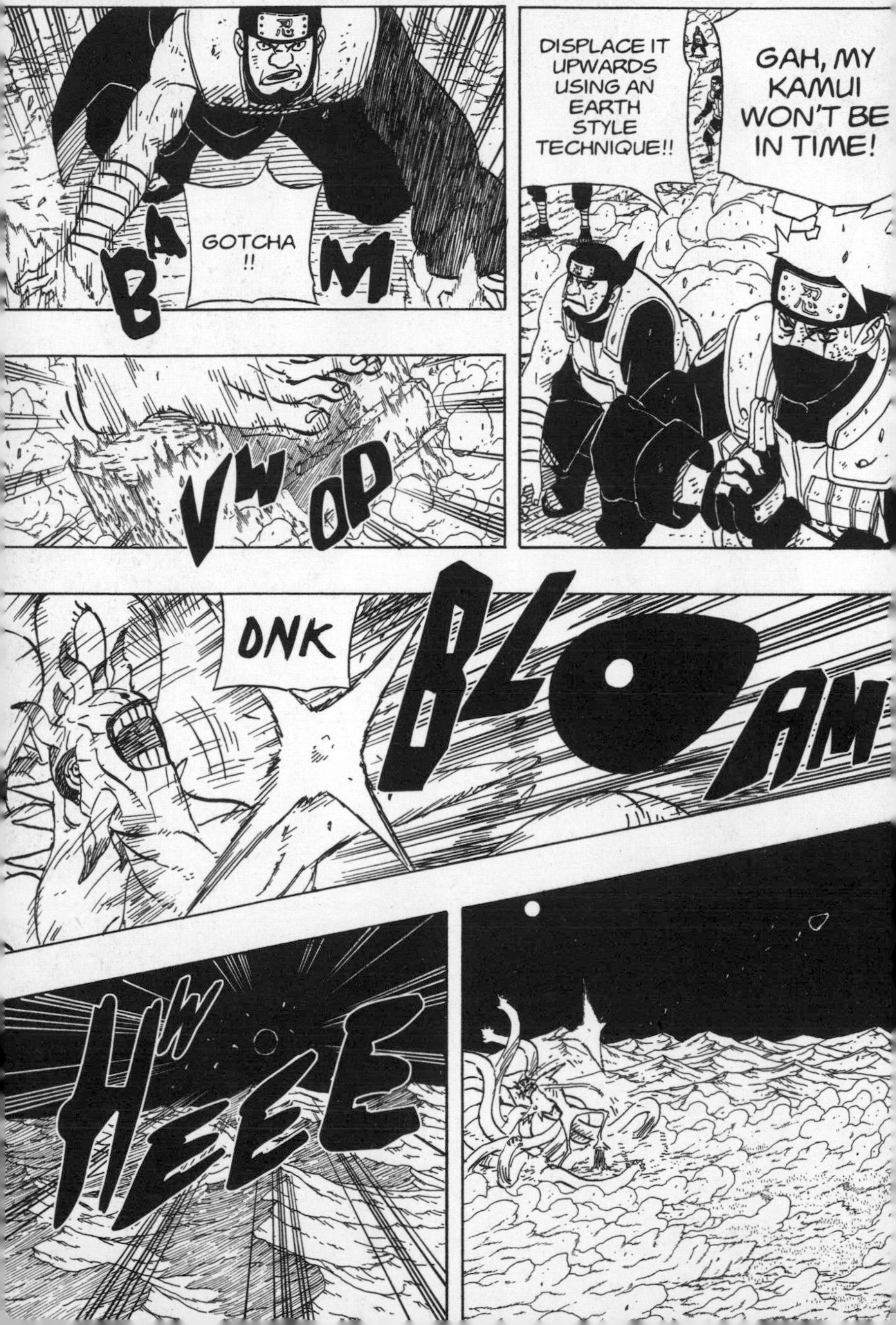
GAH, MY KAMUI WON'T BE IN TIME!
DISPLACE IT UPWARDS USING AN EARTH STYLE TECHNIQUE!!
BAM
GOTCHA !!
VWOOP
BLOAM
ONK
HWEEE

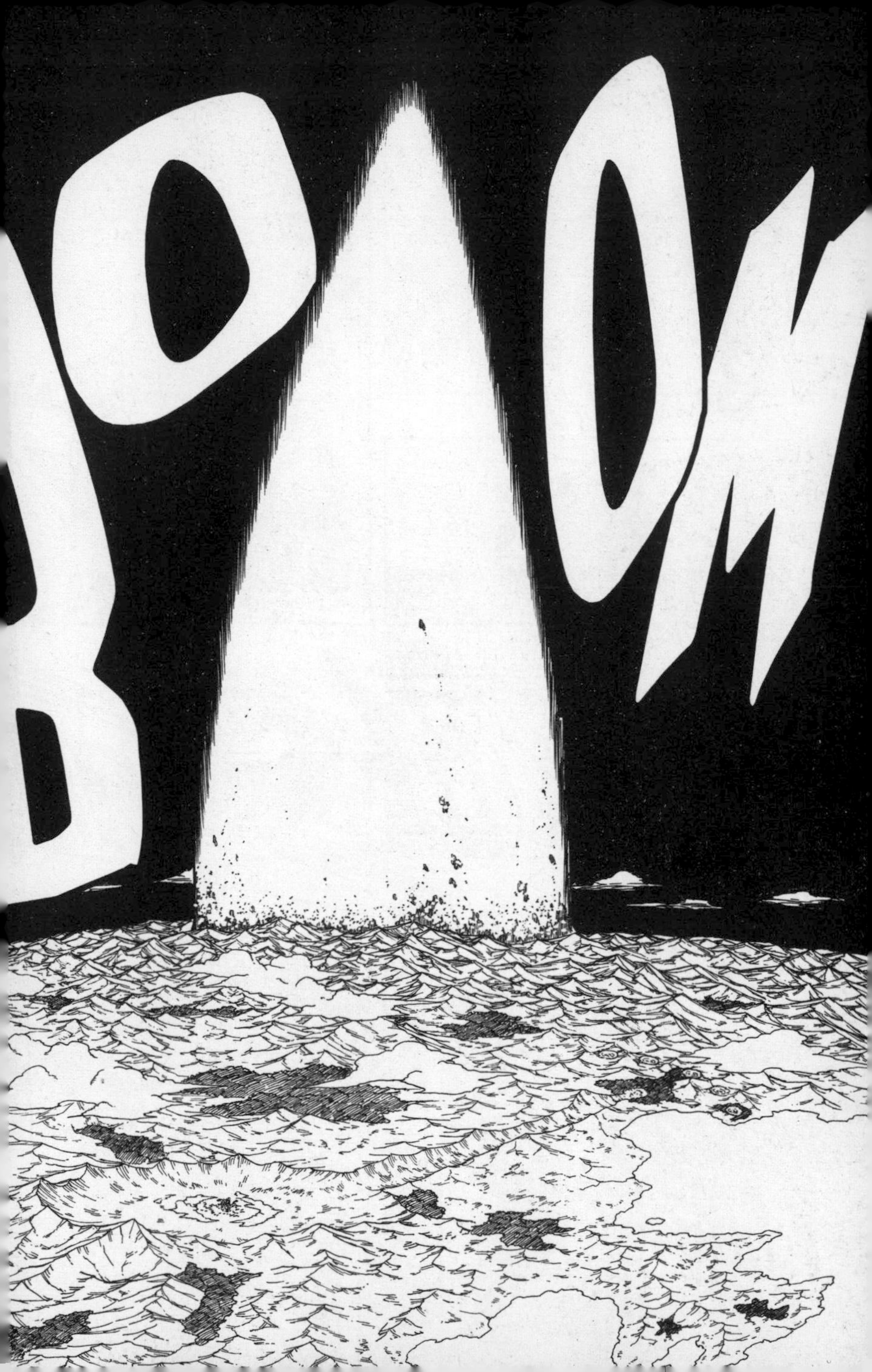
BOOM

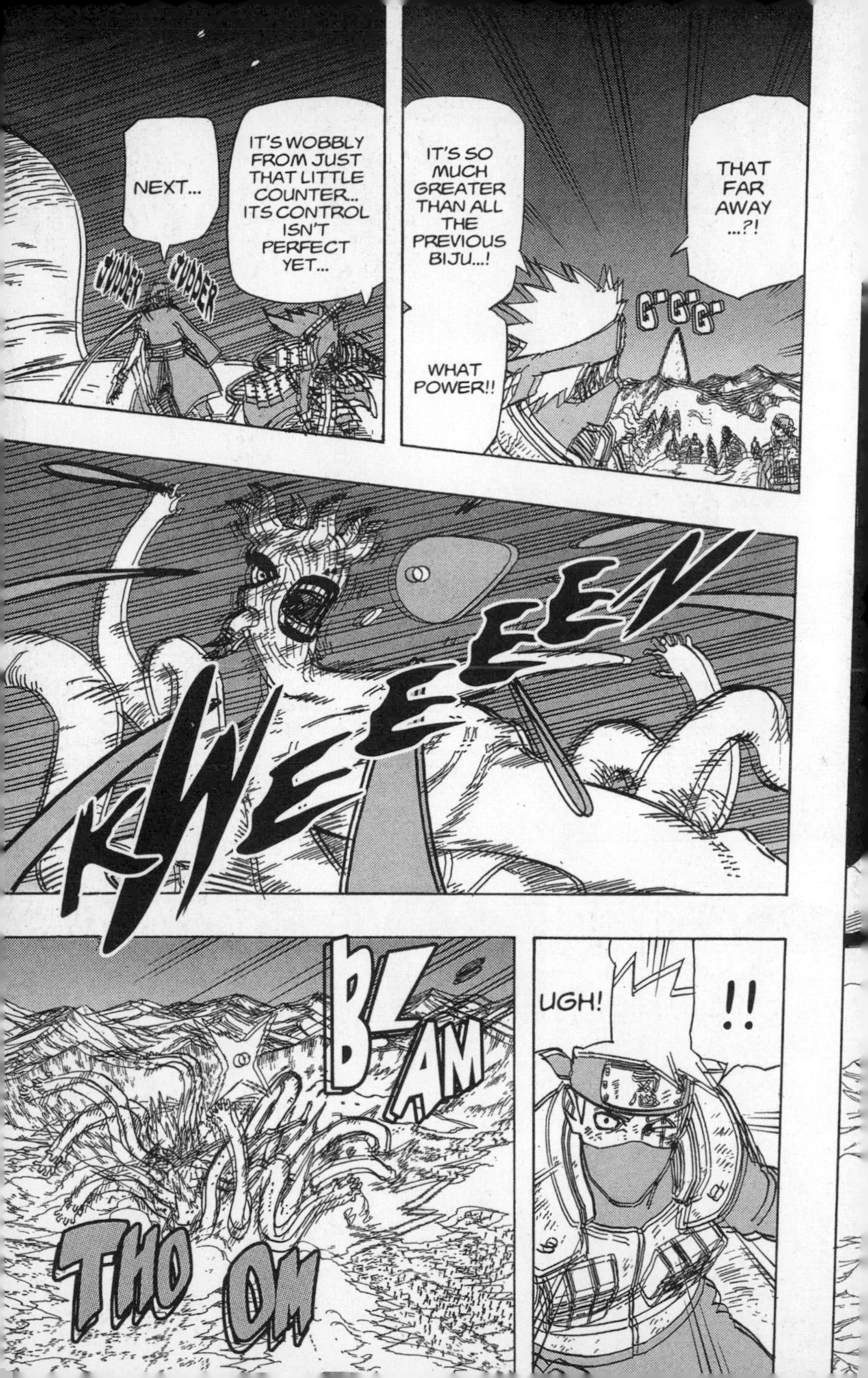
THAT FAR AWAY ...?!
IT'S SO MUCH GREATER THAN ALL THE PREVIOUS BIJU...!
G'G'G'
WHAT POWER!!
IT'S WOBBLY FROM JUST THAT LITTLE COUNTER... ITS CONTROL ISN'T PERFECT YET...
NEXT...
SHUDDER
SHUDDER
KWEEEEN
!!
UGH!
BLAM
THOOM

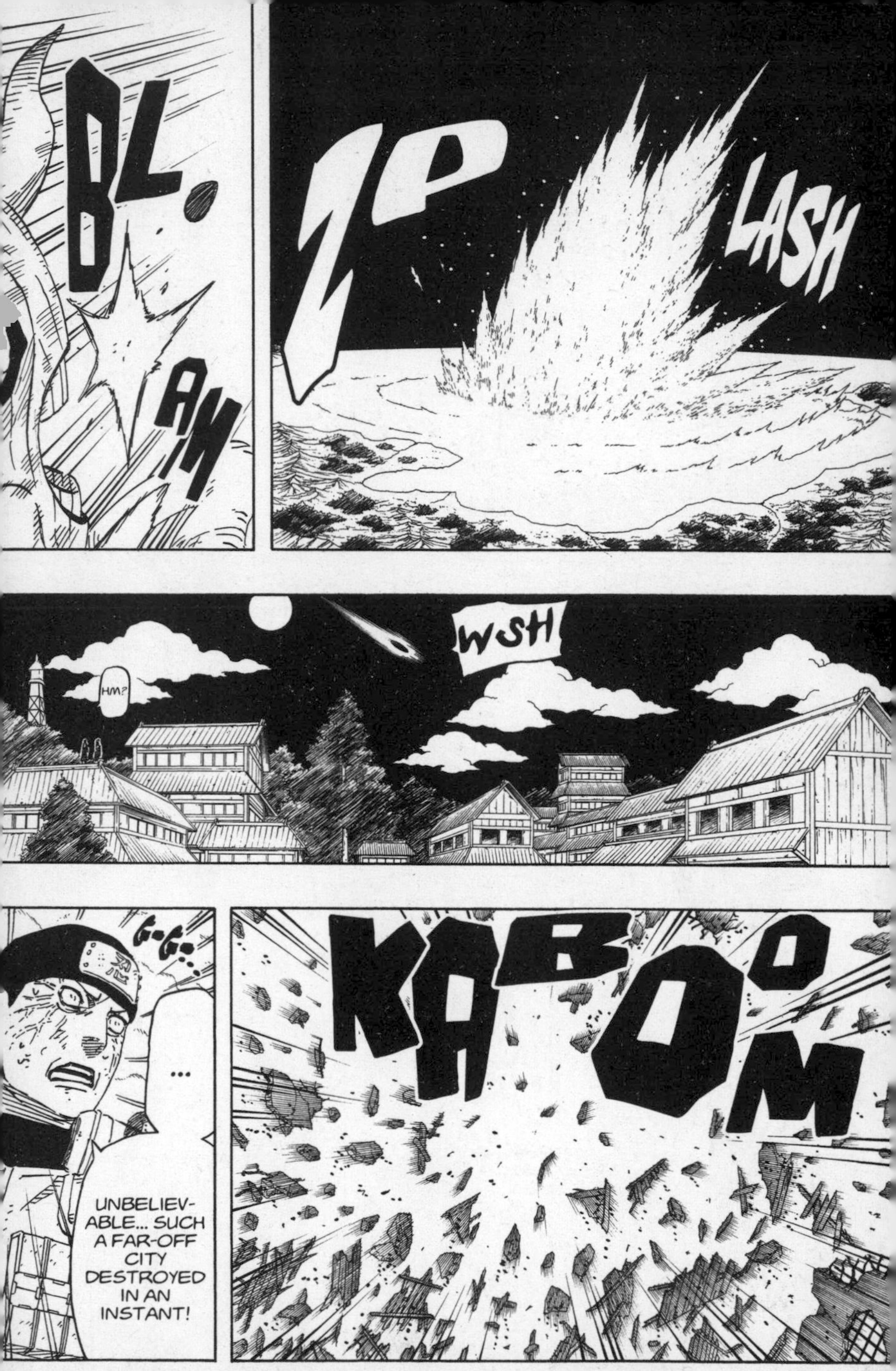
ZIP
LASH
BL.
AM
WSH
HM?
KABOOM
G-G-...
...
UNBELIEV-ABLE... SUCH A FAR-OFF CITY DESTROYED IN AN INSTANT!

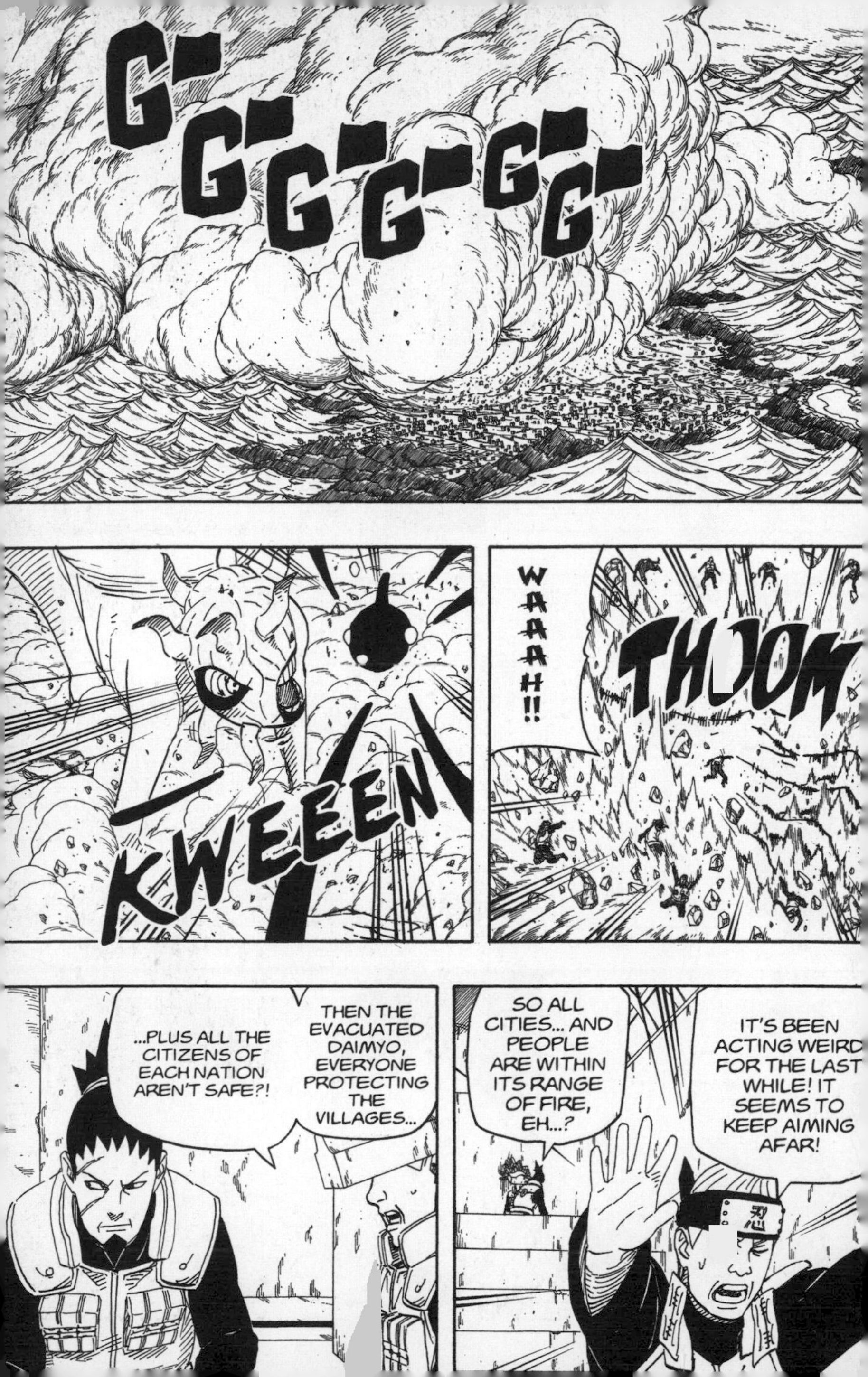
G-G-G-G-G-G-G
WAAAAH!!
THOOM
KWEEEN
IT'S BEEN ACTING WEIRD FOR THE LAST WHILE! IT SEEMS TO KEEP AIMING AFAR!
SO ALL CITIES... AND PEOPLE ARE WITHIN ITS RANGE OF FIRE, EH...?
THEN THE EVACUATED DAIMYO, EVERYONE PROTECTING THE VILLAGES...
...PLUS ALL THE CITIZENS OF EACH NATION AREN'T SAFE?!

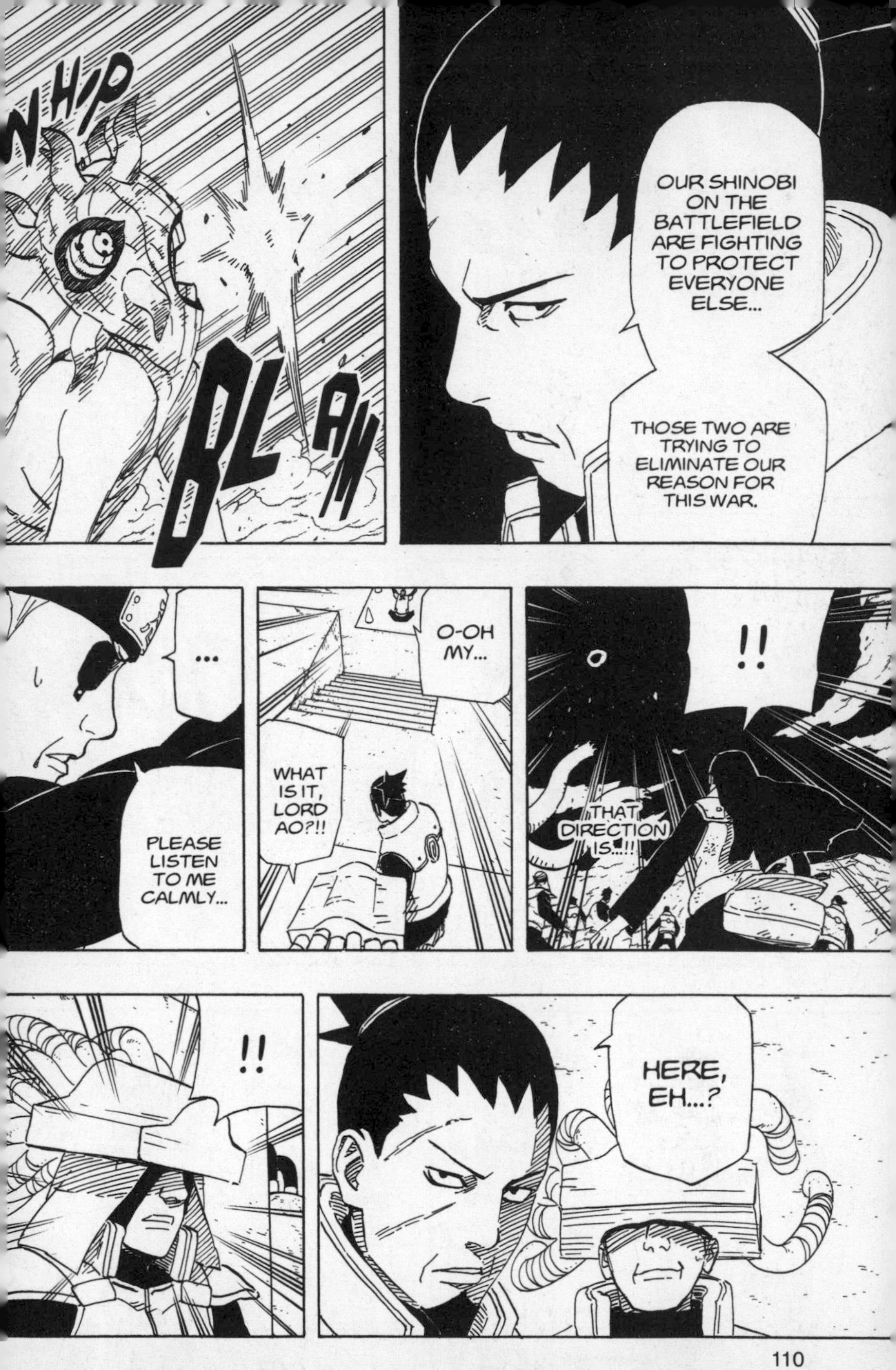
OUR SHINOBI ON THE BATTLEFIELD ARE FIGHTING TO PROTECT EVERYONE ELSE...
THOSE TWO ARE TRYING TO ELIMINATE OUR REASON FOR THIS WAR.
WHIP
BLAM
!!
THAT DIRECTION IS...!!
O-OH MY...
WHAT IS IT, LORD AO?!!
...
PLEASE LISTEN TO ME CALMLY...
HERE, EH...?
!!

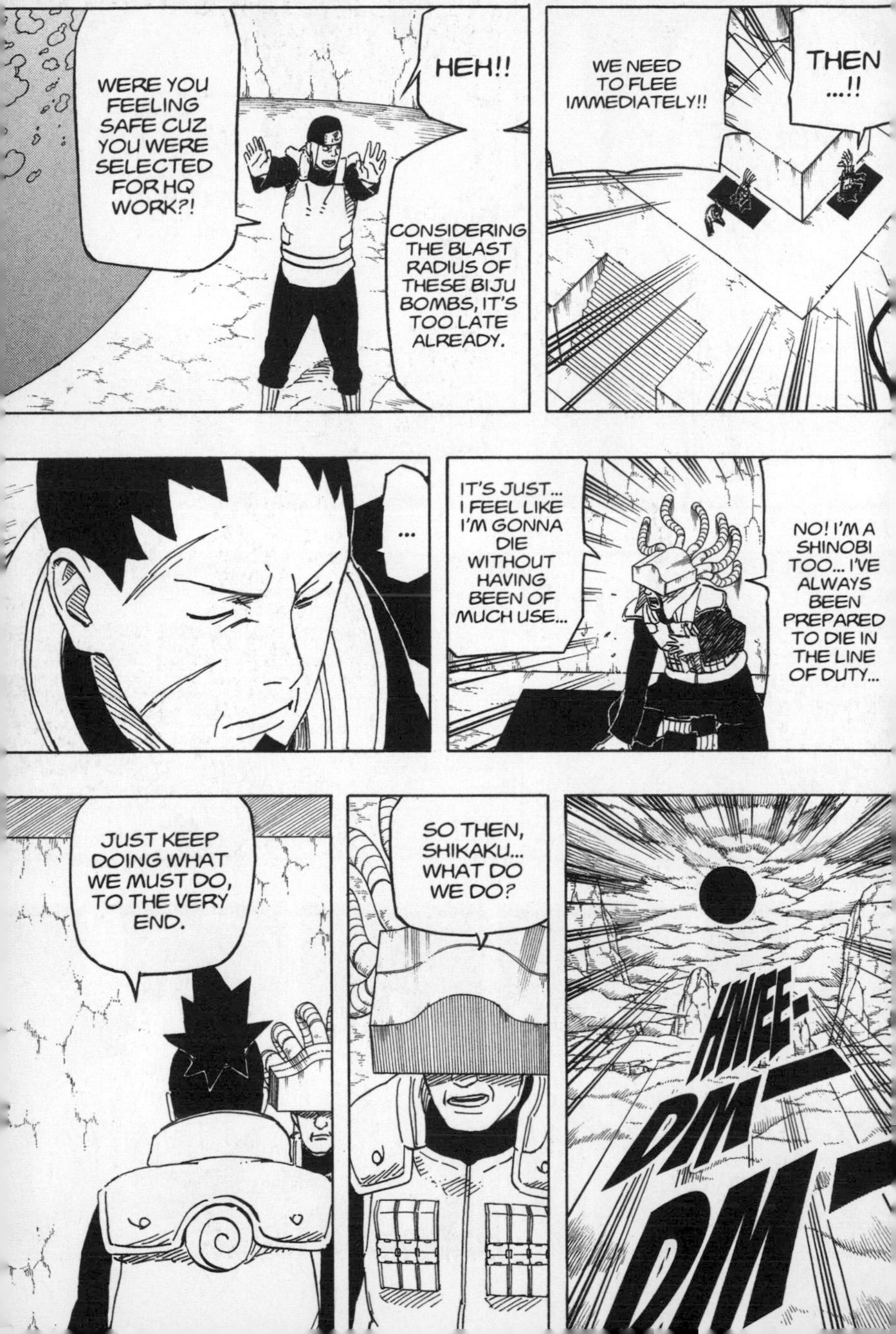
THEN ...!!
WE NEED TO FLEE IMMEDIATELY!!
HEH!!
CONSIDERING THE BLAST RADIUS OF THESE BIJU BOMBS, IT'S TOO LATE ALREADY.
WERE YOU FEELING SAFE CUZ YOU WERE SELECTED FOR HQ WORK?!
NO! I'M A SHINOBI TOO... I'VE ALWAYS BEEN PREPARED TO DIE IN THE LINE OF DUTY...
IT'S JUST... I FEEL LIKE I'M GONNA DIE WITHOUT HAVING BEEN OF MUCH USE...
...
HWEE-
DM-
DM-
SO THEN, SHIKAKU... WHAT DO WE DO?
JUST KEEP DOING WHAT WE MUST DO, TO THE VERY END.

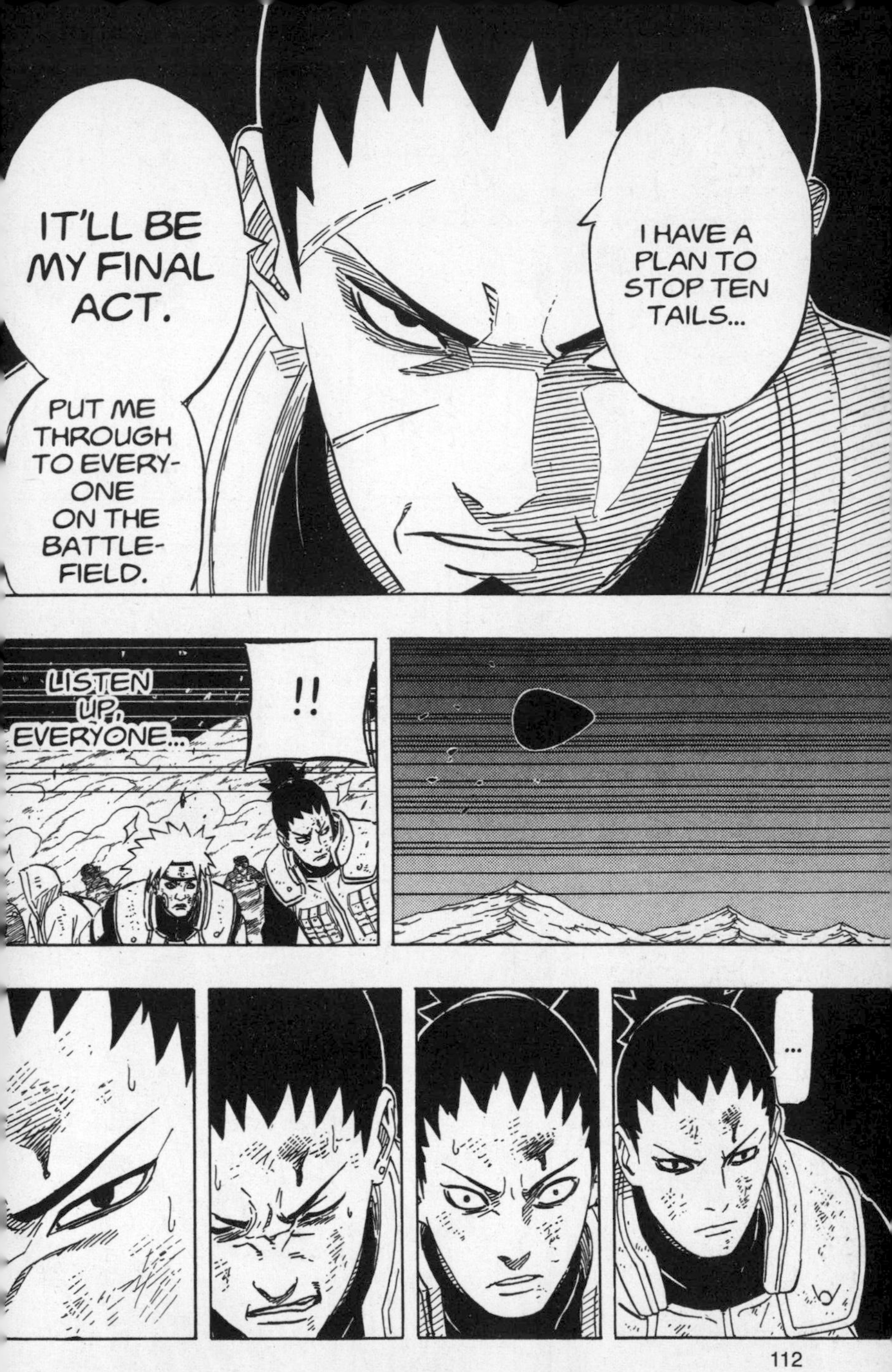
I HAVE A PLAN TO STOP TEN TAILS...
IT'LL BE MY FINAL ACT.
PUT ME THROUGH TO EVERY-ONE ON THE BATTLE-FIELD.
!!
LISTEN UP, EVERYONE...
...

FINALLY GOT THEM.

FLASH...

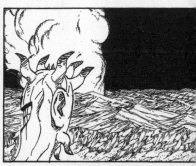

KRIK

NOW WE'VE SMASHED THE ALLIED FORCES' BRAINS.

TAP

LIKE I SAID... STRATEGY 101...

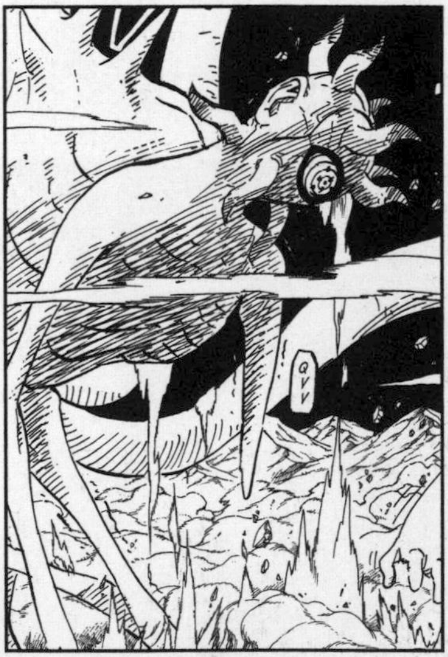
QVV

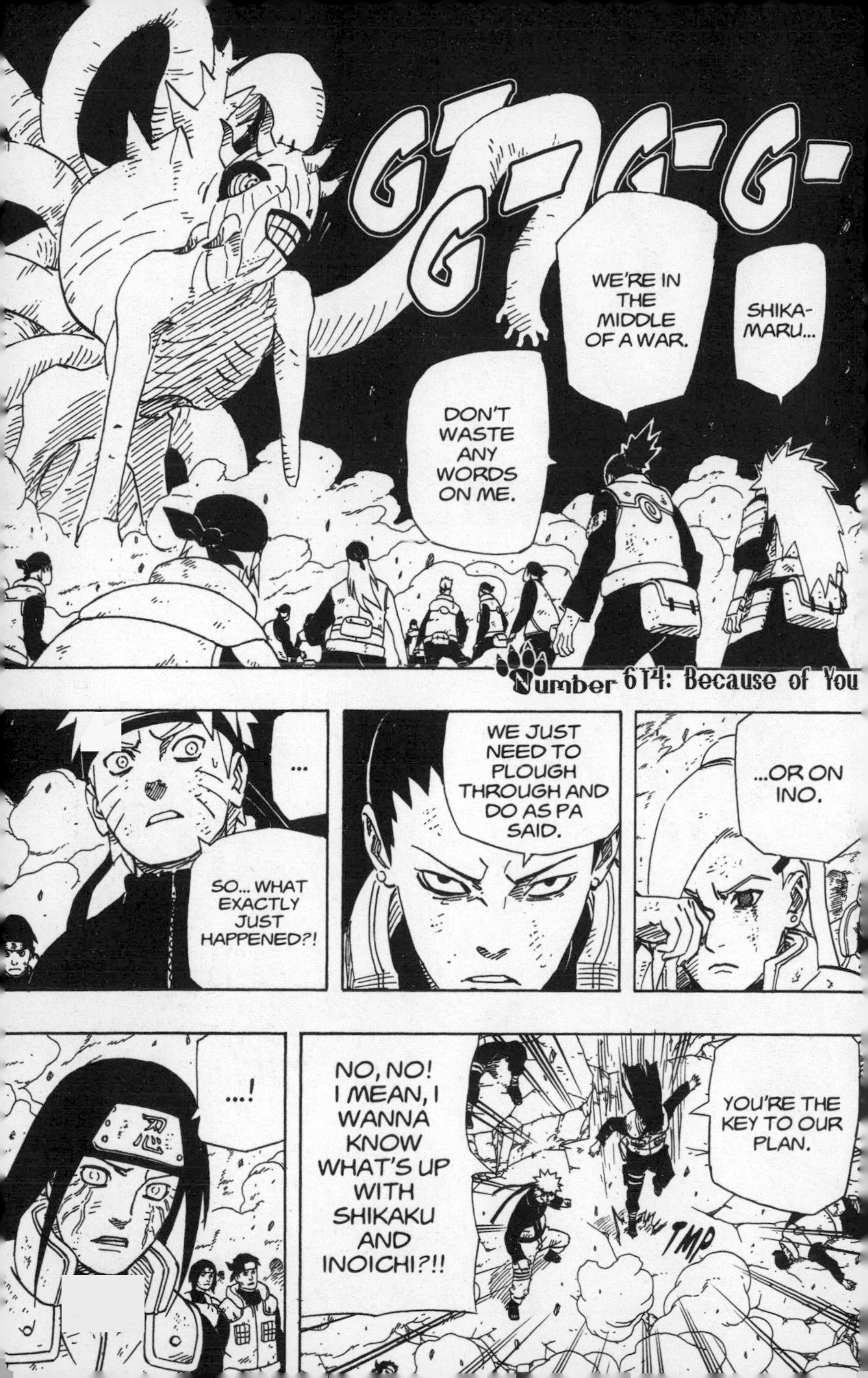

G-G-G-G-G-
SHIKA-MARU...
WE'RE IN THE MIDDLE OF A WAR.
DON'T WASTE ANY WORDS ON ME.
Number 614: Because of You
...OR ON INO.
WE JUST NEED TO PLOUGH THROUGH AND DO AS PA SAID.
...
SO... WHAT EXACTLY JUST HAPPENED?!
YOU'RE THE KEY TO OUR PLAN.
TMP
NO, NO! I MEAN, I WANNA KNOW WHAT'S UP WITH SHIKAKU AND INOICHI?!!
...!

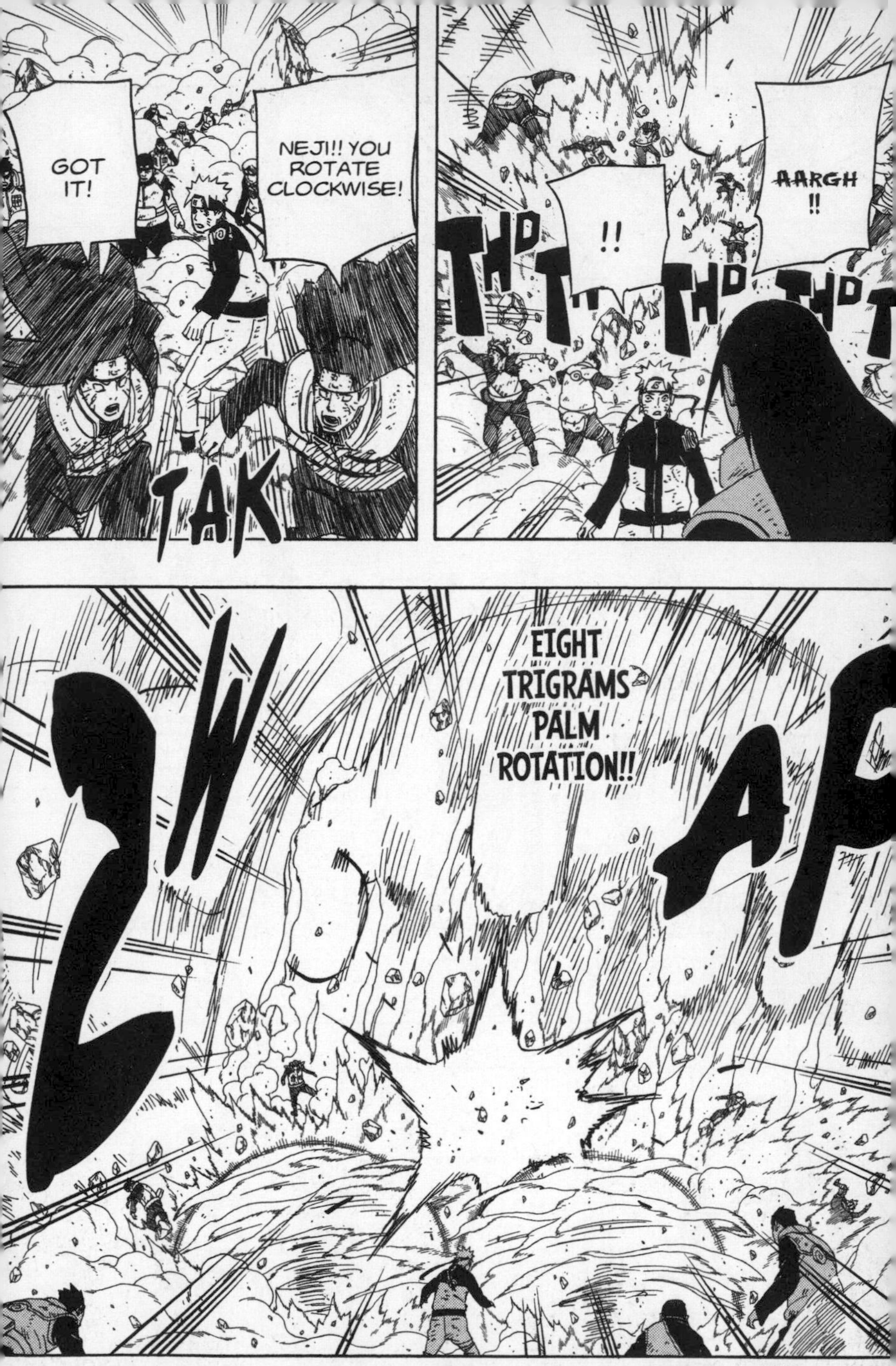

AARGH !!
THD
!!
THD
THD
NEJI!! YOU ROTATE CLOCKWISE!
GOT IT!
TAK
EIGHT TRIGRAMS PALM ROTATION!!

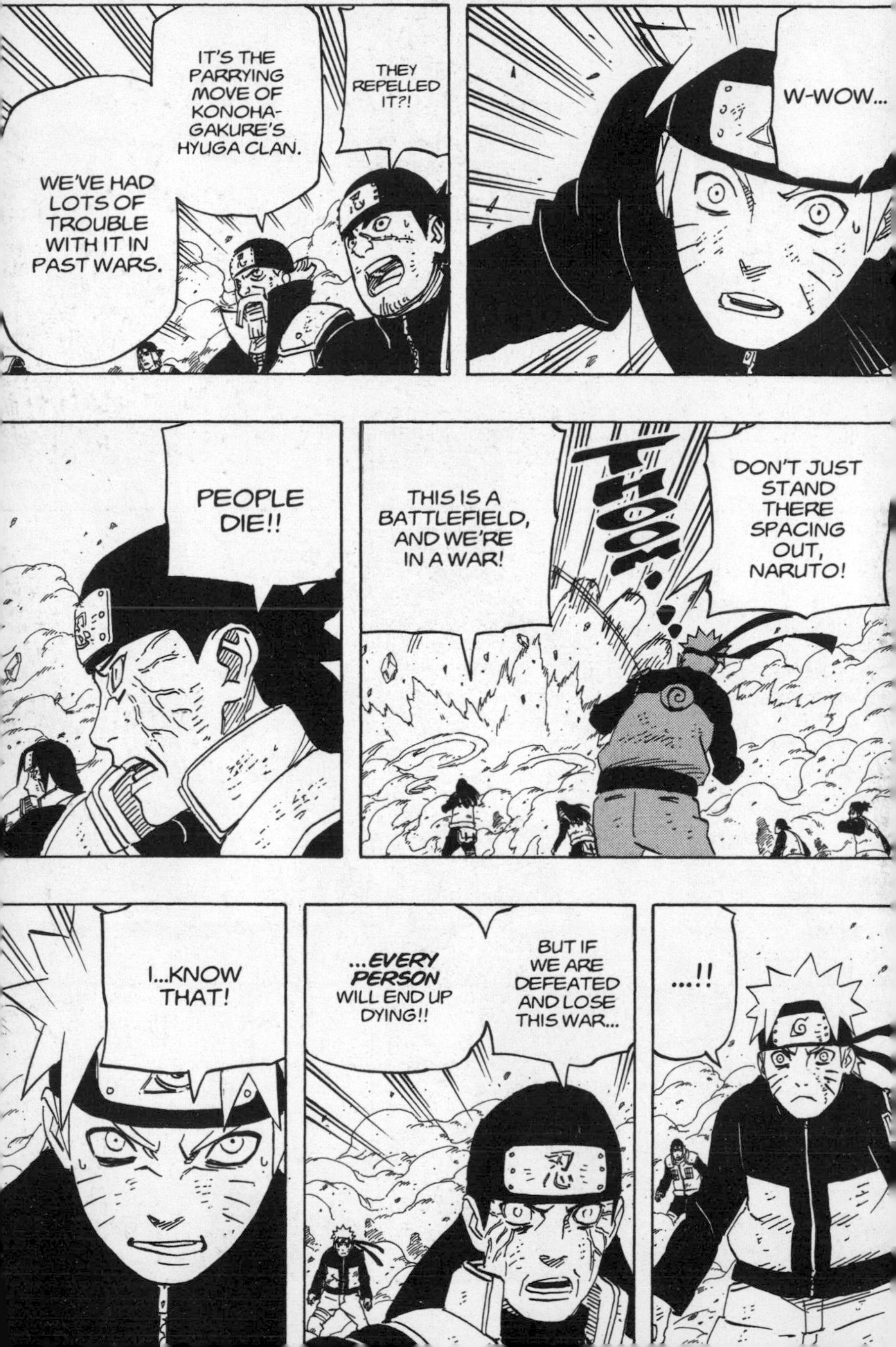
W-WOW...
THEY REPELLED IT?!
IT'S THE PARRYING MOVE OF KONOHA-GAKURE'S HYUGA CLAN.
WE'VE HAD LOTS OF TROUBLE WITH IT IN PAST WARS.
DON'T JUST STAND THERE SPACING OUT, NARUTO!
THOOM...
THIS IS A BATTLEFIELD, AND WE'RE IN A WAR!
PEOPLE DIE!!
...!!
BUT IF WE ARE DEFEATED AND LOSE THIS WAR...
...*EVERY PERSON* WILL END UP DYING!!
I...KNOW THAT!

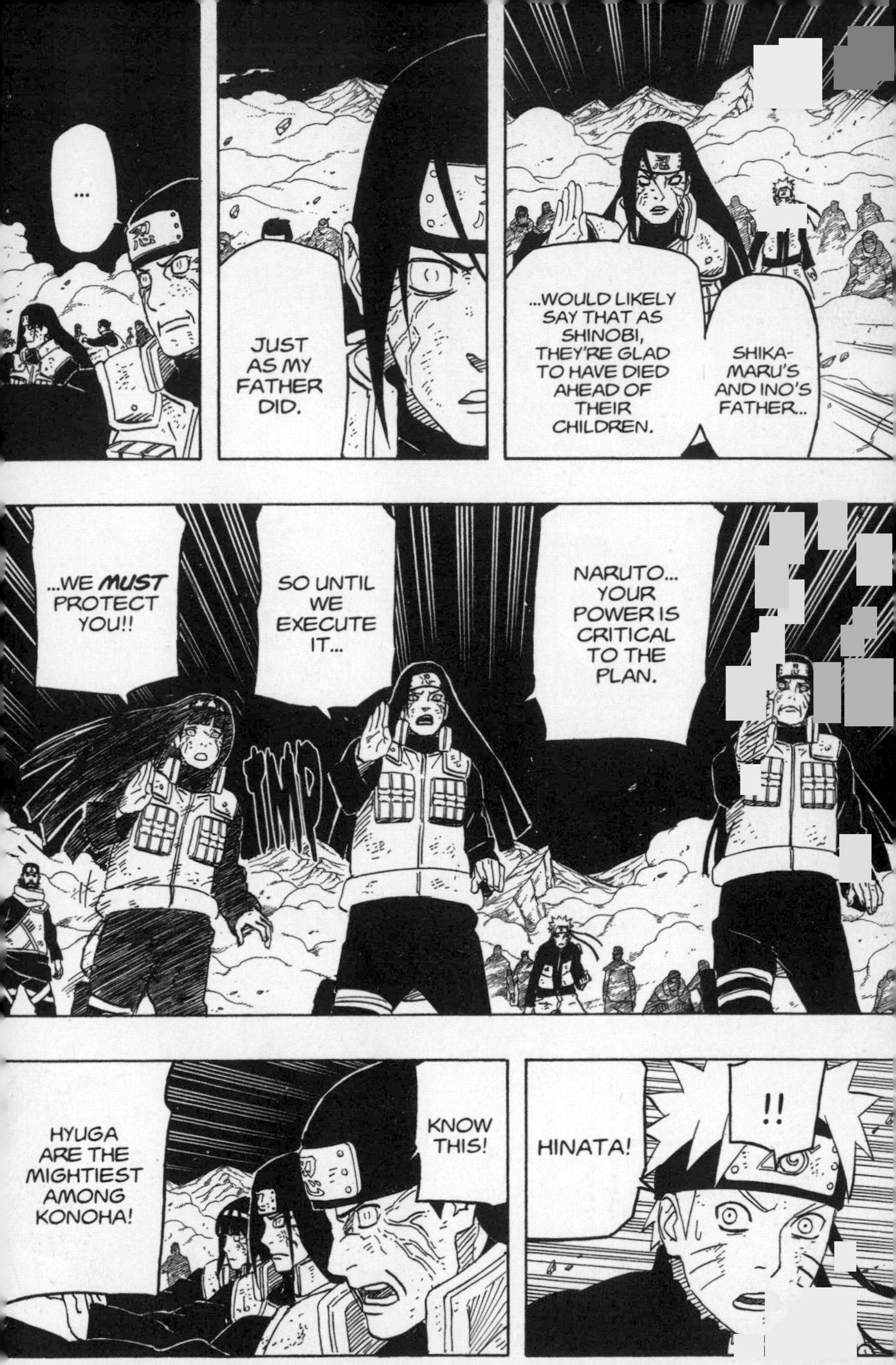
SHIKAMARU'S AND INO'S FATHER...
...WOULD LIKELY SAY THAT AS SHINOBI, THEY'RE GLAD TO HAVE DIED AHEAD OF THEIR CHILDREN.
JUST AS MY FATHER DID.
...
NARUTO... YOUR POWER IS CRITICAL TO THE PLAN.
SO UNTIL WE EXECUTE IT...
...WE MUST PROTECT YOU!!
TMP
!!
HINATA!
KNOW THIS!
HYUGA ARE THE MIGHTIEST AMONG KONOHA!

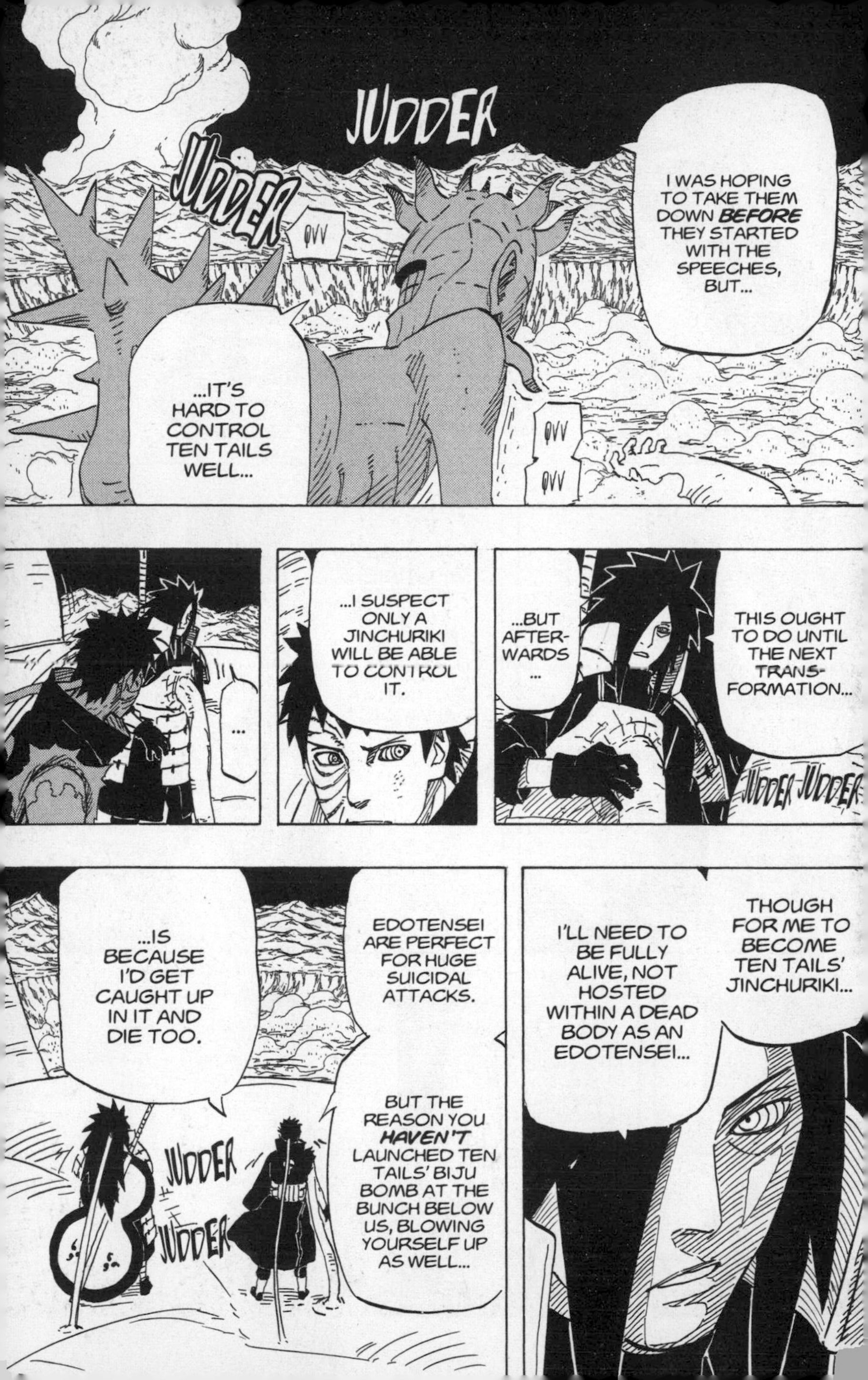

JUDDER
JUDDER
QVV
I WAS HOPING TO TAKE THEM DOWN **BEFORE** THEY STARTED WITH THE SPEECHES, BUT...
...IT'S HARD TO CONTROL TEN TAILS WELL...
QVV
QVV
THIS OUGHT TO DO UNTIL THE NEXT TRANS-FORMATION...
...BUT AFTER-WARDS...
JUDDER-JUDDER
...I SUSPECT ONLY A JINCHURIKI WILL BE ABLE TO CONTROL IT.
...
THOUGH FOR ME TO BECOME TEN TAILS' JINCHURIKI...
I'LL NEED TO BE FULLY ALIVE, NOT HOSTED WITHIN A DEAD BODY AS AN EDOTENSEI...
EDOTENSEI ARE PERFECT FOR HUGE SUICIDAL ATTACKS.
BUT THE REASON YOU ***HAVEN'T*** LAUNCHED TEN TAILS' BIJU BOMB AT THE BUNCH BELOW US, BLOWING YOURSELF UP AS WELL...
...IS BECAUSE I'D GET CAUGHT UP IN IT AND DIE TOO.
JUDDER
JUDDER

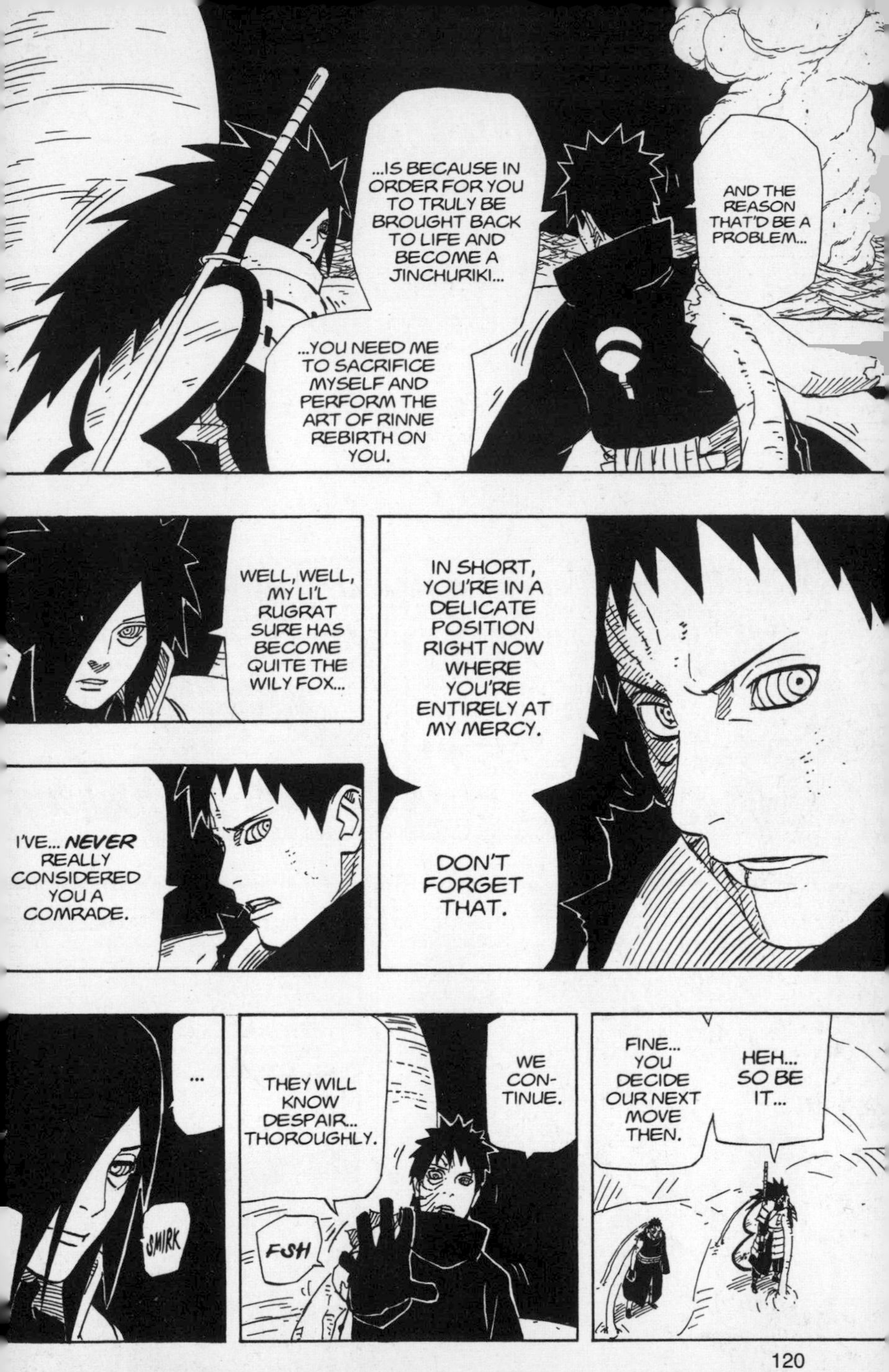
AND THE REASON THAT'D BE A PROBLEM...
...IS BECAUSE IN ORDER FOR YOU TO TRULY BE BROUGHT BACK TO LIFE AND BECOME A JINCHURIKI...
...YOU NEED ME TO SACRIFICE MYSELF AND PERFORM THE ART OF RINNE REBIRTH ON YOU.
IN SHORT, YOU'RE IN A DELICATE POSITION RIGHT NOW WHERE YOU'RE ENTIRELY AT MY MERCY.
DON'T FORGET THAT.
WELL, WELL, MY LI'L RUGRAT SURE HAS BECOME QUITE THE WILY FOX...
I'VE... ***NEVER*** REALLY CONSIDERED YOU A COMRADE.
HEH... SO BE IT...
FINE... YOU DECIDE OUR NEXT MOVE THEN.
WE CON-TINUE.
THEY WILL KNOW DESPAIR... THOROUGHLY.
FSH
...
SMIRK

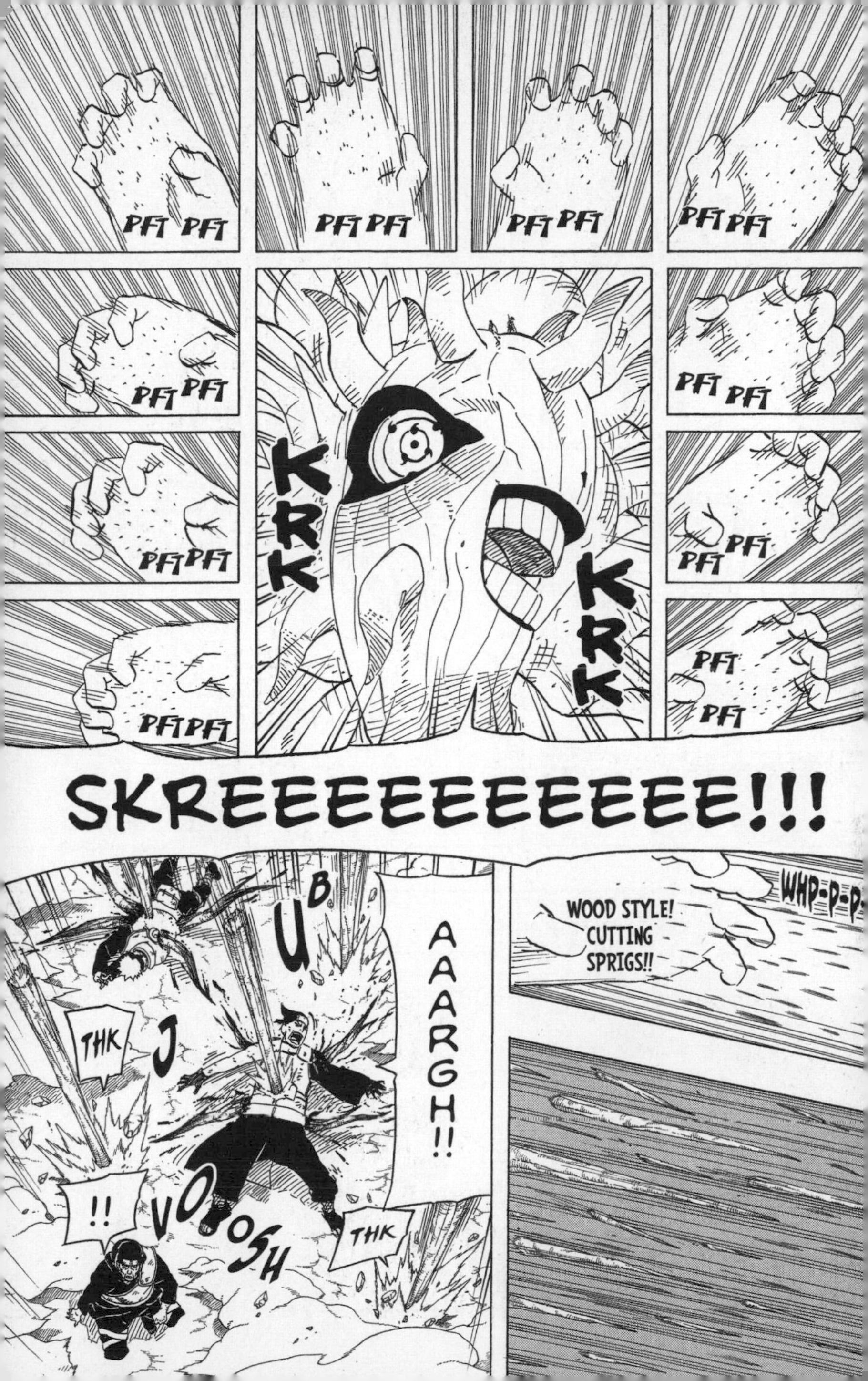
PFT PFT
PFT PFT
PFT PFT
PFT PFT
PFT PFT
PFT PFT
PFT PFT
KRK
KRK
PFT PFT
PFT PFT
PFT PFT
SKREEEEEEEEEEEE!!!
WHP-P-P
WOOD STYLE! CUTTING SPRIGS!!
AAARGH!!
B
U
THK
J
!!
VOOSH
THK

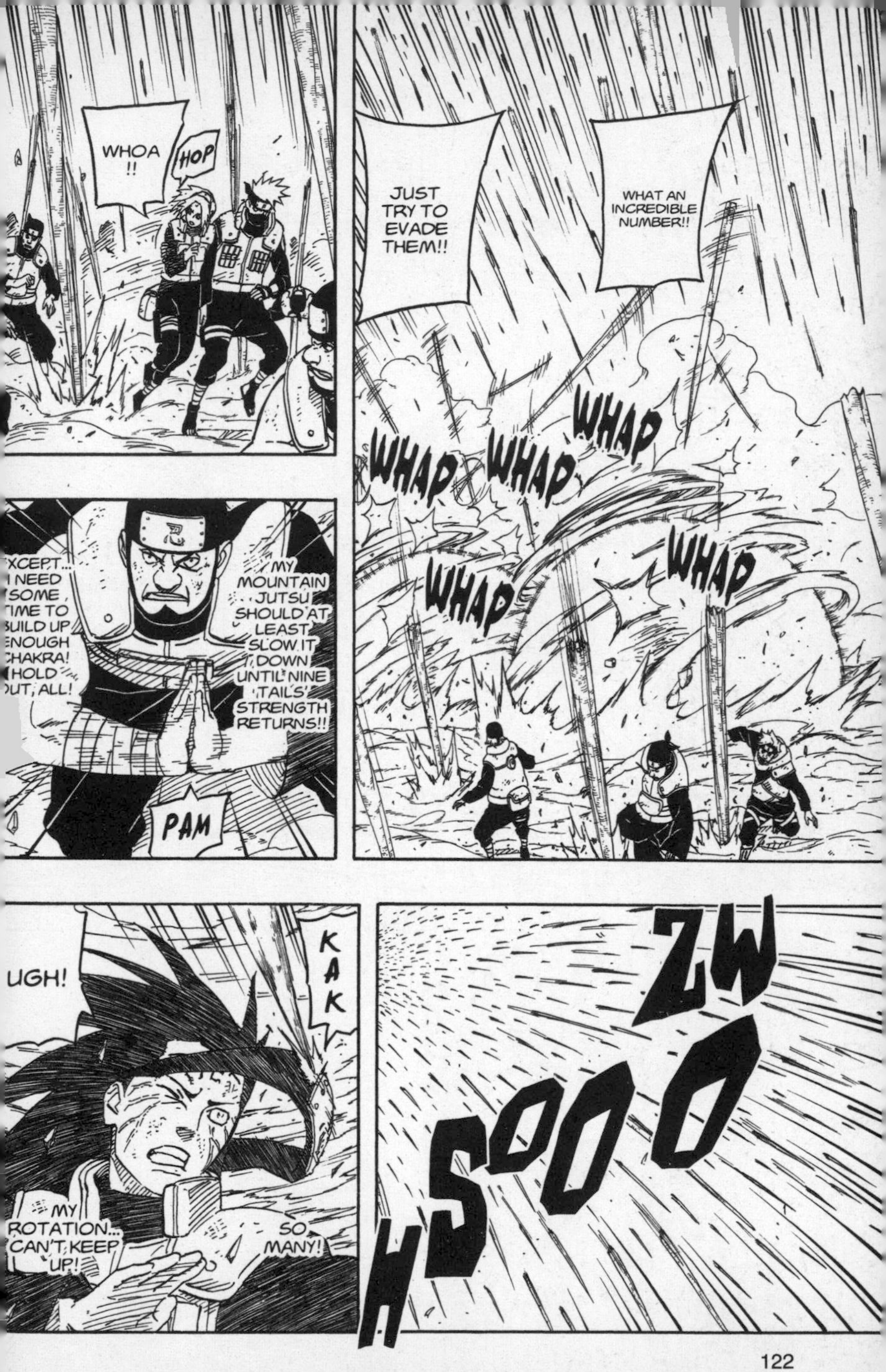
WHAT AN INCREDIBLE NUMBER!!
JUST TRY TO EVADE THEM!!
WHAP
WHAP
WHAP
WHAP
WHAP
HOP
WHOA!!
MY MOUNTAIN JUTSU SHOULD AT LEAST SLOW IT DOWN UNTIL NINE TAILS' STRENGTH RETURNS!!
EXCEPT... I NEED SOME TIME TO BUILD UP ENOUGH CHAKRA! HOLD OUT, ALL!
PAM
ZWOOOOSH
KAK
UGH!
SO MANY!
MY ROTATION... CAN'T KEEP UP!

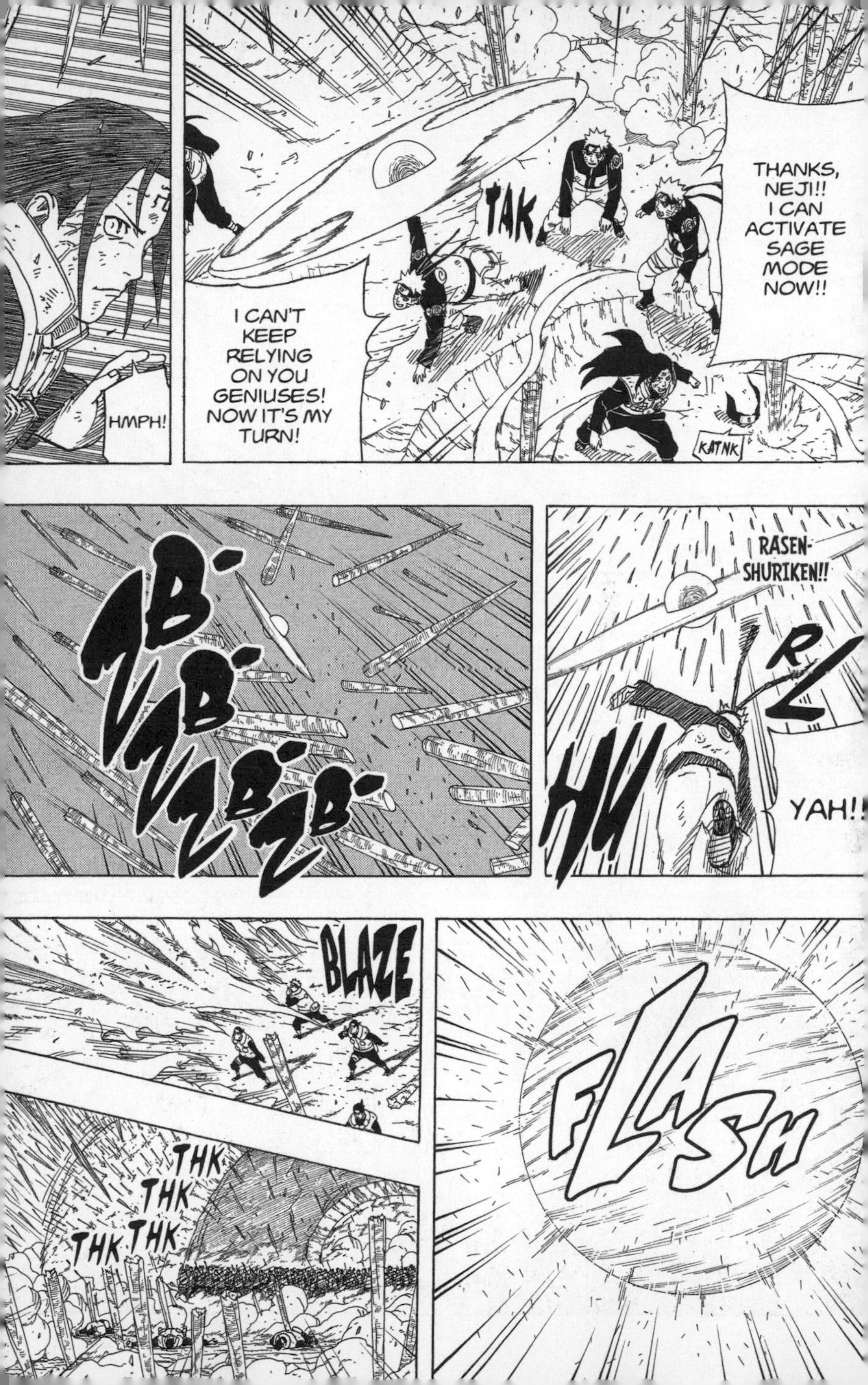
THANKS, NEJI!! I CAN ACTIVATE SAGE MODE NOW!!
TAK
KATNK
I CAN'T KEEP RELYING ON YOU GENIUSES! NOW IT'S MY TURN!
HMPH!
RASEN-SHURIKEN!!
YAH!!
FLASH
BLAZE
THK
THK
THK
THK

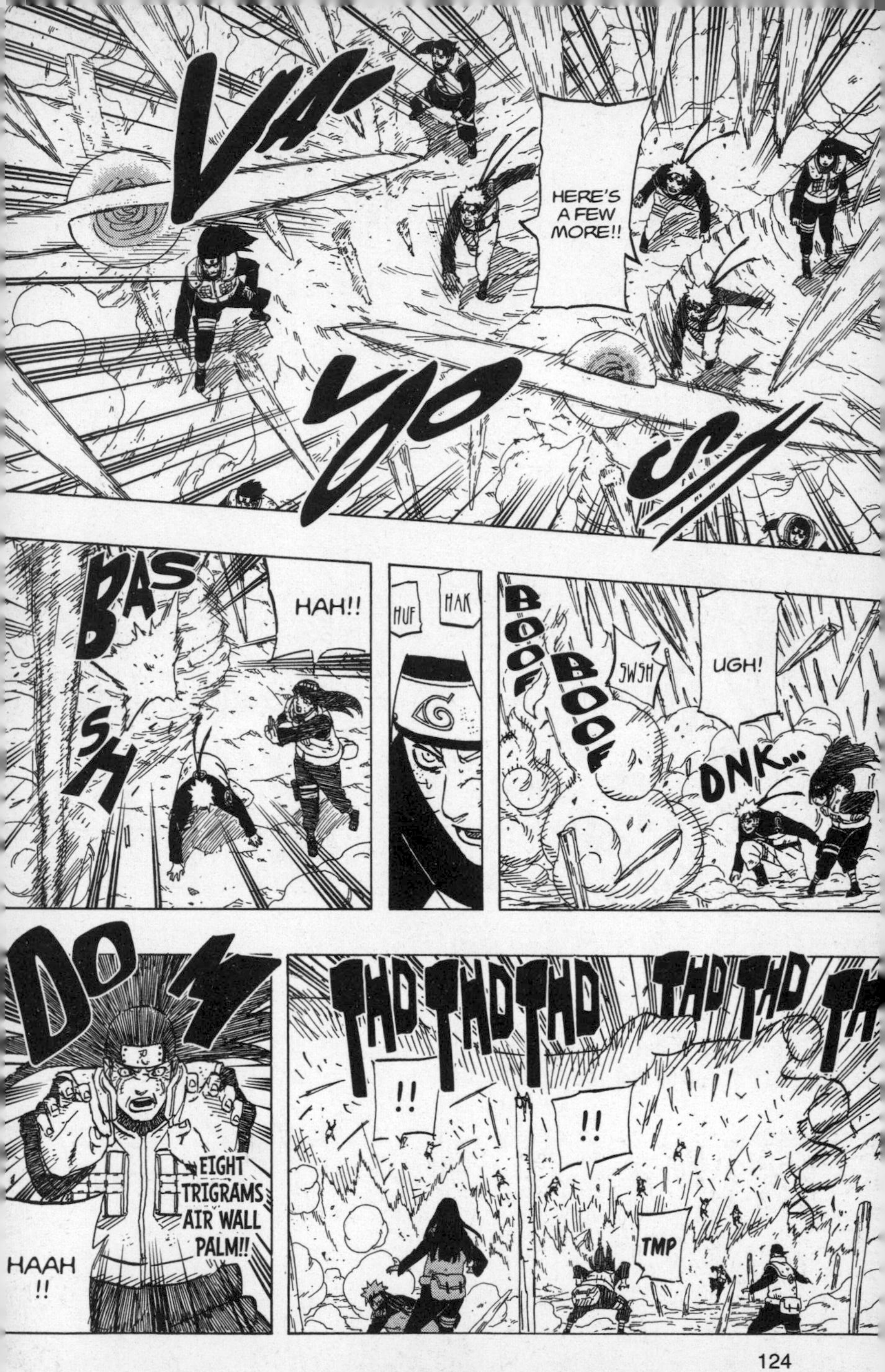
HERE'S A FEW MORE!!
VA
YO
SH
UGH!
SWSH
BOOF
BOOF
DNK...
HAK
HUF
HAH!!
BAS
SH
THD THD THD THD THD TH
!!
!!
TMP
DON
EIGHT TRIGRAMS AIR WALL PALM!!
HAAH!!

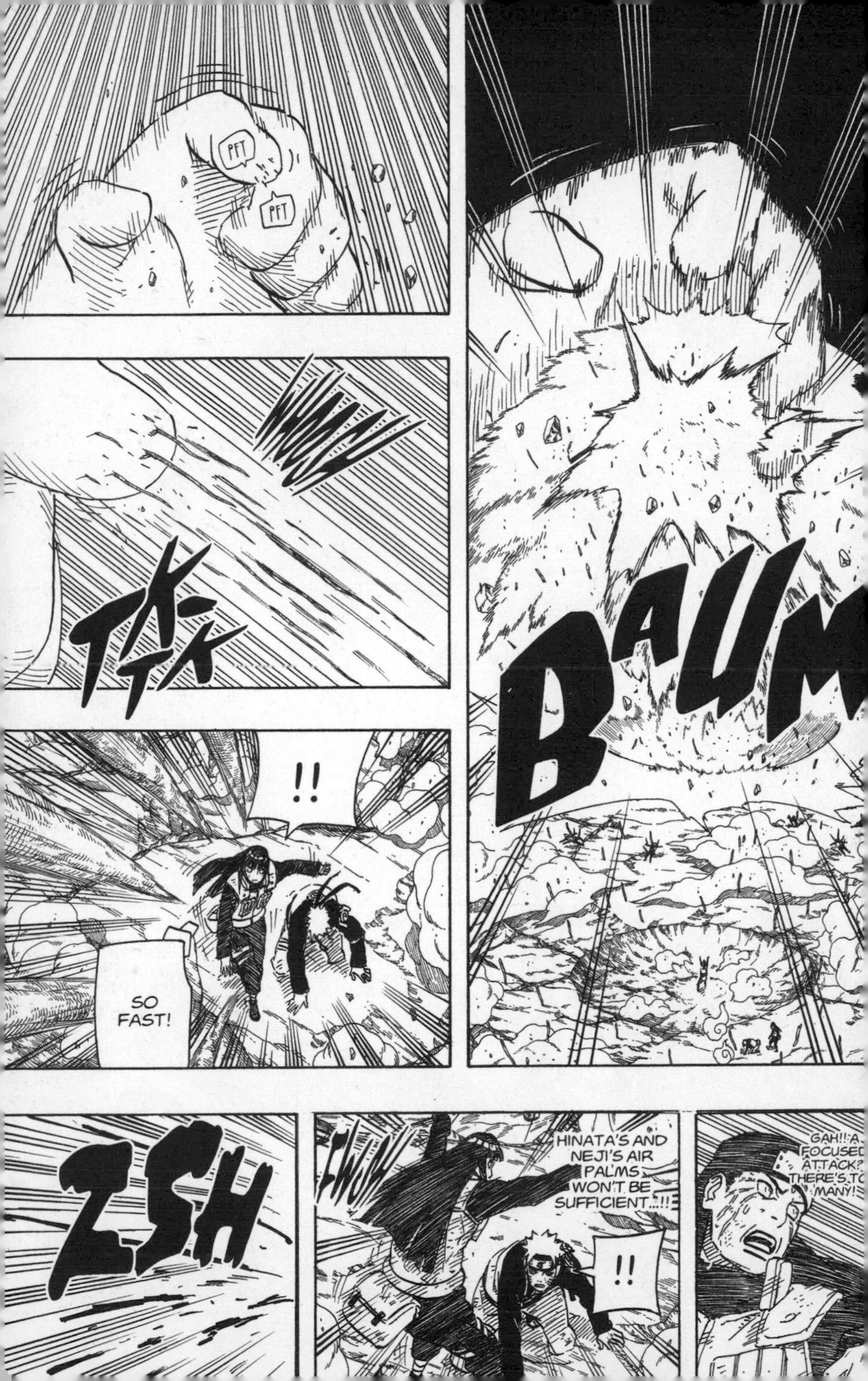
BAUM
PFT
PFT
!!
SO FAST!
GAH!! A
FOCUSED ATTACK? THERE'S TO MANY!
HINATA'S AND NEJI'S AIR PALMS WON'T BE SUFFICIENT...!!
!!
ZSH

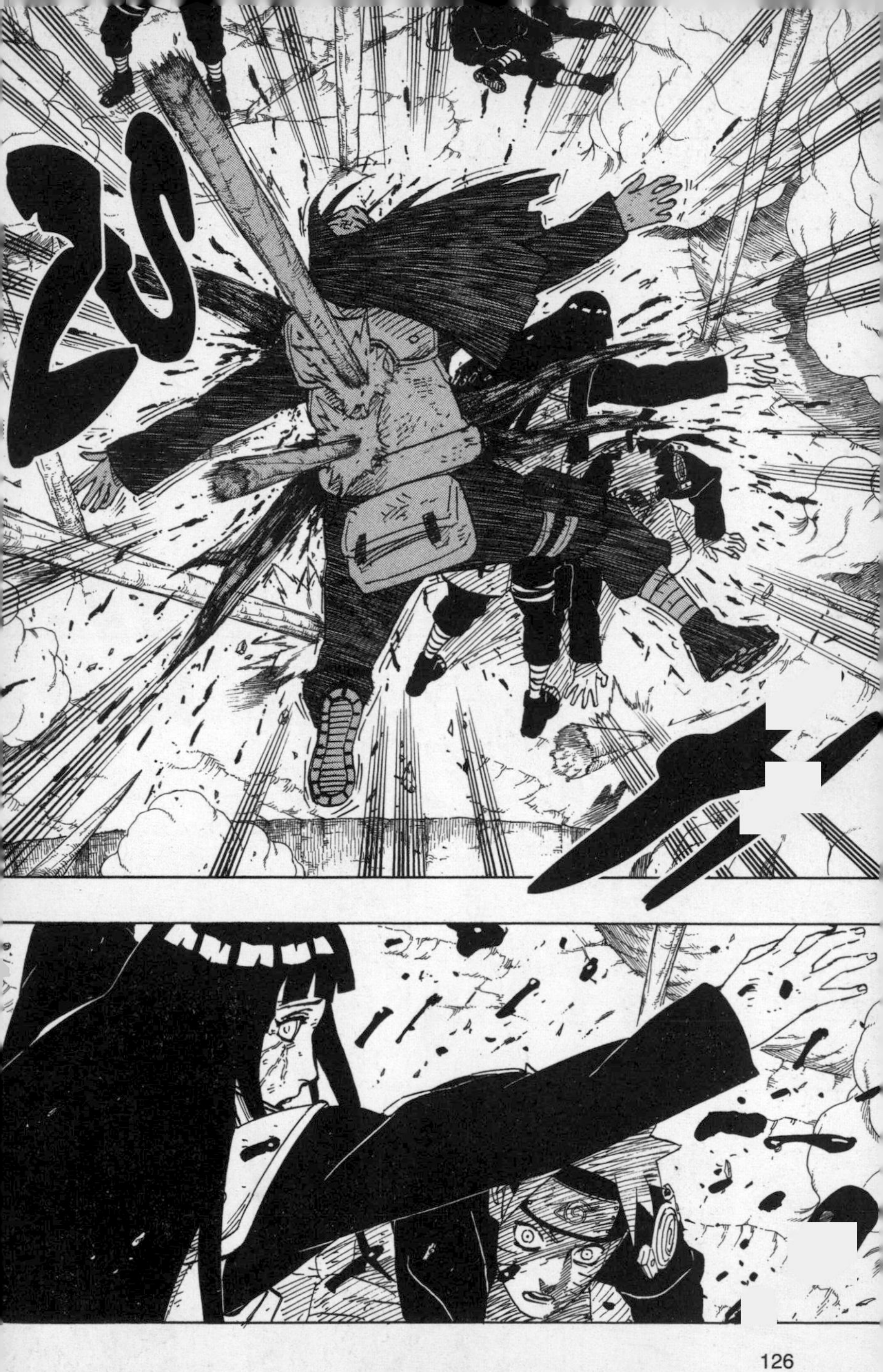

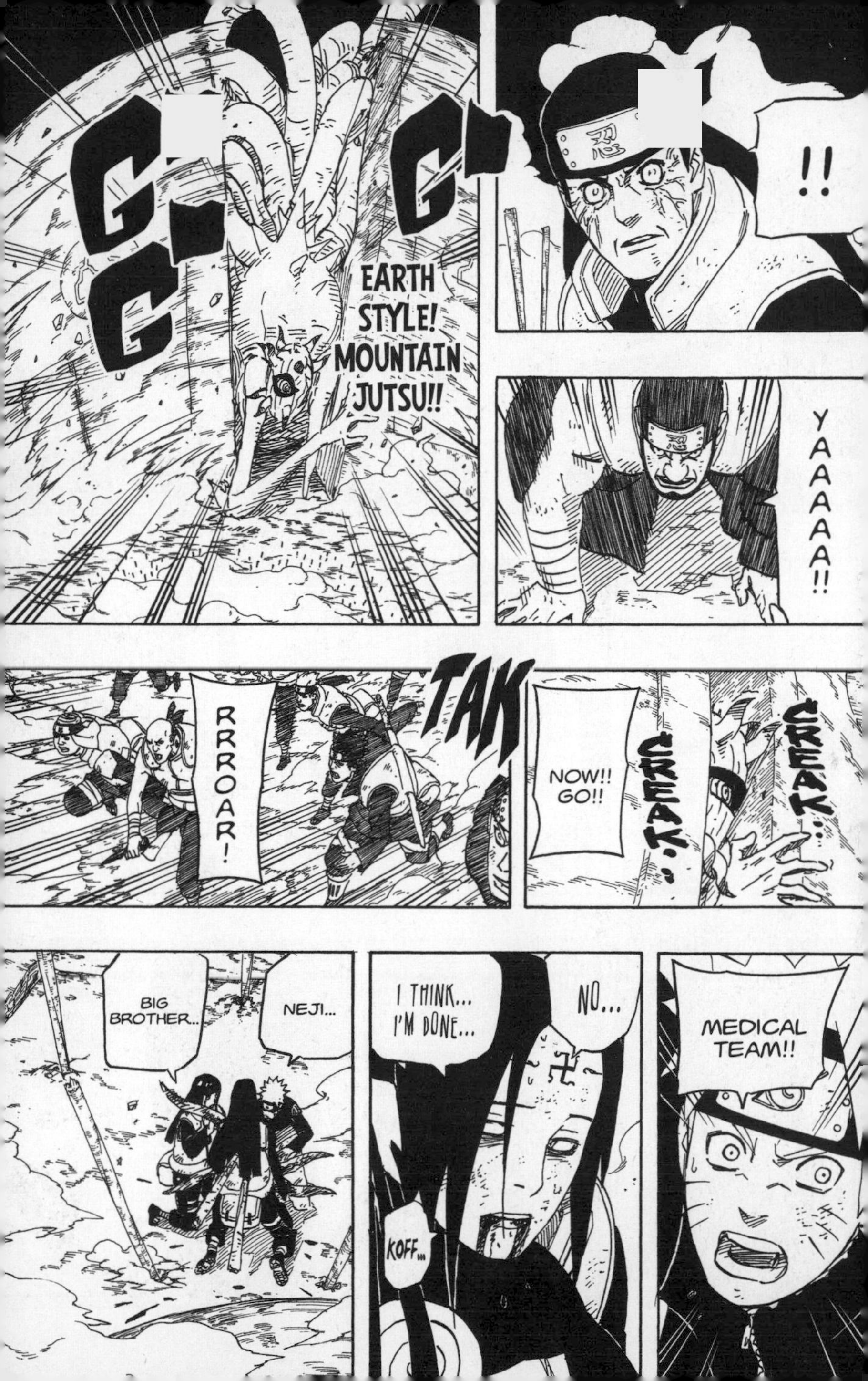
!!
YAAAAA!!
EARTH STYLE! MOUNTAIN JUTSU!!
CREAK...
CREAK...
NOW!! GO!!
TAK
RRROAR!
MEDICAL TEAM!!
NO...
I THINK... I'M DONE...
KOFF...
NEJI...
BIG BROTHER...

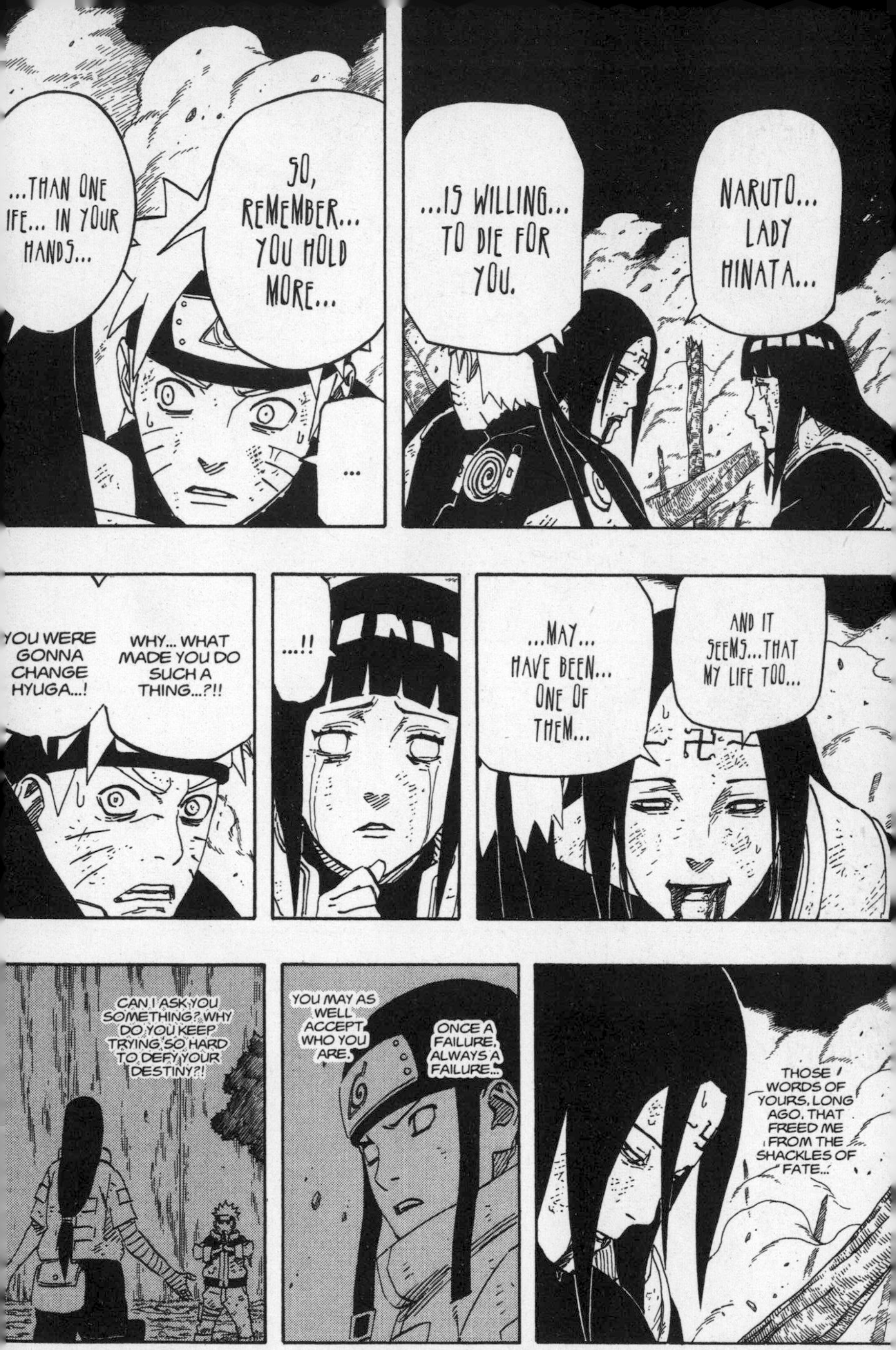
NARUTO... LADY HINATA...
...IS WILLING... TO DIE FOR YOU.
SO, REMEMBER... YOU HOLD MORE...
...THAN ONE IFE... IN YOUR HANDS...
...
AND IT SEEMS...THAT MY LIFE TOO...
...MAY... HAVE BEEN... ONE OF THEM...
...!!
WHY... WHAT MADE YOU DO SUCH A THING...?!!
YOU WERE GONNA CHANGE HYUGA...!
THOSE WORDS OF YOURS, LONG AGO, THAT FREED ME FROM THE SHACKLES OF FATE...
ONCE A FAILURE, ALWAYS A FAILURE...
YOU MAY AS WELL ACCEPT WHO YOU ARE.
CAN I ASK YOU SOMETHING? WHY DO YOU KEEP TRYING SO HARD TO DEFY YOUR DESTINY?!

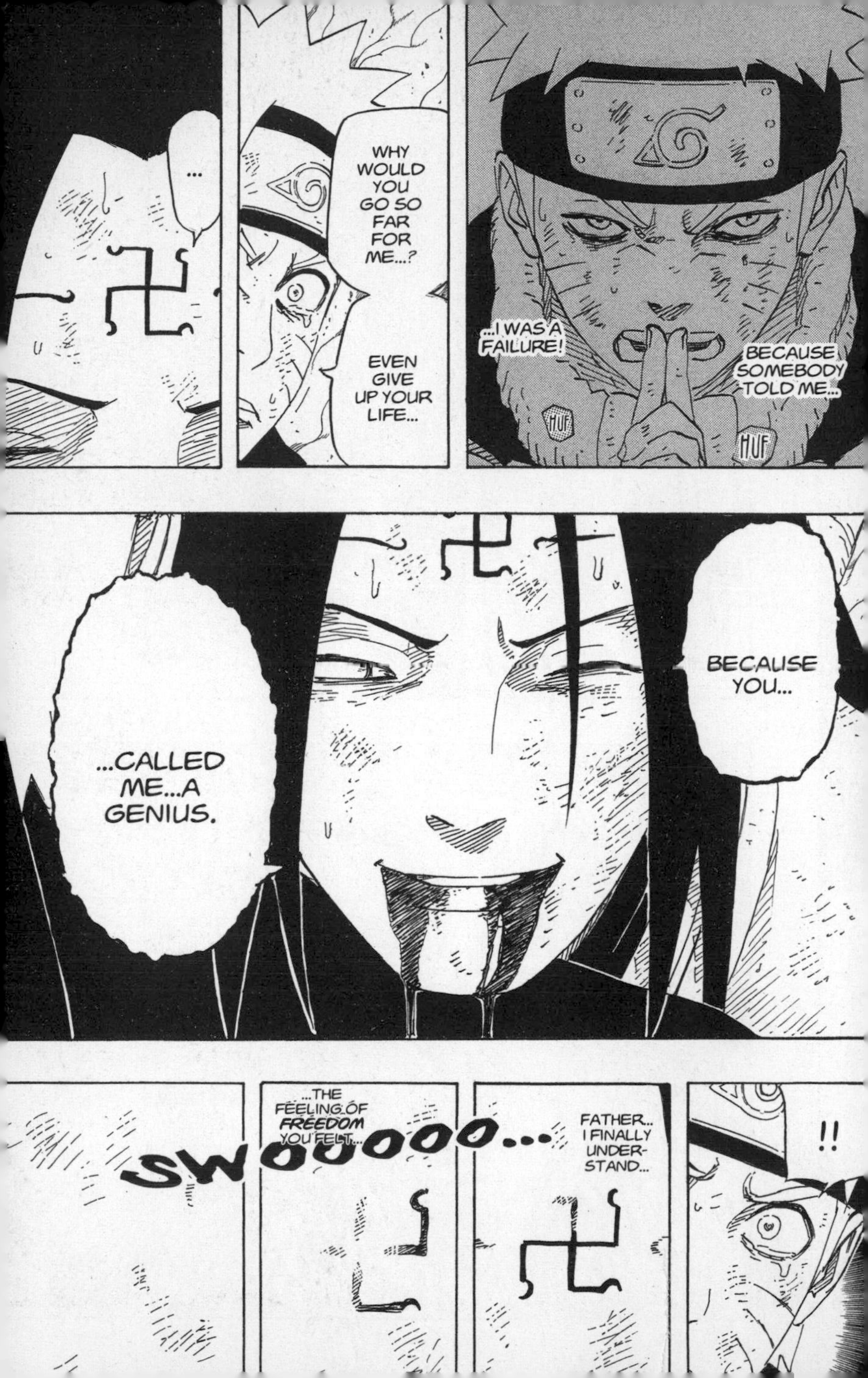
BECAUSE SOMEBODY TOLD ME...
...I WAS A FAILURE!
HUF
HUF
WHY WOULD YOU GO SO FAR FOR ME...?
EVEN GIVE UP YOUR LIFE...
...
BECAUSE YOU...
...CALLED ME...A GENIUS.
!!
FATHER... I FINALLY UNDER-STAND...
...THE FEELING OF FREEDOM YOU FELT...
SWOOOOOO...

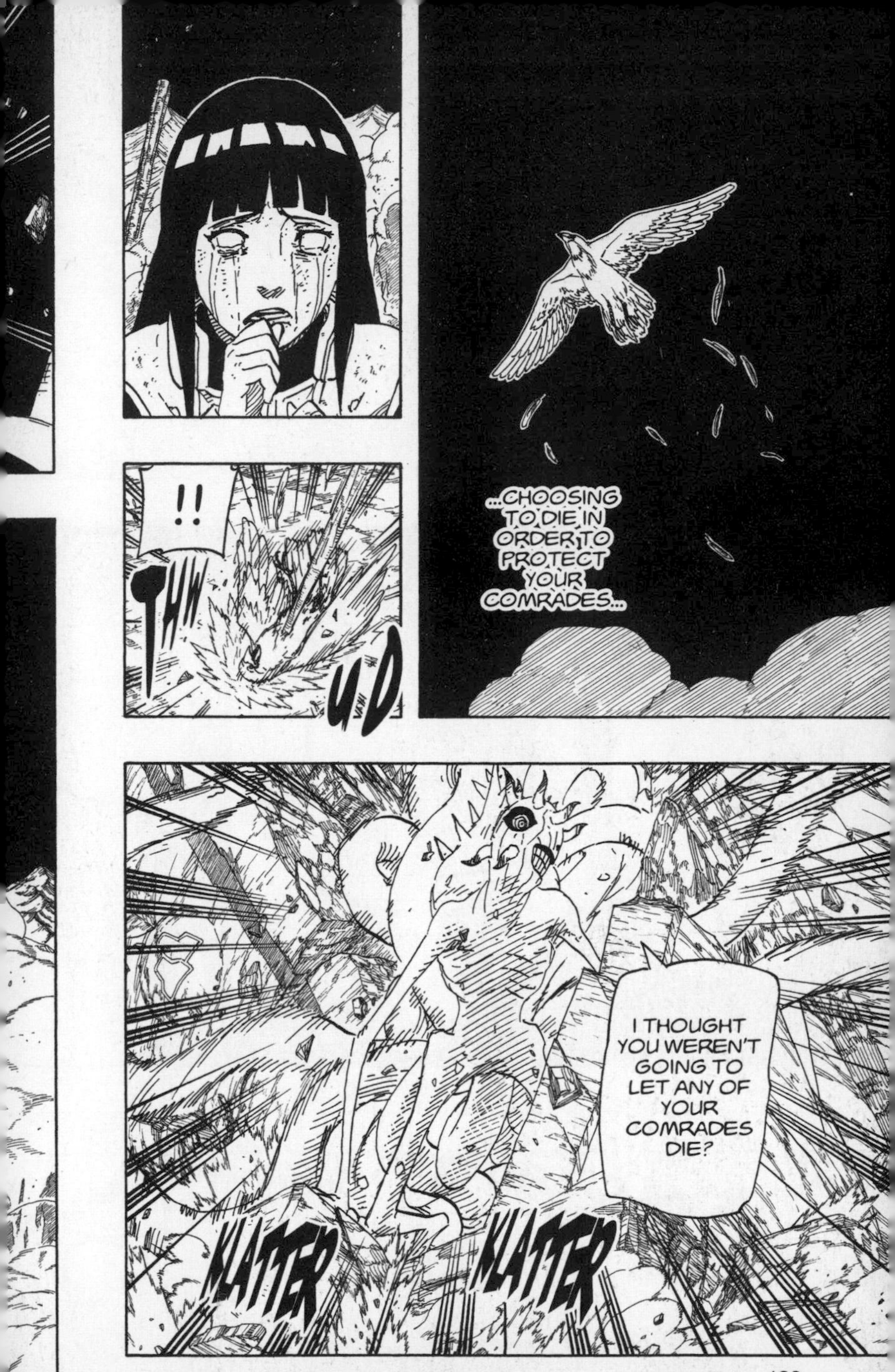
...CHOOSING TO DIE IN ORDER TO PROTECT YOUR COMRADES...
!!
THWUD
I THOUGHT YOU WEREN'T GOING TO LET ANY OF YOUR COMRADES DIE?
KLATTER
KLATTER

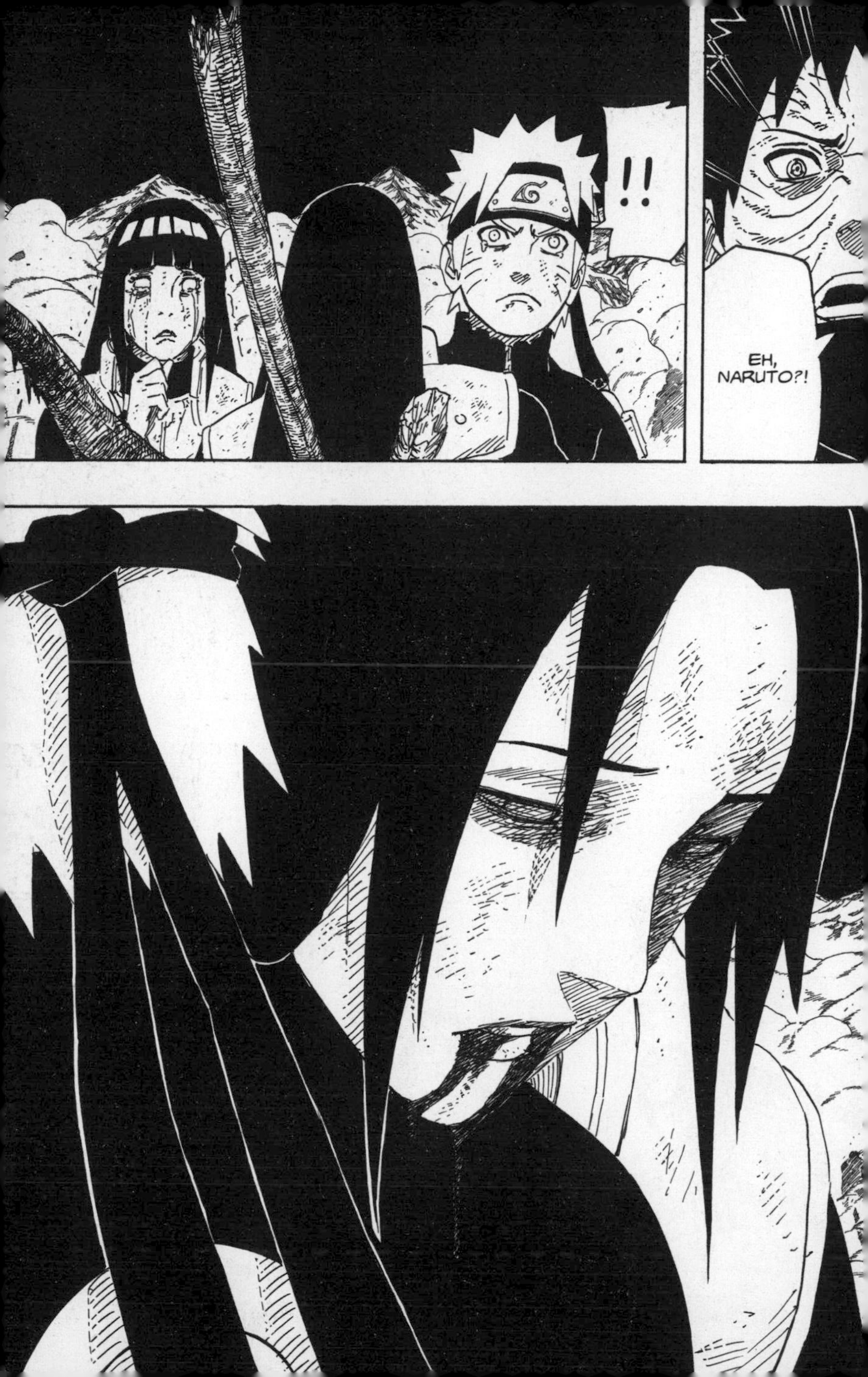
EH,
NARUTO?!
!!

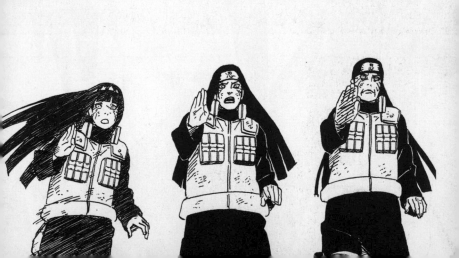

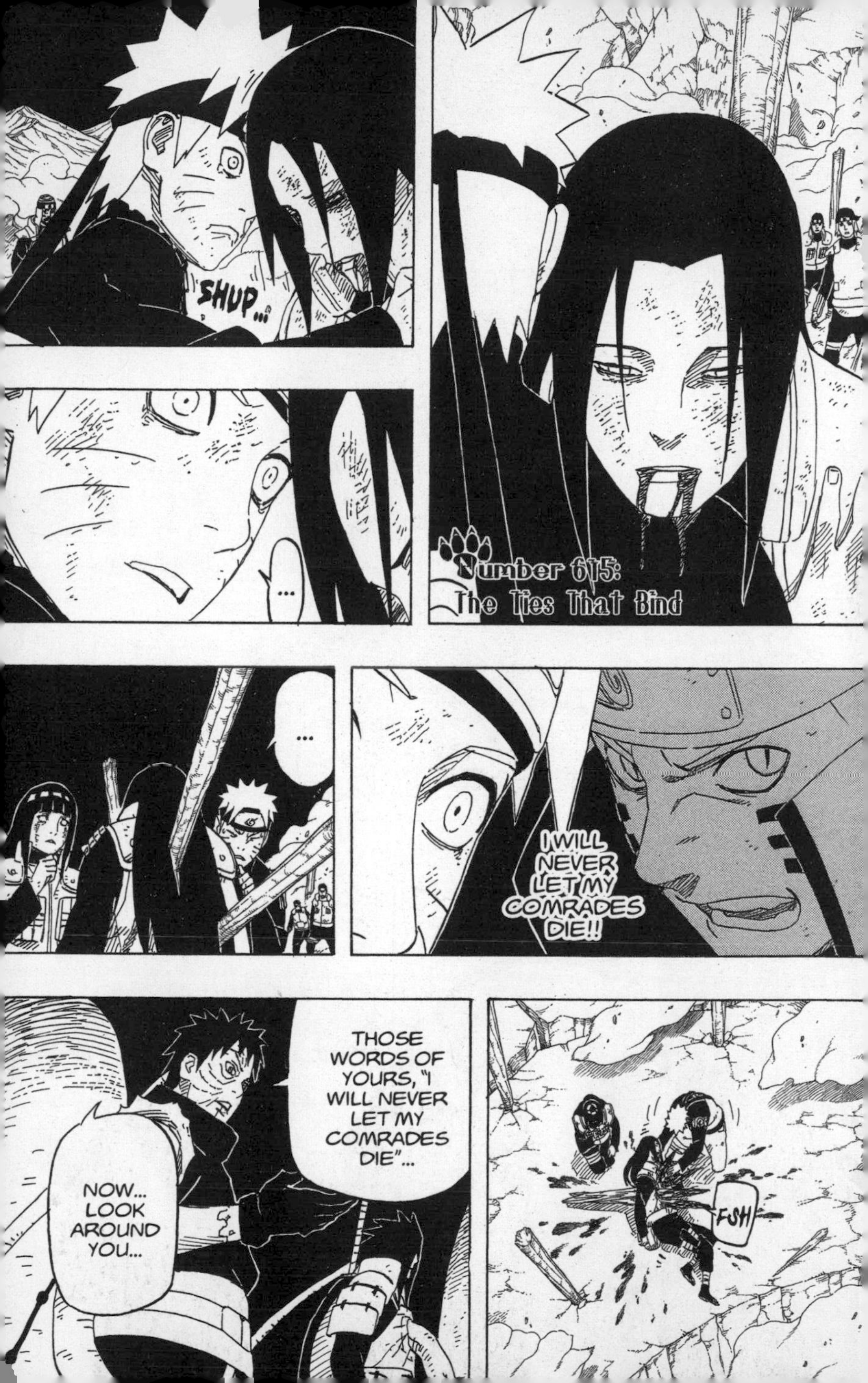
Number 615:
The Ties That Bind
SHUP...
...
I WILL NEVER LET MY COMRADES DIE!!
...
FSH
THOSE WORDS OF YOURS, "I WILL NEVER LET MY COMRADES DIE"...
NOW... LOOK AROUND YOU...

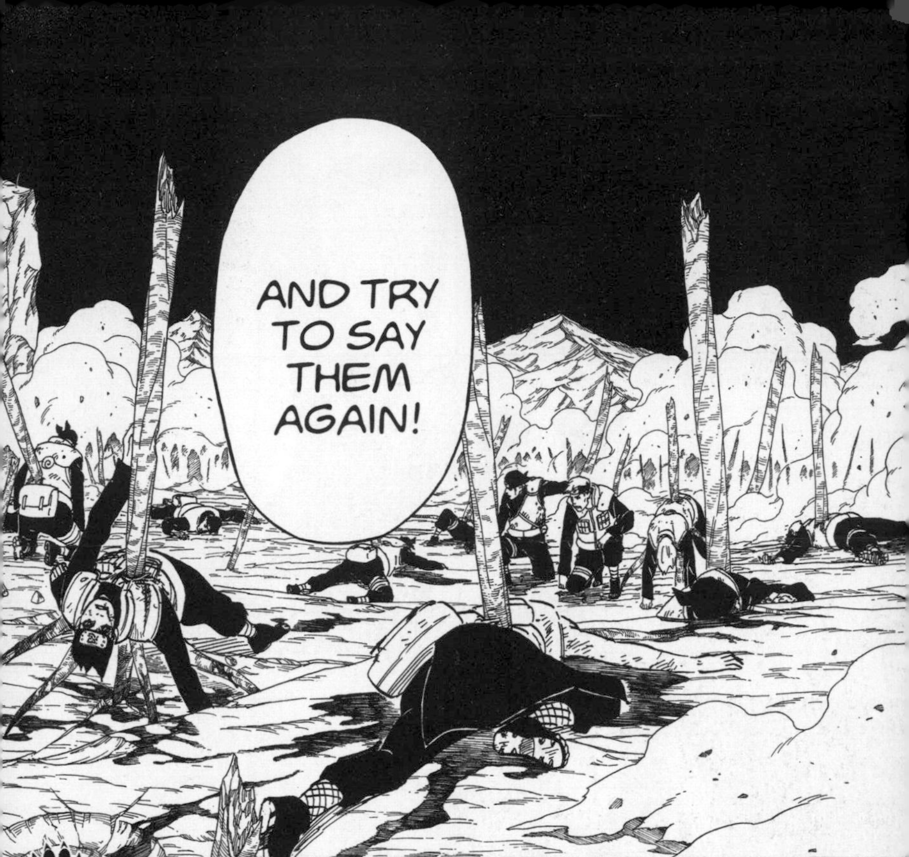
AND TRY TO SAY THEM AGAIN!

Number 615: The Ties That Bind

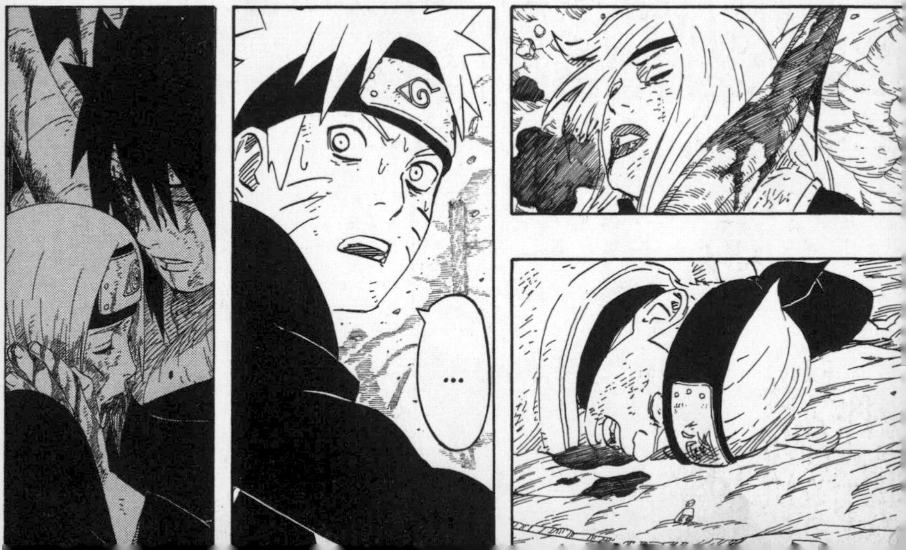
...

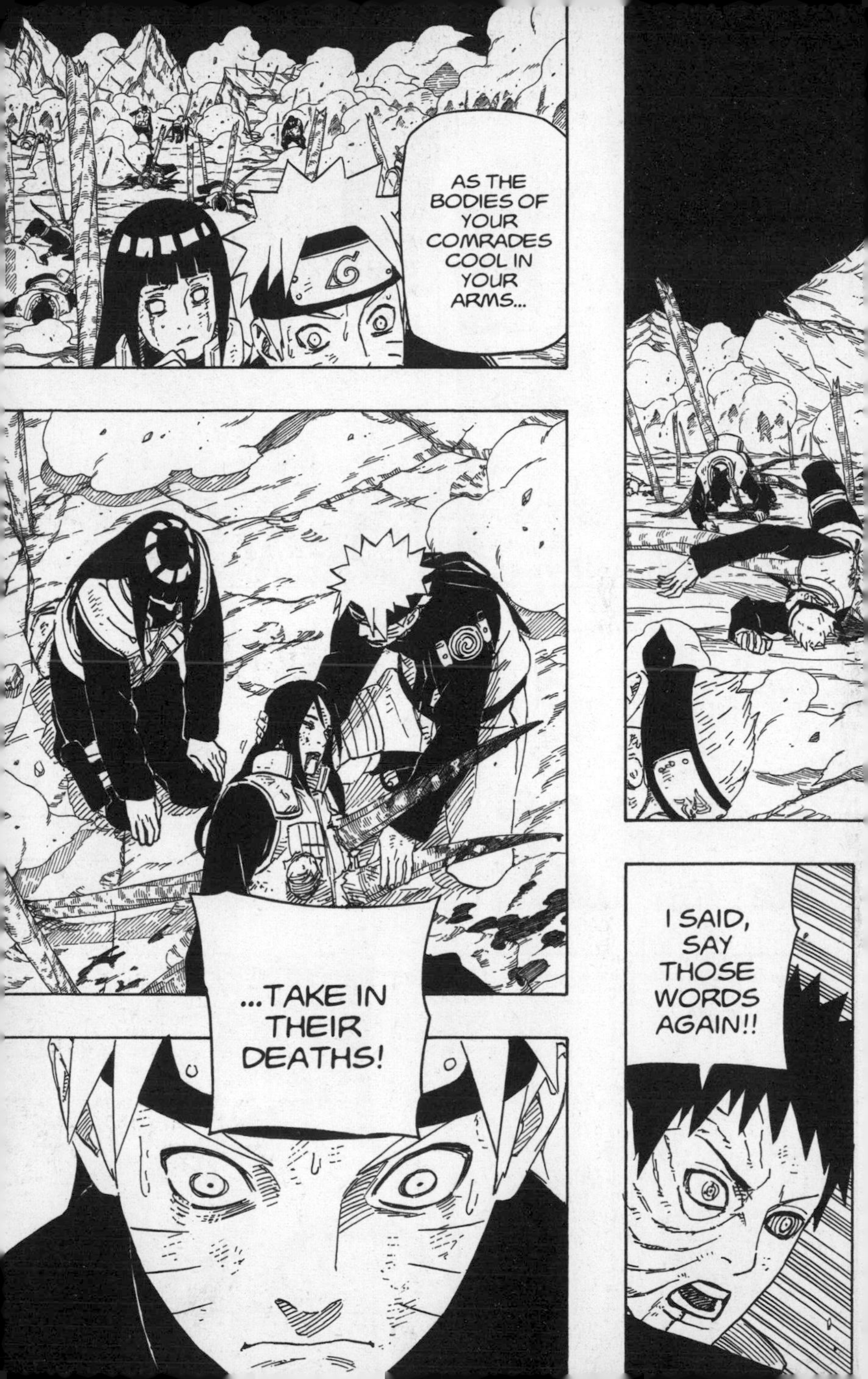
AS THE BODIES OF YOUR COMRADES COOL IN YOUR ARMS...
...TAKE IN THEIR DEATHS!
I SAID, SAY THOSE WORDS AGAIN!!

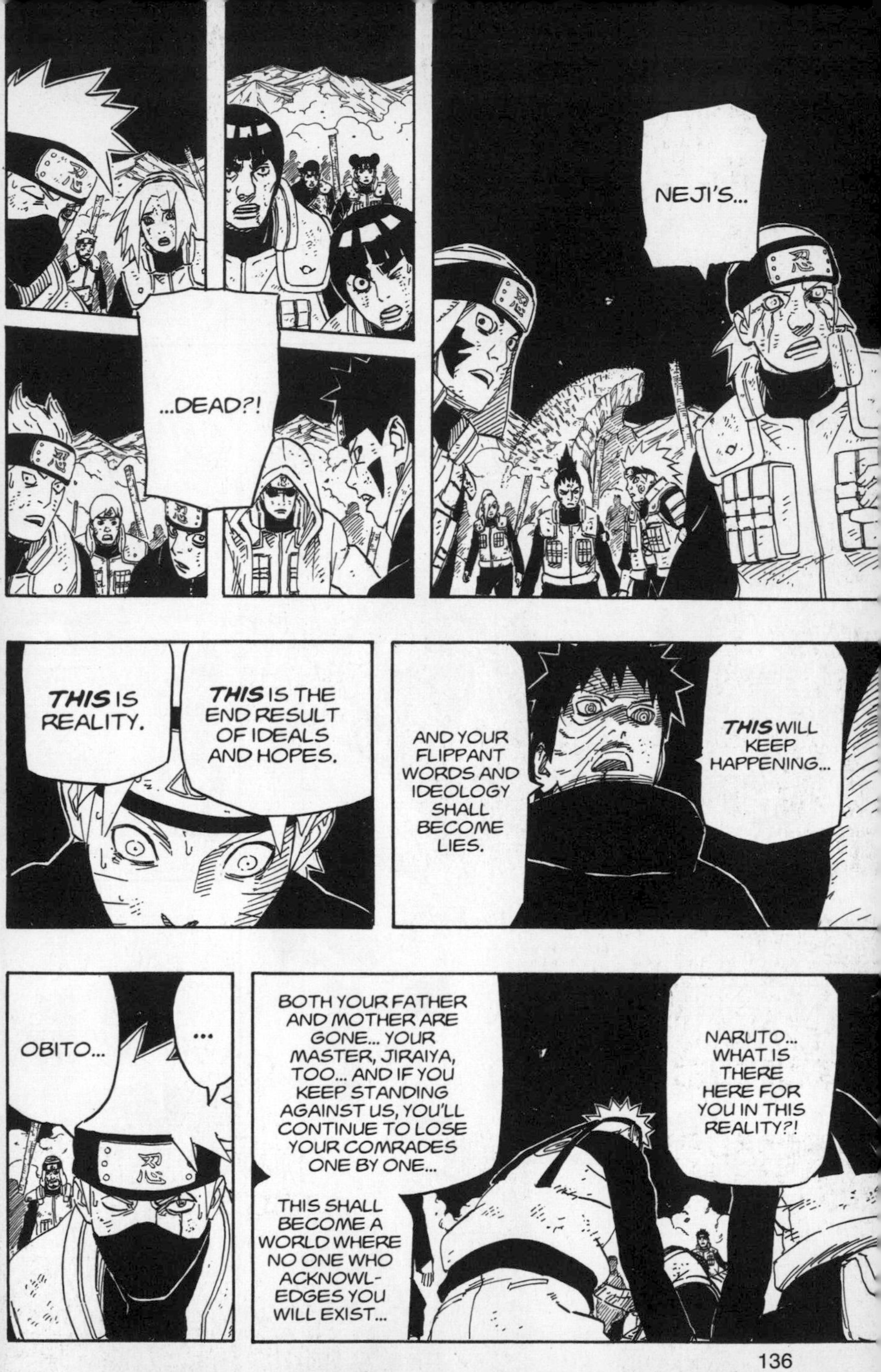
NEJI'S...
...DEAD?!
THIS WILL KEEP HAPPENING...
AND YOUR FLIPPANT WORDS AND IDEOLOGY SHALL BECOME LIES.
THIS IS THE END RESULT OF IDEALS AND HOPES.
THIS IS REALITY.
NARUTO... WHAT IS THERE HERE FOR YOU IN THIS REALITY?!
BOTH YOUR FATHER AND MOTHER ARE GONE... YOUR MASTER, JIRAIYA, TOO... AND IF YOU KEEP STANDING AGAINST US, YOU'LL CONTINUE TO LOSE YOUR COMRADES ONE BY ONE...
THIS SHALL BECOME A WORLD WHERE NO ONE WHO ACKNOWL-EDGES YOU WILL EXIST...
...
OBITO...

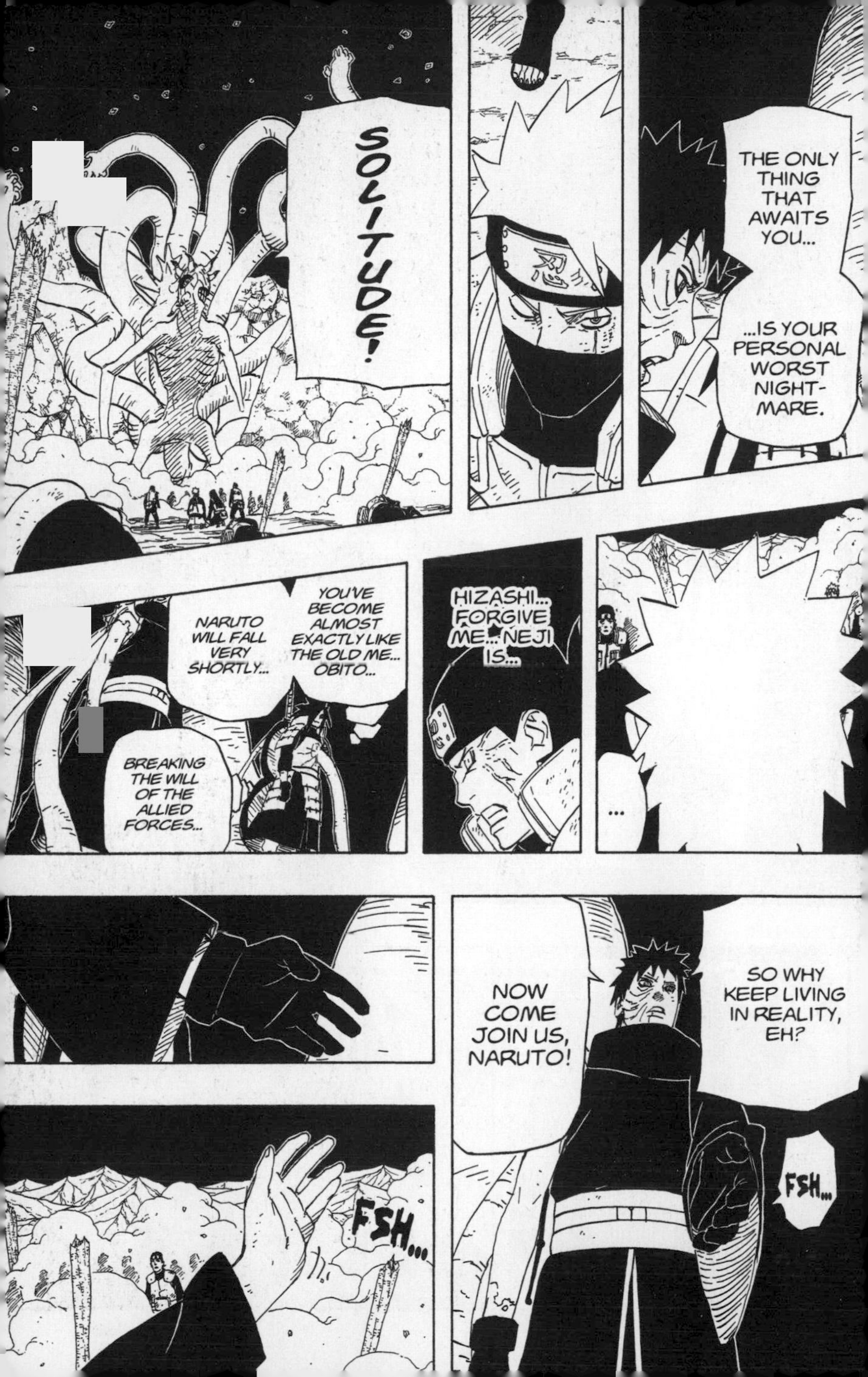
THE ONLY THING THAT AWAITS YOU...
...IS YOUR PERSONAL WORST NIGHT-MARE.
SOLITUDE!
...
HIZASHI... FORGIVE ME... NEJI IS...
YOU'VE BECOME ALMOST EXACTLY LIKE THE OLD ME... OBITO...
NARUTO WILL FALL VERY SHORTLY...
BREAKING THE WILL OF THE ALLIED FORCES...
SO WHY KEEP LIVING IN REALITY, EH?
NOW COME JOIN US, NARUTO!
FSH...
FSH...

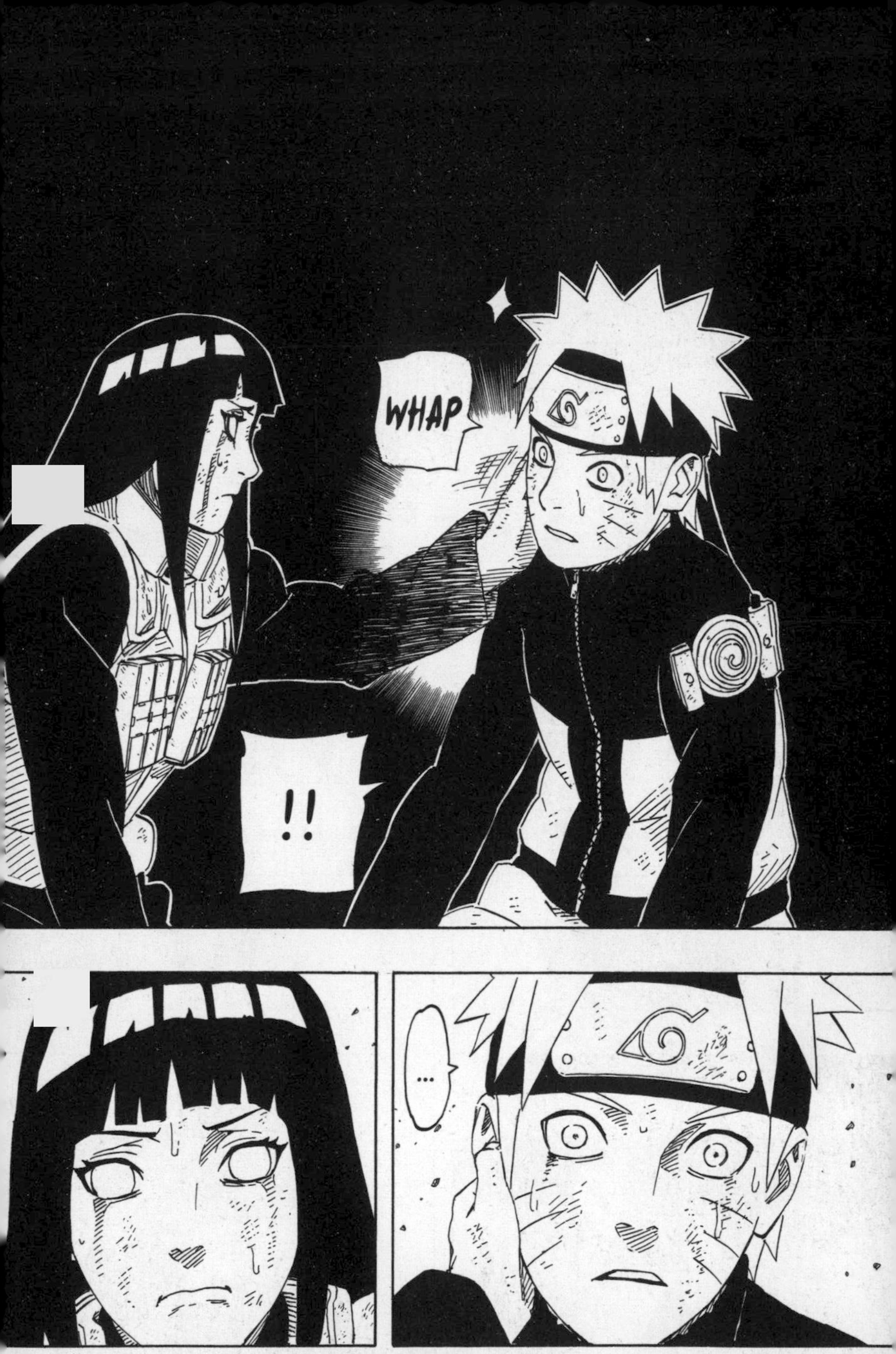
WHAP
!!
...

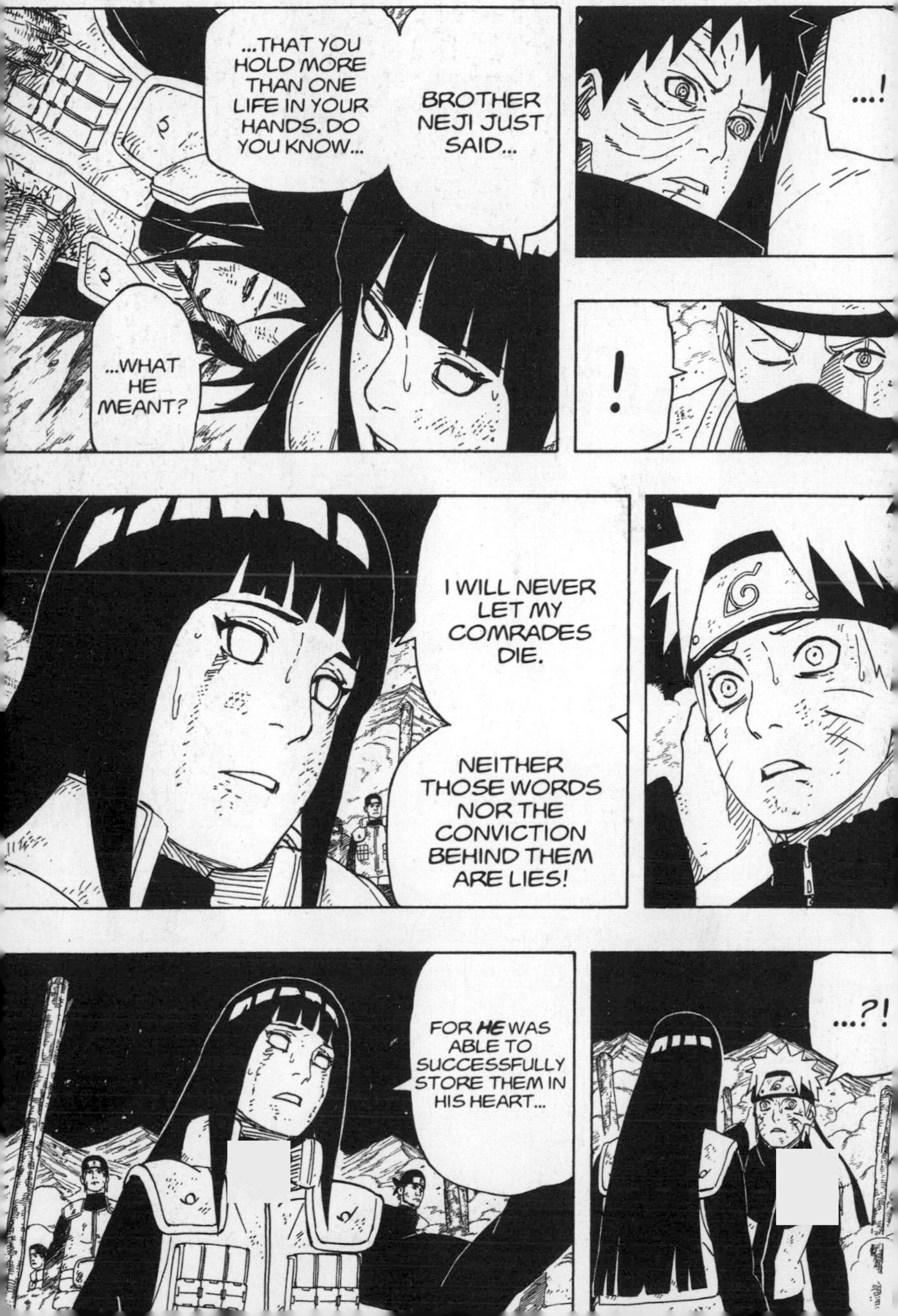
...!
!
BROTHER NEJI JUST SAID...
...THAT YOU HOLD MORE THAN ONE LIFE IN YOUR HANDS. DO YOU KNOW...
...WHAT HE MEANT?
I WILL NEVER LET MY COMRADES DIE.
NEITHER THOSE WORDS NOR THE CONVICTION BEHIND THEM ARE LIES!
...?!
FOR **HE** WAS ABLE TO SUCCESSFULLY STORE THEM IN HIS HEART...

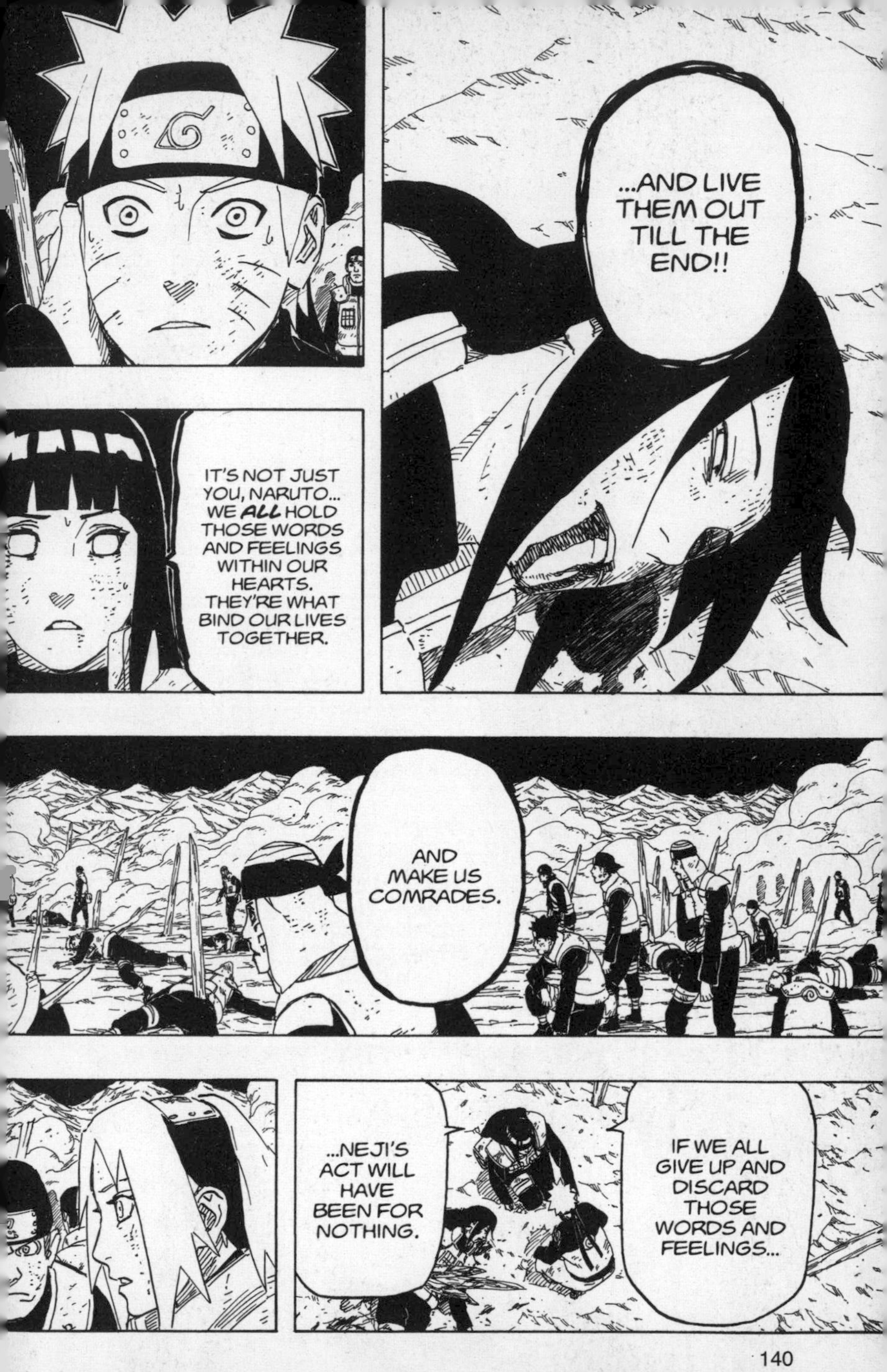
...AND LIVE THEM OUT TILL THE END!!
IT'S NOT JUST YOU, NARUTO... WE **ALL** HOLD THOSE WORDS AND FEELINGS WITHIN OUR HEARTS. THEY'RE WHAT BIND OUR LIVES TOGETHER.
AND MAKE US COMRADES.
IF WE ALL GIVE UP AND DISCARD THOSE WORDS AND FEELINGS...
...NEJI'S ACT WILL HAVE BEEN FOR NOTHING.

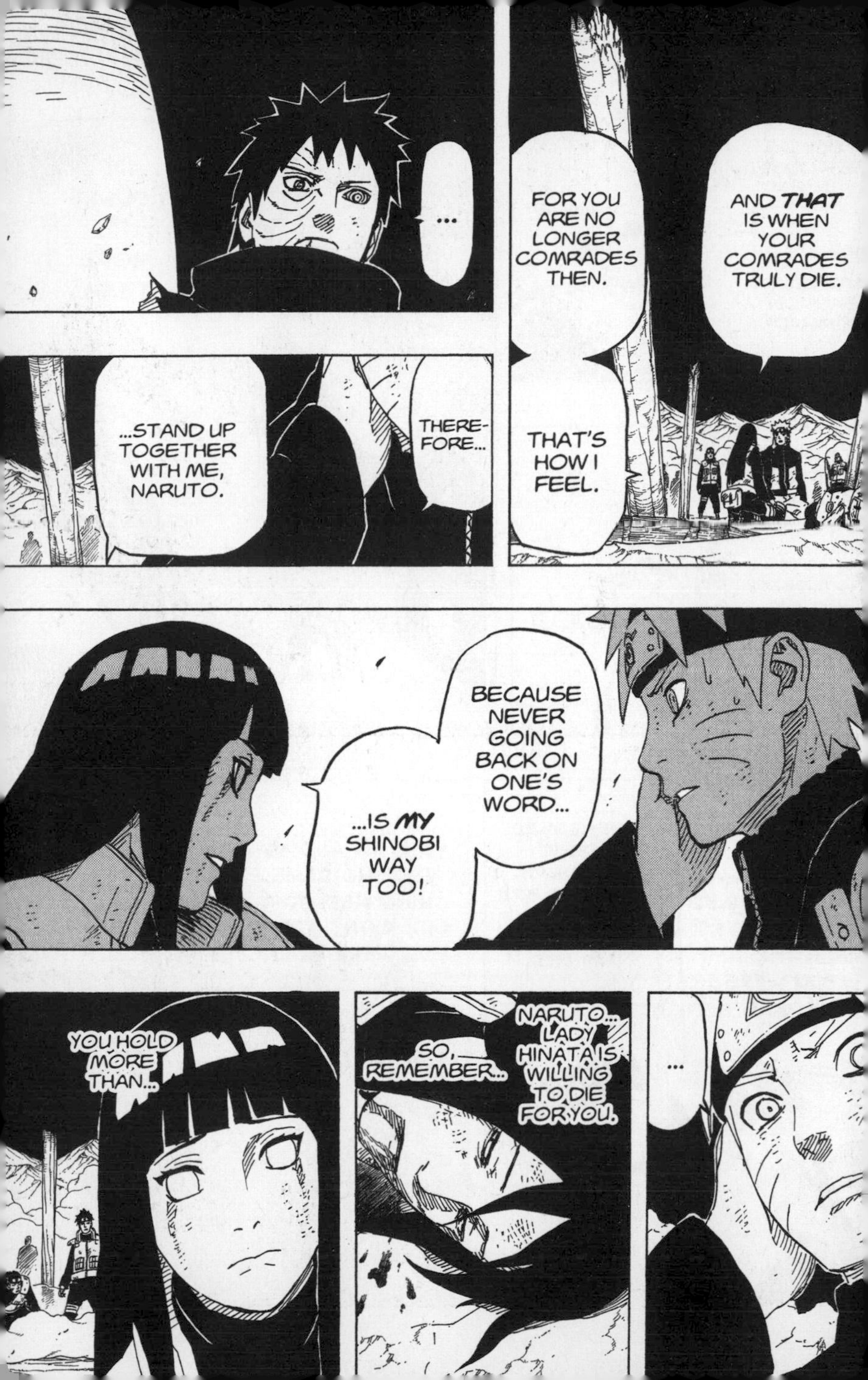
AND THAT IS WHEN YOUR COMRADES TRULY DIE.
FOR YOU ARE NO LONGER COMRADES THEN.
THAT'S HOW I FEEL.
...
THERE-FORE...
...STAND UP TOGETHER WITH ME, NARUTO.
BECAUSE NEVER GOING BACK ON ONE'S WORD...
...IS MY SHINOBI WAY TOO!
...
NARUTO... LADY HINATA IS WILLING TO DIE FOR YOU.
SO, REMEMBER...
YOU HOLD MORE THAN...

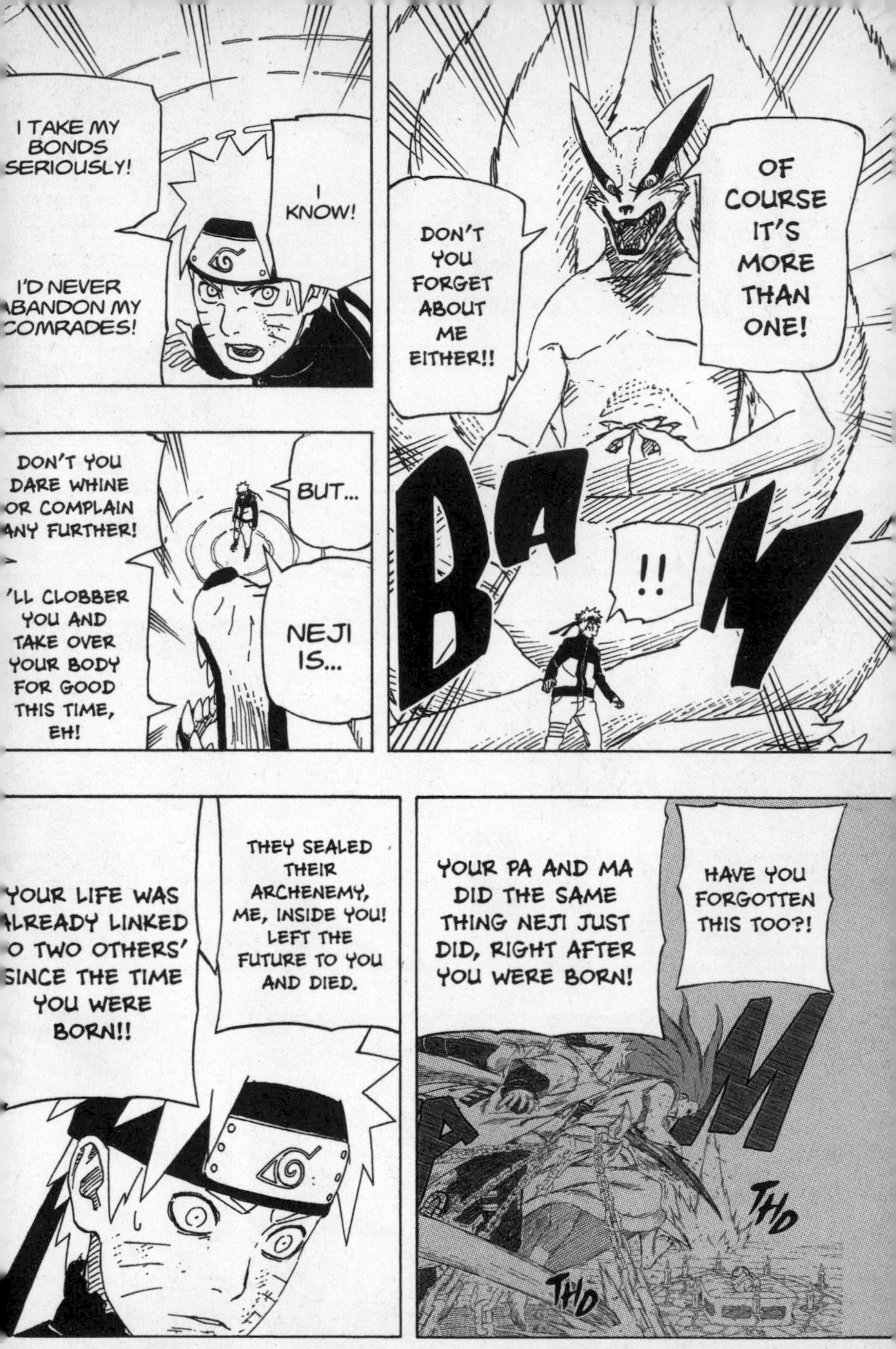
OF COURSE IT'S MORE THAN ONE!
DON'T YOU FORGET ABOUT ME EITHER!!
BAM
!!
I KNOW!
I TAKE MY BONDS SERIOUSLY!
I'D NEVER ABANDON MY COMRADES!
BUT...
NEJI IS...
DON'T YOU DARE WHINE OR COMPLAIN ANY FURTHER!
I'LL CLOBBER YOU AND TAKE OVER YOUR BODY FOR GOOD THIS TIME, EH!
HAVE YOU FORGOTTEN THIS TOO?!
YOUR PA AND MA DID THE SAME THING NEJI JUST DID, RIGHT AFTER YOU WERE BORN!
THD
THD
THEY SEALED THEIR ARCHENEMY, ME, INSIDE YOU! LEFT THE FUTURE TO YOU AND DIED.
YOUR LIFE WAS ALREADY LINKED TO TWO OTHERS' SINCE THE TIME YOU WERE BORN!!

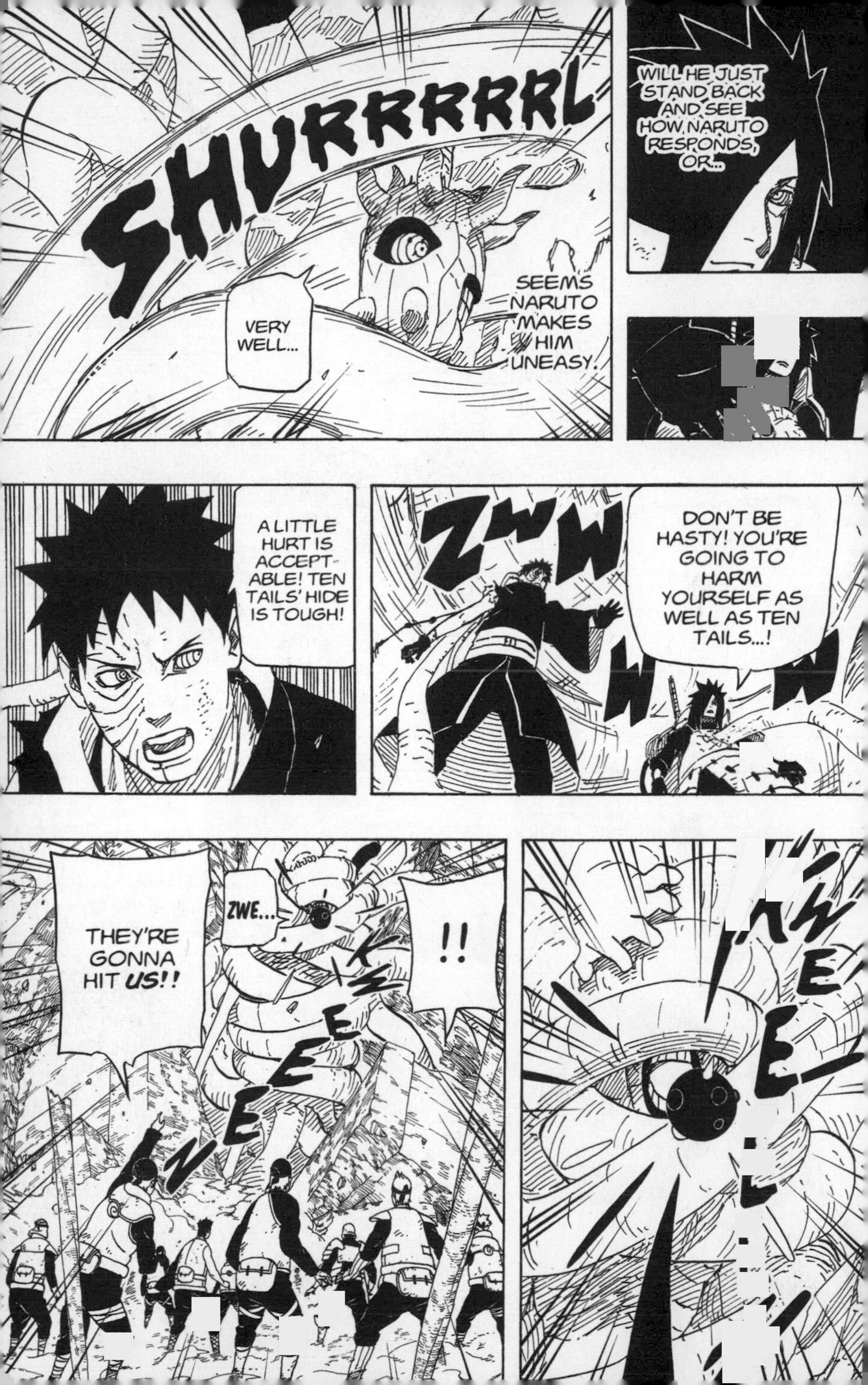
WILL HE JUST STAND BACK AND SEE HOW NARUTO RESPONDS, OR...
SHURRRRRL
SEEMS NARUTO MAKES HIM UNEASY.
VERY WELL...
ZWW
DON'T BE HASTY! YOU'RE GOING TO HARM YOURSELF AS WELL AS TEN TAILS...!
A LITTLE HURT IS ACCEPT-ABLE! TEN TAILS' HIDE IS TOUGH!
!!
ZWE...
THEY'RE GONNA HIT *US*!!

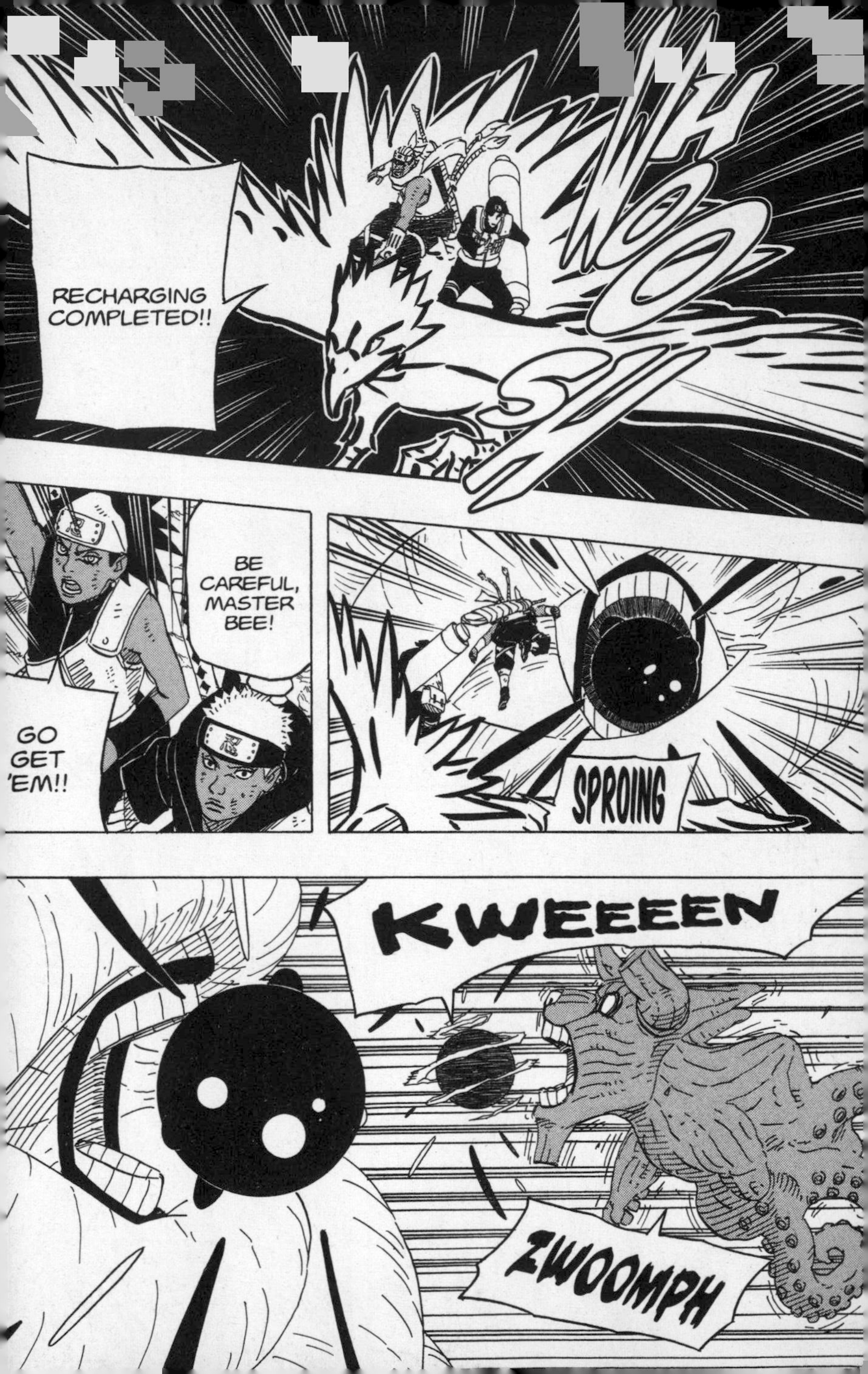
RECHARGING COMPLETED!!
WHOOSH
SPROING
BE CAREFUL, MASTER BEE!
GO GET 'EM!!
KWEEEEN
ZWOOMPH

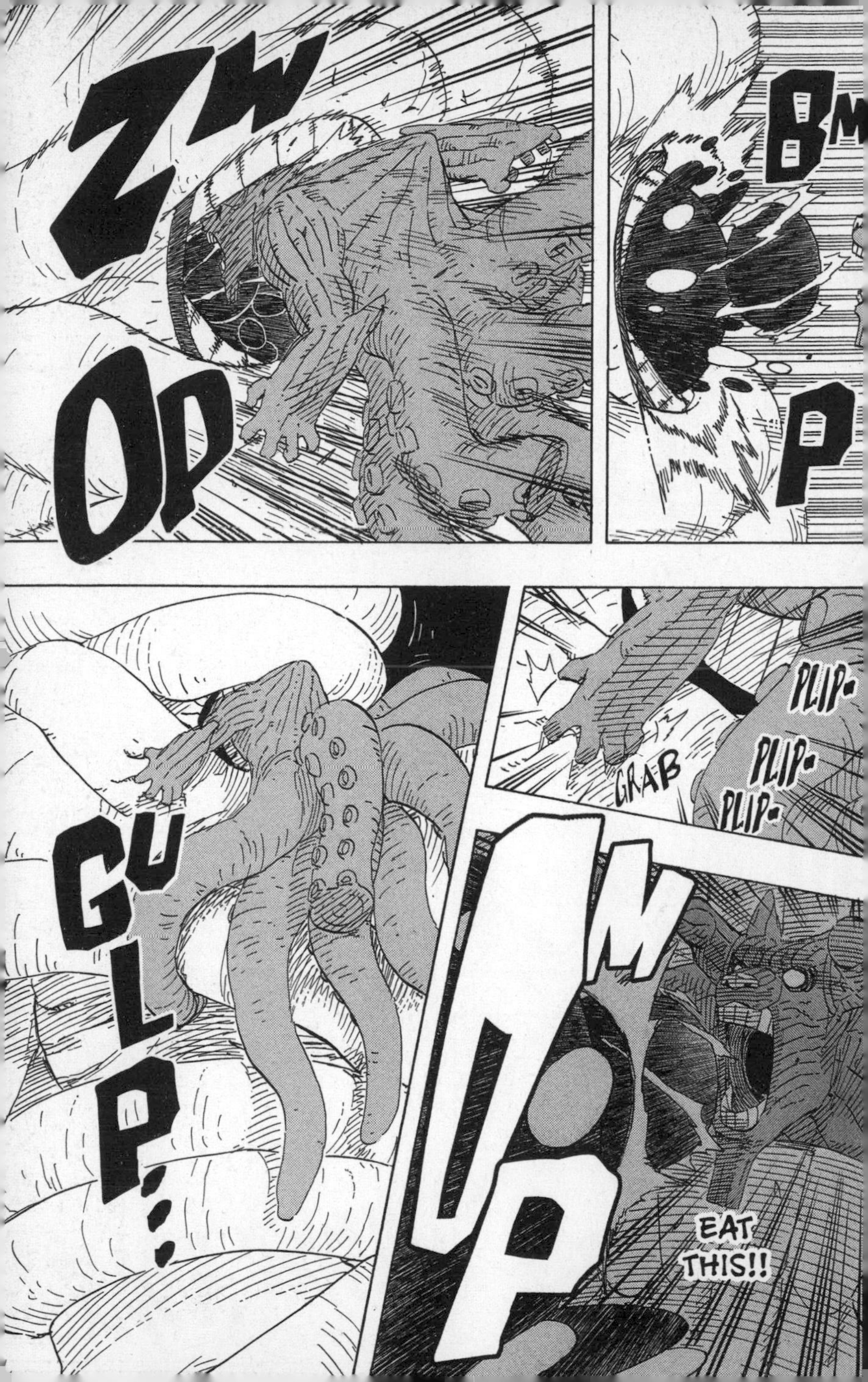
ZWOOP
PLIP-
PLIP-
PLIP-
GRAB
EAT THIS!!
GULP...

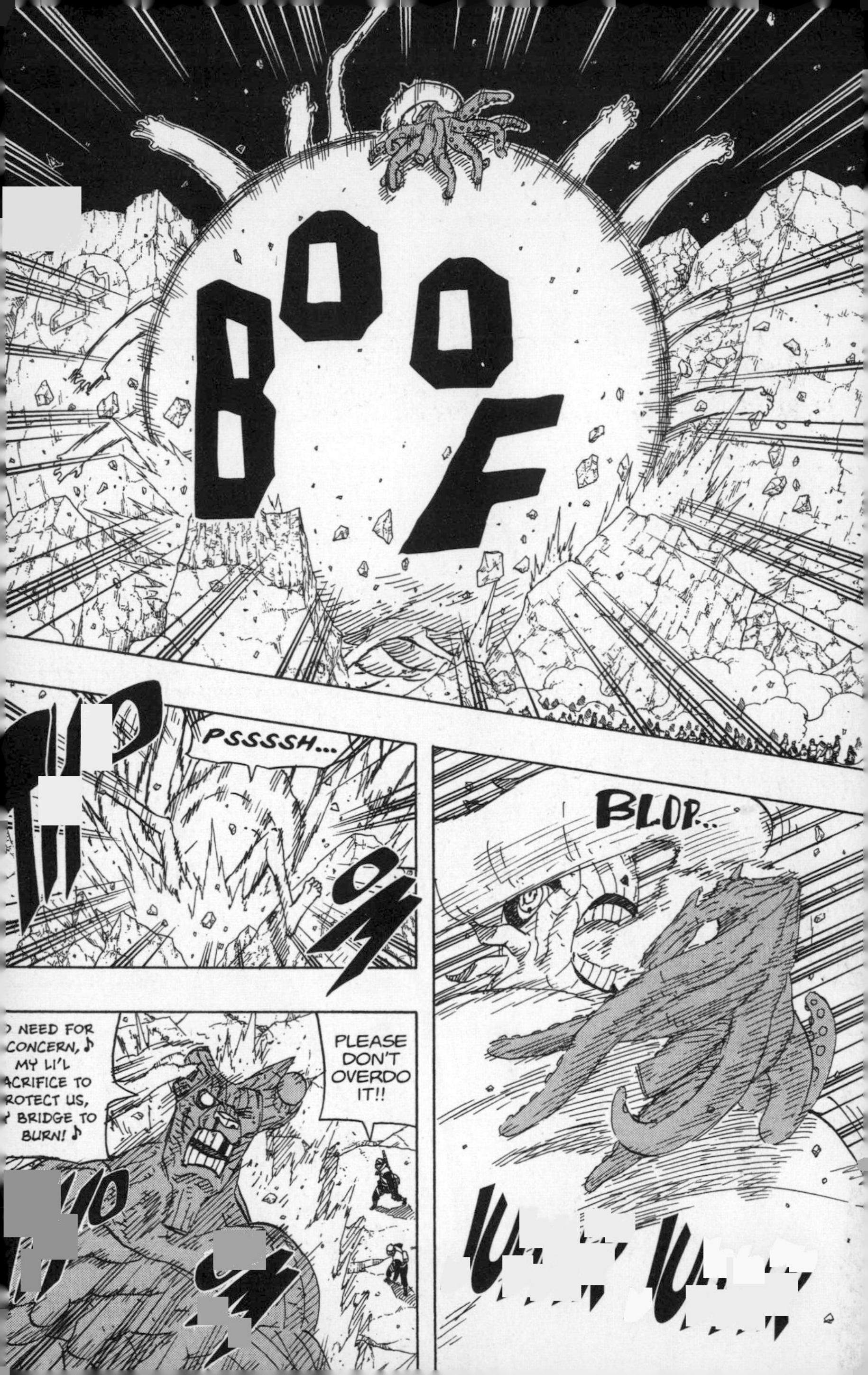
BOOF
BLOP...
PSSSSH...
PLEASE DON'T OVERDO IT!!
NEED FOR CONCERN, ♪ MY LI'L ACRIFICE TO ROTECT US, BRIDGE TO BURN! ♪

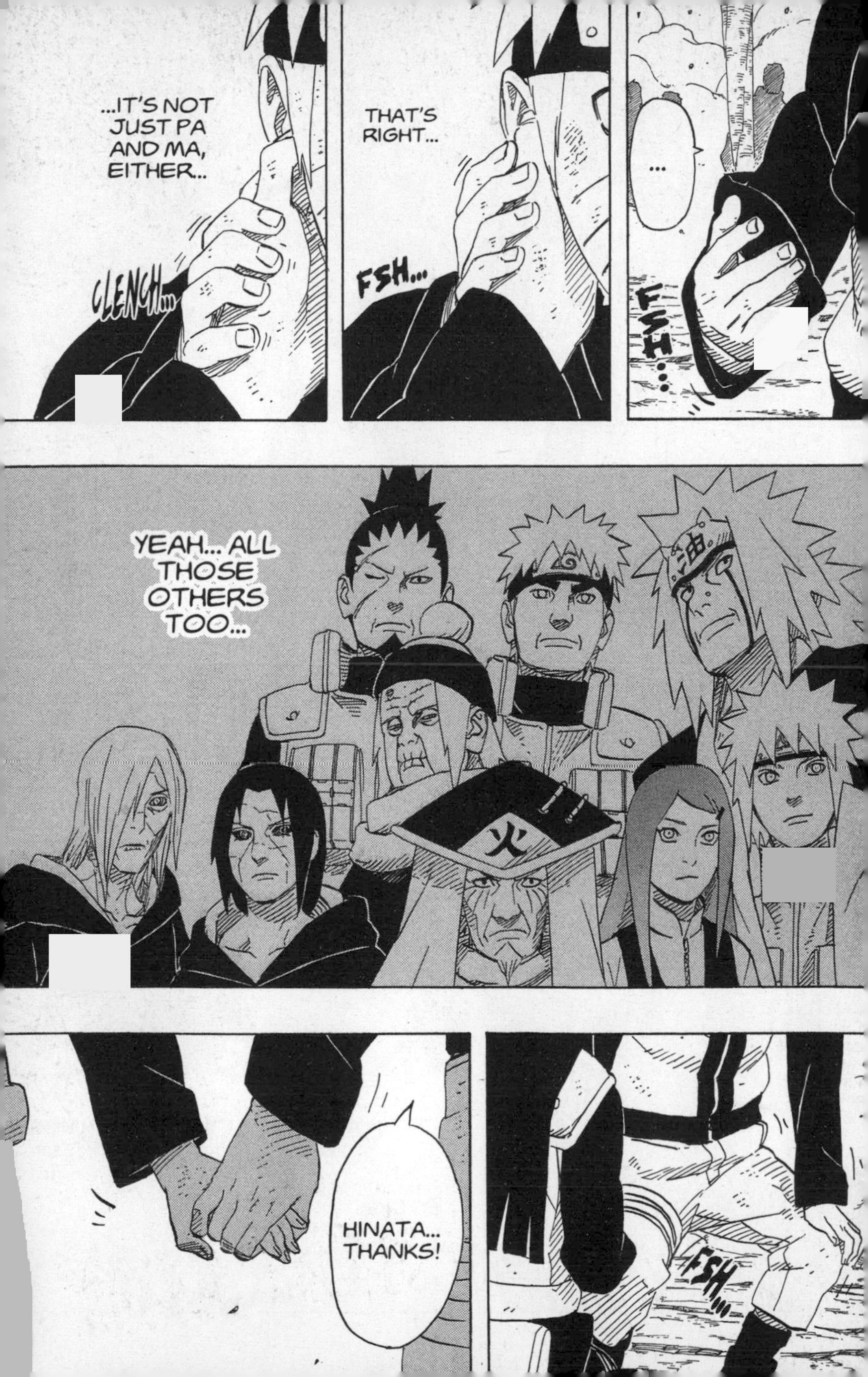
...
FSH...
THAT'S RIGHT...
FSH...
...IT'S NOT JUST PA AND MA, EITHER...
CLENCH...
YEAH... ALL THOSE OTHERS TOO...
FSH...
HINATA... THANKS!

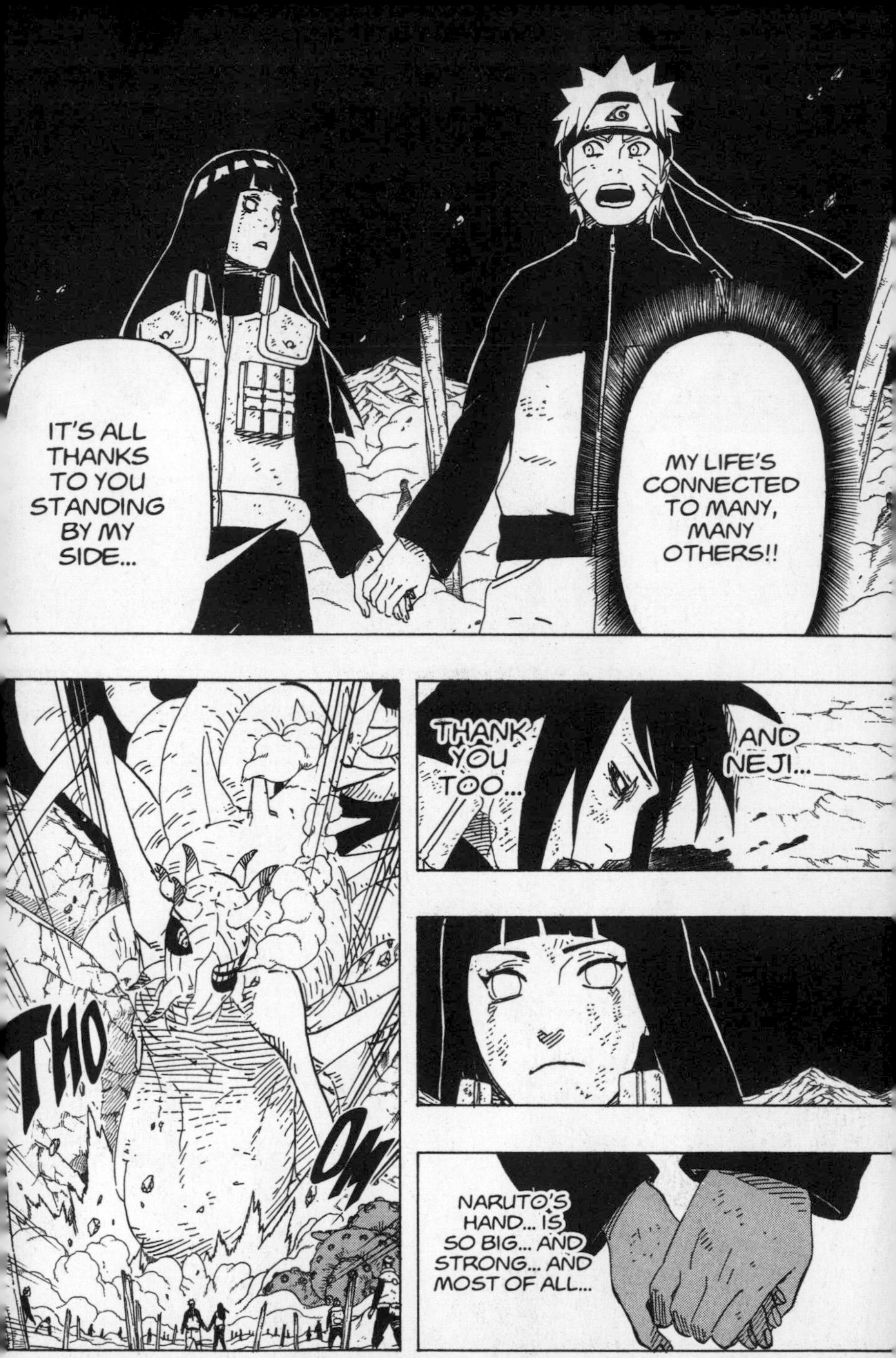
MY LIFE'S CONNECTED TO MANY, MANY OTHERS!!
IT'S ALL THANKS TO YOU STANDING BY MY SIDE...
AND NEJI...
THANK YOU TOO...
NARUTO'S HAND... IS SO BIG... AND STRONG... AND MOST OF ALL...
THOOM

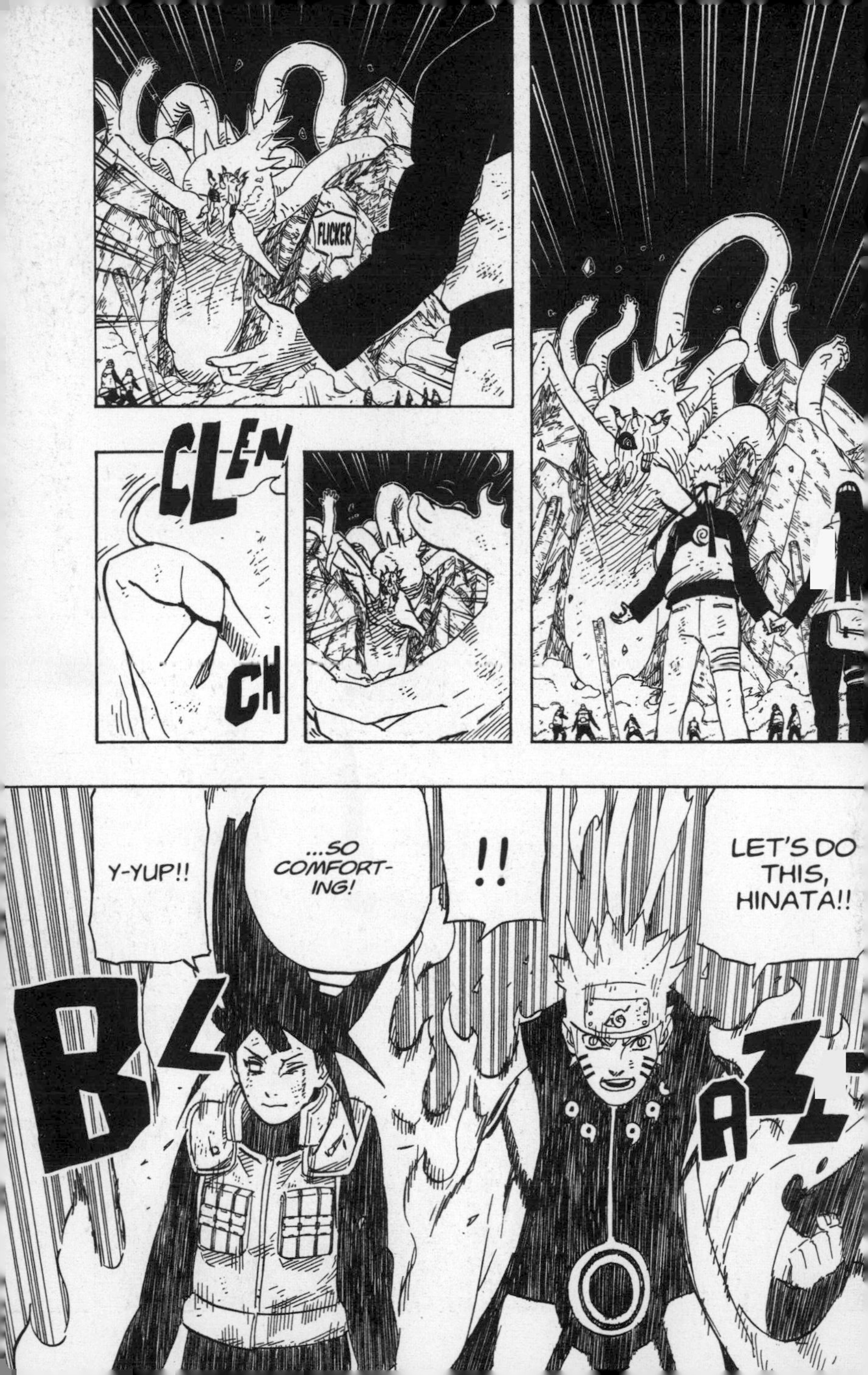
FLICKER
CLENCH
LET'S DO THIS, HINATA!!
!!
...SO COMFORTING!
Y-YUP!!
BLAZ

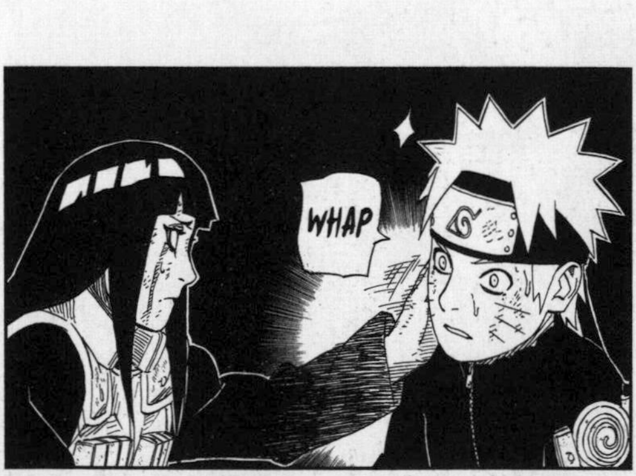
WHAP

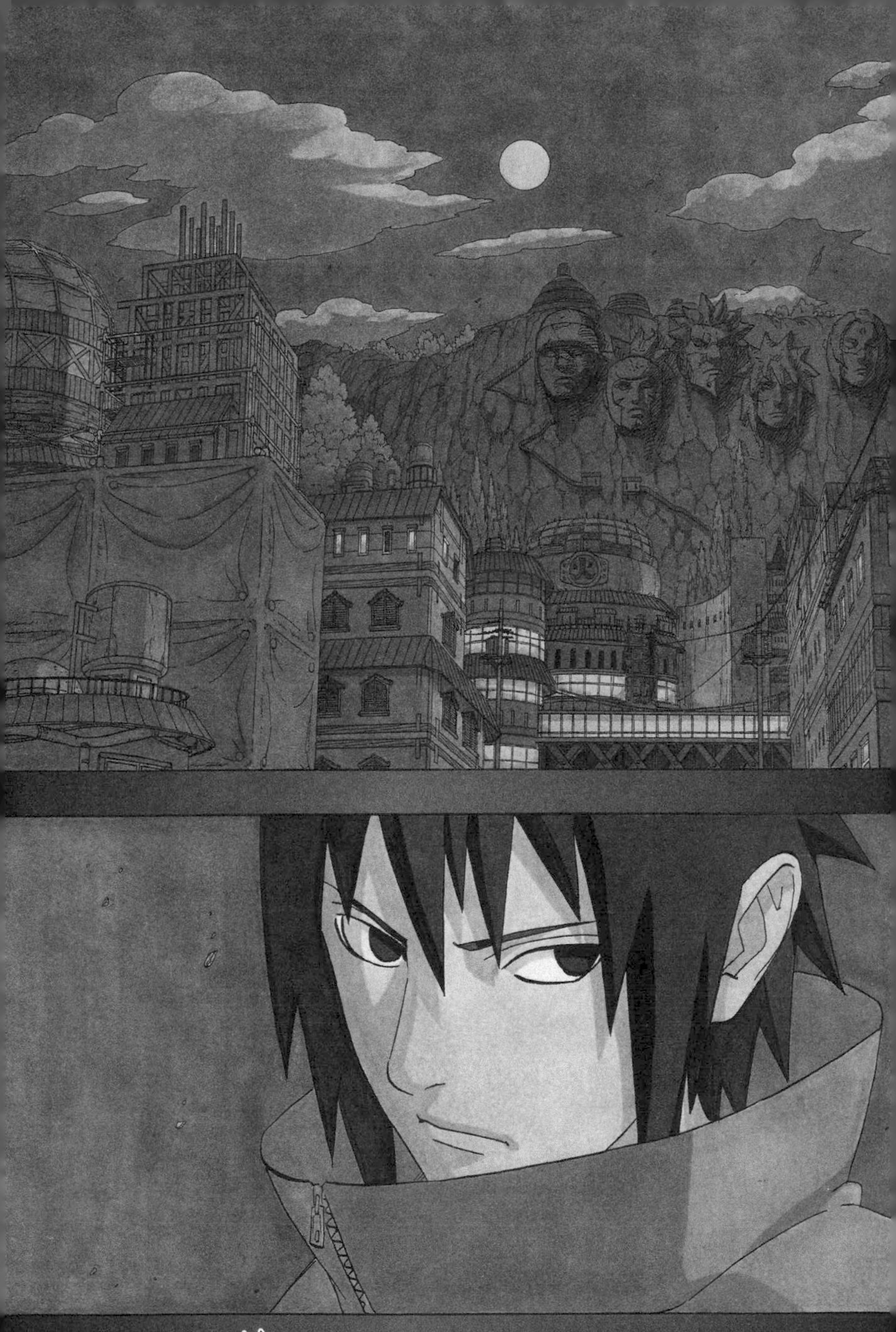

Number 616: Those Who Dance in the Shadows

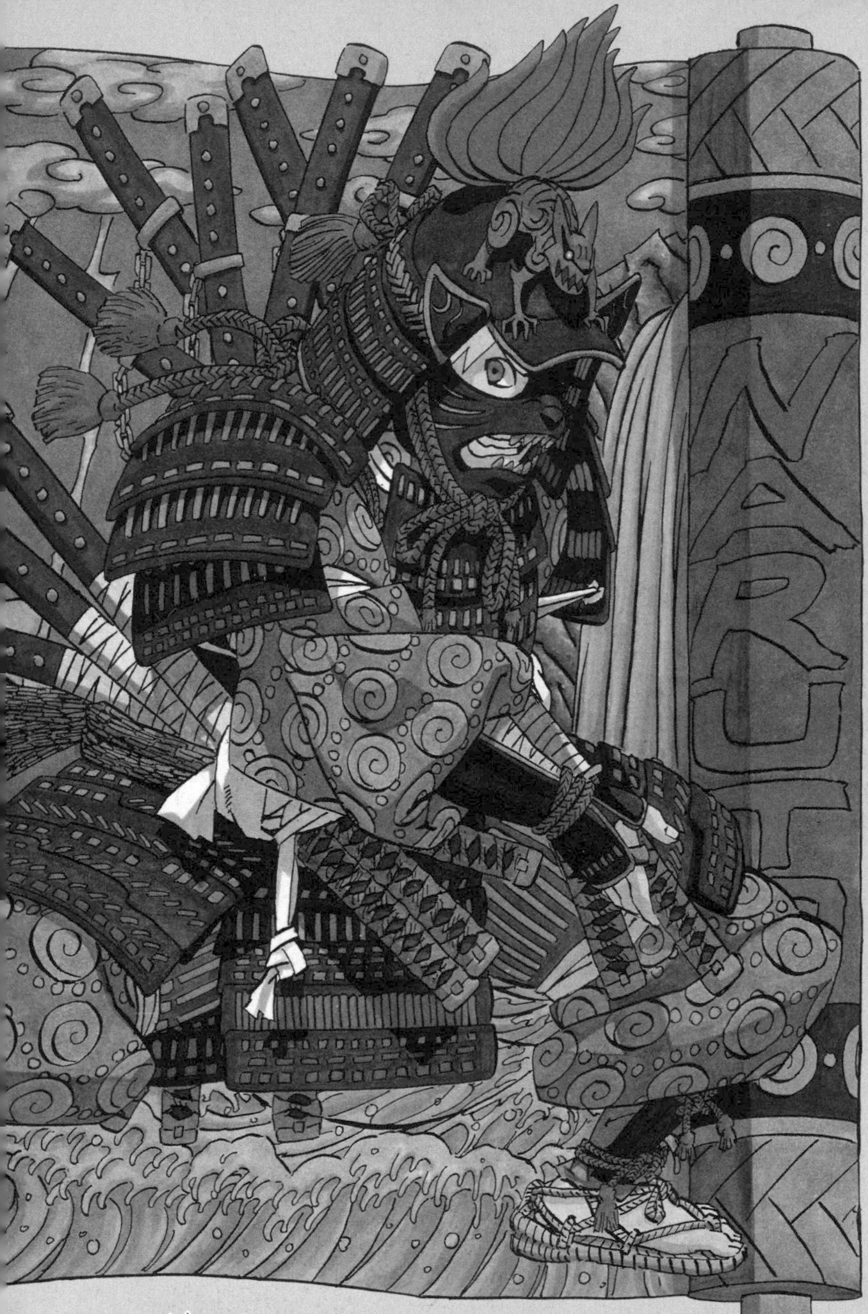
NARUTO

Number 616: Those Who Dance in the Shadows

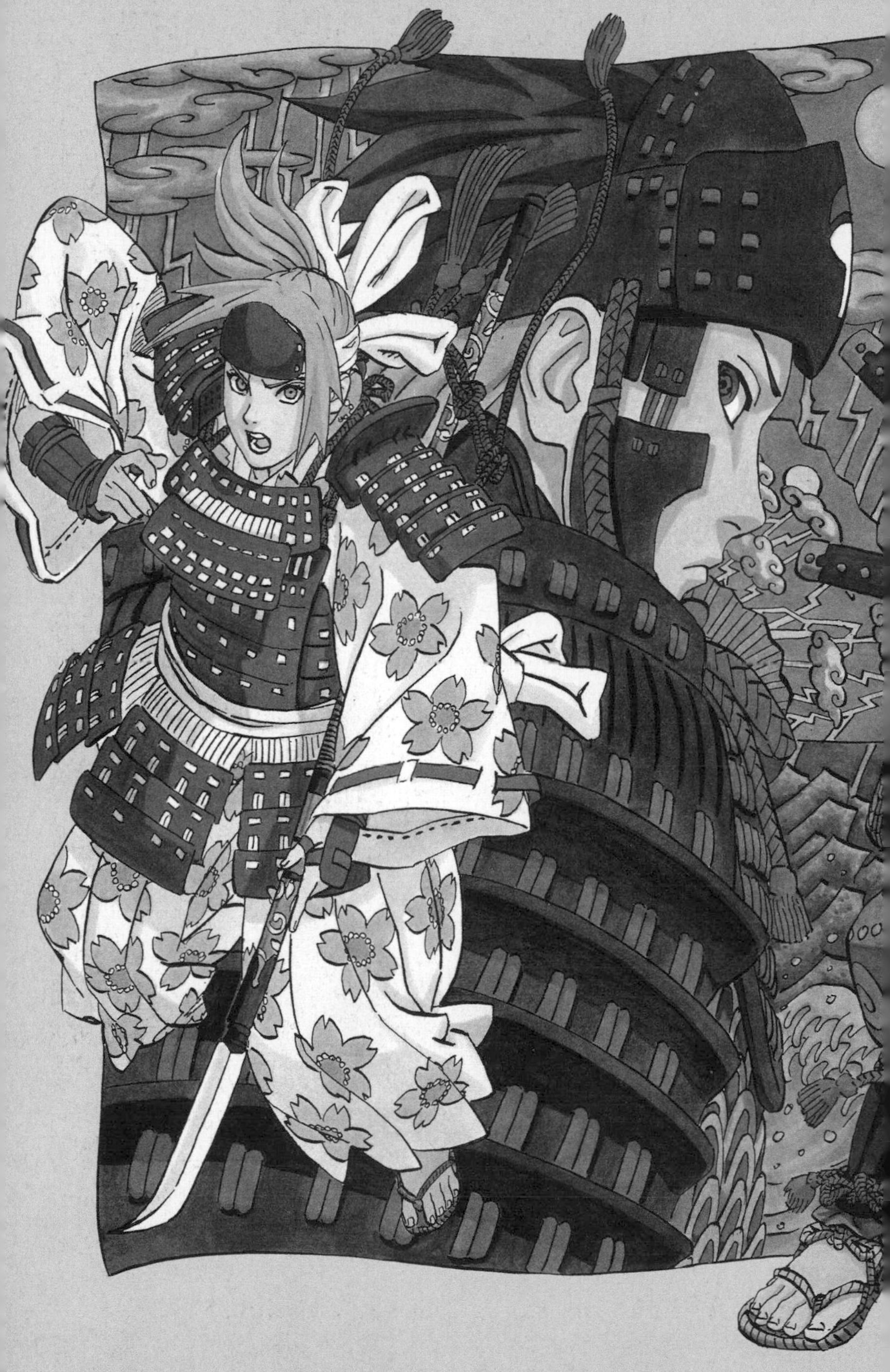

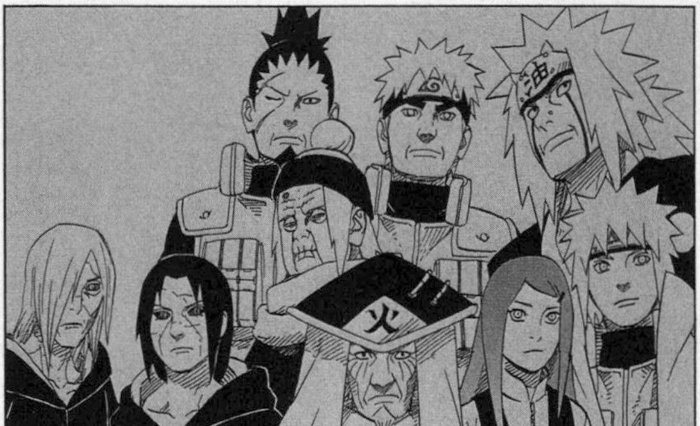
火

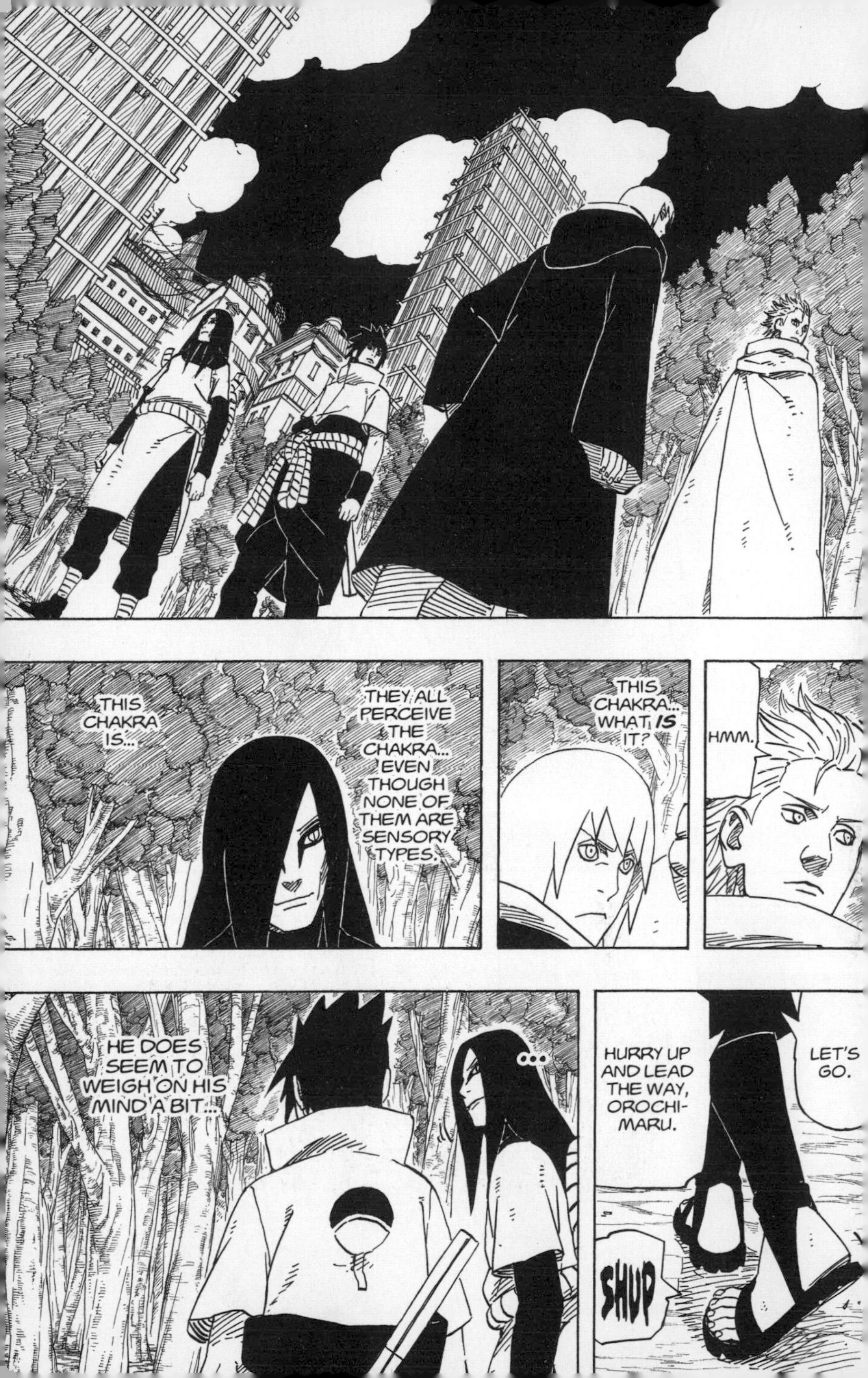
HMM.
THIS CHAKRA... WHAT IS IT?
THEY ALL PERCEIVE THE CHAKRA... EVEN THOUGH NONE OF THEM ARE SENSORY TYPES.
THIS CHAKRA IS...
LET'S GO.
HURRY UP AND LEAD THE WAY, OROCHIMARU.
SHUP
...
HE DOES SEEM TO WEIGH ON HIS MIND A BIT...

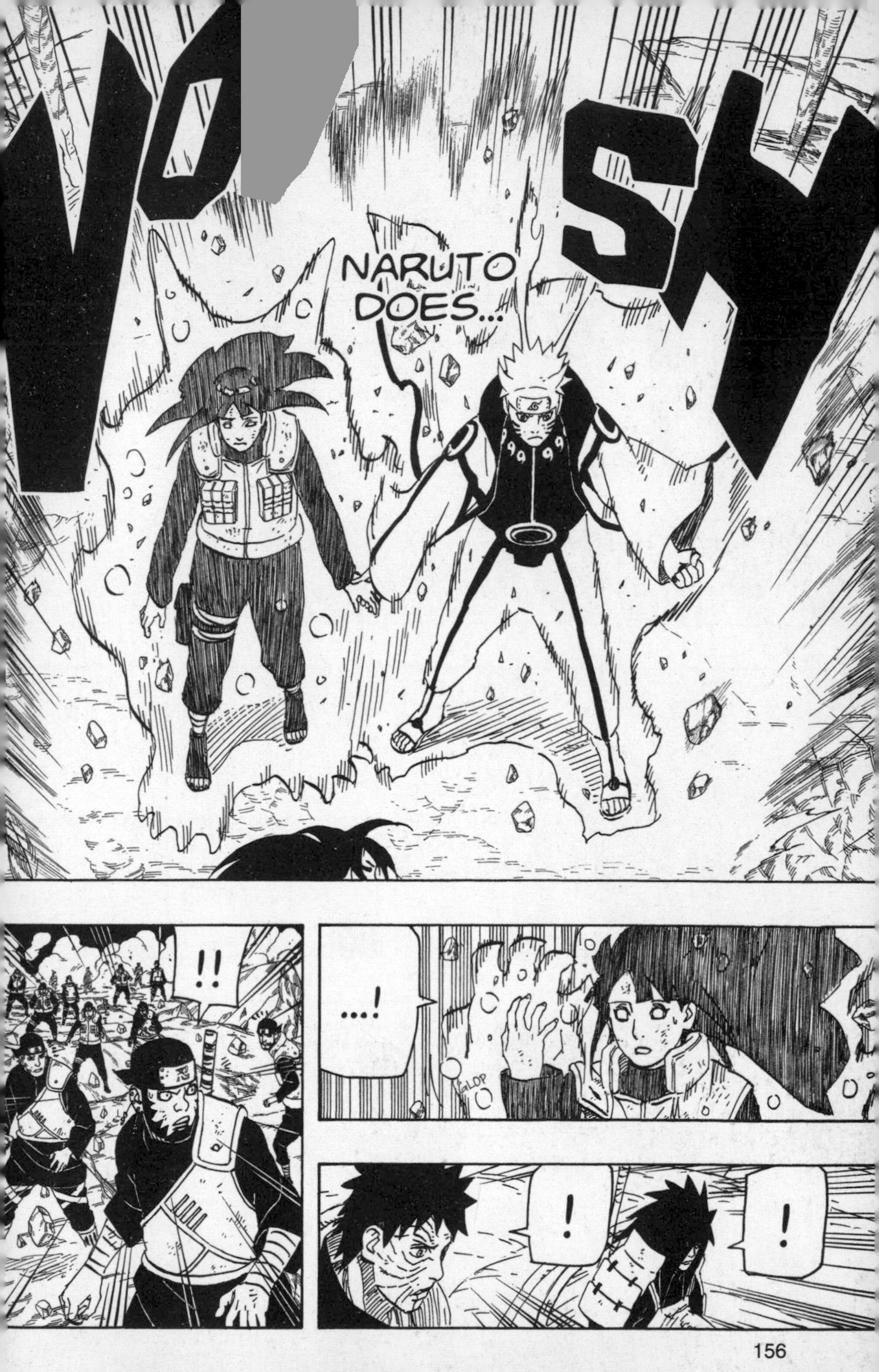
NARUTO DOES...
...!
GLOP
!
!
!!

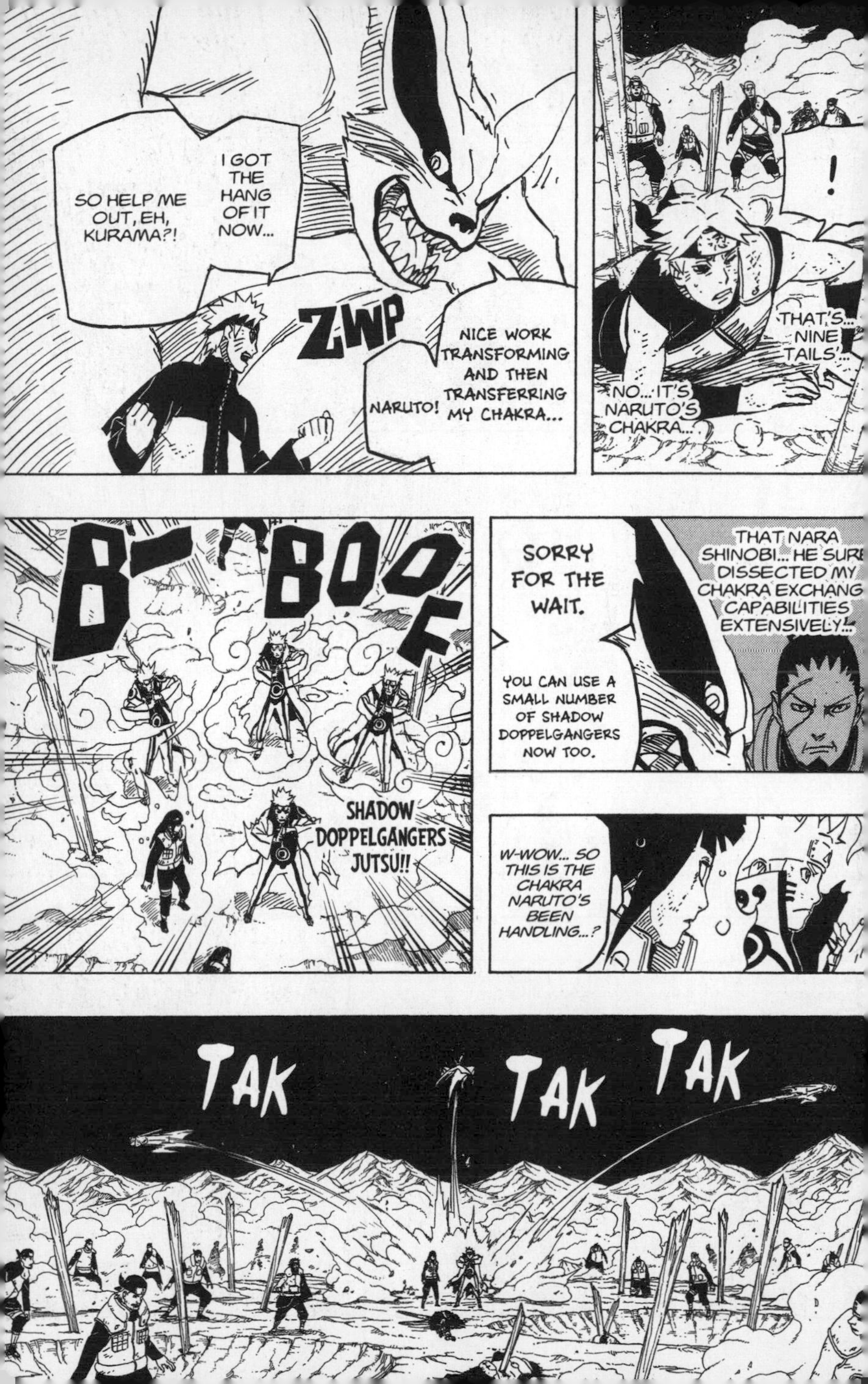
!
THAT'S... NINE TAILS'...
NO... IT'S NARUTO'S CHAKRA...
I GOT THE HANG OF IT NOW...
SO HELP ME OUT, EH, KURAMA?!
ZWP
NICE WORK TRANSFORMING AND THEN TRANSFERRING MY CHAKRA...
NARUTO!
THAT NARA SHINOBI... HE SUR DISSECTED MY CHAKRA EXCHANG CAPABILITIES EXTENSIVELY!...
SORRY FOR THE WAIT.
YOU CAN USE A SMALL NUMBER OF SHADOW DOPPELGANGERS NOW TOO.
W-WOW... SO THIS IS THE CHAKRA NARUTO'S BEEN HANDLING...?
B-BOOF
SHADOW DOPPELGANGERS JUTSU!!
TAK
TAK
TAK

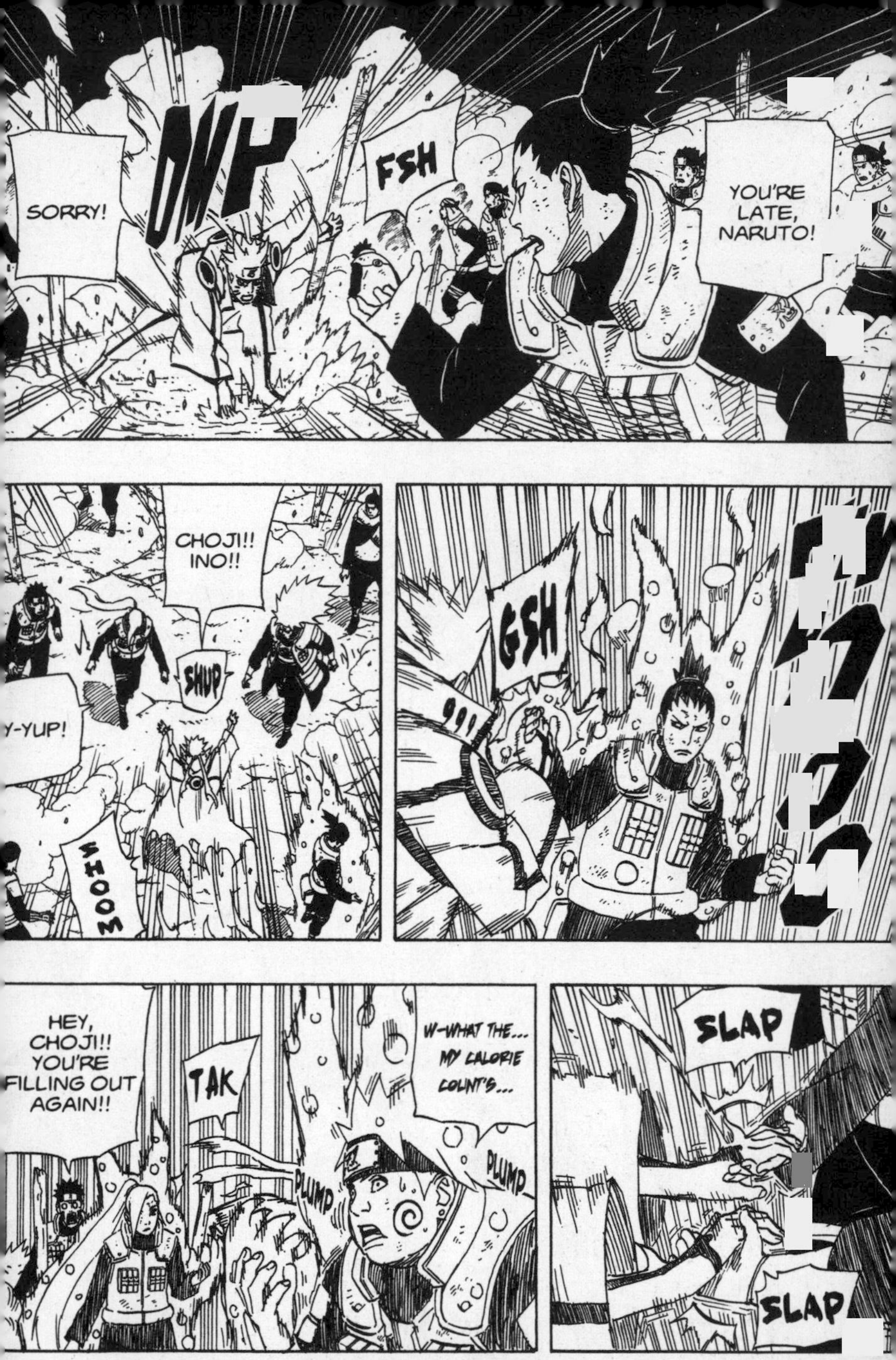

YOU'RE LATE, NARUTO!
FSH
SORRY!
GSH
CHOJI!! INO!!
SHUP
Y-YUP!
SHOOM
SLAP
SLAP
W-WHAT THE... MY CALORIE COUNT'S...
PLUMP
PLUMP
TAK
HEY, CHOJI!! YOU'RE FILLING OUT AGAIN!!

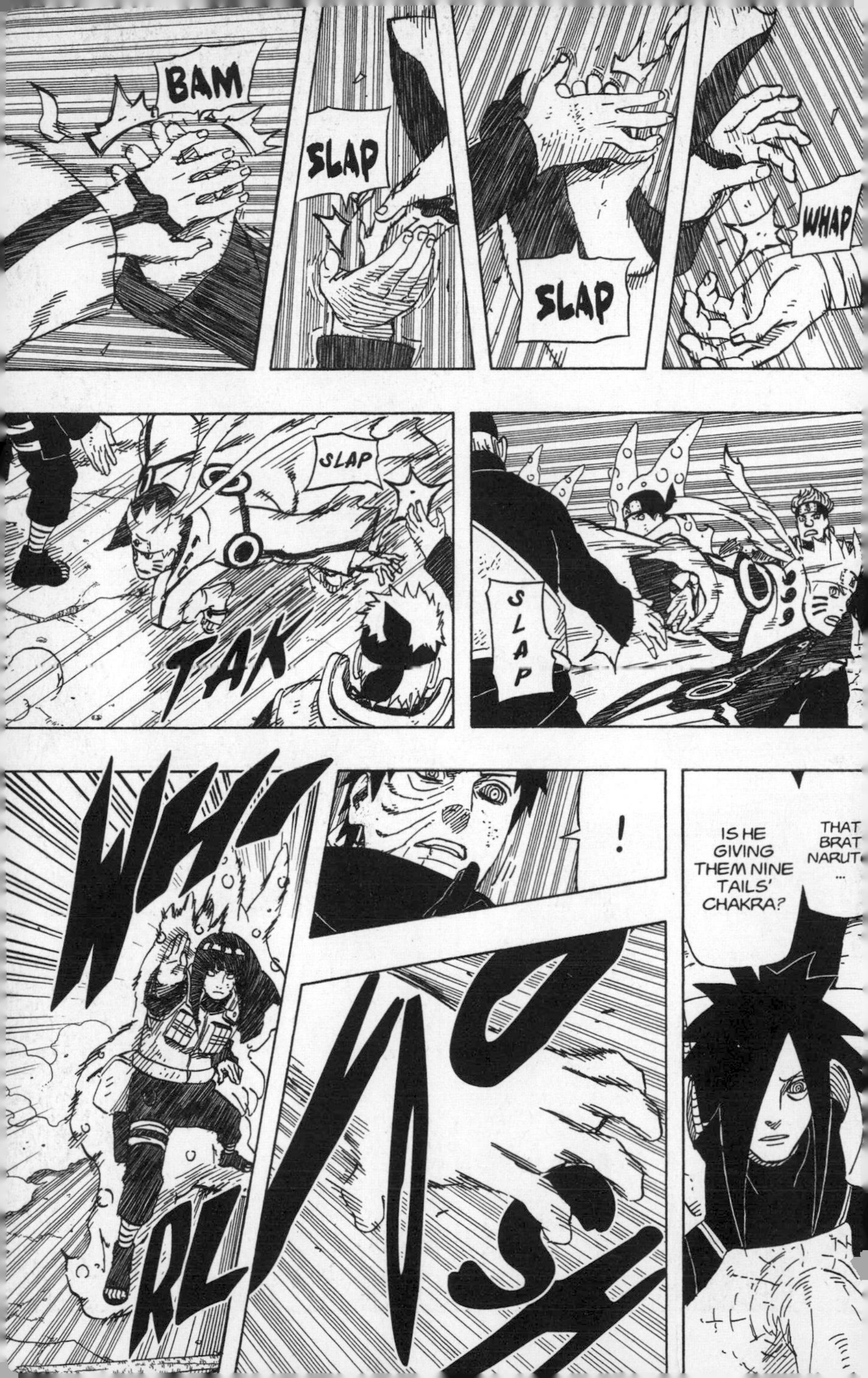
WHAP
SLAP
SLAP
BAM
SLAP
SLAP
TAK
THAT BRAT NARUT ...
IS HE GIVING THEM NINE TAILS' CHAKRA?
!

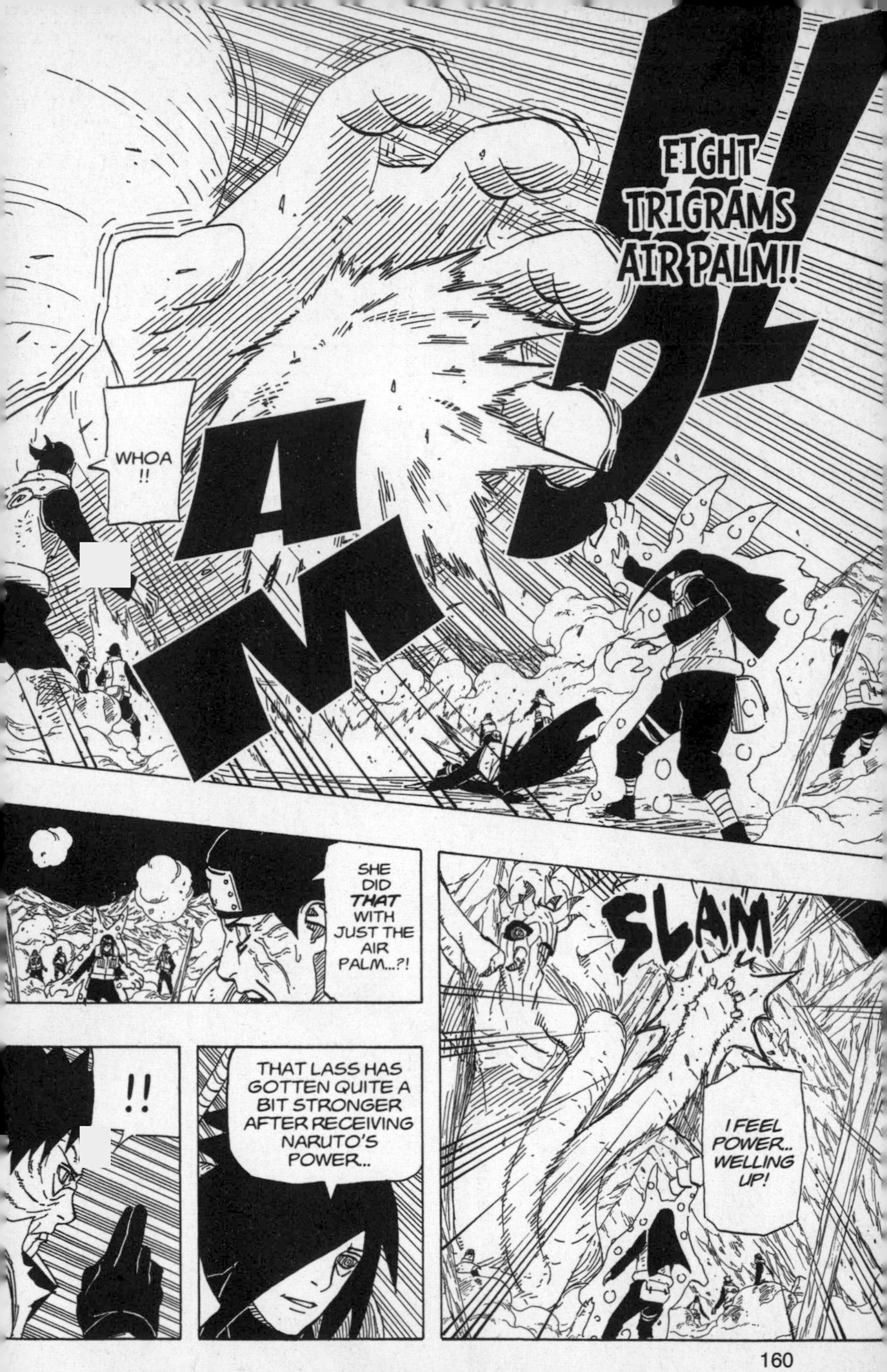
EIGHT TRIGRAMS AIR PALM!!
WHOA !!
SLAM
I FEEL POWER... WELLING UP!
SHE DID THAT WITH JUST THE AIR PALM...?!
THAT LASS HAS GOTTEN QUITE A BIT STRONGER AFTER RECEIVING NARUTO'S POWER...
!!

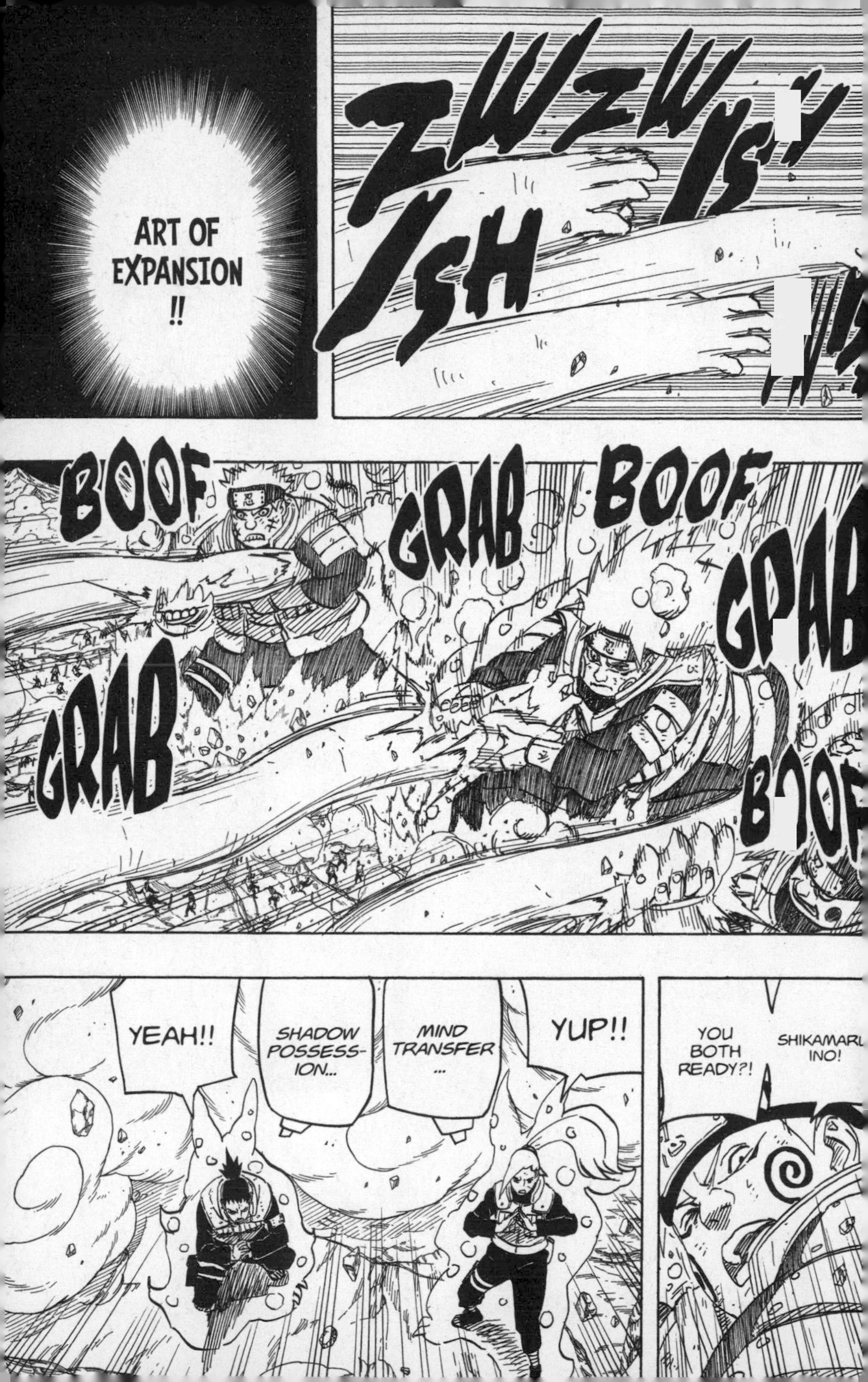
ART OF EXPANSION !!
BOOF
GRAB
BOOF
GRAB
SHIKAMARU, INO!
YOU BOTH READY?!
YUP!!
MIND TRANSFER ...
SHADOW POSSESS-ION...
YEAH!!

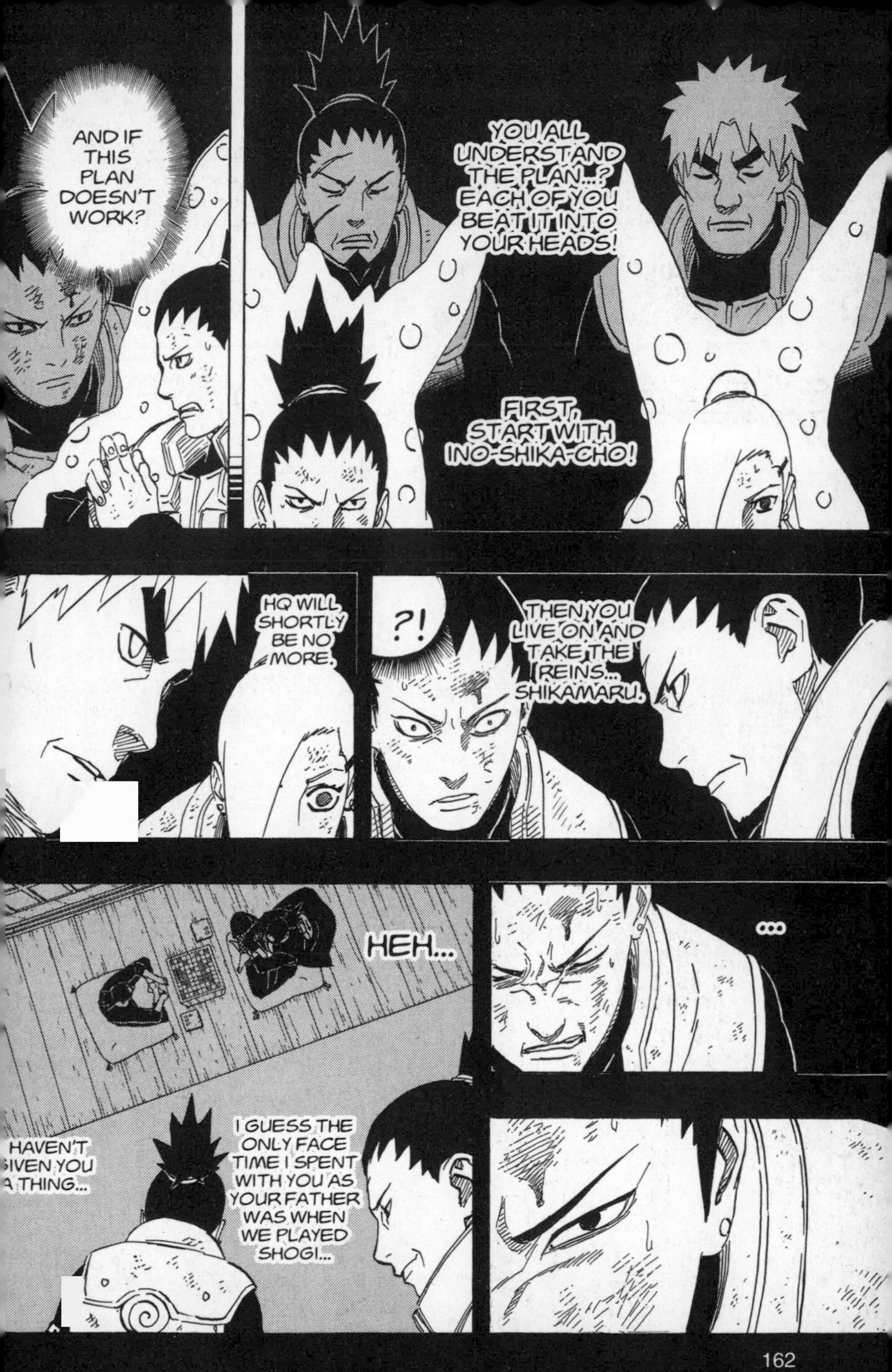
YOU ALL UNDERSTAND THE PLAN...? EACH OF YOU BEAT IT INTO YOUR HEADS!
FIRST, START WITH INO-SHIKA-CHO!
AND IF THIS PLAN DOESN'T WORK?
THEN YOU LIVE ON AND TAKE THE REINS... SHIKAMARU.
?!
HQ WILL SHORTLY BE NO MORE.
...
HEH...
I GUESS THE ONLY FACE TIME I SPENT WITH YOU AS YOUR FATHER WAS WHEN WE PLAYED SHOGI...
HAVEN'T GIVEN YOU A THING...

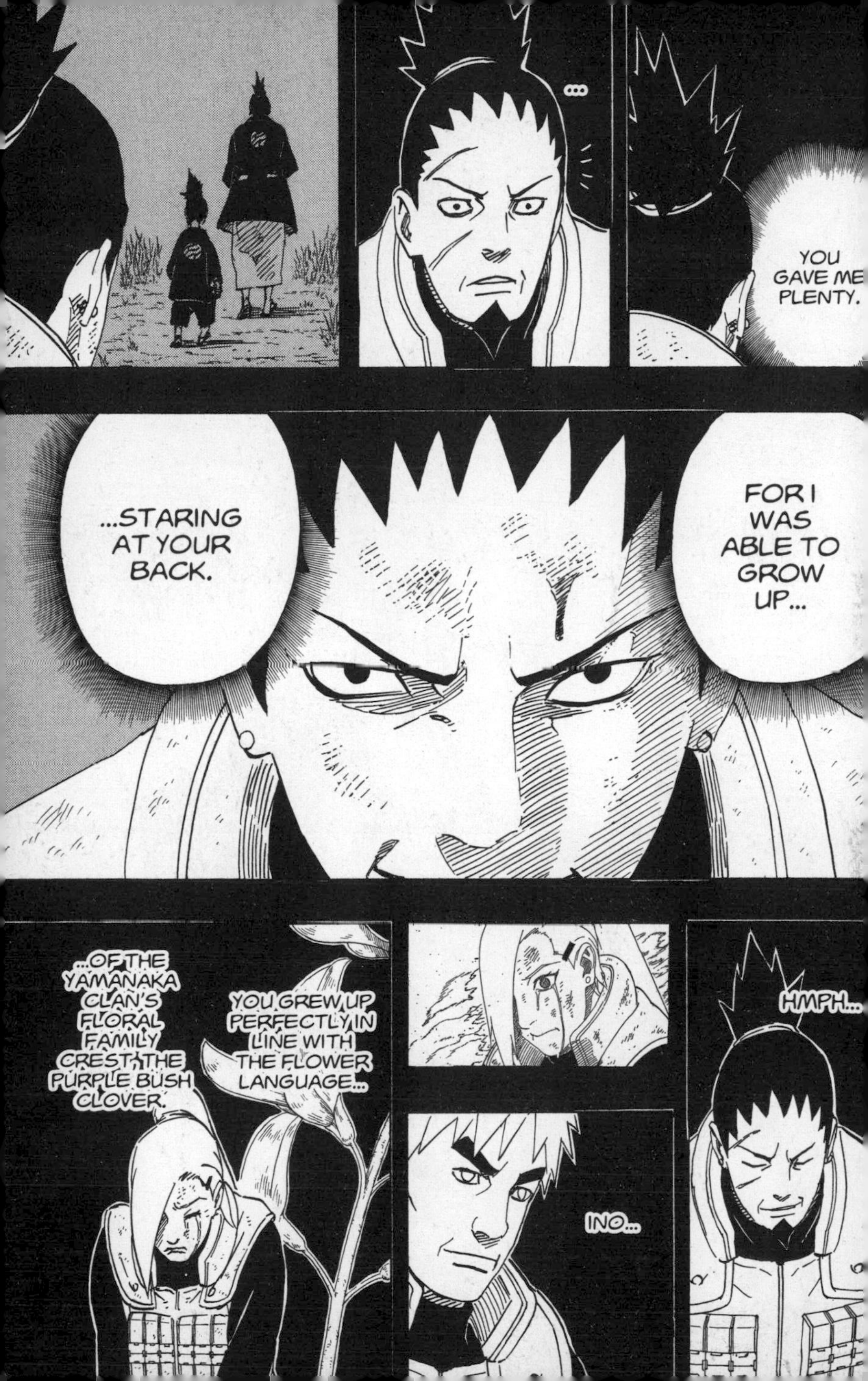
YOU GAVE ME PLENTY.
...
FOR I WAS ABLE TO GROW UP...
...STARING AT YOUR BACK.
HMPH...
INO...
YOU GREW UP PERFECTLY IN LINE WITH THE FLOWER LANGUAGE...
...OF THE YAMANAKA CLAN'S FLORAL FAMILY CREST, THE PURPLE BUSH CLOVER.

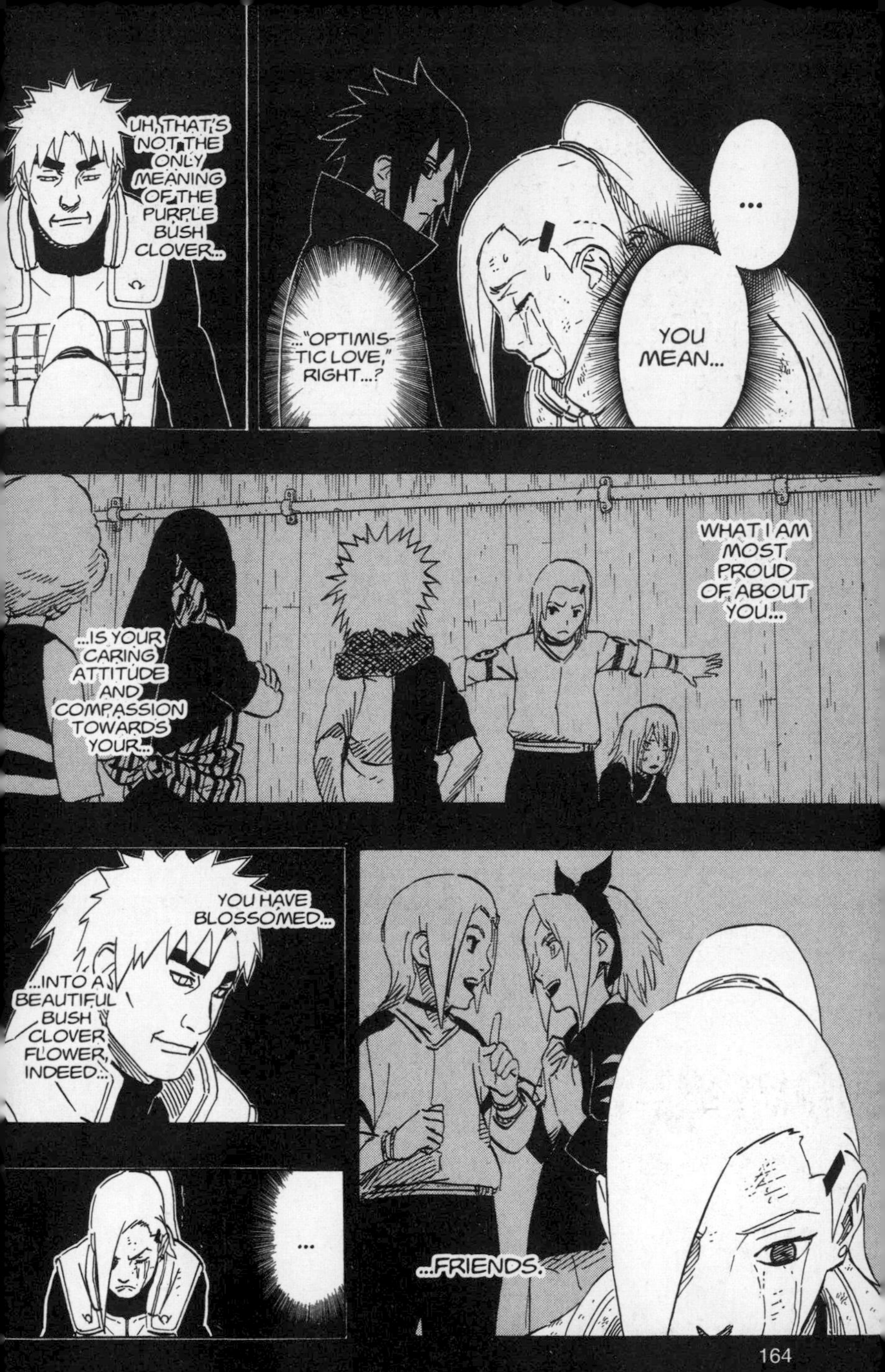
...
YOU MEAN...
..."OPTIMISTIC LOVE," RIGHT...?
UH, THAT'S NOT THE ONLY MEANING OF THE PURPLE BUSH CLOVER...
WHAT I AM MOST PROUD OF ABOUT YOU...
...IS YOUR CARING ATTITUDE AND COMPASSION TOWARDS YOUR...
...FRIENDS.
YOU HAVE BLOSSOMED...
...INTO A BEAUTIFUL BUSH CLOVER FLOWER, INDEED...
...

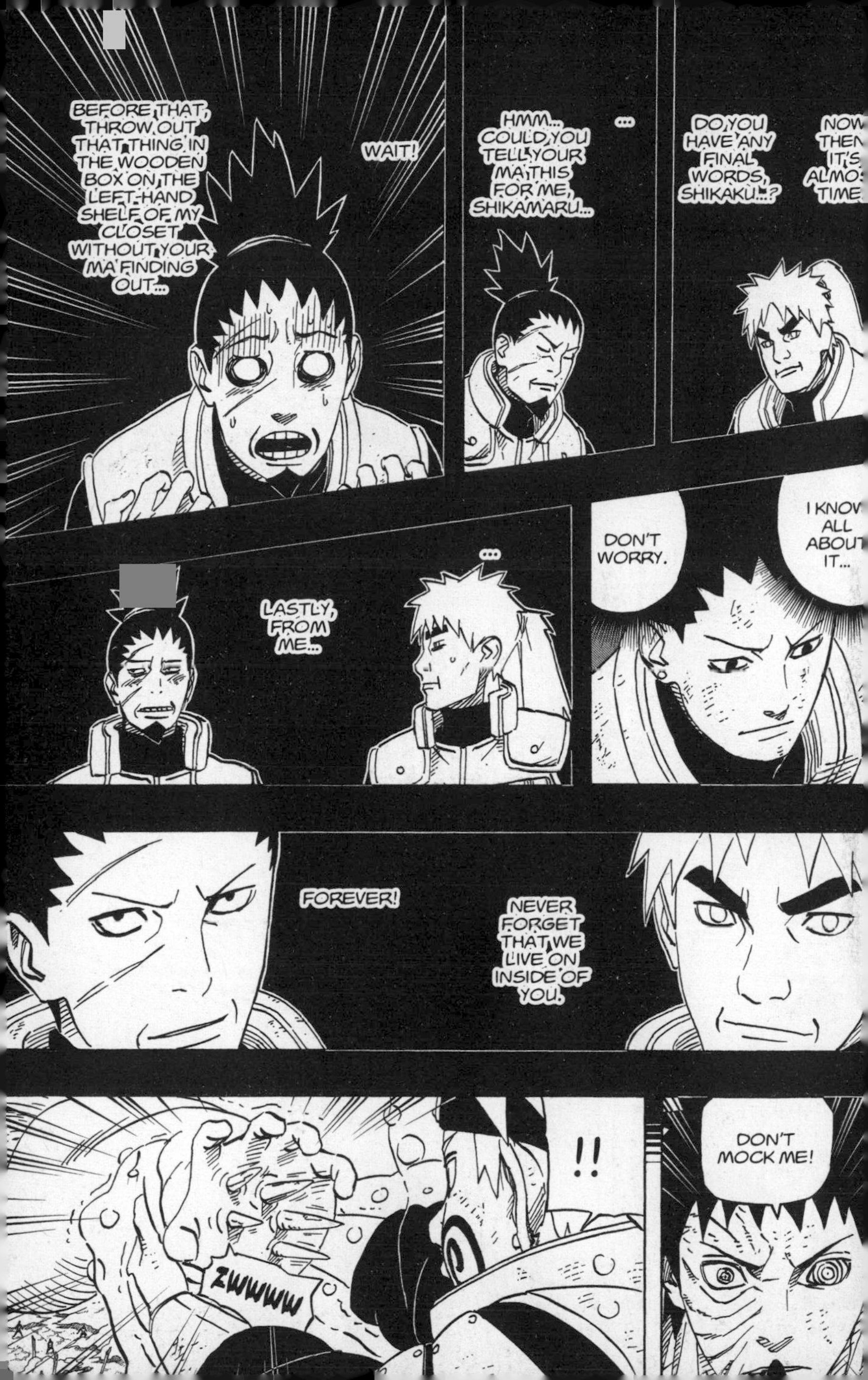

NOW THEN IT'S ALMOS TIME
DO YOU HAVE ANY FINAL WORDS, SHIKAKU...?
...
HMM... COULD YOU TELL YOUR MA THIS FOR ME, SHIKAMARU...
WAIT!
BEFORE THAT, THROW OUT THAT THING IN THE WOODEN BOX ON THE LEFT-HAND SHELF OF MY CLOSET WITHOUT YOUR MA FINDING OUT...
I KNOW ALL ABOUT IT...
DON'T WORRY.
...
LASTLY, FROM ME...
NEVER FORGET THAT WE LIVE ON INSIDE OF YOU.
FOREVER!
DON'T MOCK ME!
!!
ZWWWW

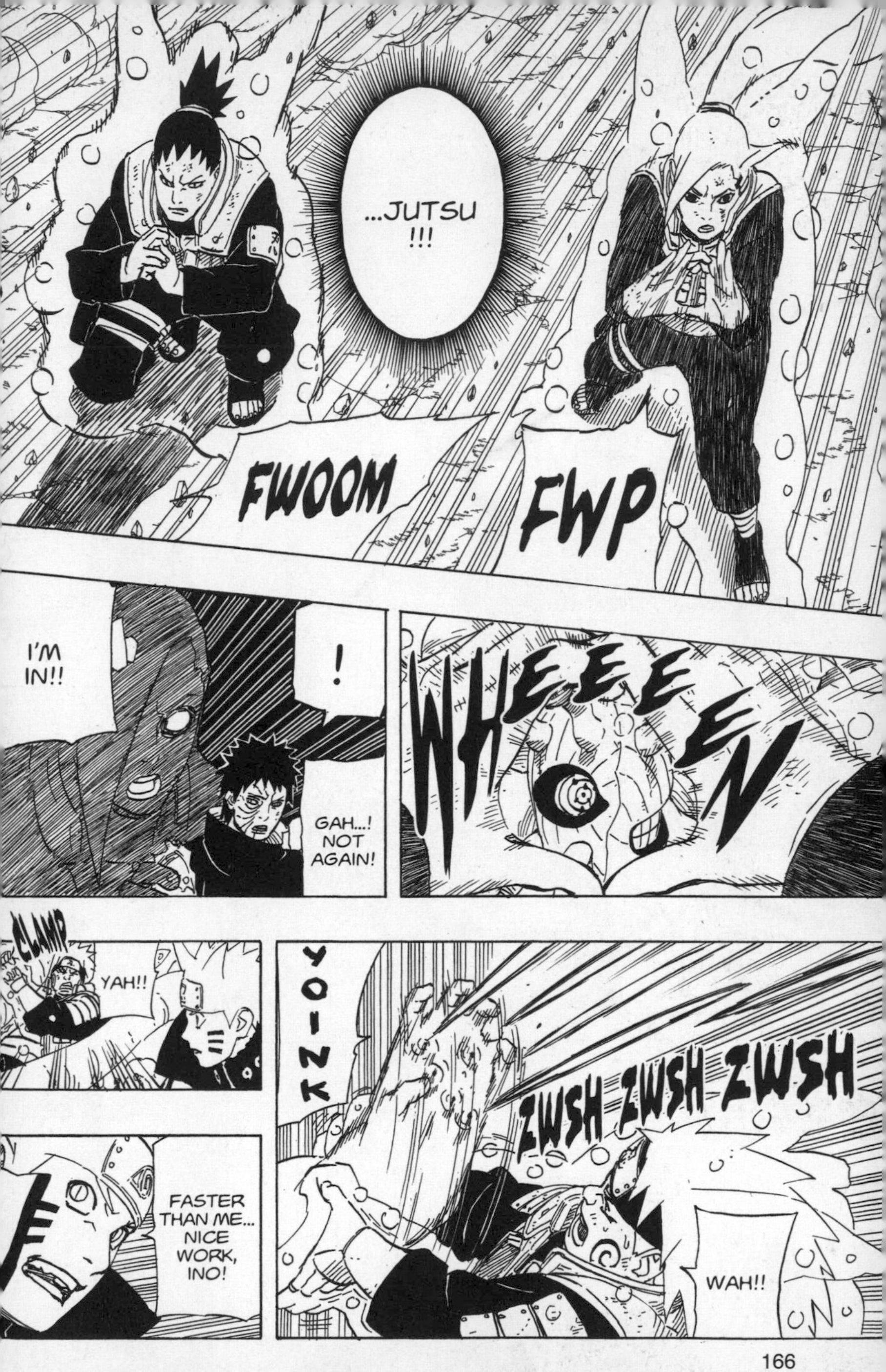
...JUTSU !!!
FWP
FWOOM
WHEEEEN
I'M IN!!
!
GAH...! NOT AGAIN!
YOINK
ZWSH ZWSH ZWSH
WAH!!
CLAMP
YAH!!
FASTER THAN ME... NICE WORK, INO!

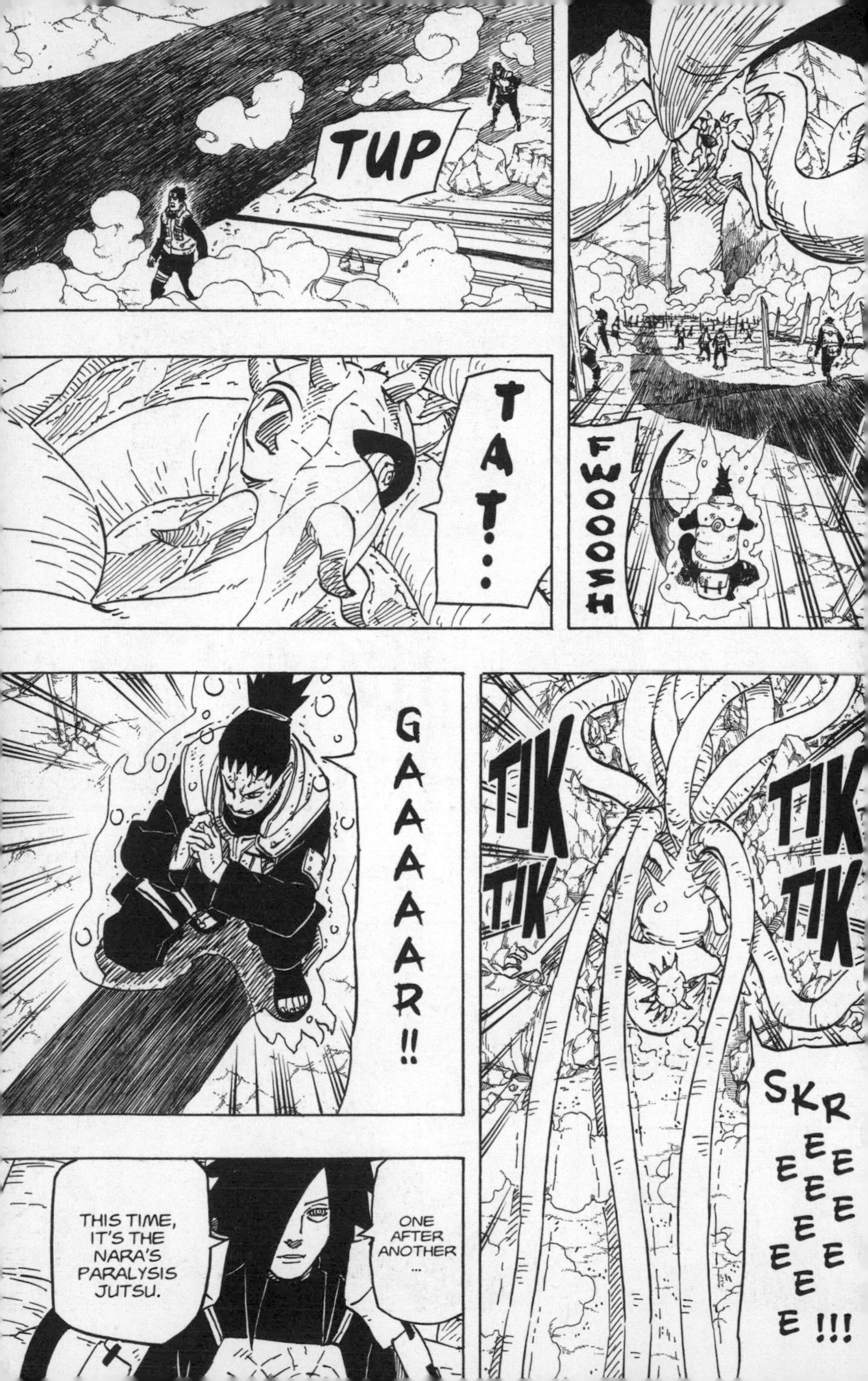
FWOOOSH
TUP
TAT...
TIK TIK
TIK TIK
SKREEEEEEEEE!!!
GAAAAR!!
ONE AFTER ANOTHER...
THIS TIME, IT'S THE NARA'S PARALYSIS JUTSU.

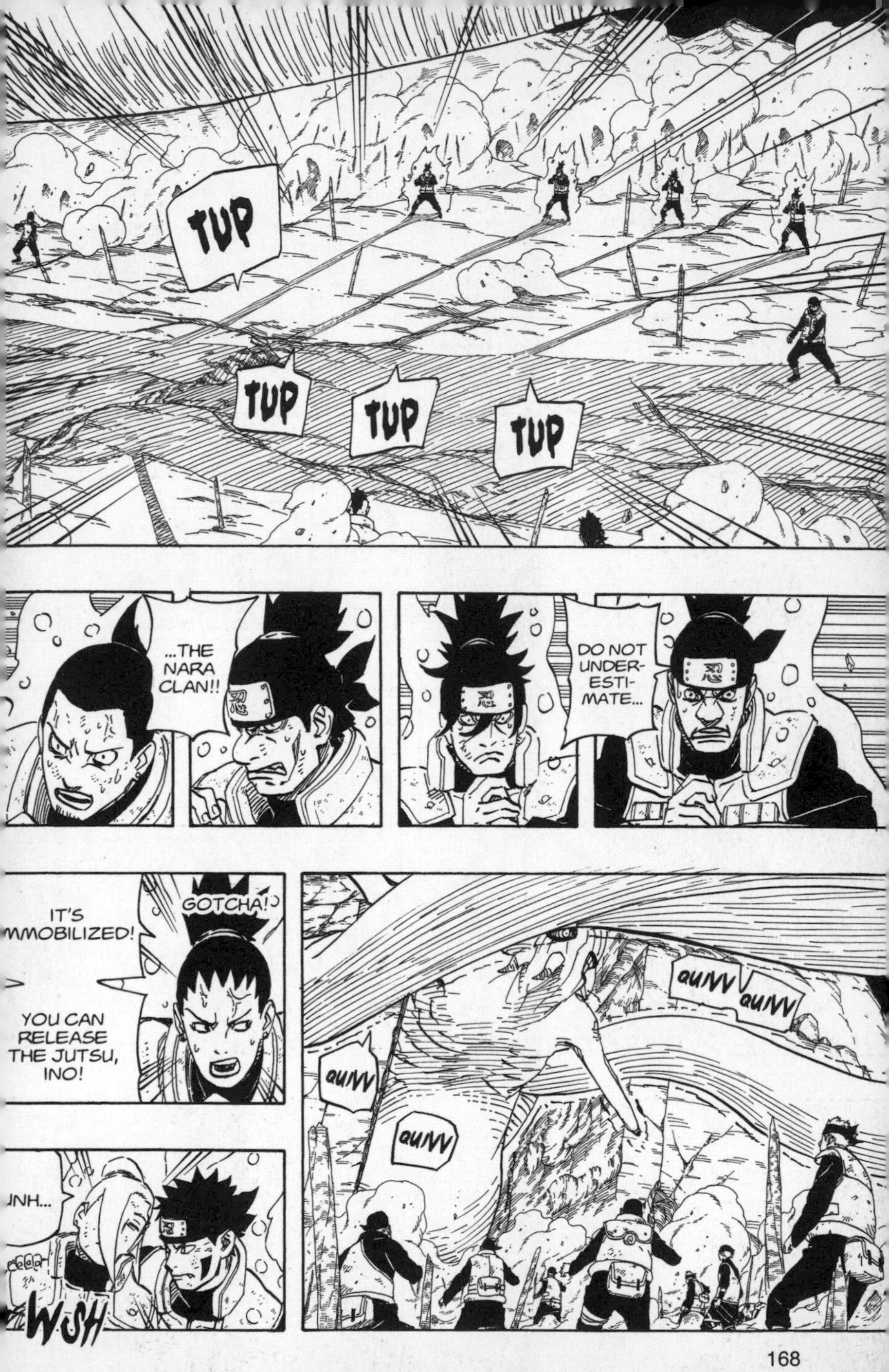
TUP
TUP
TUP
TUP
DO NOT UNDER-ESTI-MATE...
...THE NARA CLAN!!
QUIVV
QUIVV
QUIVV
QUIVV
GOTCHA!
IT'S MMOBILIZED!
YOU CAN RELEASE THE JUTSU, INO!
NH...
WSH

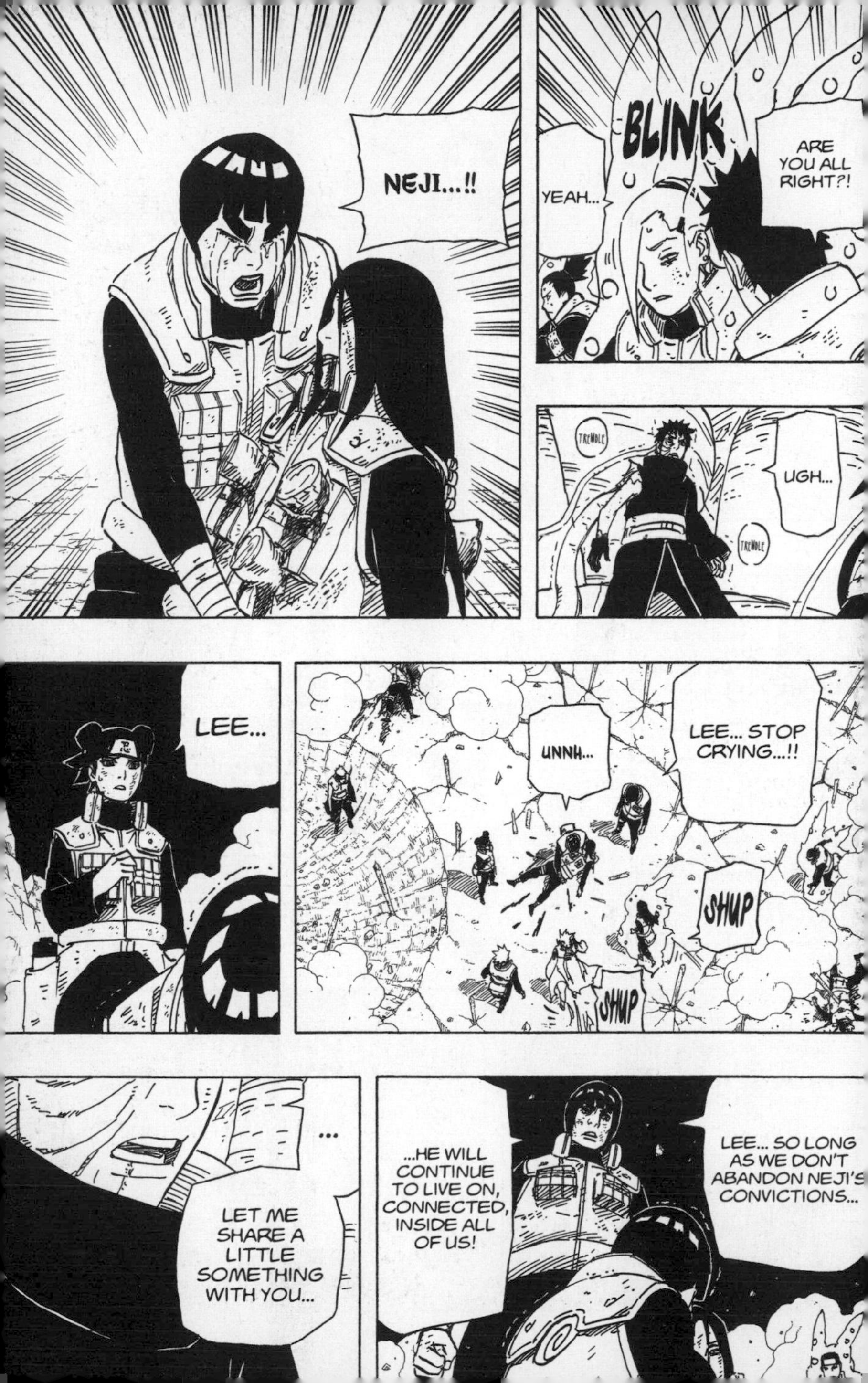
BLINK
ARE YOU ALL RIGHT?!
YEAH...
TREMBLE
UGH...
TREMBLE
NEJI...!!
LEE... STOP CRYING...!!
UNNH...
SHUP
SHUP
LEE...
LEE... SO LONG AS WE DON'T ABANDON NEJI'S CONVICTIONS...
...HE WILL CONTINUE TO LIVE ON, CONNECTED, INSIDE ALL OF US!
...
LET ME SHARE A LITTLE SOMETHING WITH YOU...

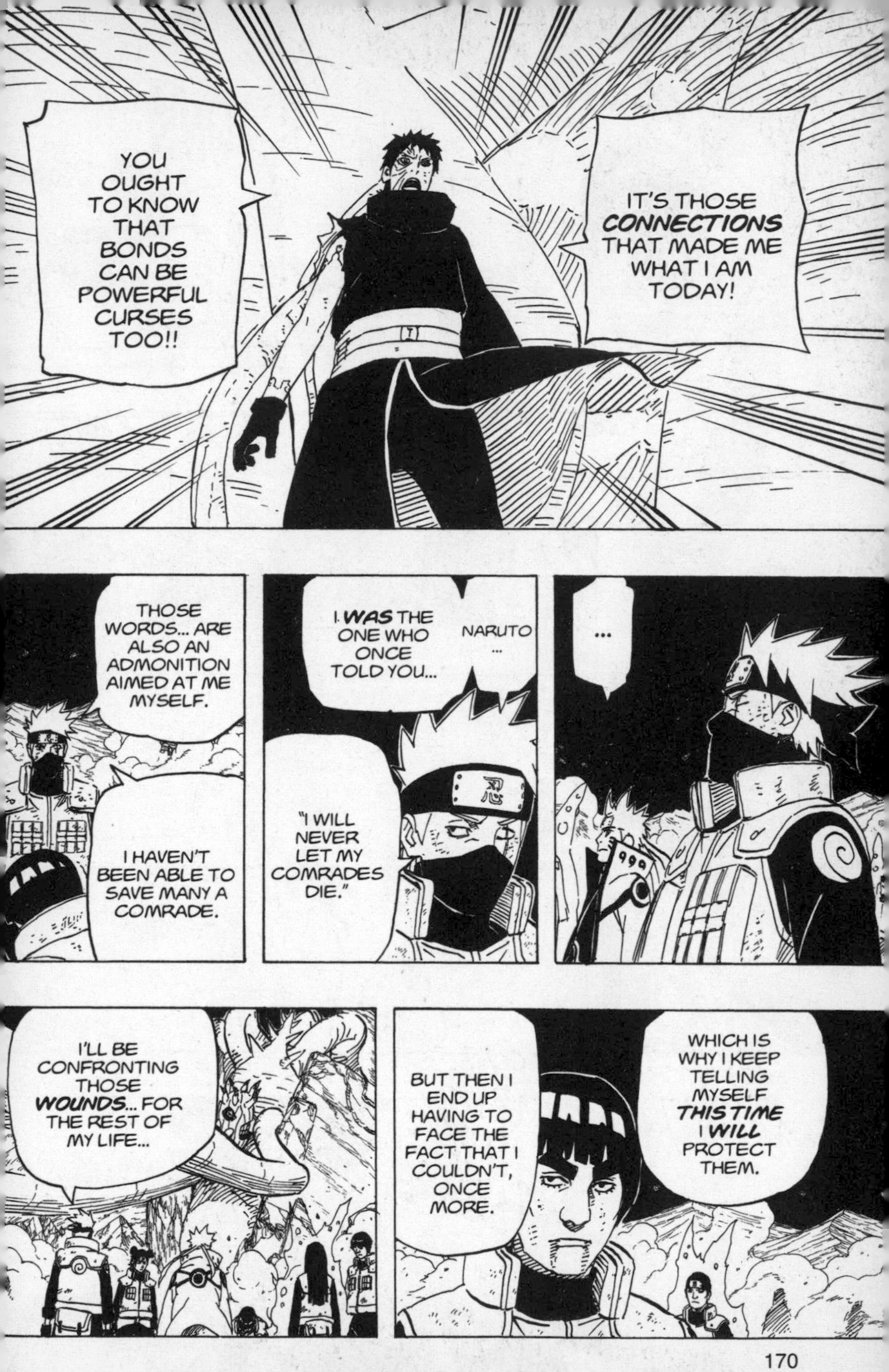
IT'S THOSE **CONNECTIONS** THAT MADE ME WHAT I AM TODAY!
YOU OUGHT TO KNOW THAT BONDS CAN BE POWERFUL CURSES TOO!!
...
NARUTO ...
I. **WAS** THE ONE WHO ONCE TOLD YOU...
"I WILL NEVER LET MY COMRADES DIE."
THOSE WORDS... ARE ALSO AN ADMONITION AIMED AT ME MYSELF.
I HAVEN'T BEEN ABLE TO SAVE MANY A COMRADE.
WHICH IS WHY I KEEP TELLING MYSELF **THIS TIME** I **WILL** PROTECT THEM.
BUT THEN I END UP HAVING TO FACE THE FACT THAT I COULDN'T, ONCE MORE.
I'LL BE CONFRONTING THOSE **WOUNDS**... FOR THE REST OF MY LIFE...

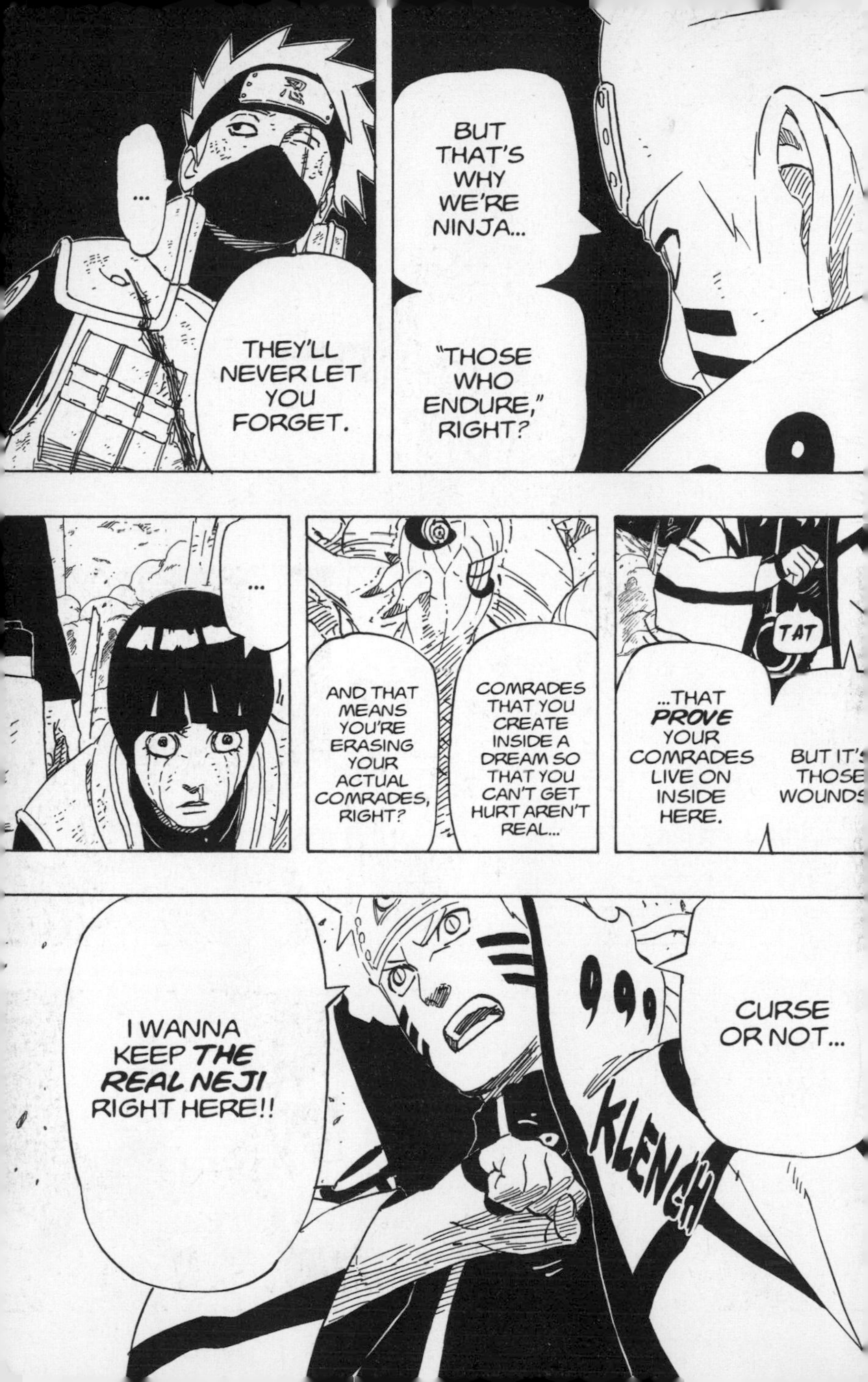
BUT THAT'S WHY WE'RE NINJA...
"THOSE WHO ENDURE," RIGHT?
...
THEY'LL NEVER LET YOU FORGET.
BUT IT'S THOSE WOUNDS
...THAT **PROVE** YOUR COMRADES LIVE ON INSIDE HERE.
TAT
COMRADES THAT YOU CREATE INSIDE A DREAM SO THAT YOU CAN'T GET HURT AREN'T REAL...
AND THAT MEANS YOU'RE ERASING YOUR ACTUAL COMRADES, RIGHT?
...
CURSE OR NOT...
I WANNA KEEP ***THE REAL NEJI*** RIGHT HERE!!
KLENCH

NARUTO

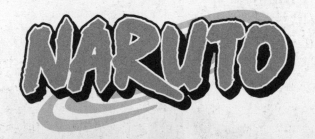

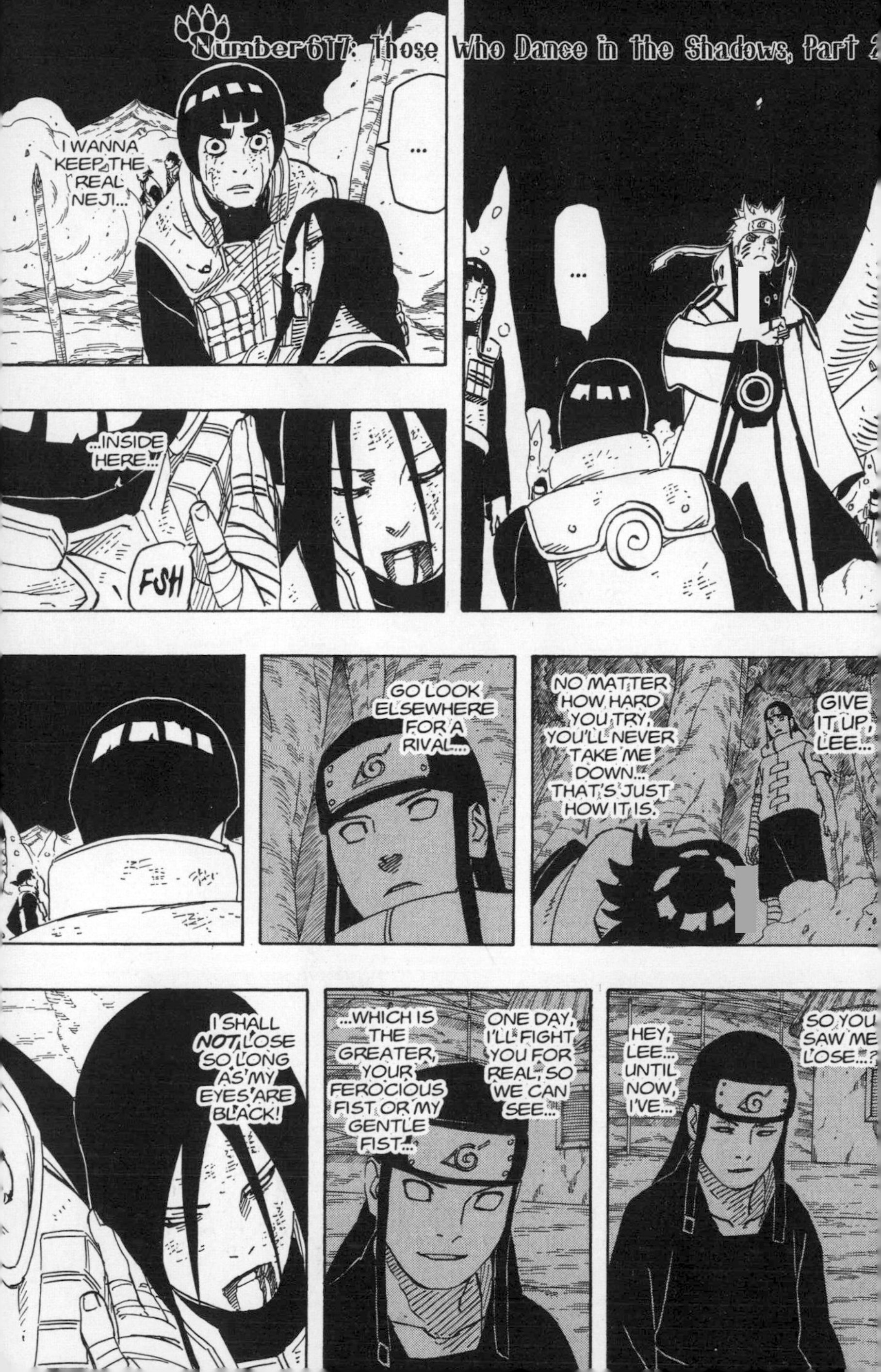
Number 617: Those Who Dance in the Shadows, Part 2
...
...
I WANNA KEEP THE REAL NEJI...
...INSIDE HERE...
FSH
GIVE IT UP, LEE...
NO MATTER HOW HARD YOU TRY, YOU'LL NEVER TAKE ME DOWN... THAT'S JUST HOW IT IS.
GO LOOK ELSEWHERE FOR A RIVAL...
SO YOU SAW ME LOSE...?
HEY, LEE... UNTIL NOW, I'VE...
ONE DAY, I'LL FIGHT YOU FOR REAL, SO WE CAN SEE...
...WHICH IS THE GREATER, YOUR FEROCIOUS FIST OR MY GENTLE FIST...
I SHALL NOT LOSE SO LONG AS MY EYES ARE BLACK!

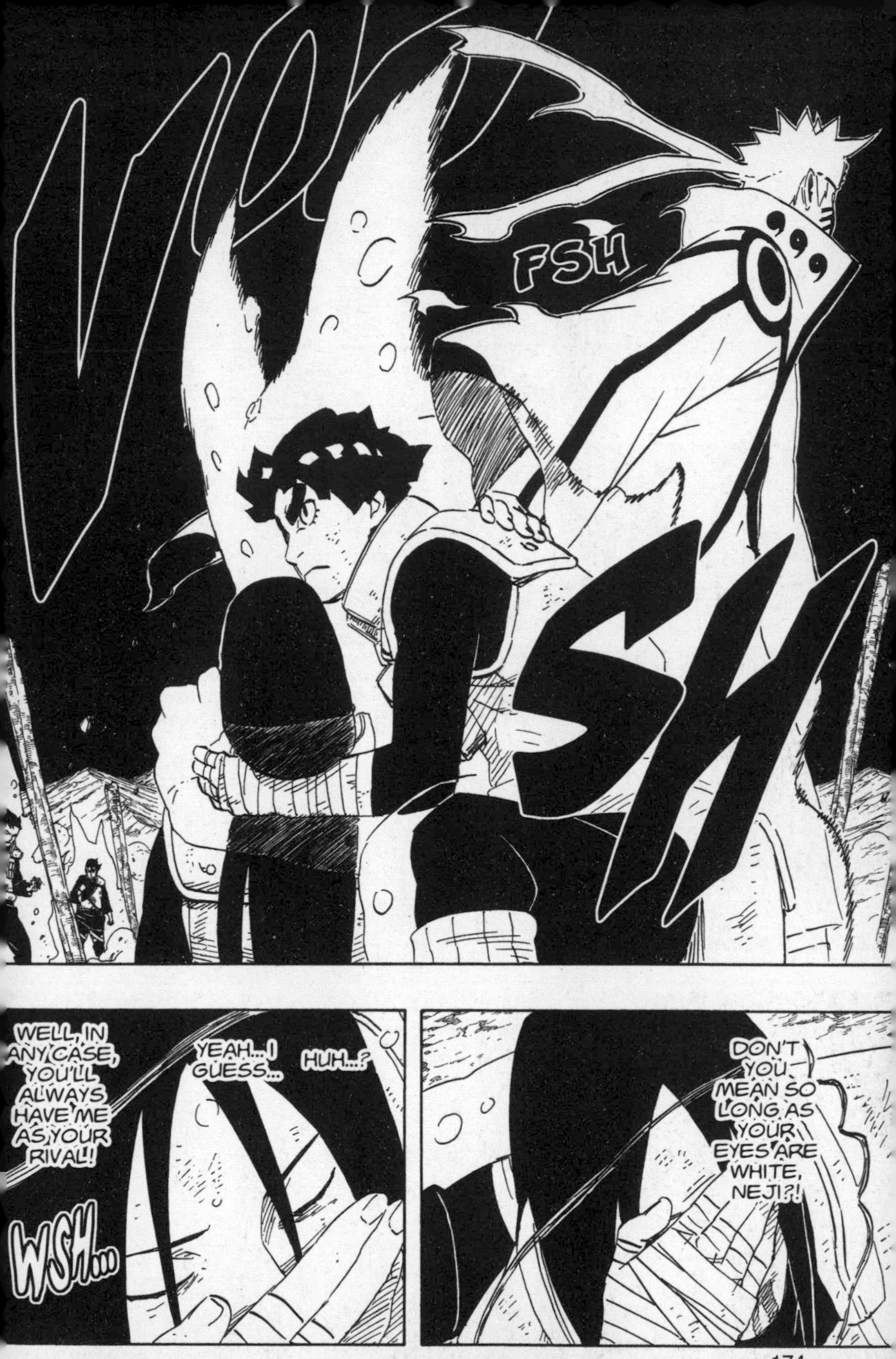
FSH
SH
DON'T YOU MEAN SO LONG AS YOUR EYES ARE WHITE, NEJI?!
HUH...?
YEAH... I GUESS...
WELL, IN ANY CASE, YOU'LL ALWAYS HAVE ME AS YOUR RIVAL!
WSH...

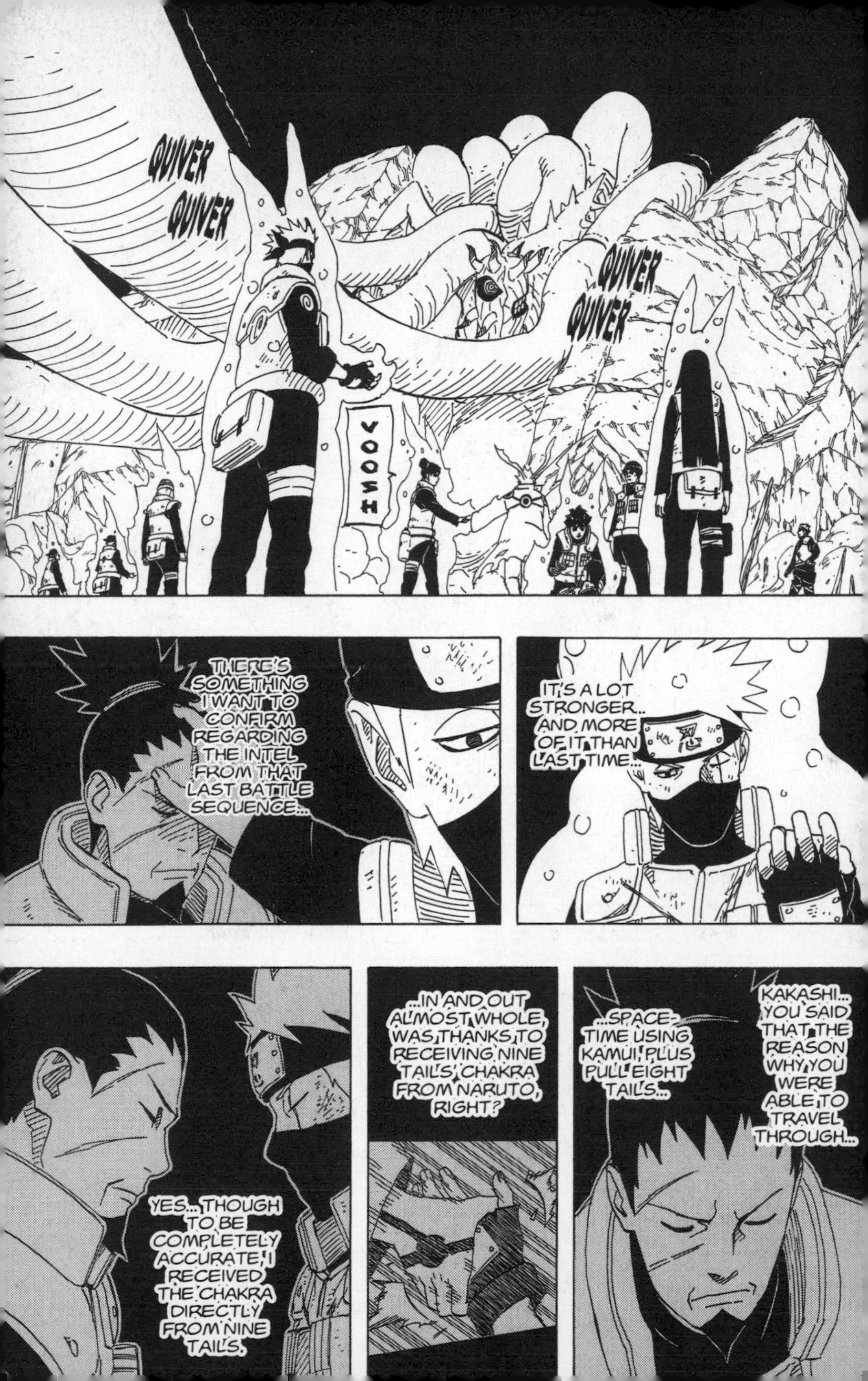
QUIVER QUIVER
VOOSH
QUIVER QUIVER
IT'S A LOT STRONGER... AND MORE OF IT THAN LAST TIME...
THERE'S SOMETHING I WANT TO CONFIRM REGARDING THE INTEL FROM THAT LAST BATTLE SEQUENCE...
KAKASHI... YOU SAID THAT THE REASON WHY YOU WERE ABLE TO TRAVEL THROUGH...
...SPACE-TIME USING KAMUI, PLUS PULL EIGHT TAILS...
...IN AND OUT ALMOST WHOLE, WAS THANKS TO RECEIVING NINE TAILS' CHAKRA FROM NARUTO, RIGHT?
YES... THOUGH TO BE COMPLETELY ACCURATE, I RECEIVED THE CHAKRA DIRECTLY FROM NINE TAILS.

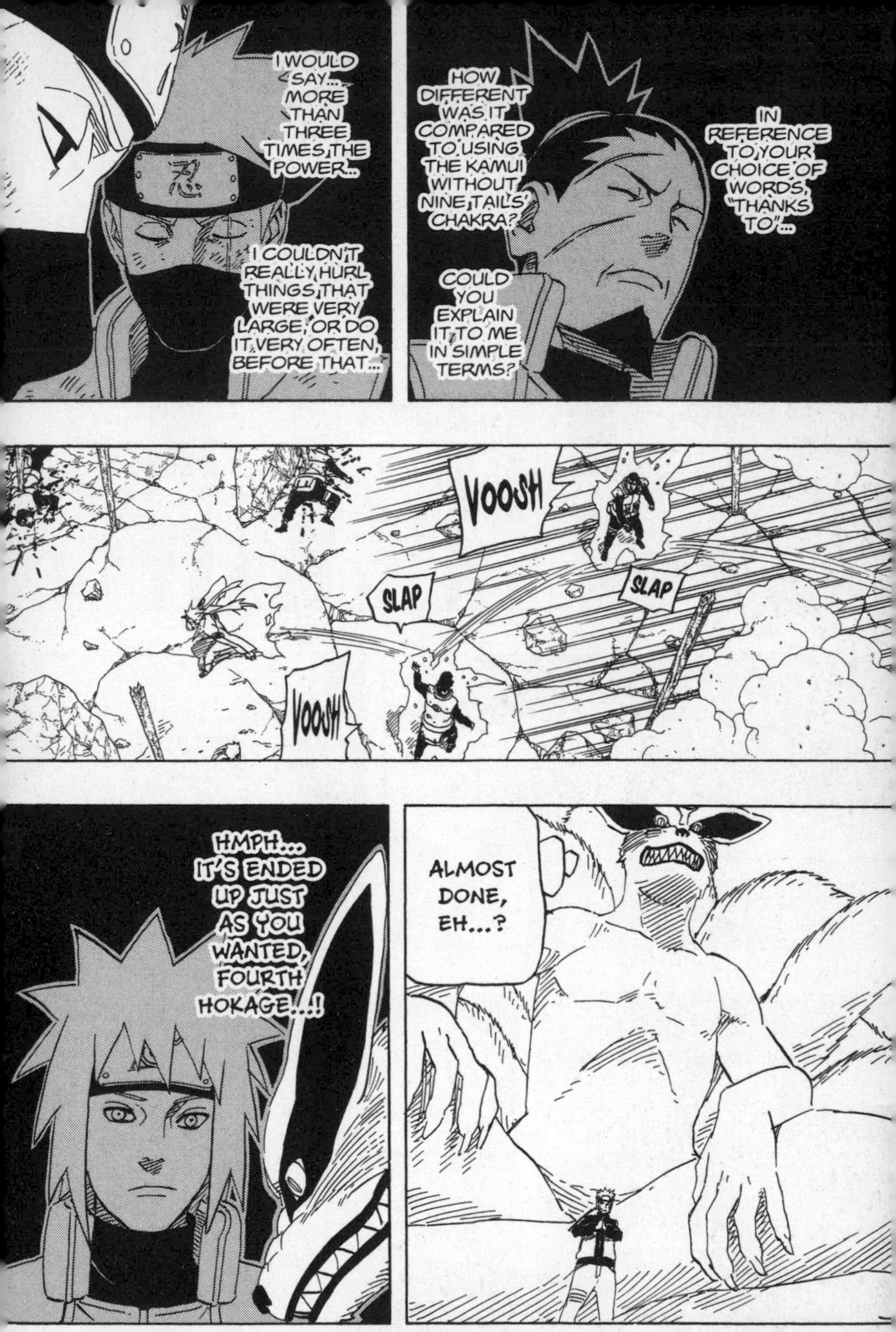
IN REFERENCE TO YOUR CHOICE OF WORDS, "THANKS TO"...
HOW DIFFERENT WAS IT COMPARED TO USING THE KAMUI WITHOUT NINE TAILS' CHAKRA?
COULD YOU EXPLAIN IT TO ME IN SIMPLE TERMS?
I WOULD SAY... MORE THAN THREE TIMES THE POWER...
I COULDN'T REALLY HURL THINGS THAT WERE VERY LARGE, OR DO IT VERY OFTEN, BEFORE THAT...
VOOSH
SLAP
SLAP
VOOSH
ALMOST DONE, EH...?
HMPH... IT'S ENDED UP JUST AS YOU WANTED, FOURTH HOKAGE...!

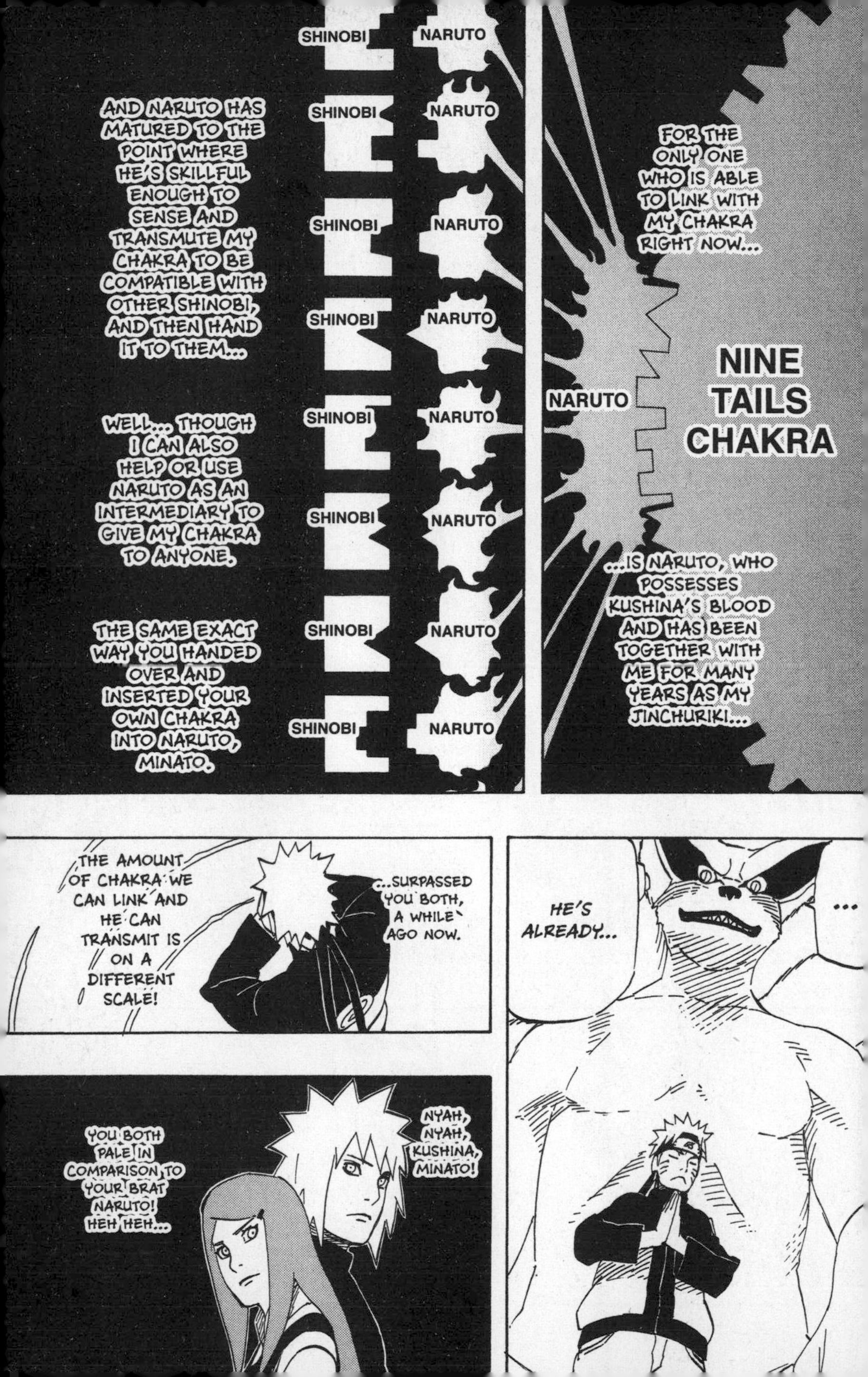
FOR THE ONLY ONE WHO IS ABLE TO LINK WITH MY CHAKRA RIGHT NOW...
NINE TAILS CHAKRA
NARUTO
...IS NARUTO, WHO POSSESSES KUSHINA'S BLOOD AND HAS BEEN TOGETHER WITH ME FOR MANY YEARS AS MY JINCHURIKI...
AND NARUTO HAS MATURED TO THE POINT WHERE HE'S SKILLFUL ENOUGH TO SENSE AND TRANSMUTE MY CHAKRA TO BE COMPATIBLE WITH OTHER SHINOBI, AND THEN HAND IT TO THEM...
NARUTO
SHINOBI
NARUTO
SHINOBI
NARUTO
SHINOBI
NARUTO
SHINOBI
WELL... THOUGH I CAN ALSO HELP OR USE NARUTO AS AN INTERMEDIARY TO GIVE MY CHAKRA TO ANYONE.
NARUTO
SHINOBI
NARUTO
SHINOBI
THE SAME EXACT WAY YOU HANDED OVER AND INSERTED YOUR OWN CHAKRA INTO NARUTO, MINATO.
NARUTO
SHINOBI
NARUTO
SHINOBI
...
HE'S ALREADY...
...SURPASSED YOU BOTH, A WHILE AGO NOW.
THE AMOUNT OF CHAKRA WE CAN LINK AND HE CAN TRANSMIT IS ON A DIFFERENT SCALE!
NYAH, NYAH, KUSHINA, MINATO!
YOU BOTH PALE IN COMPARISON TO YOUR BRAT NARUTO! HEH HEH...

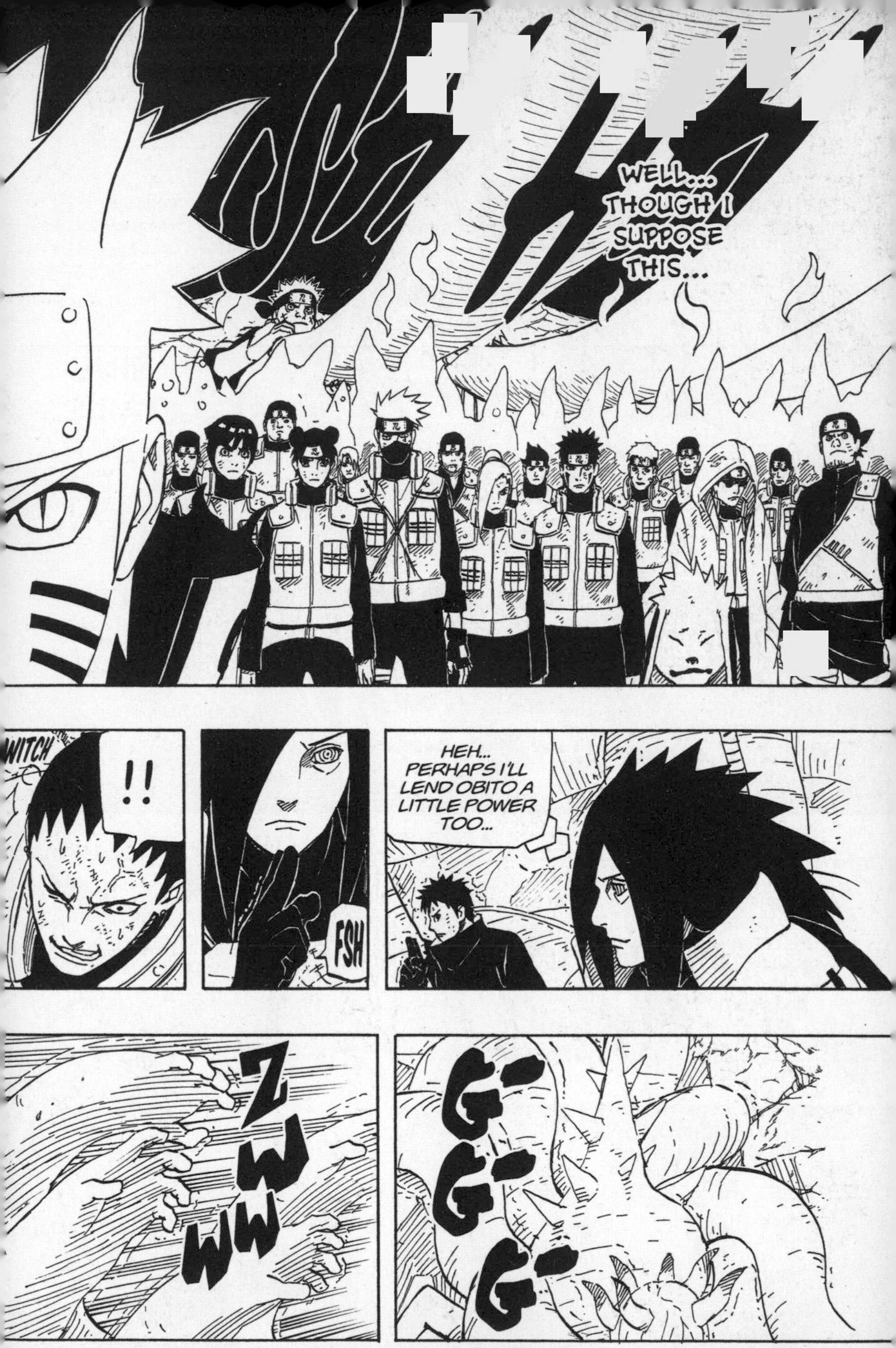
WELL... THOUGH I SUPPOSE THIS...
HEH... PERHAPS I'LL LEND OBITO A LITTLE POWER TOO...
FSH
!!
WITCH
G-G-G-
ZWWW

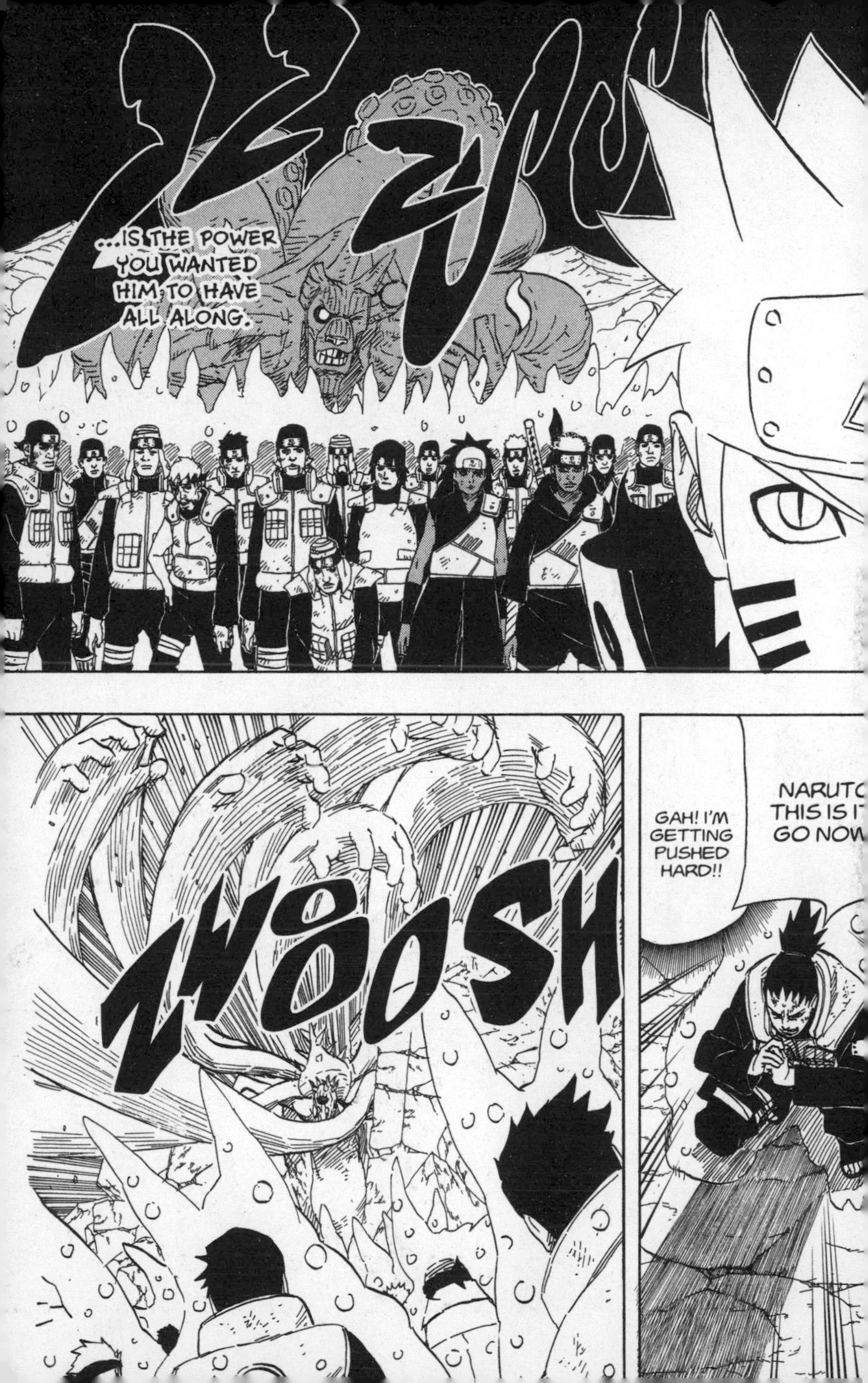
...IS THE POWER YOU WANTED HIM TO HAVE ALL ALONG.
NARUT THIS IS I GO NOW
GAH! I'M GETTING PUSHED HARD!!
WHOOSH

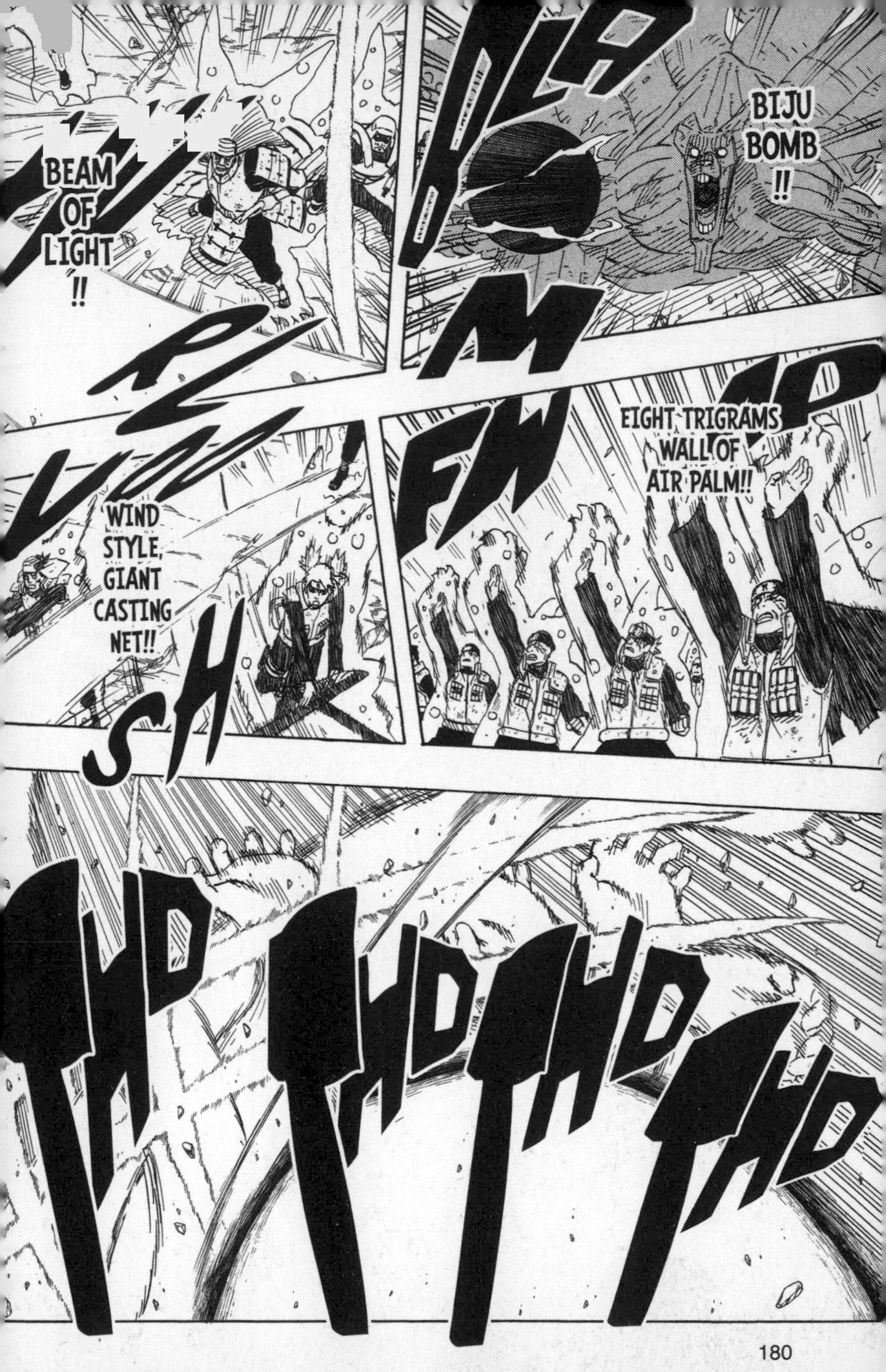
BIJU BOMB!!
BEAM OF LIGHT!!
EIGHT TRIGRAMS WALL OF AIR PALM!!
FWAP
WIND STYLE, GIANT CASTING NET!!
THD THD THD THD THD

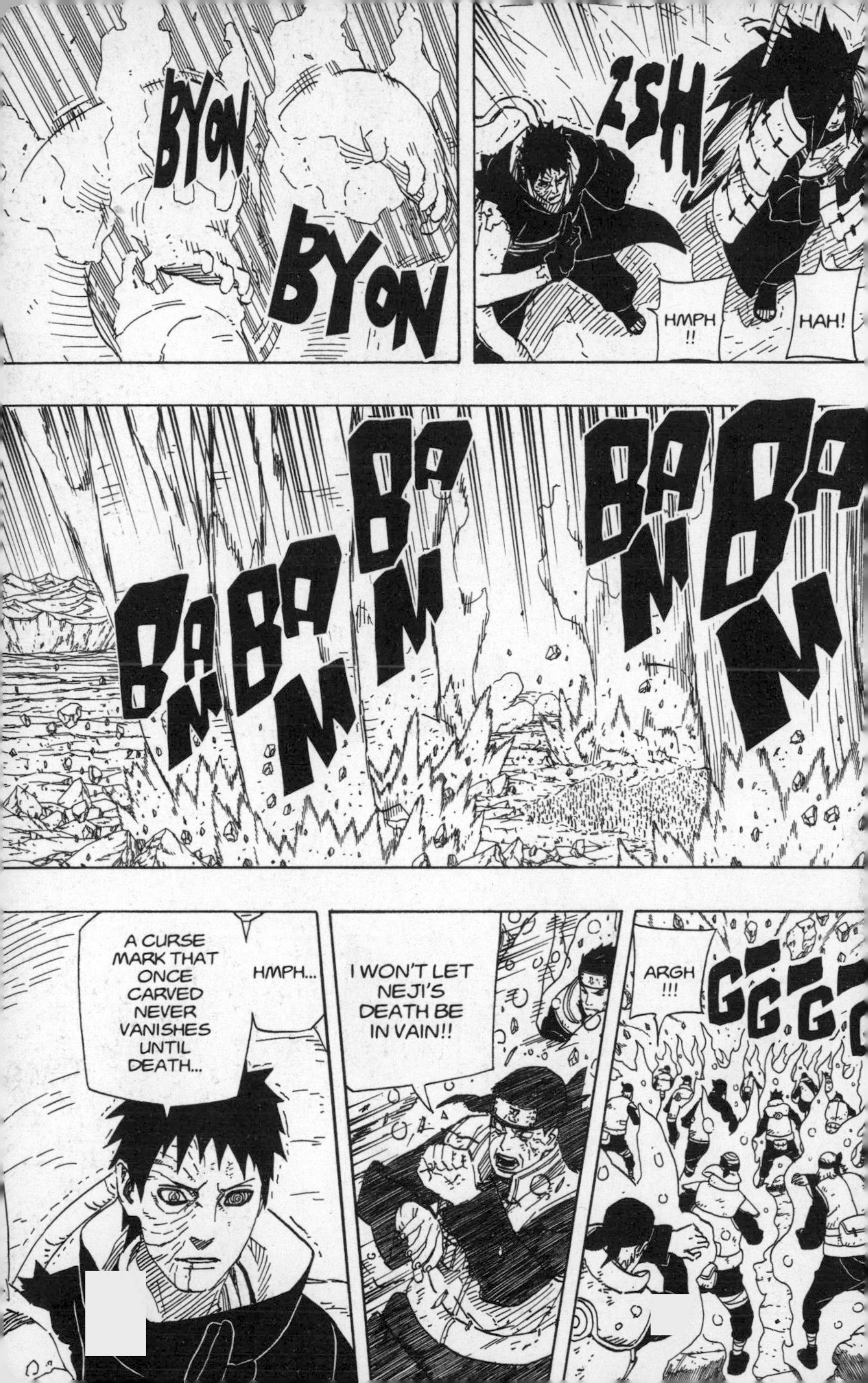
ISH
HAH!
HMPH !!
BYON
BYON
BABAM
BABAM
BABAM
BABAM
GGGG
ARGH !!!
I WON'T LET NEJI'S DEATH BE IN VAIN!!
HMPH...
A CURSE MARK THAT ONCE CARVED NEVER VANISHES UNTIL DEATH...

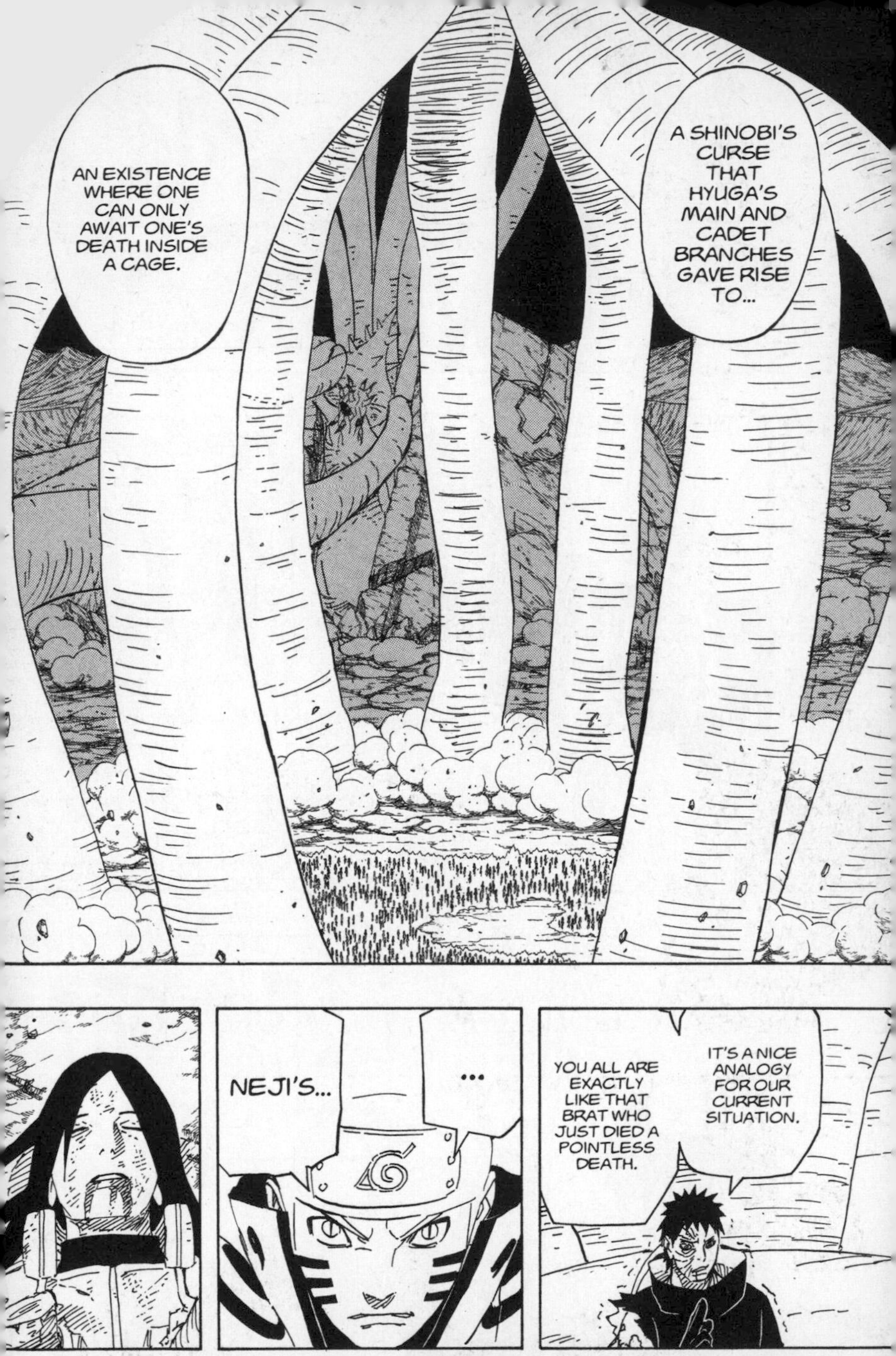
A SHINOBI'S CURSE THAT HYUGA'S MAIN AND CADET BRANCHES GAVE RISE TO...
AN EXISTENCE WHERE ONE CAN ONLY AWAIT ONE'S DEATH INSIDE A CAGE.
IT'S A NICE ANALOGY FOR OUR CURRENT SITUATION.
YOU ALL ARE EXACTLY LIKE THAT BRAT WHO JUST DIED A POINTLESS DEATH.
...
NEJI'S...

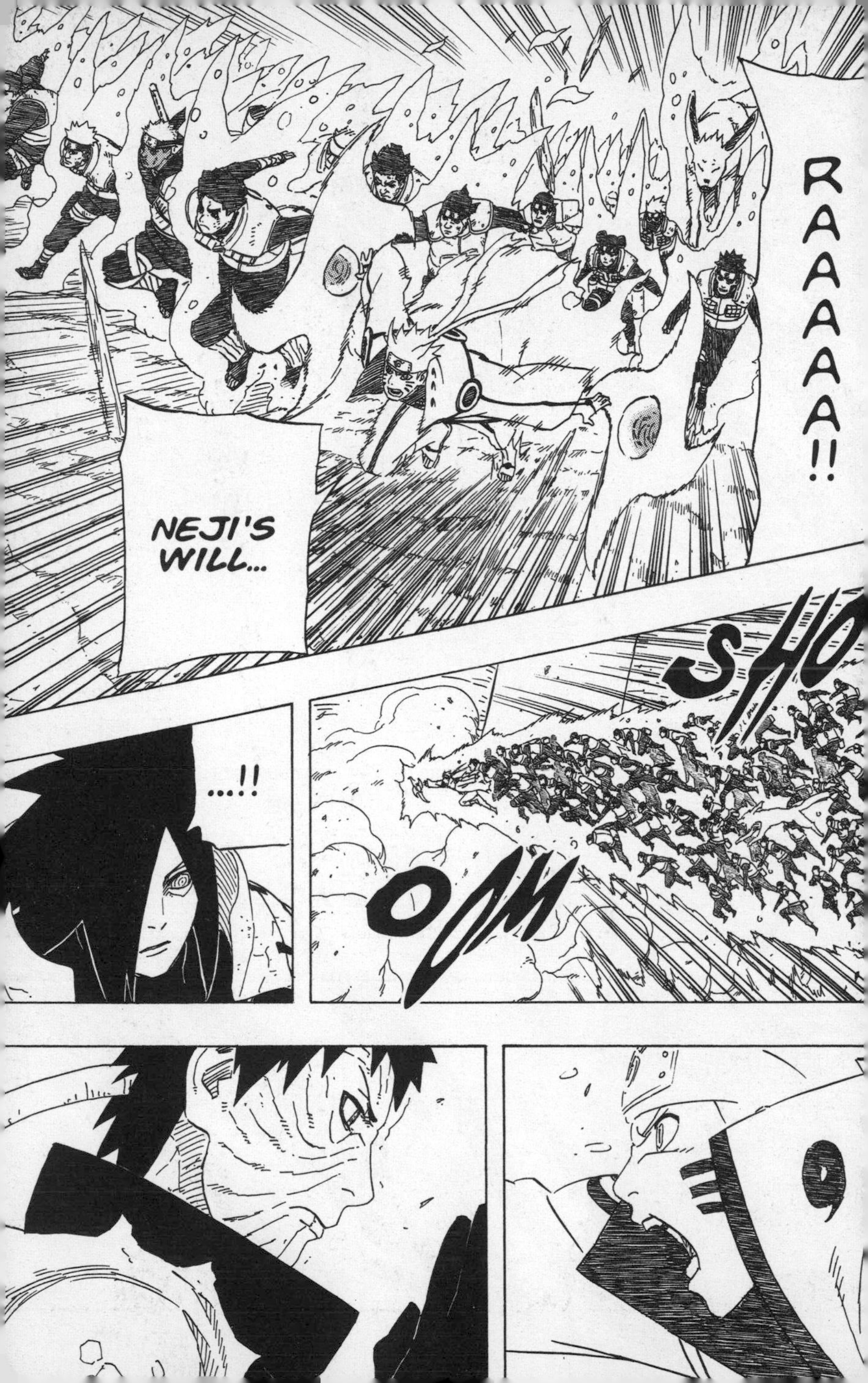
RAAAAAA!!
NEJI'S WILL...
SHOOM
...!!

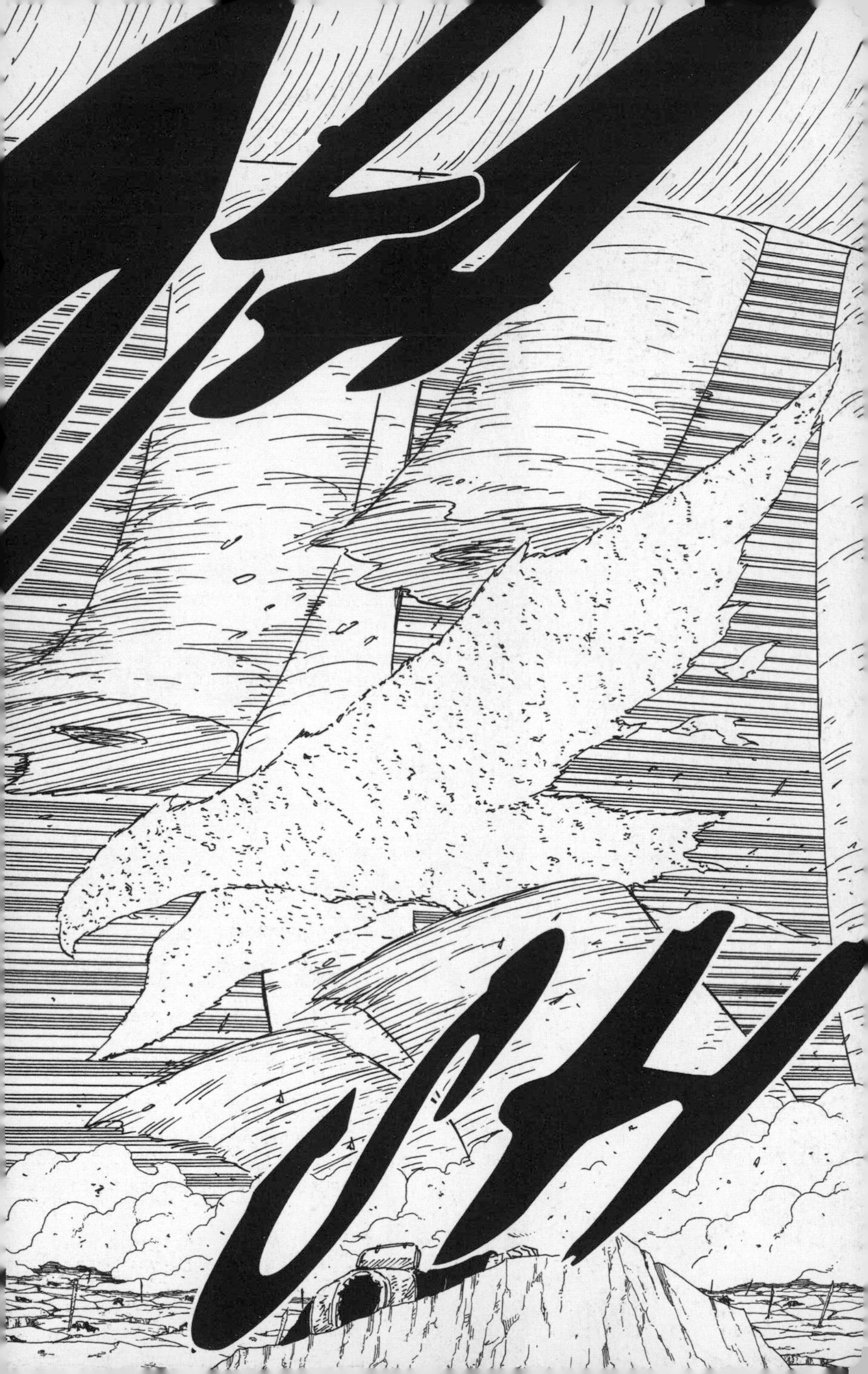

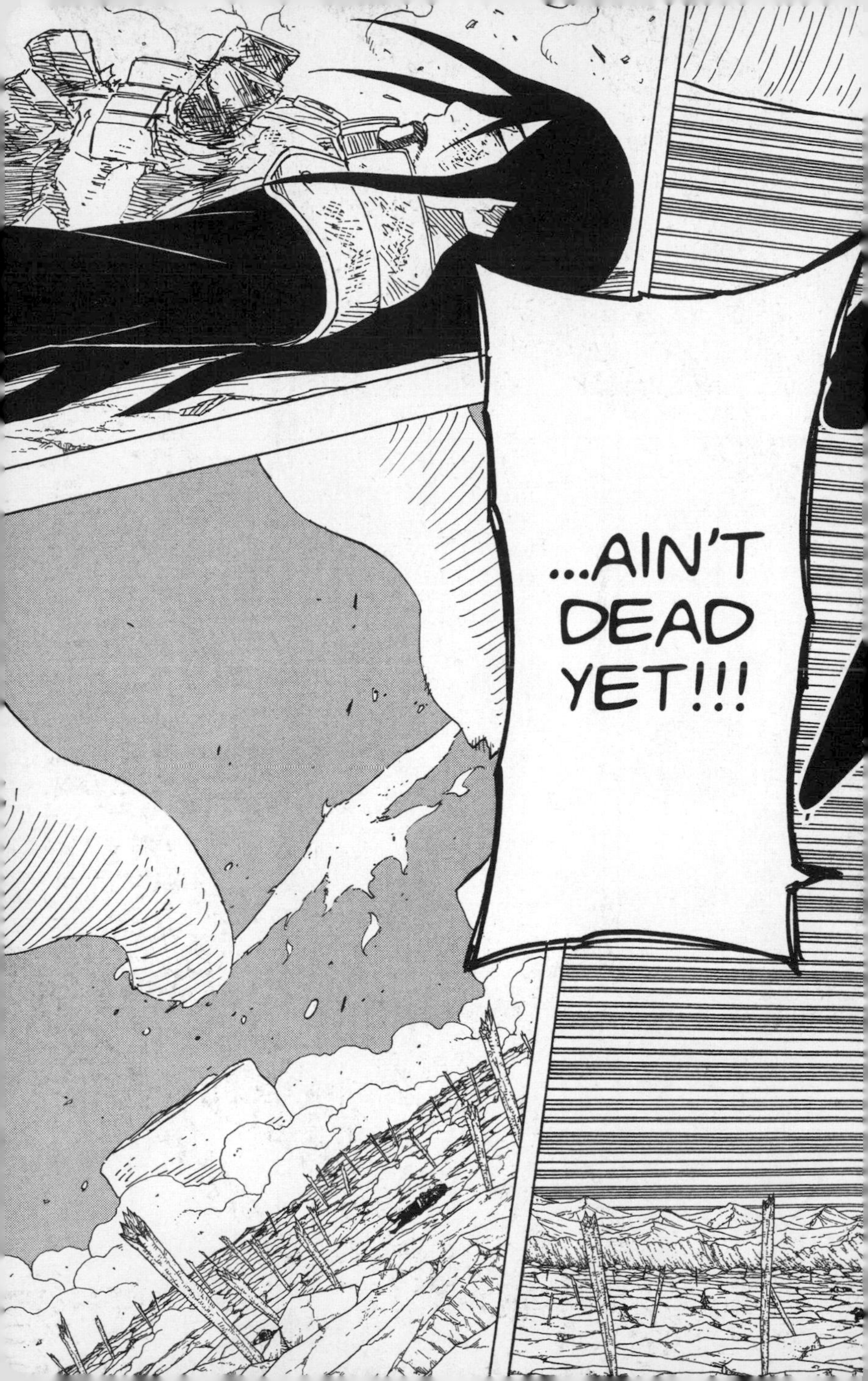
...AIN'T DEAD YET!!!

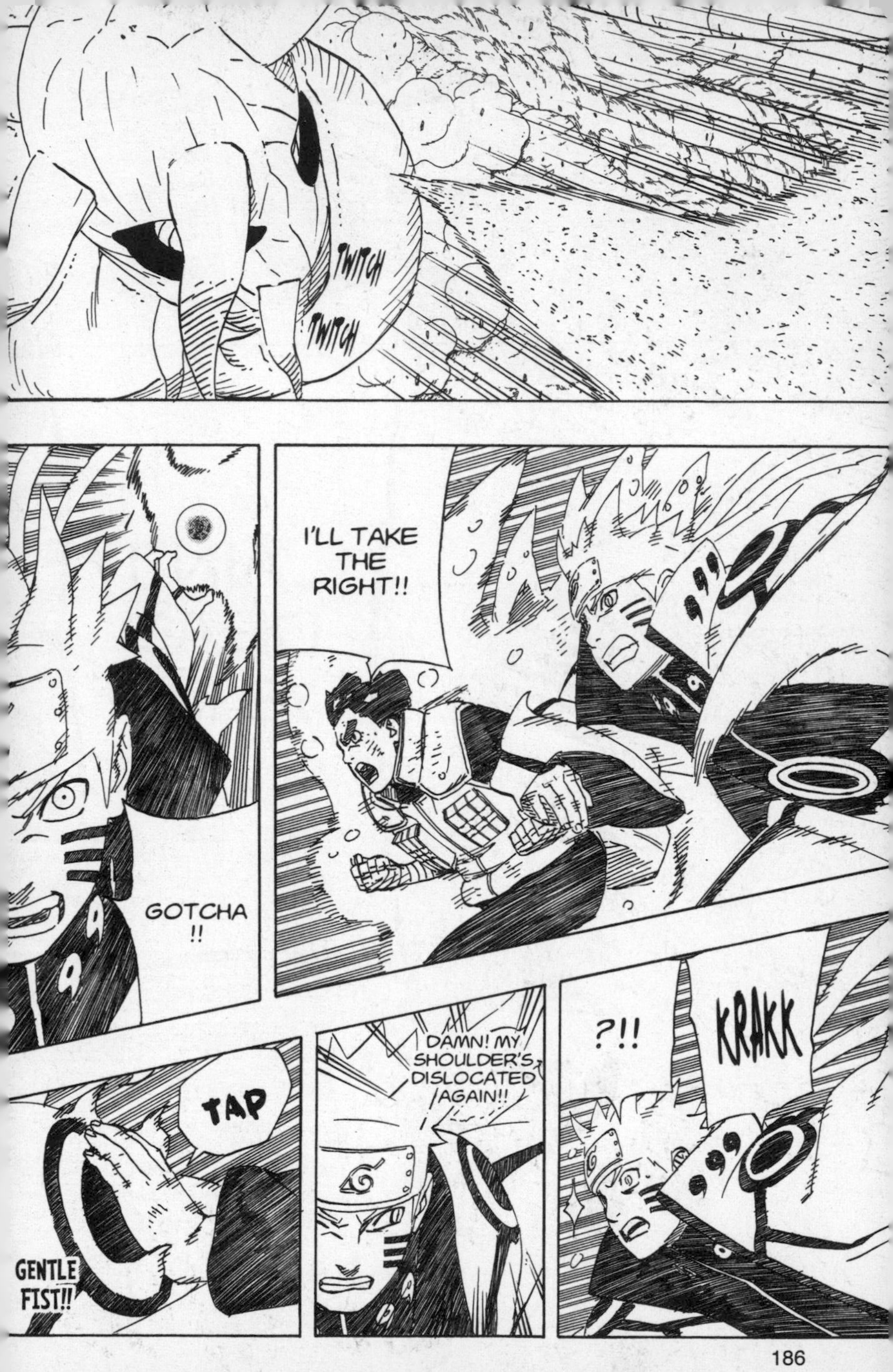
TWITCH
TWITCH
I'LL TAKE THE RIGHT!!
GOTCHA!!
KRAKK
?!!
DAMN! MY SHOULDER'S DISLOCATED AGAIN!!
TAP
GENTLE FIST!!

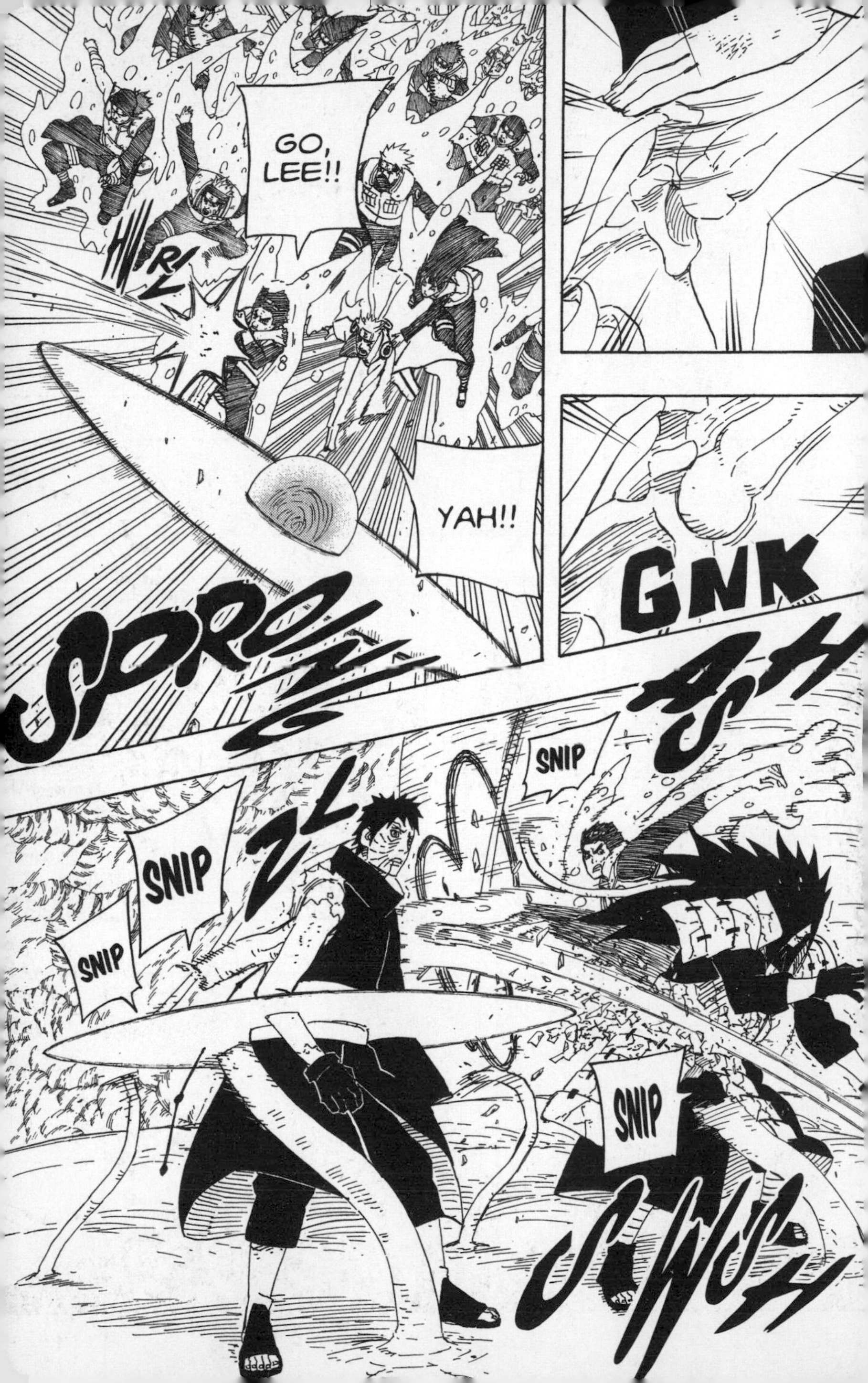
GNK
GO, LEE!!
YAH!!
SNIP
SNIP
SNIP
SNIP

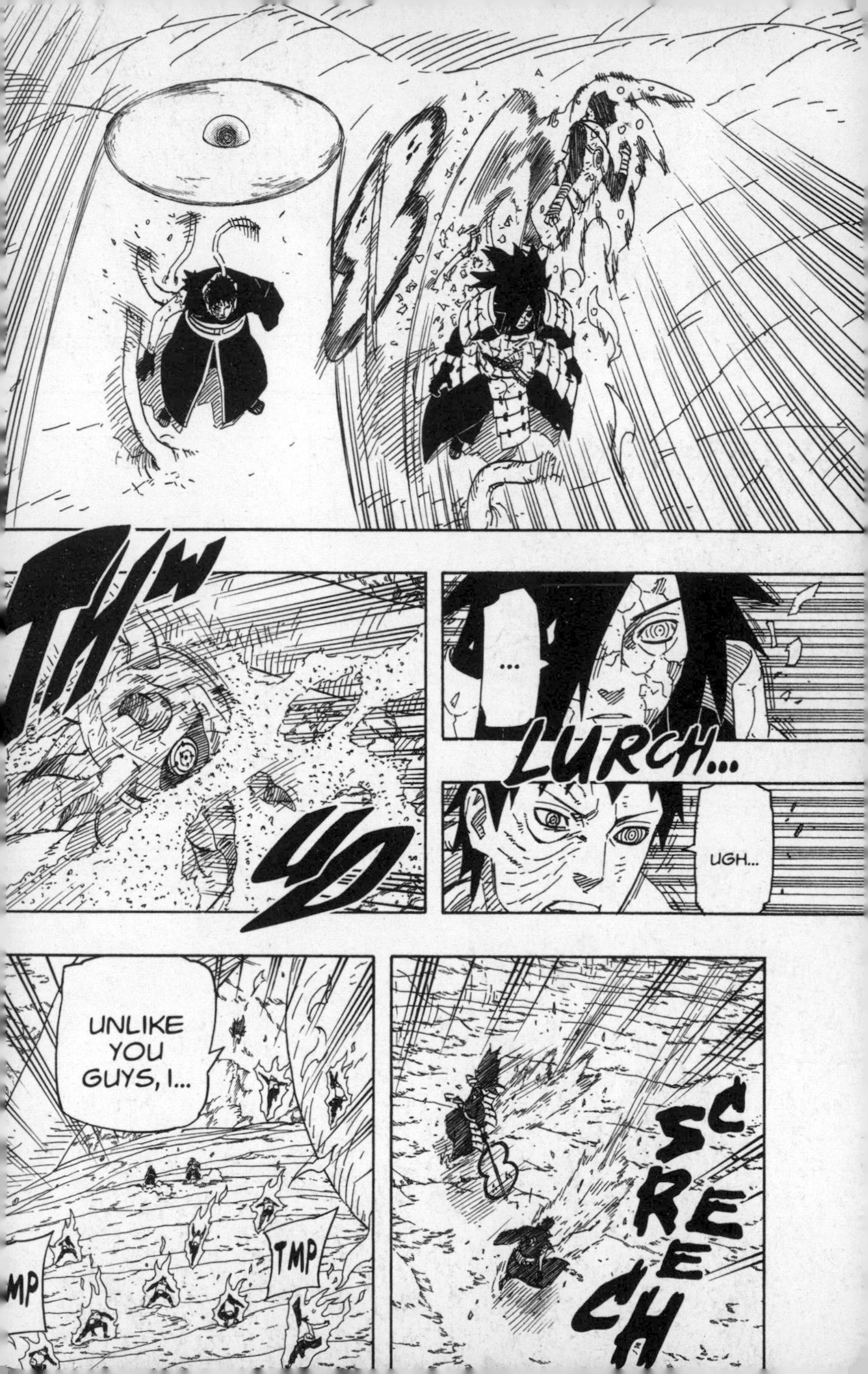
...
LURCH...
UGH...
THWUD
SCREECH
UNLIKE YOU GUYS, I...
TMP
MP

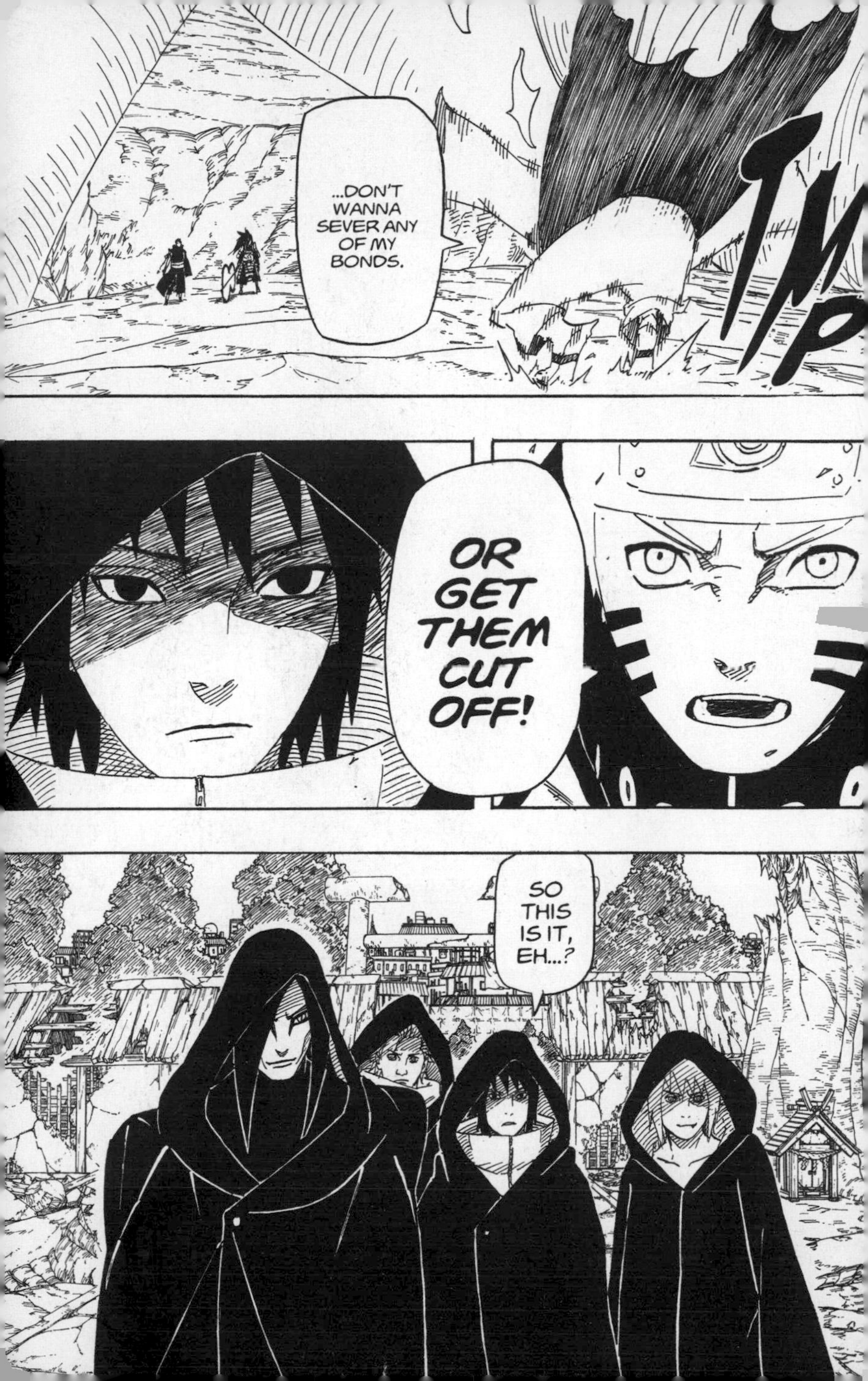
...DON'T WANNA SEVER ANY OF MY BONDS.
OR GET THEM CUT OFF!
SO THIS IS IT, EH...?

IN THE NEXT VOLUME...

HASHIRAMA AND MADARA

As the battle for the ninja world rages on, Sasuke has arrived at the location where he can finally uncover the truth. But when he learns of the dark history of the Uchiha clan, how will it affect his feelings in the present?

AVAILABLE APRIL 2014!

You're Reading in the Wrong Direction!!

Whoops! Guess what? You're starting at the wrong end of the comic!

...It's true! In keeping with the original Japanese format, **Naruto** is meant to be read from right to left, starting in the upper-right corner.

Unlike English, which is read from left to right, Japanese is read from right to left, meaning that action, sound effects and word-balloon order are completely reversed... something which can make readers unfamiliar with Japanese feel pretty backwards themselves. For this reason, manga or Japanese comics published in the U.S. in English have sometimes been published "flopped"—that is, printed in exact reverse order, as though seen from the other side of a mirror.

By flopping pages, U.S. publishers can avoid confusing readers, but the compromise is not without its downside. For one thing, a character in a flopped manga series who once wore in the original Japanese version a T-shirt emblazoned with "M A Y" (as in "the merry month of") now wears one which reads "Y A M"! Additionally, many manga creators in Japan are themselves unhappy with the process, as some feel the mirror-imaging of their art alters their original intentions.

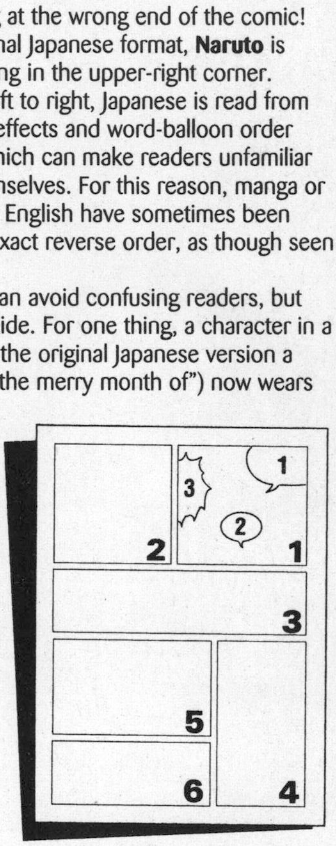

We are proud to bring you Masashi Kishimoto's **Naruto** in the original unflopped format. For now, though, turn to the other side of the book and let the ninjutsu begin...!

—Editor

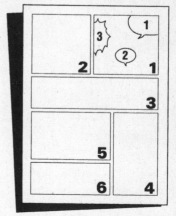